Academic Librarianship Today

Academic Librarianship Today

Todd Gilman

ROWMAN & LITTLEFIELD
Lanham • Boulder • New York • London

Published by Rowman & Littlefield
A wholly owned subsidiary of The Rowman & Littlefield Publishing Group, Inc.
4501 Forbes Boulevard, Suite 200, Lanham, Maryland 20706
www.rowman.com

Unit A, Whitacre Mews, 26-34 Stannary Street, London SE11 4AB

British Library Cataloguing in Publication Information Available

Library of Congress Cataloging-in-Publication Data Available

ISBN 978-1-4422-7874-5 (cloth : alk. paper)
ISBN 978-1-4422-7875-2 (pbk. : alk. paper)
ISBN 978-1-4422-7876-9 (electronic)

∞™ The paper used in this publication meets the minimum requirements of American National Standard for Information Sciences—Permanence of Paper for Printed Library Materials, ANSI/NISO Z39.48-1992.

Printed in the United States of America

Contents

Editorial Advisory Board

Figures and Tables

Figures

Table

Textbox

Foreword

In the last few years, information technology has become integrated into all aspects of educational life, including work in both libraries and the broader academic campus.

While academic libraries continue to collect and service print collections in the manner they have historically, new types of collections, centered on the digital, have brought about changes in the work, in jobs newly created, and in opportunities for the library to become more integrated into the teaching, learning, and research activities of colleges and universities. Now the scholarly record includes more than books and journals; such materials as research data sets, lab notes, computer models, "big" data, and digital formats form part of the library's collection.

Networked information is changing the methods of managing academic libraries, and the authors of this text confront the management issues. Todd Gilman and his contributing authors present the influence of these changes in libraries in this new textbook, which extends in many ways the challenges and opportunities for academic libraries as they continue on the movement of library transformation. Chapters on library place, the support academic libraries give to students and faculty who are working in online learning environments, distance education, MOOCs, open access, institutional repositories data curation, management of "big" data, and conservation and preservation present issues confronting the academic library today. Many of the authors exhort the academic library to move closer to the work central to the institution of higher education, and they provide advice as to how that might be done. This advice will help working academic librarians as well as students in LIS courses.

Many of the authors in this text rightly insist that the library should be at the table to help shape policies that will influence and guide the institutions' development in the technological age, and they point to institutions that see the library less as a support service and more connected directly to the academic enterprise. Good chapters rarely found in the academic library literature are included, such as those on scholarly communication and on assessment. Some approaches of the old management models can be found in the text, particularly in chapters presenting organizational structures. They are useful in a textbook for new students who will begin their careers working in the old organizational models. But new models are discussed and debated, presenting excellent content in a new library management text.

Academic Librarianship Today is an informative, comprehensive textbook including both discussion questions for students to use and for managers to consider and assignments. It is a good model in a textbook with new content, moving the management issues from the old approaches of only issues inside the library to the new approaches of issues coming to the library from the outside. The authors present thoughtful arguments, challenging discussion questions, and stimulating assignments.

Beverly P. Lynch
Professor, Department of Information Studies
Graduate School of Education and Information Studies, UCLA

Acknowledgments

I would like to thank my editor at Rowman & Littlefield, Charles Harmon, for his enthusiasm and encouragement throughout the process. I would also like to thank the members of the editorial advisory board for their invaluable comments on the book proposal and on drafts of all the chapters. The volume is infinitely stronger for their input.

Todd Gilman

Introduction

Todd Gilman

Academic libraries in North America today, both large and small, function in a continuously and rapidly changing technological and budgetary environment. The administrators, librarians, curators, and support staff who run these libraries must constantly adapt to new roles and expectations; new work flows; new electronic databases and systems; new hardware and software; new cataloging and metadata standards; and an explosion of new forms of electronic media and scholarly communication that they must collect, sustain, and make available to their patrons. To further complicate matters, we must succeed at this adaptation in an atmosphere of significantly reduced funding and rising costs for all functions, systems, personnel, acquisitions, preservation, storage, and building maintenance everywhere. Activities in these libraries have gotten so complex and specialized in recent years that it would be impossible for any one person to become an expert in all aspects of the field of academic librarianship. Yet many of us who work or wish to work in academic libraries are expected to do so—to keep abreast of the latest technology, forms of scholarly output, and work flows, not to fall behind—lest we become obsolete and find ourselves of little lasting value to our employers. The aim of this book, then, is to offer the reader the expertise of a number of highly regarded professionals in the field concerning all aspects of academic librarianship as it is practiced today in libraries of all sizes and affiliated with all types of institutions, from community colleges to four-year colleges to research-intensive universities. For if no one person can be an expert in the whole field, by offering this wide-ranging expertise in a single place, we hope the reader will learn as much as possible from the collective wisdom of these professionals and will develop a deeper and more holistic understanding of how academic libraries with all their complexities manage to thrive today amid all the challenges they face.

This new collection of contributed chapters, none previously published, explores the question of what it means to be an academic librarian today. We offer twenty experts' perspectives on the transformation of academic libraries as information organizations, why these libraries should be considered more important today than ever before, the influence of technology on how we provide academic information resources and services in a digital and global environment, and the various career opportunities available for academic librarians now and in the future. The authors offer broad and diverse views, ranging from those of senior administrators and practitioners working in North American academic libraries large and small to leaders from recognized nonprofit organizations devoted to research and strategic guidance for libraries in the digital age to faculty members from leading US library schools. Taken together, the chapters develop a fuller picture of the current state of academic librarianship in North America than has ever been available in any single resource. What emerges is a library landscape at once full of promise and exciting initiatives yet beset by seemingly insurmountable challenges—how to attract and retain the talent needed for current and future professional roles; how to keep up with ever-advancing computer technology; and how to pay for all this along with the vast quantity of books, journals, and electronic databases our ambitious and accomplished patrons demand.

At the end of each chapter, the authors offer a series of questions for discussion and one or more assignments to stimulate thought, reinforce comprehension of the chapter's content, and provide a means of applying the knowledge gained. The authors hope that the volume will be attractive to instructors in ALA-accredited and candidate programs in library and information studies and that they will adopt it as a course text. As one who has taught a graduate-level course on academic libraries for several LIS programs over the past decade, I can attest to the urgent and longstanding need for such a book. In fact, it was my dissatisfaction with the few available single- or dual-authored texts that led me to propose this new collection of chapters to the publisher as a crucial alternative. No other available course text offers anything like the breadth and depth of content and the wide variety of expert perspectives on all aspects of academic librarianship today that the volume you are reading does. We also hope that North American academic administrators, librarians, and curators will find the information and reflections on the profession presented here stimulating and essential reading. Finally, we hope that the discussion questions and assignments will prove useful, not just in graduate courses, but also to working librarians of all stripes who wish to learn more about academic libraries.

Organization

The book is comprised of three parts. Part I, "The Academic Library Landscape Today," introduces the subject, beginning with a chapter that situates US academic librarianship in its historical context and addresses the greatest obstacles the profession faces today, particularly financial and technological challenges. Chapter 2 concerns governance. In it, the author explains how academic libraries fit within the larger institutions of higher education, both colleges and universities, and how libraries seek to embrace and reflect their institutions' missions, visions, values, and academic cultures. Chapter 3 discusses organization, administration, management, and planning and focuses on how academic librarians' roles have been defined, the typical responsibilities of administrators and managers, and how to collaborate to achieve success in innovation through the strategic planning process. Chapter 4 explains the complexities of academic library funding and budgeting. The author introduces the various sources of library funds and details how budgets for collections, services, and facilities must be planned and put into effect. Chapter 5 addresses faculty research and scholarly communication, beginning with a capsule history of academic publishing and the steps involved in the peer review process. The authors then describe how teaching faculty often affect the priorities of their institutions' libraries. They end by confronting the current crisis in academic publishing, making the case that libraries must become much more proactive in finding less costly ways to provide research materials.

Part II, "Academic Librarians and Services Today," focuses on personnel and their roles serving students, faculty, and staff. It opens with public services, a topic that comprises chapters 6 and 7: the first on reference, instruction, outreach to faculty and students, and faculty–librarian collaboration; the second on collection development, circulation, and resource sharing. Chapter 6 engages with recent library science literature to convey current thinking on best practices, including such service models as traditional versus innovative ways of providing general reference services, library liaisons to academic departments, embedded librarianship, and information literacy. Chapter 7 introduces principles of collection development for general collections, as well as special collections and archives and both print and electronic formats. The author also addresses recent and future consortial lending partnerships among the largest libraries and how these libraries must now choose access over ownership of library materials in order to meet their patrons' needs. The chapter on collections leads naturally to chapter 8, on technical services, which discusses current challenges facing cataloging, metadata, systems, electronic resource management, resource discoverability, and the evolving roles professionals now assume. Chapter 9 is devoted to librarians, programs, and services in four-year college and community college libraries—colleges that are too often excluded from academic librarianship textbooks in favor of large research libraries.

Part III, "Changing Priorities, New Directions," emphasizes topics at the forefront of academic libraries in the digital age. Chapter 10 discusses recruitment, retention, and supervision of academic library staff, especially appropriate education for professional and paraprofessional employees, and the need for greater diversity, mentorship, and professional development in academic libraries. Chapter 11 focuses on physical and virtual library space design. The author explains how rethinking and reconfiguring library spaces, such as the so-called learning commons and smart classrooms, actually and potentially influence teaching, learning, and research. Chapter 12, on how academic libraries must now serve both campus and remote users, acknowledges the increasing need to accommodate patrons where they are, including students learning online who may be on campus or hundreds or thousands of miles away, and the faculty who feel an increasing need to reach them in technologically sophisticated ways. In chapter 13, on open access, institutional repositories, E-science and data curation, and digital preservation, the author emphasizes the newest means of access to and security of scholarship and raw data. Chapter 14, on assessment, promotion, and marketing, stresses the need for academic libraries to be accountable to their stakeholders in new measurable ways. The book ends with chapter 15's "Vision for the Future," a consideration of a variety of potential roles for the academic librarians of tomorrow. These roles are based on emerging activities in today's academic library and the author's sense that a number of evident incongruities in our current work environment suggest that academic librarians should be rethinking past practices and traditional roles.

Today's academic libraries will all too quickly become those of tomorrow. By developing a deeper understanding of where we are today—of the many and varied services we provide to our patrons, of the fascinating mix of colleagues with whom we interact day to day, of the challenges and rewards concomitant with emergent technologies, and of the exciting advances in scholarly communication—we can anticipate and so be better prepared for what is coming. The editor and authors join together in welcoming you to explore the vast, complex, and rapidly evolving field of academic librarianship with us. Whether you are a seasoned academic library professional; a graduate student in a library and information studies program encountering academic librarianship for the first time; a recently hired academic library employee who wants an in-depth understanding of the roles, practices, and structures that inform your new work environment; a librarian in a public library, special library, or any other library who hopes to learn more about academic libraries, we feel confident that you will find new information and many challenging ideas awaiting your discovery in the pages ahead.

Part I

The Academic Library Landscape Today

This section conveys the foundations of the subject. It begins with Deanna B. Marcum's chapter placing US academic librarianship in its historical context and identifying the most pressing issues the profession faces today, particularly financial and technological challenges. Marcum describes how the unprecedented and underestimated influx of veterans of World War II into US colleges and universities propelled the first great academic library expansion the country was to witness, along with a new focus on the needs of undergraduate students rather than graduate students and faculty, how computer technology simultaneously revolutionized these libraries, and how the growth of the Internet and World Wide Web later brought about another sea change in part by enabling the large-scale conversion of analog material to digital format. Yet she also explores the legal complications this conversion brought about, especially the Google Books initiative, and such subsequent developments as the Digital Public Library of America. She concludes with a discussion of the unsustainable financial pressure libraries have experienced as a result of the explosion of research materials (print and on-line) now available in all disciplines, particularly electronic journals in the hard sciences, and how this pressure has led to urgent efforts to share journals and books among library consortia and to make as many as possible available as open access resources, free to all.

Barbara I. Dewey's chapter on governance outlines how academic libraries fit within their parent institutions of higher education, both colleges and universities, and how libraries strive to align themselves with their institutions' missions, visions, values, and academic cultures. Dewey explains overall institutional governance; executive-level administration; collegiate and academic departmental administration; and faculty, staff, and student governance, emphasizing how important it is for library leaders to understand these structures so that they can provide effective leadership both within the library and across campus. She also identifies the various offices that support the institution, including information technology, research, finance and business, alumni affairs and development, general counsel, physical plant, and diversity, and the external bodies that control accreditation. Throughout her chapter, she points to the various ways that library administration can contribute to strategic planning, assessment, and decision-making at the institutional level.

Starr Hoffman's chapter on organization, administration, management, and planning focuses on how academic librarians' roles have been defined within the library, typical duties of administrators and managers, and how all cooperate to ensure successful innovation by means of strategic planning. Throughout, Hoffman emphasizes how recent developments have affected academic libraries, especially the growth of technology; reduced budgets; the shift in academic library structure from a hierarchical to a flat, team-based model; and the need for library personnel to respond to constant and rapid change. She also explores controversial and important current issues, including the perceived value of the master's degree in library science as a necessary credential for librarians, the increasing complexity of work that librarians expect paraprofessional staff to perform without additional compensation or promotion, the status of librarians and library administrators vis-à-vis teaching faculty, and the limitations of recent mergers between libraries and information technology departments.

Tahir Rauf's chapter on funding and budgeting describes the various sources of library funds and how budgets for collections, services, and facilities are planned and implemented. He explains the various financial management practices and budget systems libraries use and how to control collections costs via resource sharing, assessment, and data-driven acquisitions. He considers demographic and technological change in academic libraries and their effect on the allocation of library funds today and ends with a consideration of facility planning to contain costs and maximize usable space for readers.

Sarah K. Lippincott and Joan K. Lippincott's chapter addressing faculty research and scholarly communication begins with a brief history of academic publishing along with an explanation of the peer review process and its importance in controlling quality in scholarship. The Lippincotts then describe the influence of teaching faculty—who need to be productive scholars creating new knowledge—on the priorities of their universities' libraries and librarians. They note that, as researchers' challenges have multiplied due to "profound technological and economic changes disrupting the publishing system," academic librarians increasingly "act as curators and stewards of the scholarly record, as advisors to faculty and students on the publishing process, and as advocates for systemic changes that improve access to the products of research." Related to this, they grapple with the current crisis in academic publishing. They note in particular that "escalating journal prices have far-reaching implications for libraries, many of which cannot afford to purchase or subscribe to all the content their researchers require" and argue that therefore libraries must become increasingly proactive and creative in exploring less costly ways to provide research materials to scholars through advocacy for open access publishing models and institutional repositories.

1

Historical Context and Contemporary Challenges

Deanna B. Marcum

Americans know the story of industrialist Andrew Carnegie (1835–1919) and his philanthropy, which resulted in every community of any size having a public library to meet the leisure reading and information needs of its citizens. Carnegie cared about efficiency and cost containment, and he developed two sets of blueprints communities could use for their buildings—one large and one small. Now, on road trips across the country, drivers can immediately recognize the Carnegie library in hundreds of neighborhoods. Academic library buildings, in contrast, come in a wide variety of shapes, sizes, and styles. Their histories and functions cannot be separated from the historical narrative of their parent institutions. While public libraries arose to meet the wide range of community needs, academic libraries feature a specific purpose—to meet the research and curricular needs of the faculty and students who work and live on their campuses.

Academic libraries have never been independent. They serve their parent institutions and grow in collection size and budget in direct relationship to the priority these institutions grant them. Throughout the nineteenth and first half of the twentieth centuries, academic libraries purchased books in support of the curriculum, stored them on shelves in the building, and looked remarkably similar to one another.[1] During the same period, many disciplines developed lists of recommended readings and what undergraduates were expected to know came from those lists. Yet, it was in this same period, beginning around 1900, that the first major change to academic libraries became evident: Libraries began to focus on building local collections that went beyond the curriculum. Colleges and universities measured their prestige and distinction by the library collection.[2]

World War II severely disrupted the serenity and calm of the academic library. Millions of veterans returned with their educational benefits from the GI Bill in hand.[3] These same veterans were also buying houses and starting families, ensuring that eighteen years later, the first of the baby boomers would enroll in colleges and universities in droves. World War II officially ended the isolationist policies of the first half of the twentieth century, and Americans grew highly sensitized to the need for global understanding. At the same time, the technological advances that led to winning the war proved to be a driving force for the future. Science, agriculture, engineering, and business became the fast-growing areas, and universities expanded rapidly to keep up. The US government invested heavily in research related to science, technology, and national defense. Academic and research libraries that had been more related to the liberal arts curriculum came under new pressure to build research collections unlike those prior to the war.

As universities and colleges grew, and as community colleges sprang up in many states to increase access to higher education and take some of the enrollment pressures off the large public universities, library collections grew exponentially. For the research university, size equaled quality, and because all academic institutions during the second half of the twentieth century were imitating the standard-bearer—Harvard—all grew as much as their budgets would allow. The fact that libraries became more professionalized during this period contributed to increasing collections as well. Newly appointed directors of academic libraries took great pride in securing new special collections and adding volumes to the physical count. Their success was tied to growth of collections.

Before World War II, relatively few Americans were college educated. Few had imagined a future in which a college degree would be a widely held credential. Based on reputable economists' estimates of 150,000 to 700,000 returning veterans who would take advantage of the GI Bill, the public universities and colleges were totally unprepared for the 2.2 million veterans who enrolled in higher education through the benefits program.[4] Institutions of higher education were dealing with huge numbers of adult learners—men who had literally been through a war—and they had to respond with different types of learning methods, as well as library resources to support these students, who did not fit the old model of college students. By the 1960s, the baby boomers born just after the war appeared in huge numbers on the doorsteps of every form of institution of higher education, demanding more choices and expressing impatience with traditional forms of authority designed for inexperienced high school graduates.

The trend in academic institutions away from rote memorization was already well established by the mid-twentieth century, but the focus on individual research and analytical thinking received even greater attention with the influx of so many nontraditional students after World War II. College was no longer a purely residential experience. Community colleges and regional universities adapted to provide services for the commuter and working students.

The federal government fueled the research agendas of the largest research universities, and a strong link developed between the two. Government interests in scientific and technological advancement meant that corresponding departments in the academy received hefty grant funding. Laboratories were outfitted with new equipment, and libraries went up to house the ever-expanding literature, especially the new, more specialized journals that emerged in the scientific era. Big-government scientific research funded by large grants necessitated rapid results and databases. Abstracting and indexing services pioneered by Frederick Wilfrid Lancaster (1933–2013) and Robert M. Hayes (b. 1926), among others, made it possible for scientists to discover much more quickly the work going on in their fields. Libraries contributed to the ease of scientific searching in some cases by subscribing to these services or in others by creating subject-specific services; for example, the National Library of Medicine created MEDLINE, a bibliographic database of life sciences and biomedical information, and made it freely available.

A New Focus on Students

Post–World War II universities earned their distinction through research, but beginning in the 1960s, all academic institutions—from community colleges to major research universities—felt compelled to pay increased attention to the needs of undergraduate students. The decade of the '60s witnessed the deaths of preeminent civil rights and political leaders. Military action in Vietnam raised social concerns about a draft policy that required all American men between the ages of eighteen and twenty-five to register for military service. An exemption for college students caused thousands of young men to enroll in an academic institution. Campus protests of civil rights injustices and military involvement in Southeast Asia led large numbers of students to find their voices in opposition to the status quo. They demanded more of a voice in their educational programs, as well. Why should they study the works of so-called dead white men exclusively? What could they learn from women writers, gay writers, or racially ethnic writers? The slogan "Don't trust anyone over thirty"[5] signaled the deep distrust of authority by young people, and that attitude accounted for some of the profound changes that took place on academic campuses and in their libraries. Faculty had to be concerned about student engagement, something that only the liberal arts colleges had been concerned with until this time. By the 1970s, academic institutions were talking about teaching and learning, and this movement continued to grow to the end of the twentieth century. Innovative faculty experimented with new forms of teaching and learning, and they acknowledged that students learn in different ways. Academic libraries of all types offered new services that addressed different learning styles and different needs. The library building now housed writing and study clinics, advising centers, and language labs.

While community college libraries and liberal arts college libraries were finding their way in offering more tailored services for their students, university libraries came to the realization that undergraduates had distinctive needs that were not easily met by the university's research library. As early as 1949, the first undergraduate library was built on the Harvard campus.[6] The 1960s witnessed a rapid growth of separate undergraduate libraries on many of the state-supported institutions of higher education. Warren Kuhn, then library director at Iowa State University, explained, "If the university experience is to be one in which the profound relationship between books and life-long learning can be initiated for students, the undergraduate library would seem a valid means for stimulating and reinforcing this process and in opening up for students the wider bibliographical territory beyond."[7] The rapid rise of the undergraduate library on large campuses was notable for the emphasis placed on providing customized services for students, not just the faculty.

Liberal arts college libraries led the way in establishing collaborations between faculty and librarians in developing information literacy programs for undergraduates. Evan Farber, director of Earlham College Library, launched a bibliographic instruction program on his campus that required a librarian-led component to courses taught at Earlham.[8] During his three-decade tenure, Farber was the profession's most important ambassador for the library's role in teaching and learning, and academic libraries across the United States emulated the bibliographic instruction program that he developed for Earlham.

Technology as a Transformative Force

The information explosion made searching in a card catalog obsolete. Fast-moving discoveries and new technology replaced the quiet life of the scholar who toiled in solitude for decades. From the 1800s, scientists and inventors tried to find ways to deal with large amounts of data—ways to sort and analyze it. The pioneering English codebreaker Alan Turing (1912–1954) in 1945 designed the prototype of a modern computer as he sought to understand the types of information that are computable. By the end of World War II, the ENIAC (Electronic Numerical Integrator and Computer) drew attention in the general press. Although designed for use by the US Army to calculate artillery firing tables, the ENIAC featured in national newspapers as a "giant brain" that could calculate huge amounts of data in short order. Scholars soon understood the possibilities of this number-crunching capability. Scientists wanted this type of capability in their labs. And libraries wanted this sort of capability to make massive amounts of bibliographic and abstracting and indexing information available to support scholarship.

The Library of Congress (LC) hired Henriette Avram (1919–2006) in 1965. She had worked for the National Security Agency (NSA) in the 1950s, where she was introduced to an IBM 701 and became one of the first computer programmers. In the 1960s, while working for a software company, Datatrol Corporation, she was given the assignment of designing a computer science library. She consulted the Library of Congress to understand how bibliographic information was constructed. It quickly became apparent that she had a great deal to offer the nation's library, then in the process of trying to determine how to provide access to the millions of bibliographic records for the materials in its collection. Working closely with professional librarians, Avram invented MAchine Readable

Cataloging (MARC) records, and her system became the foundation for a technological revolution in libraries.

After bibliographic records were converted to machine-readable computer code, for the first time, librarians could easily share these catalog records with libraries across the United States and around the world. In 1967, the Ohio College Association hired Frederick Kilgour (1914–2006), medical librarian at Yale University, to create a library network of fifty-four academic libraries in the state so that they could share resources. He hired Avram as a consultant to help him think through the use of technology for accomplishing this task. He ultimately created a worldwide bibliographic system that currently comprises more than 16,000 institutional members in more than 100 countries: OCLC. While the acronym originally stood for the Ohio College Library Center, in 1981 it changed to the On-line Computer Library Center.

After OCLC, other bibliographic networks emerged. These were designed either to serve specific regional needs or, as in the case of the Research Libraries Group (RLG), to improve on the bibliographic records in order to meet the needs of scholars in the largest research universities. Over time, the regional networks and RLG were folded into OCLC, making it the single-most important source of bibliographic data.

While the original intent of OCLC was to provide a rich database of bibliographic records so that libraries could take advantage of others' cataloging, saving millions of dollars for libraries collectively, scholars could use the same database to find out where information resources were housed. This easily accessible information meant that scholars could readily see what their colleagues in other institutions had access to. This knowledge of what others had led to competition, especially among research libraries. Research universities were competing for federal dollars and also for talent. The best scholars wanted easy access to scholarly resources, and they demanded that from their institutions.

Other types of libraries were affected indirectly. Liberal arts colleges were increasingly rewarding faculty not only for teaching but also research. The faculty wanted access to more scholarly resources. Community colleges emerged all across the country after the late 1960s to meet the demand for access to higher education. They enrolled more students than all of the other types of higher education combined, but their library budgets were tiny in comparison to those of their counterparts. Librarians wanted to take advantage of the technology that allowed them to know what was available where and the value system of the profession that encourages sharing. OCLC made it clear that technology could facilitate sharing, so networks and consortia were created to allow access for the students and faculty who did not happen to be part of a well-endowed institution. The social climate in the post-Vietnam era emphasized access and fairness; technology made it possible.

The ever-escalating cost of library materials also reinforced the impetus for sharing. The cost of books to support the humanities and social sciences remained relatively stable, but scientific and technology fields were not satisfied with books that took a long time to write and a long time to publish. Information needs in these fields were too rapidly changing, so journal literature became the preferred choice for disseminating research results in these fields. And the fields and subfields of specialization within a discipline grew rapidly, each defined by a new journal or journals. Libraries saw their serials budgets growing rapidly in the 1970s and '80s, eating into the budget allocated to monographs.

Emergence of the Internet and the Possibility of a Digital Library

The Council on Library Resources (CLR), a nonprofit organization established by the Ford Foundation in 1956 to make grants to libraries to help them adopt automation, awarded a grant to J. C. R. Licklider (1915–1990), a professor at MIT, to develop a library of the future. Funded in the late 1950s, the grant report issued in 1961 took the form of a monograph, *Libraries of the Future* (1965), published by MIT Press. Charged by the council to explore how developing technologies might shape libraries in the year 2000, Licklider's group envisioned a much closer interaction between scientists and the information itself than print libraries could offer. He imagined an automated system that allowed scientists to interact directly and immediately with accumulated knowledge.

While the Library of Congress and OCLC were making good progress toward a global system for sharing bibliographic information, the scientific community was building on computer capabilities and communications technologies to allow information seekers to go directly to the information itself—the very thing librarians had always wanted to deliver to their users. The development of the Internet and the World Wide Web gave rise to a massive conversion of analog material to digital format. Websites could be searched, and the information itself could be found, not just the bibliographic information that would let a user know the location of the information. It would be difficult to exaggerate the importance of this technological shift for academic libraries. For decades, librarians had played an intermediary role, helping their students and faculty to identify and secure the information resources they needed. In the connected world, users believed they could find what they wanted for themselves, at any time, from anywhere. Librarians, of course, know the limits of the open web, and they have to remind users that much of the information they seek will only be found in subscription-based databases, such as those ProQuest and EBSCO have developed, LexisNexis, JSTOR, and others provided through library purchases.

Librarians saw the opportunities wrought by the technology, of course, but it was not so easy to figure out how to make the transition from the analog books and journals on shelves to digital library resources. Librarians began wondering how they could digitize their resources to make them more widely accessible. One of the first massive digitization efforts began at the Library of Congress in the early 1990s. Librarian of Congress James Billington established a group of technology experts to advise the library on ways to digitize the primary source materials in its special collections and distribute them to primary and secondary schools. First relying on CD-ROMs (prepressed optical disks containing data in so-called read-only format) for distribution, the library launched the American Memory Program, in which documents related to America's history and culture were scanned, imprinted on these CD-ROMs, and sent through regular mail to schools around the country.

Members of Congress warmly embraced this project because it gave them something to deliver to their home districts. They saw the distribution of the contents of the Library of Congress to every schoolchild in America as an important public good. It helped that newly elected Speaker of the House Newt Gingrich was an ardent supporter of the project. He added $5 million to the library's annual appropriation. Following his lead, individual philanthropists and other foundations contributed to the effort. The Library of Congress set a goal to digitize 5 million items from the library's collections over the next five years. While the original intent of this project was to provide digitized versions of primary source materials to schools and the general public, the primary users of the collection were college students and faculty.

The highly publicized nature of LC's American Memory Project stimulated other academic and research libraries to think about what portions of their collections should be digitized and made widely available. Individual donors, seeing the power of Internet visibility, insisted as part of the contract that the collections they contributed to libraries be digitally accessible via the Internet. Users quickly became accustomed to having access to many materials that had until then been available only on-site at the holding library. They appreciated seeing the digitized highlights of individual collections, but they wanted more. When Google announced at the Frankfurt Book Fair in December 2004 the Google Print Library Project—that it planned to work with six major research libraries to digitize their entire collections and make them accessible—this sealed the deal. This announcement constituted an expansion of the Google Print Program, which until then had assisted publishers in making books and other offline information searchable online. Libraries, like it or not, would become digital.

What we have known since 2005 as Google Books, then, began as Google Print. Google planned to scan the content of books so they could be indexed and searched. Publishers and authors raised objections on copyright grounds. Libraries questioned what this initiative would mean for the local institutional collections. On the one hand, the Google project would actually accomplish what librarians had aspired to forever—to make the collections of knowledge universally available. On the other, why would an individual library make any difference if all knowledge were to be available on the Internet?

The Google Books Project ran into a number of legal and public relations problems. Universities and their libraries were asked to sign nondisclosure agreements, which bound both the institutions and Google to secrecy so the general public had no knowledge of the terms under which Google would scan the collections. Publishers saw in the plan complete disregard for intellectual property rights, even though Google had pledged to make publicly accessible only so-called snippets of copyright-protected content. In 2005, authors and publishers, through the Authors Guild and the Association of American Publishers, filed a suit to halt the Google Books Project, and legal battles ensued that went on for a decade. Technologists saw in the Google Books Project the first glimmer of hope that a universal digital library could be realized, with the only drawback being that a single commercial company had created a monopoly. Many technologists called on Google to join forces with others to make Google Books a public good project.

The academic library community became sharply divided on the issue. The five large libraries that signed on initially (Harvard, the University of Michigan, the New York Public Library, Oxford, and Stanford) knew that the cost of digitizing their collections on their own would be prohibitively expensive. If Google would do this for them, with the promise that each library could have a copy of the digital files to use as they saw fit, then they counted themselves as the beneficiaries of an enormous gift. They would use those files to build a local digital library and make access much more convenient for their students and faculty. Few of these institutions, however, would actually have the infrastructure to host the massive digital files that resulted from the digitization effort. Brewster Kahle (b. 1960) of the Internet Archive[9] had long aspired to create a universal digital library. He had actively supported Carnegie Mellon's Professor Raj Reddy (b. 1937) in his Million Book Project, which entailed sending libraries' books to India and China for inexpensive scanning and then depositing the digital files with the Internet Archive. Kahle approached Google about joining forces, but being rebuffed, he established the Open Content Alliance (OCA), which offered an alternative for libraries that wanted their collections to be Internet accessible.

As noted earlier, Harvard was one of the founding Google Books participants. University librarian Sidney Verba (b. 1932) signed the agreement before his retirement, and digitization efforts were underway when newly appointed university librarian Robert Darnton (b. 1939) appeared on the scene in 2007. Darnton questioned the agreement that Google and Verba had made and began national-level discussions about the opportunities for the library community to join together to create a massive, free digital library that would be a distributed responsibility rather than the work of any one organization. He convened a meeting of library leaders, technologists, and foundation representatives in October 2010 at Harvard to discuss the possibility of creating a national digital library. The word *national* conjured up too many bad associations for too many librarians, and the most important decision reached at that meeting was that the initiative would be called the Digital Public Library of America (DPLA). Steering committees to put flesh on the bones of the new organization were appointed, and eventually a governance structure was developed. With funding from the Institute of Museum and Library Services (IMLS) and the National Endowment for the Humanities (NEH), scanning hubs were created that allow small libraries, historical societies, and museums to have their collections scanned so that cultural organizations of all sizes will be represented in the new Digital Public Library of America. Thus far DPLA amounts to a collection of metadata that act as pointers to the cultural organization that actually holds the material.

These mass digitization projects are important historical events because they foreshadowed what would happen to academic libraries. Students growing up in the age of the Internet would expect the vast web of resources to be available to them. The notion of being limited to the library's local collection would be anathema to them. The large aggregations of digital content would rival the local collections for students' attention and use, and academic libraries would have to justify in entirely new ways their budget requests on their local campuses. Academic libraries struggled with decisions concerning the best way to be involved in the digital revolution. Library users were giving them great credit for opening the knowledge vaults to make scholarly content easily and freely accessible. But how to pay for digitization efforts became a conundrum. While demonstration grants[10] were relatively common in the early years of digitization, the larger institutions with massive special collections had been the most likely recipients. The congressional interest shown for the American Memory Project faded as quickly as it appeared, and there seemed to be no hope of securing government funds for a massive digital library program such as the one developed in Europe, Europeana. Larger academic libraries enjoyed some reallocation of funds that had been used for preservation of print collections to digitization centers that were staffed to scan materials continually. Smaller college and community college libraries could hardly set up their own operations. In their cases, they secured digital content for their users by subscribing to vendor-provided services, such as EBSCO and ProQuest, which converted the microfilmed collations from years past, or through agreements they reached with libraries to scan topical or time-bounded collections.

Acquisitions librarians became contract negotiations specialists, as the books and serials budgets gave way to subscriptions to digital resources. Community colleges as well as comprehensive universities began offering more online courses, and they needed to offer electronic resources to support the work of their remote students. Libraries of all types and sizes learned that their users on and off campus preferred the ease of electronic access. Users were not interested in what the library actually owned; instead, they wanted access to the vast web of resources. As the web of Internet-based resources continued to grow, academic libraries on individual campuses were forced to reconsider their roles and responsibilities.

Financial Pressures and Uncomfortable Questions

The disruption was first felt in the budget. The ubiquitous hype surrounding the power of the Internet convinced many administrators and trustees that "everything" was freely available as long as one had access to a computer. In budget justification meetings, libraries were interrogated about why a library was any longer needed. And if it was needed, could it not be drastically reduced? The rhetoric about the library being the heart of the campus no longer convinced a number of leaders who paid the bills. When the financial crisis of 2008 made its effects known on college campuses, the questions became sharper and more urgent. Some of the largest and oldest private universities, such as Harvard, saw their endowments lose more than 20 percent of their value. The public institutions that lived on annual tuition fared slightly better, but the public was becoming restive about the cost of tuition, and boards of trustees felt obligated to contain or even lower tuition fees. The recession led to the elimination of jobs in huge numbers; companies were no longer hiring new college graduates. Families balked at paying high tuition costs given that they could not envision a clear career path for graduates, and politicians called on universities and colleges to downplay the value of the liberal arts, urging them to pay greater attention to the sciences and technology—those fields that would help rebuild American's economic strength. President Obama focused on the role of community colleges in preparing American workers with immediately needed skills. All of these factors created enormous challenges for academic libraries.

Administrators questioned the need to build collections of materials that would not be used immediately. Libraries responded by moving even more quickly to licensing databases that allowed access to students and faculty for a subscription fee and to patron-driven acquisition (PDA) plans, which require a library to pay only for those materials used by the students and faculty on a particular campus. Consortia of institutions formed by type or region became more focused on collective purchases and licensing agreements. The financial crisis sparked a much stronger interest in financial accountability, and librarians in every type of academic institution found themselves having to justify in new and detailed ways how their expenditures helped the institution meet its goals.

Significant drops in humanities majors, especially those in English and history, meant that these longtime favorites of librarians would not be receiving the collections support they had enjoyed in the past. STEM (science, technology, engineering, and mathematics) programs received both federal and state support, while humanities programs shrank. Smaller colleges in particular consolidated humanities departments into broad programs in order to reduce faculty costs. And these changes in the academy affected library operations. While the humanities departments generally speaking had demonstrated interest in working with librarians to provide information fluency training for their students, the STEM departments were more interested in access to additional databases. The students learned to use these resources as part of their classroom instruction, so there was little need for librarians' involvement.

Meanwhile, faculty members were also finding ways to meet their needs beyond their institutional libraries. Beginning in the 1990s, several disciplines in the sciences launched efforts to bring all of their literature together in digital form, including preprints, published articles, and related materials. Paul Ginsparg (b. 1955), a physics professor at Cornell, created arXiv, a preprint repository for mathematics, physics, astronomy, computer science, quantitative biology, statistics, and quantitative finance. Launched in 1991, the repository grew rapidly, and eventually Cornell University Libraries hosted it with financial assistance from other institutions whose faculty depend on the collection. Discipline-based repositories in other fields became popular in succeeding years. Academic libraries, especially the largest ones, recognized that they could play an important role on their campuses by collecting the intellectual output of their faculty and making it accessible to others while also saving money for their institutions. For some libraries, this proved to be the best route for supporting open access. By asking scholars to deposit their scholarship in a form not protected by third-party copyright, libraries could become distributors of high-quality, free scholarly resources. Harvard and the University of California System led the way in establishing repositories for faculty research based on votes in all of the colleges to support open access.

Other institutions, such as the University of Maryland System, have focused on policies that encourage the use of open educational resources (OER) for their students, helping them to avoid the cost of expensive textbooks. The University of Maryland University College (UMUC), primarily an online college that focuses on working adult learners, has become notable for its adoption of embedded OERs for all its courses. UMUC's small cadre of full-time faculty develop the courses, while many adjuncts around the world teach them. The University of Maryland librarians have played an essential role in helping faculty to identify the high-quality open educational resources that are available to support teaching and learning.

Publishers have come to see open access as the inevitable future, and they are increasingly putting portions of their protected content on the web as a way to bring users directly to their sites. They are concerned about maintaining their reputations as purveyors of high-quality, peer-reviewed content. Most of the scholarly publishers have adopted some form of open access for some of their journals, depending on author payments (known as article processing charges, or APCs) for publication to cover costs for the content being openly accessible. Such journals as *PLOS ONE* (published by the Public Library of Science) and *PeerJ* distribute open access scholarly resources in the sciences. *PLOS ONE* relies on author fees as its business model; *PeerJ* charges either a per-article price (no matter how many authors are involved) or a membership price for authors, who can submit as many articles for publication as they like. These models, which work well in the sciences because most of the researchers have federal grants to support their research and cover these costs, are not well suited to the humanities, where grants are either small or nonexistent.

Transition from Collections to Services

The focus on STEM disciplines by so many institutions created a crisis in the library community. Humanistic disciplines had received disproportionate attention from librarians for many years. Most academic librarians were themselves trained in the humanities or social sciences and did not possess deep knowledge of the sciences. Much of the scholarly literature in the humanities grows out of scholarly societies or university presses, while the scientific literature comes mainly from commercial publishers. As more federal funding went into scientific research, the cost of science journals escalated rapidly, and because science researchers were securing large grants for their universities, these researchers could demand that their libraries purchase or license the materials they needed. The model for science publications worked reasonably well for the largest research libraries (although they were not pleased with the high costs, either), but the subscription costs for regional comprehensive, college, and community college libraries simply could not be sustained. Over time, academic librarians, individually or as part of professional organizations, began to mount campaigns against the publishers. Some limited their campaigns to commercial publishers, but others saw publishers in general as the enemy. While we might easily imagine that, when both libraries and publishers had to face the need to move entirely into the digital era, they would find common ground for collaboration, this has not happened. Distrust has developed on both sides, and librarians have campaigned for open access models for disseminating scholarly materials. Furthermore, a number of academic libraries in both research universities and colleges have become publishers themselves in order to make scholarly information more broadly and freely accessible.

What has remained constant during the post–World War II era is the ability of academic libraries to adapt. In the 1950s and '60s, academic libraries were challenged with growth—more institutions of higher education, each needing a library for the acquisition and storage of curricular and research materials. Additional staff had to be hired to serve the growing student populations and to meet the expanding needs: As new and nontraditional groups of students began enrolling in universities, colleges, and community colleges, their corresponding libraries developed missions and purposes that would contribute to their parent institutions' success. Automation and digitization changed the course of academic library history perhaps more than any other factor. Beginning with the creation of OCLC for widespread reuse of catalog records, technical services staffs, which had been the backbone of academic libraries, began to diminish, and now only the largest libraries with highly specialized collections or heavily invested in international cultures and languages employ sizeable numbers of catalogers. Community colleges and smaller college libraries have generally opted to buy materials that come with publisher-generated catalog records or simply rely on copy cataloging for records for their own online catalogs.

Google and other search engines have put information directly into the hands of students and faculty. From the perspective of the Internet-savvy undergraduate, there is little need to consult reference librarians for most assignments. Many academic librarians, once generalists who guided and assisted undergraduates and specialists who identified the most appropriate research materials for their faculties, have morphed into service providers—knowledge navigators who work in partnership with faculty and students in their departments in support of their work, whatever that may be. Consequently, the librarians who work as partners with the academics must be deeply immersed in the discipline in order to be successful.

Providing services and developing pathways to information resources have largely replaced building local collections. Collaborative programs to create print monograph repositories that can be used at the point of need for a number of institutional libraries (e.g., the University of California's northern and southern regional facilities) and subscription services to digitized journals that obviate the need for individual libraries to house the bound volumes (e.g., JSTOR) have cleared shelf space in academic libraries to make way for collaborative study spaces, more technology, quiet rooms for individual reflection, coffee bars, and cafés. The building that was designed to shelve books efficiently has become a community center for learning. Librarians serve as advisors, mentors, and partners in the academic enterprise, and they mark their success based on the extent to which they help their institutions to do a better job of recruiting, retaining, and graduating students.

Discussion Questions

1. How have academic libraries measured their success in the last fifteen to twenty years? Why have these measures been important? What new measures should be used in the current environment? In what way would the new measures reveal the effectiveness of the library?
2. Librarians have been trained to work in a collections-based institution. What are the new educational requirements in a services-based model of the academic library?
3. How has technology changed the role of the academic librarian and his or her relationship with users?
4. How have massive digital libraries affected the role of the institutional academic library?

Assignment

Thinking about the shift from a collections focus to a services focus, identify a specific academic library, and write a five- to ten-page paper describing the changes that would be needed in organizational structure to effect that shift. What skills must the librarians possess in order to be effective?

Notes

1. From 1906 until 1941, the Carnegie Corporation awarded grants to 248 college libraries to build their book collections in support of undergraduate education. The foundation's Advisory Group on College Libraries drew up a list of books recommended for undergraduate education, and this list became the measure of quality of library collections.
2. Stephen E. Atkins, *The Academic Library in the American University* (Chicago: American Library Association, 1991), 23, http://digicoll.library.wisc.edu/cgi-bin/History/History-idx?type=turn&entity=History.AcadLib.p0039&id=History.
3. The Servicemen's Readjustment Act of 1944 (P.L. 78-346, 58 Stat. 284m), known informally as the GI Bill, was a law that provided a range of benefits for returning World War II veterans (commonly referred to as GIs). Benefits included cash payments of tuition and living expenses to attend a university or high school or vocational education, as well as one year of unemployment compensation.
4. Thomas N. Bonner, "The Unintended Revolution: In America's Colleges since 1940," *Change: The Magazine of Higher Learning* 18, no. 5 (September–October 1986): 46, doi:10.1080/00091383.1986.9940575.
5. Attributed to Jack Weinberg, leader of Berkeley's Free Speech Movement of the 1960s.
6. Keys D. Metcalf, "The Undergraduate and the Harvard Library, 1937-1947," *Harvard Library Bulletin* 1 (Autumn 1947): 288–305.
7. Warren B. Kuhn, "Undergraduate Libraries in a University," *Library Trends* 18, no. 2 (1969): 188–209, http://lib.dr.iastate.edu/libadmin_pubs/9.
8. Evan Farber, "Faculty-Librarian Cooperation: A Personal Retrospective," *Reference Services Review* 27, no. 3 (1999): 229–34.
9. Internet Archive, established in 1996, is a nonprofit organization with a mission to build an Internet library, a digital equivalent of a public library.
10. This is a grant, generally of limited duration, made to establish or demonstrate the feasibility of a theory or approach.

2

College and University Governance

THE ROLE OF THE ACADEMIC LIBRARY

Barbara I. Dewey

Academic libraries constitute a fundamental part of college and university transformation and success in the twenty-first century. This chapter focuses on colleges' and universities' governance structures in all respects and how these structures relate to the library. Typical collegiate governance structures are examined, including overall institutional governance, executive level administration, collegiate and academic departmental administration, research, finance, development, general counsel, institutional support unit configurations, faculty governance (including senates and committees), staff governance (including labor unions), student governance, alumni and development governance, ethics, equity and diversity, compliance, and accreditation requirements. Organizational structure varies widely in terms of an institution's size and level of formality.

The institution's strategic planning process and the importance of library relevance to its vision, mission, goals, and foundational principles are discussed. This chapter provides a comprehensive overview of college and university governance and the important ways library convergence is achieved within the governance process and university stakeholder interaction. The alignment of libraries with the institutions' strategic plans are detailed, including identifying and managing initiatives. Finally, we summarize strategies for participation and communication with different sectors of the institution.

Institutional Governance in Higher Education

Universities, colleges, and community colleges conform to a variety of governance models. All institutions that are accredited or that seek accreditation are first and foremost placed under the auspices of an accrediting body. Accreditation constitutes the recognition that an institution maintains certain standards, and its goal is to ensure that the education institutions of higher education provide meets acceptable levels of quality. Accrediting agencies are bodies that establish operating standards for educational institutions, determine if these standards are met, and publicly announce their findings for the benefit of prospective students and faculty. There are two types of accreditation—institutional (college- or university-wide) and specialized (specific professional school, major, or college).[1]

Library leaders or members of their staff (or both) support the accreditation process by supplying institutional information (including information about the library), serving on committees set up to write the required self-study, and meeting with the visiting committees. The opportunity to participate on accreditation committees can be a valuable way for librarians to connect with people from throughout the institution and learn more about a myriad of initiatives occurring in different campus sectors. This knowledge provides librarians with new avenues for campus support and participation.

The characteristics of boards differ between private and public institutions. Private institutions typically have some type of governing board operating under a set of bylaws or principles. Public institutions, depending on their states of origin, also have a governing board. Some states group public institutions together by type (for example, community colleges, state universities, technical colleges) and have one board overseeing each group. Appointment configurations and methods vary. Private institutional boards often have a nominating committee and then a vetting process before selection of board members. Boards governing public institutions vary in their makeup and selection process. Methods of selection include but are not limited to

- election by the board,
- selection by the board,
- election by alumni,
- election by all voters in the state,
- residence by geographic area or districts served by the institution,
- appointment by the state governor,
- selection by state constituency groups (business, agricultural, education, etc.),
- appointment by the board itself,
- appointment by faculty senate, and
- appointment by student government.

Meeting frequency for boards varies a great deal. In some cases, boards only meet once or twice per year but may have an executive committee who meets more frequently. In other cases, boards have committees who specialize in various aspects of university operations, such as

- academic affairs and student life;
- outreach and community relations;
- laws, ethics, and compliance;
- planning;
- finance and capital (space) planning; and
- compensation and human resources.

A board makes important decisions affecting the trajectory of the institution and therefore the library. Of primary importance is the board's responsibility for financial health and institutional control. "Academic governance in the United States is built on the principle that governing boards exercise their functions with and through the chief executive," notes Robert T. Ingram, former president of the Association of Governing Boards of Universities and Colleges.[2] It is important to be knowledgeable about the institutional governance structure, its bylaws, meeting agendas, and topics to be addressed. Some boards routinely approve administrative decisions, while others take a much more active role in the process.

Depending on the board's agenda, the library might be asked to provide background information for topics from the archives or other resources. In other cases, topics may be directly related to the library, such as decisions about new facilities or renovated spaces and technology strategies. We should consider the assumption that all board members are knowledgeable about libraries to be false. Librarians should be ready for a lot of misconceptions, such as the notion that print is no longer relevant and therefore libraries need no additional space. Another misconception is that everything is digital and therefore students no longer use the library. The library may also work with certain board members who are library donors. If board committees are in place, then the library may find that one or more handles business of high relevance to library operations. Important board decisions should also be followed, such as setting the institution's budget and determining tuition and fee rates. Board meetings, or at least parts of them, can be open to the public. It can be instructive to attend and observe firsthand the way governance works at this level. Additionally, library visibility to board members benefits their understanding of the library's centrality to student and faculty success.

Government Relationships

Public institutions of higher education have special relationships with state governments. In some cases, a representative of the state serves on the institution's governing board. Public and private institutions that accept federal funding (virtually all colleges and universities) have responsibilities to federal laws and mandates that they must fulfill in order to keep this funding. In some cases, the library can assist in ensuring compliance with these mandates; for example, with preservation and dissemination requirements for research publications and data supported by federal research funding.

Institutions accomplish their management of government relations at several levels. In large institutions, professional lobbyists specializing in state or federal government relationships enjoy a place in the president's office or another high central administrative office. Also, colleges and universities rely on lobbyists from representative organizations, such as the Association of American Universities (AAU), the Association of Public and Land-grant Universities (APLU), the Consortium of Liberal Arts Colleges (CLAC), and the Association of American Community Colleges (AACC), and disciplinary organizations, such as the Association for Research Libraries (ARL), the American Library Association (ALA), the Scholarly Publishing and Academic Resources Coalition (SPARC), and many others. These lobbyists represent the interests of higher education and associated constituencies to state and federal governments. Often libraries will be asked to provide background information on issues or may bring forward matters that affect the colleges or universities, such as open access and copyright, in order for lobbyists to explore these with appropriate government officials. In any case, it is important for library leadership to make contact with lobbyists in their institutions as well as in the library profession so as to efficiently address issues as the institutions see fit, including issues that arise suddenly.

State Relations

Public colleges, community colleges, and universities sometimes have special relationships to their states. For example, some states provide funding to help support interlibrary loan from the larger higher education–based library to communities through their public libraries. A variety of relationships might exist with the state libraries or the states' departments of education. Elected state representatives are often interested in the colleges or universities in their districts and may have questions about library policies, especially access of its collections to the local constituencies. Libraries who are federal, state, or local document depositories have important interactions with these constituencies.

Executive-Level Governance

All colleges and universities have one individual who is responsible for the operations of that institution. Titles vary, but they are typically president, chancellor, or chief executive officer (CEO). Multi-campus institutions may have a "system" parallel to the flagship campus: a president and associated administrators with their own administration. System–campus relationships must be well understood by the library so its responsibilities are carried out appropriately. In some cases, the flagship campus has responsibility for all campus libraries, and in other cases, each library reports to the campus administration. In both cases, libraries in systems need to work collaboratively and understand system leadership expectations and political realities related to funding and access. The top executive officer, whether president or chancellor, has the major responsibility for the outward face of the institution, including community relationships and fund-raising.

The second level of administration is crucial to actually leading the institution's operations. Individuals at this level, depending on the size of the institution, often have vice president titles. The positions normally include chief academic officer or provost, chief financial officer (CFO), research officer, chief information officer (CIO), diversity officer, general counsel, outreach officer, and strategic communications strategist. At larger institutions, there is often another layer of executives carrying titles like vice provost for a variety of areas; and, at some institutions, the library director is included as a vice provost.

The chief academic officer or provost plays three primary roles—presidential partner, trustee liaison, and budget leader.[3] The library is often part of the chief academic officer's portfolio, and library leaders should make sure they are supporting the academic affairs agenda of the institution. Most often the library reports directly to the chief academic officer and should not only brief him or her on library matters but also assist in institution-wide academic initiatives and priorities. Even if the library reports to another office, such as the chief information officer, a close relationship with academics is essential.

A third level of administration consists of collegiate deans or directors leading the various academic colleges and their respective programs and departments. Deans typically have associate deans reporting to them, with responsibilities for carrying out the academic missions of their respective areas, including curriculum, research, and faculty development and affairs. This cohort of executives most often includes the library director, and thus, they are peers with important relationships to nurture. Deans are often asked to speak out on strategic directions and policy directions. The library leadership should be integral to these discussions and be willing to take a stand when necessary with their dean peers on academic issues, even those that are controversial. Deans understand that, if their positions differ from those of their superiors, then they could be dismissed from their deanships.

Finance and Business Operations

A college's or university's budget process and oversight are incredibly important for all of the academic and support units in the institution. "Ownership" of the budget is normally placed in the hands of the president or provost, but it could also reside jointly with the vice president for budget and business operations (titles vary). The institution's board has overall fiscal responsibility, too. All campus units need to understand the budget process in detail, including how and when budget decisions will be made. A number of important areas fall within finance and business operations, including an office devoted to budget matters, controller (chief financial officer), investment management, audit functions, risk management, human resources, physical plant operations and space planning, and auxiliary services (food services, dorms, etc.). Governance in this area also relates strongly to state and federal legal requirements and institutional policy and procedures. The library's budget comprises a major and visible part of an institution's budget and, in more and more cases, bears a relationship to other units' budgets because of increasing partnerships.

Information Technology Organization and Governance

Information technology (IT) units are tasked with finding, creating, and sharing services and tools and with offering training that meets the evolving technological, academic, and business needs of students, faculty, and staff. IT units typically bear responsibility for networking and phone services, cybersecurity, classroom technology, enterprise business systems (for human resources, student services, and finances), identity management services, course management systems (Canvas and Blackboard, for example), and help desk operations. The head of IT usually serves as a vice president or vice provost reporting to either the chief academic officer, the vice president for business and finance, or both. Libraries have close ties to IT units because of both the need to support their rich technological environments and the emergence of an increasing number of partnerships in which IT functions within library space. In some cases, the library director is also the head of IT or reports to the head of IT. IT governance varies from none to a formal body of stakeholders charged with offering advice concerning strategies and directions. Faculty senates sometimes have an IT committee or an IT–library committee to advise them on important matters. Institutions with a student technology fee sometimes have a group of students from student governance to provide input concerning the expenditure choices from the fee.

Academic Departments and Programs

Heads of academic departments, sometimes known as chairs, are the most important and influential academic leaders because they are responsible for their disciplines or programs in terms of teaching and research. Heads are also heavily involved in faculty and student assessment. For example, they lead the promotion and tenure process for their disciplines and monitor student success. Whether large or small, the library should interface closely with academic departments to support discipline-specific teaching and research. The emphasis on multidisciplinary initiatives is growing rapidly, and libraries are well positioned to provide leadership to bring academic departments or key individuals together because libraries have a broad perspective of the entire academic enterprise.

Faculty Governance

Colleges and universities apply some version of a shared governance model by which stakeholders work with executives on decision-making in certain arenas and on consultation in others. Faculty senates serve as a focal point for shared governance and consist of faculty elected by their peers to represent them. Faculty senates usually do some version of the following:

- serve as a legislative body representing the faculty,
- act as an advisory and consultative body to the president and other executives, and
- serve as a forum for the exchange of ideas and discussion of issues.

The president of the senate and other faculty senate officers lead the faculty senate and interact with the administration on a regular basis. Faculty senate work is done largely in committees. A primary responsibility of faculty is the curriculum. It is often stated that faculty "own" the curriculum, so any changes, modifications, or developments for undergraduate and graduate programs must proceed through the appropriate curriculum committee. One committee is devoted to faculty affairs; others, to personnel and benefits, research, educational equity, undergraduate education, strategic planning, and athletics. Committees or task forces may also be formed related to areas of strategic priority and interest to the institution, such as engaged scholarship (i.e., out-of-classroom academic experiences that complement in-classroom learning) or health and wellness.

Individual colleges often have a governance group with ties to the institution's faculty senate. Libraries where librarians enjoy faculty status can also have a library faculty organization that is connected to the institution's faculty senate. Often topics related to the library appear on the agendas of these groups and will require education, support, and interaction from the library.

Staff Governance

Staff at colleges and universities are represented by staff councils, which advise the administration and, in particular, human resources leadership. Staff councils often do the following:

- provide a forum for discussion of staff-related issues;
- represent, collectively, staff issues and concerns;

- make recommendations concerning staff issues to the administration;
- ensure adequate staff participation on key university committees, such as strategic planning.[4]

Staff represented by a labor union have specific and strictly defined ways of interacting with the administration and participating in governance. Large libraries may have staff represented by multiple unions.

Libraries have, of course, a special interest in supporting their own staff and sometimes have governance structures in place, such as a staff counsel to advise the library administration. Library staff might also serve on the institution-wide staff counsel. Staff, in general, are important stakeholders for the library and significant in varying degrees to the successful execution of its duties.

Student Governance

Students have representation on an elected body that goes by different names, such as student senate or student association. At larger institutions, there will also be a body representing graduate students. Student senates enact legislation regarding student matters through such committees as academic affairs, student affairs, and diversity affairs. Student government bodies work closely with the president, provost, and especially the vice president for student affairs. Student leaders work on a wide variety of agendas, including those related to their hopes and desires for the library specifically or for initiatives related to the library, such as open access, hours of operation, and sufficient seating. Securing student support can be an effective way to initiate positive changes for the library.

Academic Affairs Governance

As noted earlier, faculty play an important role in academic affairs, especially in overseeing the curriculum and the promotion and tenure process. However, certain administrators also have specific responsibility for steering undergraduate and graduate learning as well as faculty support and development (including, once again, oversight of the promotion and tenure process). At larger institutions, this responsibility may fall to committees comprised of appropriate representatives from each college or program who make decisions regarding academic policy and procedures. A similar committee or group of representatives focuses on graduate education. Some institutions have governing committees for online programs. Library representation on these committees is important to ensure appropriate involvement and improve the overall effectiveness of such groups. Individual colleges or departments may also have advisory committees of alumni and other professionals or educators. These advisory committees may serve the entire college or be focused on a specific program, such as colleges of business, education, and liberal arts.

Research Governance

The research enterprise is a big part of higher education, especially for those institutions with a strong research focus. Such institutions have an office or at least an individual charged with supporting faculty and student research and ensuring appropriate research conduct and compliance with state and federal requirements. Offices of research also play a role in

- educating faculty and students about research grant opportunities in the public and private sector;
- assisting faculty and staff with patents, funding opportunities and awards, and research protections;
- connecting industry to the institution's researchers;
- protecting and licensing the institution's technologies; and
- representing the institution to grant agencies.

Barbara I. Dewey

Research offices work with federal, state, and private funding agencies and foundations to ensure that grants and awards are properly and successfully expended. Increasingly, mandates and legal requirements accompany awards. Compliance is essential to avoid withdrawal of funds or even more serious consequences. Library representation on an institution's research counsel helps to ensure appropriate support for research and data management, including awareness by principal investigators and academic administrators of data management services, benefits of using the institutional repository, and specialized support for all aspects of the cycle of research from problem conception to research dissemination and preservation. Such library representation also increases proposal writers' awareness of library collections support.

Human Resources and Staff Development Leadership

College and university human resources (HR) departments are responsible for the recruitment, hiring, development, and employee and labor relations functions of the institution. These central HR departments are a resource for administrators, faculty, and staff who are, in many cases, carrying out these functions at the unit level. Library leadership needs to be aware of the policies and procedures governing personnel, as well as federal and state requirements pertaining to central human resources, affirmative action officers, and those tasked with overseeing discrimination and sexual harassment complaints. Library leaders can work with central HR to improve services and opportunities benefiting the entire institution. The library can also be an excellent venue for staff development and educational offerings.

Physical Plant Operations

All colleges and universities have a unit devoted to physical facilities or what is often known as the physical plant. Physical plant operations include buildings and grounds maintenance, facilities planning, campus planning and design, energy provision, and campus environmental health and safety. The head of the physical plant unit typically reports to a vice president for budget and administration. If the unit is a public institution, then important work goes on to prepare documentation for state government on building and other projects.

Positive relationships with physical plant operations are crucial to the library's success and even to its basic operations. Negative or adversarial relationships can lead to lack of support for library building and grounds maintenance. The end result can be catastrophic to the health and well-being of staff and collections. Although not part of the academic side of the house, where elitism can impede relationships across job boundaries, physical plant employees should be respected and included in library activities and planning efforts. For example, support by a college or university administration for a new library or a library renovation project will not surface without library leaders first generating excitement and support of the physical plant director and his or her team.

Diversity and Inclusion Leadership

Fostering diversity and inclusion has become an important endeavor at colleges and universities. All of academic leadership is charged with contributing to a positive climate of diversity, equity, and inclusion throughout the institution for faculty, staff, and students, as well as increasing capacity for diversity. Often there is an individual or an office charged with leading and coordinating these efforts. Within the institution, the responsible person supports and evaluates diversity and inclusion initiatives and serves as an advocate for a range of populations, including historically underrepresented racial and ethnic minorities; persons with disabilities; persons from low-income families who would be first-generation college students; veterans; lesbian, gay, bisexual, and transgender persons; and women.[5]

The library is ideally suited to provide leadership in diversity and inclusion, not only in diversifying the library itself but also by motivating the institution as a whole to increase diversity efforts. Libraries represent the diversity of knowledge and the human experience. Librarians and staff are active on campus committees and commissions related to diversity and bring important values and resources to the table through programming, collection development, assistance with recruitment, and other activities. Librarians' professional philosophies and ethics of creating a welcoming environment, championing academic freedom, and providing access to information and scholarly resources from many perspectives make them the obvious choice to assume the role of ambassadors for inclusion and diversity.

Global Programs and Presence

More and more colleges and universities are putting strategic focus on global programs. Initiatives include study abroad, recruitment, enrollment, and support of international students; development of strategic international affiliations and partnerships; and international fund-raising. At larger institutions, a high-level administrator, such as a vice president or vice provost, leads global program efforts. The library is an important partner in these efforts. Activities include providing resources for study-abroad participants, participating in orientation programs for international students, making connections with libraries in partner institutions around the world, and developing robust collections to support work in regions of interest.

Athletics

Governance for intercollegiate athletics varies by size and type of institution, as do reporting relationships. At large institutions, an athletic director may report directly to the president and also have an athletic advisory board of alumni or others with a passion for and perhaps expertise in athletics. Smaller institutions may have individuals supporting athletics who also have other roles, such as faculty or staff. Athletics programs at institutions that are members of the National Collegiate Athletics Association (NCAA) operate under specific rules regarding student athletes and how they interface with their academic and athletics programs. Libraries on campuses with athletics departments should be knowledgeable about athletics' personnel and programs in order to provide support for student athletes' success, participate in such athletics programming as tutoring or library instruction, and support athletics administrators and coaches. In some cases, library donors are also supporting athletics (and the same is true with collegiate and disciplinary donors). Also, libraries can provide a home for an institution's sports records, thereby creating a potentially powerful archive of high interest to alumni and donors now and in the future.

Ethics and Compliance

Colleges and universities are subject to a myriad of state and federal laws and requirements. Additionally, individual institutions have implemented more rigorous methodologies for legal and stakeholder accountability. Many more processes are now in place to safeguard the well-being of students, faculty, and the public who interact with the institution at various times. These processes, including training, are put into place by the growing number of professionals with extensive expertise in ethics and compliance. Smaller institutions are also subject to the legal and moral ethics and compliance expectations but might make heavier use of consultant or faculty expertise in setting up the required systems of training, background checking, and general education on the topic. Library staff sometimes get involved in aspects of ethics and compliance by supporting records management programs and providing support for tools to detect plagiarism.

Risk Management and Audit

Institutions have some type of risk management operation whose mission is to enable the college or university to protect revenue and assets and to facilitate good business judgments, permitting the efficient use of resources to accomplish its goals. The audit function is closely tied to risk management, but in many institutions, it has a separate office and reporting line. Audit operations perform value-added, risk-based audits designed to independently review, test, and evaluate the financial, electronic, and operational controls throughout the institution. Audit functions include examination and assessment of (for example)

- business risks facing the institution;
- compliance with policies, procedures, laws, and regulations;
- safeguarding and use of institutional assets;
- accuracy, reliability, and integrity of institutional records and reports;
- development and implementation of methods, systems, and procedures;
- suspected fraud or waste; and
- adequacy of internal controls.

Risk management personnel often bear responsibility for reviewing contracts and license agreements. In the digital age, library content is often tied to contracts and licenses, making it essential for the library to work closely and collaboratively with risk managers. Libraries will also periodically be subject to audits.

General Counsel

Most colleges and universities have a general counsel's office. The general counsel's office is typically responsible for overseeing all legal affairs of the institution. The general counsel also provides legal advice to the president, the board, and other administrators. Most general counsel incumbents work under the philosophy of providing advice and options for moving through legal issues, which can be related to personnel, procurement, intellectual property and trademarks, conflicts of interest, construction, real estate and zoning, employment and personnel issues, affirmative action, medical malpractice, human subjects in research, Title IX, Clery Act (keeping and disclosing information concerning campus crime), civil rights, sexual harassment claims, all types of liability, FERPA (Family, Educational Rights and Privacy Act), HIPAA (Health Insurance Portability and Accountability Act), and a whole host of other topics. College and research libraries do at times have legal issues and should develop knowledge and a strong working relationship with the appropriate contact in the general counsel's office. For example, the number of claims related to ownership of digitized collections on the open web are increasing. Personnel issues (including union grievances), contract and license issues, and information technology–related problems needing counsel's assistance are not uncommon. Academic libraries increasingly have questions related to copyright, open access, publishing, and other aspects of scholarly communication to such a degree that some are hiring copyright attorneys who work with the institution's general counsel's office but are based in the library.

Alumni Affairs and Development

Colleges and universities all have alumni and some type of alumni association with accompanying governance. Most have a professional executive director of the institution's alumni association. Organizational models differ, but staff will be devoted to supporting the alumni, volunteer officers (often elected), and those who serve on executive committees or councils. Alumni often have strong connections with serious commitment to their institutions. This commitment is fundamental to an institution's ability to raise private funds for their strategic initiatives. While the fund-raising effort is strongly connected to the alumni, it is not organized in the same way and often has a separate governance structure. As noted earlier, there is typically a high-level executive responsible for both alumni and development. Normally a vice president, the executive works with a development board of volunteers, who advises him or her on fund-raising strategies and helps to identify potential donors. In some cases, a benefit of alumni membership can be the ability to use the library. The library might partner with the alumni association on such projects as lecture series or the creation of a digital alumni library that makes popular databases and digital collections available to those no longer on campus (or to graduates). It is crucial that the library become part of the institution's fund-raising priorities throughout the campaign cycle and beyond.

Strategic Communications

Institutions of higher education must have visibility in order to be successful in recruiting students and faculty. Attracting grant and donor funding also depends on agencies and individuals knowing about the institution and its activities. Strategic communications manages the college or university brand and serves as the central contact for the media. Communications administrators also work with crisis management and messaging for difficult situations and catastrophic events. Sometimes the library is part of the incident and therefore needs close ties to strategic communications along with other institution units. The library can provide resources needed to pull stories together. Likewise, strategic communications can promote library stories, services, and activities to the broader community.

Planning, Assessment, and Institutional Research

Planning, assessment, and institutional research offices provide support to university decision-making through data collection and analytic activities, research projects, and strategic planning, as well as consultation, facilitation, and training services. The planning office often provides detailed reports and background materials for a variety of governance uses, including the institution's governing board, president's cabinet, or dean's council. The planning office is also involved in a wide variety of assessment activities supporting the institution's overall operations and its mandates from accrediting bodies, state and federal governments, and other organizations. In particular, the growing emphasis on student learning outcomes assessment has become a key focus for these offices. The library supports planning through its resources but can also benefit from its services, especially assistance with assessment programs.

Strategic Planning

Strategic plans constitute an institution's blueprint for the future and articulate the mission, vision, and values, as well as foundational principles, imperatives, strategic priorities, and supporting efforts that will enable institutions to thrive in a highly competitive environment. The president, chancellor, or chief academic officer will lead strategic plan development for an institution in consultation with the institution's board, but the process involves many other stakeholders along the way. The strategic plan charts the institution's course typically for the next three to five years. Therefore, it is crucial that libraries, colleges, and other units be heavily involved in its development and implementation. Unit plans accompany the institution-wide strategic plan with more specific blueprints for that particular unit. The unit plans, including the library's, should clearly connect to and support the institution's strategic plan. All of these plans, if they are going to be effective, should be living documents and not just completed and placed on a shelf. Implementation and assessment strategies are necessary processes for supporting the plan's, and therefore the university's, success. Often, financial resources are directed toward the institution's priorities, so campus administrators must have a clear understanding of the convergence of library needs and these priorities.

Library involvement in institutional strategic planning is powerful because the library supports all aspects of the institution's mission, encompassing all disciplines and programs. The library can shift its own emphasis to the emerging university vision, foundational principles, and thematic priorities because of its broad mission. Library representation on a strategic planning oversight group can be useful because of the library's ability to contribute in multiple ways but also for practical reasons of providing needed resources to the group.

Governance Participation Strategies

The ability to participate in advancing an institution's strategic priorities requires being at the right tables: where key decisions and planning take place. Library leadership should be in a position to identify these tables by having detailed knowledge of institutional operations and priorities. At some institutions, the library is already well embedded in institutional decision-making and at the appropriate tables. However, other institutions have not included the library in major decision-making bodies. An effective strategy is proposing to the group leader that the library should have a role by emphasizing the benefits for achieving the group's goals. Another strategy would be to ask to attend a meeting as a guest to learn more about the group's activities and therefore how the library can contribute.

Roadmap to Relationships with Administrators and Stakeholders

How does library leadership develop relationships with administrators from the various areas of the institution? A proactive approach is essential for successful interactions and subsequent outcomes. Preparing briefing documents, with the emphasis on *brief*, in advance on appropriate topics saves time and ensures that the correct information is provided. Library leaders should be willing to go to the offices of the identified administrators. They should prepare questions in advance for the administrators, including asking about their respective office priorities in the near and long term. They should be prepared to answer questions about the relevance of the library to that office or operation. The administrator may have questions or need additional information; any supplementary information should be sent promptly after the meeting. Making these connections face to face will strengthen the relationship and help the library to support the different areas of the university. Library leaders should also be visible at important social and cultural events.

Summary

College and university governance and administration is a multifaceted and complex topic. This chapter lays out governance structures at various levels of the organization and key areas of administration. Library leaders must have a comprehensive understanding of their institutions' governance structures; relevant areas of administration; and a wide variety of committees, councils, and groups that provide its direction. Clearly, there are significant roles for libraries to support and contribute to these structures, offices, and groups. Librarians can and should assume a leadership role, not only within the library, but also throughout the campus. Mapping library priorities and efforts to the institution's strategic plan and helping to shape that plan is a powerful way to lead as well as support stakeholders. The breadth of knowledge that librarians offer to support all disciplines should now include an expansive understanding of the workings of the college or university administration and support areas, along with sound communication strategies to connect effectively with busy administrators. The combination of these two large areas of knowledge—institutional governance and library priorities—enables librarians to contribute strategically to the success of the institution on all fronts.

Discussion Questions

1. List the top three library stakeholders (individuals or groups) and why each is on this list.
2. What are effective ways for library leaders and librarians to participate at the key venues for college or university decision-making?
3. What are specific strategies and formats for communicating effectively with campus administrators?
4. How does the library contribute to the success of the institution, and how is this contribution assessed?

5. If you were a new library dean or director, what would be your strategies for learning about and interacting with the various governance sectors of the institution?

Assignments

Scenic Community College

Scenic Community College (SCC) is a two-year institution located in Flower, CT. SCC recently completed a five-year strategic plan with goal areas of

- increasing enrollment;
- strengthening leadership and resource generation;
- improving industry alliances;
- strengthening information technology networks;
- improving science achievement by students; and
- increasing diversity of students, faculty, and staff, including improved recruitment and retention.

SCC's plan, like many, does not specifically mention the library, so library leadership needs to translate its impact and contributions to each of SCC's goals.

Select a community college, college, or university. Locate its strategic plan. Map the library's initiatives to the institution's strategic plan, including discussion of relevant offices for partnership and support. Cite best practices from the literature in each of the initiative areas.

Eastern Mountain State University

Eastern Mountain State University (EMSU) is the only land grant university in the state and a large, comprehensive research university. EMSU provides undergraduate and graduate education for 60,000 students, supported by 2,500 faculty and 5,000 staff. Founded in 1830 as an agricultural and engineering school, EMSU now features ten colleges (education, liberal arts, architecture, business, engineering, health sciences, human development, information sciences, sciences, and the online college). EMSU has many highly ranked programs at the graduate and undergraduate levels.

EMSU's library was built in the 1930s and lacks appropriate space for twenty-first-century students who require technology-rich individual and collaborative areas. A new library has been proposed to address this problem but has not yet been approved by the university's president's council. The president's council is comprised of the president, provost, athletics director, vice president for business and finance, vice president for development and alumni relations, vice president for research, vice president for student affairs, vice president for educational equity, and vice president for undergraduate education. Agenda items coming before the council are only allocated a few minutes due to a robust agenda.

Prepare and present a two-minute compelling "elevator" speech appropriate for the president's council describing the library's vision, its relevance to the university's strategic plan, and why it is crucial to the success of the institution. Remember: At stake is approval of a new library building for EMSU!

Notes

1. US Department of Education, *The Database of Accredited Postsecondary Institutions and Programs*, http://ope.ed.gov/accreditation.
2. Robert T. Ingram, *Governing Public Colleges and Universities* (San Francisco: Jossey-Bass, 1993), 21.
3. James Martin and James E. Samels, *The Provost's Handbook: The Role of the Chief Academic Officer* (Baltimore: Johns Hopkins University Press, 2015), 35.
4. Lincoln University Staff Council, http://www.lincolnu.edu/web/staff-council/staff-council.
5. Office of Educational Equity, Penn State University, http://equity.psu.edu.

3

Organization, Administration, Management, and Planning

Starr Hoffman

Introduction

This chapter shows how developments over the course of the past decade have affected academic libraries, particularly the role of technology, limited budgets, and the necessity of responding to an environment of constant change. It provides an overview of the administrative functions and trends of academic libraries, their changes in recent years, and the role of strategic planning in determining the organization's direction. Some topics addressed here are subjects of debate within librarianship, such as the status of paraprofessional staff and mergers of libraries with information technology departments.

Librarian and Staff Roles

Not all librarians work directly with patrons, technology, or cataloging. This section addresses the variance in roles of librarians in positions at different levels of an academic library's organizational hierarchy, from the library faculty and staff to department heads to assistant or associate deans to chief administrators.

Library Faculty and Staff

The collective term *library staff* may be used to describe both librarians and other staff members working in the library. The majority of library staff are directly involved in library operations; for instance, working with patrons, loading or editing catalog records, or maintaining hardware and software in the library. Librarians in these functional positions typically have a primary responsibility aligned with the department or division in which they sit. They often have no administrative or managerial responsibilities, although some may supervise student employees. In large libraries with extensive hierarchies, however, functional librarians may manage subunits that make up larger units and have managerial duties in addition to their functional tasks. These librarians can be considered "department heads" as listed in a later section.

Paraprofessionals are library staff who do not hold the master's degree in library science. Sometimes referred to as "support staff" or "classified staff," they usually bear titles like library assistant, associate, specialist, or technician instead of librarian. Paraprofessionals may perform tasks similar to those that librarians do in their area. Paraprofessionals' status has been a source of debate and controversy—paraprofessionals are often paid lower wages than librarians, despite their responsibility for many of the same duties.[1] Some paraprofessionals may possess more years of experience than a librarian in their department doing similar work or even have master's degrees (often earned during their employment) yet still be paid less than a librarian. Because of this, part of the ongoing debate has been the question whether to grant some paraprofessionals the title of librarian.[2]

One of the chief arguments against such a move is that the graduate degree in library science provides more than a mere education in library tasks. The MLS provides socialization into the profession, which includes an introduction to research methods, a theoretical framework for librarianship, and an introduction to the profession's ethics and values (such as access and intellectual freedom). This socialization, particularly the adoption of library values, is in large part why some librarians believe that professionals who hold a non-LIS doctorate should obtain an MLS before transitioning to a librarian position.[3] Additionally, the degree's theoretical base and education in research methods can provide a foundation for new librarians in an environment that often expects the presentation and publication of academic work. Ultimately, although many LIS curricula are in need of reform, the MLS grants significant value, particularly as a socialization tool in professionalism and the principles of librarianship. Still, we must develop new ways to appreciate and reward the expertise of library paraprofessionals and better and more timely methods to promote MLS-degreed paraprofessionals into professional positions.

Many libraries also employ nonlibrarian professionals for positions that require specific expertise. Such positions may include data analysts, nonlibrarian researchers, some technology-oriented positions, or accountants, among others. These positions often require a bachelor's degree in a specific field and may require a master's in the area of expertise.

Unions for Library Faculty and Staff

At some academic libraries, librarians, other professional staff, and support staff have organized into unions in order to protect their interests, which may be related to wages, benefits, issues of managerial control, or working conditions.[4] While these organizations are not the norm, they are a large number; in 2010, 25.1 percent of libraries reported unionization of librarians and professional staff, and 14.4 percent reported the unionization of support staff.[5] Academic librarians tend to organize with academic faculty; the three most common bargaining units for academic librarians are the American Association of University Professors (AAUP), the American Federation of Teachers (AFT), and the National Education Association (NEA).[6] Because unions influence pay and working conditions, their presence or absence greatly affects library faculty and staff.

Department Heads

Department heads are middle managers who supervise paraprofessionals or librarians. They coordinate the work of their department, which may include determining whether the department's work fulfills the direction of the library's strategic plan. They are usually promoted to these positions from functional librarian positions, although some areas, such as technology departments, may be led by an individual without a master's who has relevant expertise. Duties of department heads are described in more depth in the later section on library administrators and managers.

Assistant and Associate Deans

Depending on the size and structure of the library, there may be a single associate dean to whom all department heads report or there may be a senior-level administrative team with several administrators, each of whom is responsible for different areas of the library. In cases where there is a single associate dean, he or she may be effectively in charge of the internal operations of the library, while the dean assumes responsibility for all external-facing library activities, such as fund-raising and communicating with other academic administrators on campus. Some small libraries or libraries that favor a less hierarchical structure have eliminated such positions entirely, preferring to have department heads report directly to the library's dean.

Titles for administrative positions below the chief administrator of the library typically follow the title of that position, preceded by a qualifying word (often *assistant*, *associate*, or *deputy*). Thus, a large library may have a dean, an associate dean, and several assistant deans. The variance in title of these positions may result from any of several factors. The qualifiers *assistant* and *associate* may indicate the seniority of the position (similar to the professorial ranks, in which associate is more senior than assistant), while *deputy* typically indicates that the position serves as second-in-command and may act in the dean's position in his or her absence. The variance between the second half of the title, *dean*, *university librarian*, *director*, and other titles (such as *vice provost*) is less clear and is discussed more thoroughly in the next section.

Alternatively, some libraries call these positions division directors. While associate deans often focus on the whole of library operations, assistant deans or division directors frequently oversee specific areas of the organization. These are typically large divisions (collections of departments) with department heads reporting directly to the assistant dean or division director.

Deans, Directors, and University Librarians

In universities and colleges, the chief administrator of an academic library typically reports to the chief academic administrator for the institution, usually a provost. Some may alternatively report to the president or a vice president, depending on the size and structure of the institution. This varies at community colleges, depending on whether the library is structured under academics, support services, or information technology, which is discussed in more detail in the section on organizational structure.

The title for the chief position of an academic library may be influenced by the faculty status of librarians there, by the type of the institution (university, college, community college), or by other factors. *Dean*, *university librarian*, and *director* are perhaps the most common but not the only terms for the head of an academic library: others include *chief of the library* and *vice provost*.[7] Much of the literature on chief academic library administrators refers to them generally as "directors;" thus, I use that term in this chapter in a generic sense.[8]

The title of *dean* implies a peer relationship with the deans of other academic colleges. For instance, a dean of libraries would be expected to be an equivalent position to the dean of the College of Arts and Sciences, and both might serve on a deans' council.[9] *Dean* may also indicate the faculty status or tenure-track status of librarians at the institution.[10] For instance, three studies found that institutions whose library directors were titled *dean* were also more likely to grant faculty status to librarians, to grant tenure to librarians, to have the same or parallel librarian ranks as those for the teaching faculty, and to have librarians who serve on the faculty senate.[11] However, the title of *dean* does not necessarily indicate that any of these distinctions apply, and even at one institution, the title for the same position may change over time. For instance, when Michael Gorman agreed to serve as the library director at California State University in Fresno, he requested that the position's title be changed from *university librarian* to *dean*.[12] Gorman's motivation for the request was his desire to be perceived as a peer of the academic deans: "I asked to be called dean because I wanted to be a participating member of the dean's council. It's enabled me to be a more useful member of the university."[13] Gorman does note that this position title change was granted only because librarians at the institution had tenure-track status and so were already peers of the teaching faculty. Perhaps, then, Gorman's choice of the word *useful* might be interpreted as code for *explicitly equal*.

Another contributing factor to how academic deans view library deans may be their educational background.[14] The Association of College and Research Libraries (ACRL) has identified the master's in library science as the terminal degree for academic librarianship as a profession; however, some position descriptions for deans (and similarly titled library directors) list a doctorate as preferred or required.[15] Typically the doctorate may be in any subject to emphasize a peer relationship with the other deans. However, many deans without doctorates have positive peer relationships with academic deans; thus, there is some debate about appropriate education for deans. Ultimately, the importance of specific educational backgrounds seems to vary from institution to institution and from dean to dean.

The title *dean* is used in institutions of various types, from large universities to small colleges to community colleges. The title varies somewhat, from *dean of libraries* to *library dean* or *dean of library services* and, in the case of some community colleges, *dean of the learning resource center.*[16] As noted previously, the variance in title appears to have more to do with the status (tenure-track or not) of librarians at the institution than it does with an institution's type.

The title *university librarian* does not bear a clear relationship to faculty status, tenure, or participation in faculty. Although Mary K. Bolin's original study of land grant institutions showed that the title *university librarian* was positively associated with faculty status and participation in faculty senate, her follow-up study of research universities indicated a negative relationship between this title and both librarian tenure and participation in faculty senate.[17] In general, the title *university librarian* appears to emphasize the professional nature of the role, parallel to such institutional positions as university attorney or registrar.[18] As the title itself implies, *university librarian* appears more frequently in university libraries, while the title *college librarian* features in some college libraries.[19]

Sometimes the head of the library bears the title *vice provost*—this may be either as a replacement for the *dean* or *university librarian* title or as an addition to it. For example, in 2014 the position of chief administrator of Columbia University Libraries/Information Services changed title to *vice provost and university librarian* from the previous title of *university librarian.*[20] A *vice provost* title may connote that the institution views the library as directly connected to academic work rather than as a support service.

The title of *director* often indicates that librarians supervised by this position do not possess faculty status.[21] This use of the title parallels its use in other areas of higher education institutions; the title *director* will often be used for positions in student affairs or administrative units, which often include such areas as institutional research or academic assessment.[22] Moreover, the title may imply that this person has functional librarian duties in addition to his or her administrative role (for instance, serving as a reference librarian). Thus, this title typically features in small libraries with a limited hierarchy. *Director* appears commonly, though not exclusively, in community college libraries. It seems likely that this prevalence stems primarily from the size of library staff; a survey of eighty-six community college libraries found that about 60 percent had a staff of ten people or fewer.[23] Additionally, *director* may refer to the head of a smaller branch or subject library within a system of multiple libraries; for instance, director of the Health Science Library, who in turn reports to the dean of libraries.

Duties and Roles of Library Administrators and Managers

Librarians in their first middle-management position often express surprise at how different the position seems from their previous work as a librarian, as well as from their training in library school. Managers' primary duties involve directing the work of their staff. In the case of a department head, this means coordinating each staff member's work so that the department as a whole reaches its goals (which are usually part of the library's overall strategic plan, described later). To that end, department heads often assume responsibility for planning department projects and must then track their progress. At the end of the academic or calendar year, department heads typically must submit annual reports that summarize their department's achievements, often explicitly relating these accomplishments to the strategic plan. Some libraries allot department heads a budget for equipment, office supplies, travel, and so on, while other libraries manage these funds centrally.

Managers also have a number of duties related to their staff (both librarians and paraprofessionals). These may include hiring, disciplining, and firing staff; alternatively, hiring may be the responsibility of a search committee. Managers must also evaluate the performance of their staff, usually on an annual basis, and may apportion salary increases. Some managers also manage the schedule for service areas, determining who will staff an area at a given time. Managers typically approve sick leave and vacation days and may also adjudicate travel or professional development requests. Effective managers also motivate their staff and help to ensure their success by removing barriers to their work. Managerial duties vary widely in number and scope, not only based on the type of institution, but also among each individual library.

Administrators manage the library as an organization overall. Therefore, these employees often deal with such matters as budgeting, fund-raising, operations management (security and building facilities), interactions with the rest of the campus (particularly with other academic administrators), and determining and communicating the organization's direction.[24] Often, the library's vision and direction will be communicated through a strategic plan, a document designed to outline specific goals for the organization during the next two to five years (this planning process is covered in more detail later). Sometimes, assessment, the evaluation of progress made toward strategic goals, also features as an administrative function, with an assessment librarian reporting to the director or to another administrative position. (Assessment is covered in more depth in chapter 14.)

Administrative roles do differ by institutional type, though perhaps this can also be attributed to differences in organizational size. Often, administrators at smaller college and community college libraries must perform multiple roles simultaneously because they have fewer staff to fill them.[25] Thus, administrators may perform administrative duties (for instance, budgeting and communicating with other campus administrators) alongside functional librarian duties, like working shifts at a reference desk. Some institutions may have only one librarian, in which case he or she must assume responsibility for all library roles. Having no additional staff may eliminate managerial duties, but the compression of these roles often also means that some tasks must be relinquished; for instance, fund-raising. Additionally, smaller organizations may not need or be able to sustain a formal strategic planning process.

Organizational Structure and Recent Trends

Academic library structure has traditionally followed a hierarchical model in higher educational organizations, often divided between public and technical services. However, in recent years, many libraries have discarded this model for a more flat organization; that is, an organization in which there are few, if any, layers of middle managers between functional employees and administrators. The reasons for this shift vary from budgetary (remove middle-management positions to recoup their salaries) to operational (facilitate communication, be able to respond quickly to change).

The study of organizational structure and development in higher education owes much to Robert Birnbaum's 1988 book *How Colleges Work*. Here, Birnbaum discusses five models of learning organizations:

1. collegial, in which authority and decision-making are shared throughout the organization;
2. bureaucratic, a structured hierarchy where authority follows strict lines;
3. political, in which power and influence are the ultimate goals;
4. anarchic, which appears chaotic and loosely organized; and
5. cybernetic, in which Birnbaum combines what he views as the strongest characteristics of each of the preceding four models.

Academic libraries tend to both take on features of their parent institution's organizational structure and also form their own. The traditional structure of academic libraries, particularly in universities, has been bureaucratic: hierarchical with clear lines of authority.[26] This structure has been explored in depth in library science literature and exhibited in numerous organizational charts. However, college libraries have historically broken from this model and taken on more collegial characteristics. Contributing factors include the typically smaller staff size in college libraries and the tendency for more collegial organization of their parent institutions, as Birnbaum notes.[27]

Community college libraries' organization varies. Although their organizational charts often indicate clearly bureaucratic, hierarchical qualities (inherited from their parent institution's structure), the structure of these libraries also mainly results from the influence of their missions and their reporting structures.[28] University and college libraries often fall under the academic structure, with the director viewed as a peer of the deans of academic colleges; however, while some community college libraries report to the chief academic officer, others fall under student services (usually reporting to the dean of students) or under the information technology area, discussed later.[29] The reporting structure of the library greatly affects both its mission and its organizational structure.

The division of personnel into familiar divisions constitutes another common aspect of academic library organizational structure, the most common among these divisions being public services (typically reference or research support and instruction) and technical services (acquisitions, cataloging, discovery).[30] Additional divisions often include technology support, administration or operations (human resources, security, facilities), and access services (circulation, interlibrary loan). There are many variations, but overall, the literature and the profession appear to consolidate the organizational view into the divide, whether real or imagined, between public and technical services.

In the past decade, much literature has discussed a shift in academic library structure from hierarchical to flat, team-based organizations (similar to Birnbaum's collegial model). In actuality, although much literature in the past decade discusses such changes, we should not consider this an entirely new trend. In 1994, Richard Sweeney published an article titled "Leadership in the Post-Hierarchical Library," in the first paragraph of which he discusses libraries that have moved to flat structures.[31] Another book from the early 1990s mentions the growing popularity of moving from the hierarchical decision-making of a bureaucratic model to a collegial shared-governance model with a loose structure.[32] Regardless of when this shift began, it continues to be popular, while many libraries also continue to function well using a more traditional structure.

The literature provides many reasons for moving to a team-based model. For one thing, moving away from a model defined around siloed functional areas (public services, technical services) to one populated by smaller teams created for emerging services or functions that cross these traditional boundaries breaks down organizational barriers to communication. Additionally, team-based organizations can be more agile and responsive to environmental shifts and stakeholder needs.[33] However, there are also disadvantages. Sometimes team-based structures face problems making decisions and accomplishing tasks because of a lack of a clear line of authority, which can result in a lack of a coherent organizational vision and plan.[34] Librarians in functional positions may be reluctant to take on tasks previously assigned to specific managers or administrators. Furthermore, the number of direct reports for the top-level administrator(s) may be unwieldy and overwhelming.[35] By contrast, the clear authority and reporting structure can be a strength of traditional, hierarchical libraries, though they cannot always respond as quickly to changes in their environment. This section explores some examples and their transitions.

KU Libraries (the University of Kansas) started investigating a restructuring process in 2011 in order to be more adaptive to institutional needs.[36] The ultimate restructuring resulted in the creation of four divisions and two administratively focused offices, which, while redeploying staff in new ways, still generally follows a hierarchical structure. However, the library simultaneously created cross-functional teams that draw on staff from all divisions to lead strategic or ongoing initiatives.[37] These teams help break down communication silos between divisions and ensure that a broad range of staff talents and expertise can be harnessed through specific initiatives.

The University of Arizona Library underwent a complete reorganization, moving to a full team structure, in 1993.[38] The impetus for this restructuring was the arrival of a new library dean and the steep increase in serial costs nationwide, which the library's budget could not absorb. The team-based structure helped to address the budget issue because, as department head positions were eliminated, the library was able to realize some salary savings. Librarians at this library did describe some growing pains during the restructuring process, including a sense of loss during the initial reorganization,[39] an overwhelming amount of information resulting from distributed decision-making,[40] and some negative effect on individuals' self-esteem and individual professional identities.[41] Ultimately, however, the team-based structure at the University of Arizona Library produced a distributed decision-making process and encouraged team members to learn continuously and develop themselves professionally. No examples of team-based structures in college libraries or community college libraries could be found in the literature. Such structures seem less likely to be present in smaller libraries, which have fewer staff to populate multiple teams.

Academic Libraries and IT Departments

Some colleges and universities have taken a completely different approach to academic library organizational structure by merging their information technology (IT) departments with their libraries. Budgetary considerations combined with the increasingly prominent role technology now plays in libraries (public-use computers, OPACs, e-books, online research databases, etc.) have driven these mergers and serve as their primary justification. Such mergers became a particularly popular theme in the literature, though not necessarily in practice, in the 1980s and 1990s, when librarians and campus administrators grew increasingly concerned about the possible impact of technology and, in particular, the Internet, on libraries.[42] It was assumed that, as the library became dependent on technology, there would be a swift move to electronic-only collections. The reality, that overwhelming amounts of information online and in traditional formats still necessitate mediation through a librarian, has meant that these predicted mergers have taken different shape than futurists originally predicted.

As a few institutions began to adopt this model in the late 1990s and throughout the first decade of the new century, library and IT mergers became highly controversial.[43] Some librarians saw these mergers as privileging technology over traditional library values, like access and service, threatening the existence of libraries as service institutions and the future of librarianship as a profession. Others saw the mergers as opportunities to provide cutting-edge technology to their patrons, to take advantage of economies of scale, and to survive budget cuts, particularly during the recession of the late 2000s.[44] The issue of library–IT mergers provides a succinct example of how perspectives and outcomes can differ broadly based on the specific institution, its mission, and individual circumstances. Indeed, it might inform our approach to many controversial issues throughout academic librarianship, in that oftentimes there may be no single solution to a given problem because institutions and individuals vary so greatly.

Although the literature of the late 1990s and 2000s often discussed merged library–IT organizational structures, Bolin's 2005 study of land grant institutions (primarily comprehensive universities, though a few colleges were included) indicated that 88 percent of these institutions have traditional library organizational structures.[45] By contrast, the University of Southern California (USC) provides one high-profile example of a library–IT merger gone awry. USC merged the library and IT area into what they called the Information Science Division (ISD) in 1997 but dissolved it again into separate divisions in 2006.[46] The merger resulted from the need to improve efficiency and service while cutting costs. Unfortunately, however, the merged organization met neither of the original divisions' needs. Moreover, a culture clash ensued between librarians (service-oriented, viewing technology as a means to an end) and technologists (viewing technology as its own end). This problem has vexed multiple similar mergers, due not only to different technological orientations but also to differing schedules, pay ranges, and conflicting opinions of what constitutes sufficient customer service.[47]

Literature on IT–library mergers largely asserts that such mergers are primarily successful in small college libraries.[48] However, Gettysburg College, a liberal arts institution with about 2,200 students, had an experience similar to USC's: The library and IT were merged in 1994 and separated in 1997. An employee attributed the failure to several factors: excluding staff from the planning process, a loose team-based structure that lacked clear leadership, and cultural differences.[49] Nearly a decade later, however, a mixed-methods study of thirty-nine liberal arts institutions with merged library–IT structures showed that their administrators (academic deans or chief information officers, most with library backgrounds) found these merged organizations to be effective.[50] Thus, it is difficult to draw broad conclusions about such mergers based on the type of institution.

Community college libraries tend to be organized under one of three umbrellas: academic programs, IT, or student services. Each of these models both provides distinct advantages and creates problems. For instance, community college libraries organized under IT tend to enjoy a stronger technological infrastructure and newer technology for student use; however, these libraries often suffer weaker ties to the college's academic departments and thus have little support for public services.[51] Positions at these libraries tend to be more IT-focused, dealing with systems, electronic resources management, or technical support. While the literature lists no specific cases of community college libraries merged with information technology departments, surveys of merged organizations have been conducted. Thus, while there may be no specific cases to summarize here, the literature indicates that such structures exist in community colleges. For instance, Douglas Kaylor's 2007 study of community college libraries in Ohio revealed that, out of the fifteen libraries surveyed, four had merged to some degree with the IT department, and most of these were large institutions (at least 5,000 students).[52] Kaylor noted that this finding directly contradicts the literature, which states that most merged library–IT organizations occur in small institutions.

Strategic Planning in Libraries

In recent decades, strategic planning has emerged as a process intended to provide direction for the library and to align its goals with those of its parent institution. This section briefly reviews a typical strategic planning cycle, the importance of so-called SMART goals, and some obstacles commonly encountered during the process. Strategic planning cycles vary quite a bit between institutions, so this section describes the process in general terms in order not to imply that all libraries use this exact process. The popularity of the strategic planning process in academic libraries mirrors its general pervasiveness in higher education, which has been influenced by many factors, among them shrinking institutional budgets and rising costs, complex accreditation standards, rapidly evolving technology, and public demand for accountability. Common aims of the process include increasing efficiency and ensuring that the organization constantly improves and thus better serves its constituents (students; staff; faculty; and, in many cases, the local community). Strategic planning is typically described as a "cycle," in reference to a continual process of improvement.

Libraries undertake the process of strategic planning in order to produce a plan, a document that outlines their broad objectives as well as specific goals (often at a department level) that detail how progress will be made, and ideally includes metrics against which to measure success.[53] Plans may be as short as a single page or as long as several hundred pages. Ideally, the plan should be digestible in such a way that the organization regularly refers to it while working toward the goals; the literature reveals instances of libraries immediately shelving the document due to its length or perceived irrelevance and consulting it either only at the end of the planning cycle or not at all.[54] The plan should not be a stale document but rather a living strategy that guides the daily decisions of everyone in the library.

The strategic planning cycle typically begins by determining the high-level objectives that the library wishes to meet. On occasion, the library may wish to mirror some of the objectives in the parent institution's strategic plan. For instance, if one of the institution's aims is to increase faculty research productivity, then the library might create an objective to provide more robust support services for faculty research, with a specific goal to create faculty workshops on the grant-writing process. The library's strategic objectives may be determined either top-down (by the director or other library administrators) or bottom-up (by working collaboratively with staff from all levels of the library). Involving the entire organization in the planning process often helps individual staff members not only to feel involved but also to more easily take ownership of the resulting objectives, which can build greater enthusiasm and buy-in for the plan. There may be a multitude of processes by which these objectives are decided, and many factors must to be taken into consideration, such as the parent institution's strategic objectives or state-mandated education requirements.

After determining objectives, libraries typically break these down into smaller pieces or goals. These smaller pieces may be listed as general themes and interpreted by different library areas as they see fit, or each department may write specific goals for its area that fit within the broad objectives. The language used to designate these pieces of the strategic planning process varies—*goals*, *objectives*, *actions*, *initiatives*, *measures*—but all these terms serve as a broad roadmap for the organization and indicate some specific actions to be taken to achieve its aims.

Goals will often be written to fit the SMART standard; that is, specific, measurable, attainable, relevant, and timely.[55] The word *specific* indicates that goals should not be so broad or generic that they become meaningless. For instance, the statement "The library should encourage learning" might seem at first glance to be a worthy goal, but it could be significantly improved if it were more specific. The statement "The library should increase the number of information literacy sessions for freshman courses" reads as specific and concrete, and thus librarians can effectively act on it by taking particular steps. The first version of the goal is worded so vaguely that it would be hard to determine whether the library ever achieved it.

Measurable means that there should be some criteria to determine if a goal has been met. The plan should offer details about how to track progress toward the goal and, ultimately, judge its success. Thus, in this example in which the goal expresses the intention to "increase the number of information literacy sessions for freshman courses," the criterion would be how many information literacy sessions are offered. In order for the goal to be truly measurable, the wording could be adjusted to "The library should double the number of information literacy sessions for freshman courses offered the previous year." Thus, this goal's success can be judged at the end of the year by comparing the number of sessions conducted during the two years in question. Some goals may be measured by quantitative means (based on numbers or "how much") or by qualitative means (based on an evaluation of quality or "how good"); these measurements are discussed in more depth in the chapter on assessment. Library goals may also be specifically crafted to measure the library's impact on student learning outcomes and other institution-wide goals.[56] However, some goals may be difficult to measure; for instance, creating a more welcoming library environment for patrons. This could be viewed alternatively as a goal that needs refinement to better fit the SMART standard or as a meaningful goal that shows a weakness of SMART.

Attainable means that a goal can realistically be achieved. Goals should be crafted such that, given the library's current budget and staff, the organization could conceivably accomplish the goals within the time specified in the strategic plan. Thus, to continue the example, unless the library has significantly increased its staff recently, setting a goal to increase the number of information literacy sessions by five times would be unrealistic and as a result probably not attainable. Another factor to consider is that achieving this goal may not be completely within the library's control. For instance, if information literacy sessions are to be implemented in courses, then the decision to schedule them may lie with the faculty instructing those courses. Such factors should be considered when judging attainability.

Relevant has to do with how worthwhile the goal is and how consistent with respect to both other goals and the library's long-term plans. For instance, if the parent institution were a four-year undergraduate institution and most of the library's goals center on information literacy, support for student learning, and campus outreach, then creating a goal "to build deep research collections" would not make sense. Instead, a goal to "provide basic introductory texts and collections that support the undergraduate curricula" would be more in keeping with the institution's mission.

Timely means that there should be a specific date set by which the goal ought to be achieved. In some cases, all goals have the same timeline as the plan itself, but in others, the plan might include staggered goals in order to provide milestones along the way. This strategy enables the organization to celebrate successes throughout the plan timeline and helps to ensure progress. Either way, including a timeline at some level will be important to make certain that the goal will be measured.

Once objectives and goals have been decided and the plan is finalized, the time comes for implementation. This may involve many parts, such as department heads beginning to delegate the work necessary to achieve their specific departmental goals. Some libraries may form a committee to regularly assess progress toward goals, while others may assign one or more administrators to this task.

Near the end of the strategic planning cycle, the organization will measure progress toward those goals and determine whether they have been met according to the details set forth in the strategic plan. If a planning committee has been formed, then its members may do this work; otherwise an assessment librarian may be responsible for this step. In some cases, the individual departments may assess their own progress and report back to the organization. Often, the outcomes and assessments will be compiled into an annual report of the organization's progress. This report may be kept purely internal, sent to key campus administrators, or published on the library's website.

As stated earlier, a strategic planning process might be implemented in any number of ways. Ideally, by achieving these goals, the library becomes more relevant to its key constituents (be they students, faculty, staff, or others), more efficient, and more effective. Strategic planning constitutes one tactic among many in higher education to make institutions more accountable to their students and the public.

Conclusion

While there may be commonalities in the administration of different types of academic libraries—for instance, the basics of the strategic planning process are quite similar—some aspects, such as organizational structure, vary widely according to the institution's type, size, and mission, among other factors. The traditional hierarchical model of academic library organization has been expanded to include collegial and team-based models as well as instances in which libraries have merged with information technology. And though staff sizes vary, the roles and duties of paraprofessionals, librarians, middle managers, and administrators remain mostly comparable across libraries.

Discussion Questions

1. Librarians who assume managerial or administrative roles often mention that fulfilling such a role was not part of their initial career goals. What are some of the ways that librarians might prepare for taking on such roles? Are there offerings in your current LIS program designed to prepare you for such a possibility?
2. What are some advantages and disadvantages of hierarchical versus flat organizational structures, apart from those identified in this chapter?
3. How might institutional size, funding (private or public), or type (university, college, or community college) affect organizational structure or operations?

4. In your opinion, what makes someone a "librarian"? Is it a master's in library science, a titled position as a librarian, performing a specific kind of work, or something else?
5. Consider the institution at which you are a student. Do you think a library–IT merger would be a useful structure for that institution? Why or why not?
6. Strategic planning and SMART goals started in business before their adoption in higher education. Can you identify other business theories or approaches that have been employed in libraries or higher education more generally?

Assignments

1. Find organizational charts for two academic libraries. The two institutions should differ from each other in institutional type (university, college, or community college) or size (number of full-time enrolled students, or FTE). You should be able to find organizational charts on library websites, usually in the "About" section, or by searching the website for "organizational chart." Write a two- to three-page reaction paper about why you chose these institutions, compare their structures and organizational levels, discuss any factors that may have affected their choices of organizational structure, and discuss what those choices tell you about these libraries.
2. Pretend that you have recently been named the director of an academic library. Given the organizational chart and the circumstances listed in the following (fictitious) case study, would you reorganize the library? Write a three- to five-page explanation of how you would reorganize and why or why not. Note: Case studies generally do not have one right or wrong answer. Your work will be evaluated based on your demonstrated understanding of the various factors involved and how you use the information presented in this chapter to create a solution.

Case Study: Institution X

Institution X is a small private university with 3,500 full-time enrolled students. The library is funded through a student use fee. Enrollment has slightly dropped over the past decade from 3,900 students, and tuition has remained at the same level, thus the library budget has steadily dropped. The library has already made some minor cuts to its collections but will

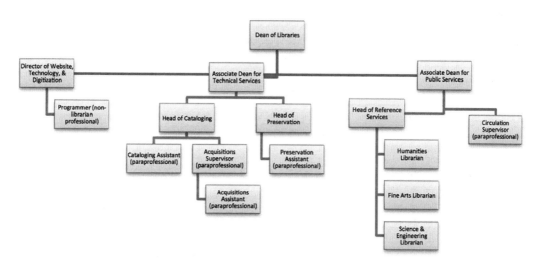

Figure 3.1 Organizational chart for Institution X Libraries

have to start looking at personnel salaries to save costs. Other departments, such as IT, have also suffered budget and personnel cuts.

The university president has just launched a new strategic plan aimed at making the campus more technologically focused, which includes providing each incoming student with a free tablet or laptop, and has asked the library to convert all its remaining print journals to electronic format and to order only e-books (no print). Additionally, the university has begun a new program in aviation engineering, and the newly hired faculty are heavily involved in grant-funded research, which provides a potential opportunity for the library to offer new faculty services.

Notes

1. Nancy Huling, "Paraprofessionals at the Reference Desk: Not 'Whether,' but 'How,'" *Alki: WLA Journal* 12, no. 2 (July 1996): 19–20.
2. "What Is a Librarian?" *Annoyed Librarian, Library Journal*, June 17, 2009, http://lj.libraryjournal.com/blogs/annoyedlibrarian/2009/06/17/what-is-a-librarian; Nena Schvaneveldt, "What Makes You a Librarian?" *INALJ*, September 27, 2013, http://inalj.com/?p=40581.
3. For more reading on this debate, see Todd Gilman, "A Matter of Degrees," *Chronicle of Higher Education*, May 18, 2005; Todd Gilman and Thea Lindquist, "Academic/Research Librarians with Subject Doctorates: Experiences and Perceptions, 1965–2006," *portal: Libraries and the Academy* 10, no. 4 (2010): 399–412; Jean-Pierre V. M. Herubel, "Doctoral Degrees and the Academic Librarian, or, 'Is There a Doctor in the House?'" *Indiana Libraries* 25, no. 3 (2006): 42–44; Mary D. Johnson, "Turning Ph.D.'s into Librarians," *Chronicle of Higher Education*, October 16, 2003; Thea Lindquist and Todd Gilman, "Academic/Research Librarians with Subject Doctorates: Data and Trends 1965–2006," *portal: Libraries and the Academy* 8, no. 1 (2008): 31–52; Jennifer Mayer and Lori J. Terrill, "Academic Librarians' Attitudes about Advanced-Subject Degrees," *College and Research Libraries* 66, no. 1 (2005): 59–73; James G. Neal, "Raised by Wolves: Integrating the New Generation of Feral Professionals into the Academic Library," *Library Journal* 131, no. 3 (2006): 42–44.
4. Rachel Applegate, "Who Benefits? Unionization and Academic Libraries and Librarians," *The Library* 79, no. 4 (2009): 443–63; Kathleen de la Peña McCook, "Unions in Public and Academic Libraries," School of Information Faculty Publications, Paper 108 (2010), http://scholarcommons.usf.edu/si_facpub/108.
5. Kathleen de la Peña McCook, "There Is Power in a Union—2008–2009," *Progressive Librarian* 32 (2009): 55.
6. McCook, "Unions," 6.
7. Susan Carol Curzon and Jennie Quiñónez-Skinner, "Academic Libraries," in *Encyclopedia of Library and Information Sciences*, 3rd ed., edited by Marcia J. Bates and Mary Niles Mack, 11–22 (New York: CRC Press, 2010).
8. Bryce Nelson, *The Academic Library Administrator's Field Guide* (Chicago: American Library Association, 2014).
9. Mary K. Bolin, "A Typology of Librarian Status at Land Grant Universities," *Journal of Academic Librarianship* 34, no. 3 (2008): 224.
10. For more detail on the complex debate regarding faculty status and tenure for academic librarians, see Todd Gilman, "Academic Librarians and Rank," *Chronicle of Higher Education*, January 4, 2008; William H. Walters, "Faculty Status of Librarians at U.S. Research Universities," *Journal of Academic Librarianship* 42 (2016): 161–71.
11. Bolin, "Typology," 224–27; Mary K. Bolin, "Librarian Status at U.S. Research Universities: Extending the Typology," *Journal of Academic Librarianship* 34, no. 5 (2008): 418–23; Deborah Lee, "Faculty Status, Tenure, and Compensating Wage Differentials among Members of the Association of Research Libraries," in *Advances in Library Administration and Organization* (Advances in Library Administration and Organization, vol. 26), edited by Edward D. Garten, Delmus E. Williams, James M. Nyce, and Janine Golden, 151–208 (Bingley, UK: Emerald Group, 2008), 180–81, 185, 199.

12. Mark Y. Herring and Michael Gorman, "Conference Call: Do Librarians with Tenure Get More Respect?" *American Libraries* 34, no. 6 (2003): 70-72.

13. Ibid., 72.

14. For more reading on this topic, see Annie Downey and Starr Hoffman, "The Value of the PhD for Academic Librarians," paper number 2009-262, presented at the annual conference of the Association for the Study of Higher Education, Vancouver, BC, Canada, November 2009; Gilman, "Matter of Degrees"; Gilman and Lindquist, "Academic/Research Librarians"; Starr Hoffman, "The Preparation of Academic Library Administrators" (PhD diss., University of North Texas, 2012); Lindquist and Gilman, "Academic/Research Librarians."

15. Chih-Feng P. Lin, "Changes in Stated Job Requirements of Director Positions of Academic Libraries in the US," *Journal of Information, Communication, and Library Science* 8, no. 1 (2001): 9-25.

16. Judy Born, Sue Clayton, and Aggie Balash, eds., *Community College Library Job Descriptions and Organizational Charts, CJCLS Guide 4* (Chicago: American Library Association, 2000).

17. Bolin, "Typology," 222-26; Bolin, "Librarian Status," 418-22.

18. Bolin, "Typology," 224.

19. Ibid.; Bolin, "Librarian Status," 418-22.

20. John Coatsworth, "Libraries Update: University Librarian Search and Faculty Advisory Committee," *Columbia University: Office of the Provost*, November 17, 2014, https://provost.columbia.edu/node/180.

21. Bolin, "Typology," 222-26; Bolin, "Librarian Status," 418-22; "Reading Titles," *Confessions of a Community College Dean* (blog), April 6, 2010, https://www.insidehighered.com/blogs/confessions_of_a_community_college_dean/reading_titles.

22. M. Christopher Brown II, *Organization and Governance in Higher Education*, 5th ed., ASHE Reader Series (Boston: Pearson Custom, 2000).

23. Born, Clayton, and Balash, *Community College Library Job Descriptions*.

24. Sharon Gray Weiner, "Leadership of Academic Libraries: A Literature Review," *Education Libraries* 26, no. 2 (2003): 9-11.

25. Jennifer Arnold, "The Community College Conundrum: Workforce Issues in Community College Libraries," *Library Trends* 59, no. 1 (2010): 220-36.

26. John Budd, *The Changing Academic Library: Operations, Culture, Environments*, no. 56 (Chicago: Association of College and Research Libraries, 2005); James Thompson, *An Introduction to University Library Administration*, 2nd ed. (Hamden, CT: Linnet Books, 1975); James Thompson, *University Library History: An International Review* (New York: C. Bingley, 1980); Louis Round Wilson and Maurice F. Tauber, *The University Library: The Organization, Administration, and Functions of Academic Libraries* (New York: Columbia University Press, 1956).

27. Robert Birnbaum, *How Colleges Work: The Cybernetics of Academic Organization and Leadership* (San Francisco: Jossey-Bass, 1988), 91-93.

28. Arnold, "Community College Conundrum," 220-36; Born, Clayton, and Balash, *Community College Library Job Descriptions*; Michael A. Crumpton and Nora J. Bird, *Handbook for Community College Librarians* (Santa Barbara, CA: Libraries Unlimited, 2013), 7-20.

29. Arnold, "Community College Conundrum," 220-36; Crumpton and Bird, *Handbook*, 7-20.

30. Curzon and Quiñónez-Skinner, "Academic Libraries," 14; Barbara B. Moran and Elisabeth Leonard, "Academic Librarianship," in *Encyclopedia of Library and Information Sciences*, 3rd ed., edited by Marcia J. Bates and Mary Niles Mack, 1-10 (New York: CRC Press, 2010).

31. Richard T. Sweeney, "Leadership in the Post-Hierarchical Library," *Library Trends* 43, no. 1 (1994): 62.

32. Stephen E. Atkins, *The Academic Library in the American University* (Chicago: American Library Association, 1991), 95-99, 163.

33. M. Sue Baughman, "Assessment of Teams and Teamwork in the University of Maryland Libraries," *portal: Libraries and the Academy* 8, no. 3 (2008): 293-94.

34. Ibid.

35. Catherine Quinlan and Hugh McHarg, "The Emerging Library: Structure, Culture, and Lessons Learned from the Dissolution of a Combined Libraries–IT Organization," *Journal of Library Administration* 52, no. 2 (2012): 147-61.

36. Erin L. Ellis, Brian Rosenblum, John M. Stratton, and Kathleen Ames-Stratton, "Positioning Academic Libraries for the Future: A Process and Strategy for Organizational Transformation," *Proceedings of the IATUL Conferences*, paper 13, 2014, http://docs.lib.purdue.edu/iatul/2014/plenaries/13.

37. KU Libraries, *User-Focused Organization Structure* (organizational chart), https://lib.ku.edu/sites/lib .ku.edu/files/images/general/KULibraries-org-structure-jan-2016.pdf.

38. Joseph R. Diaz and Chestalene Pintozzi, "Helping Teams Work: Lessons Learned from the University of Arizona Library Reorganization," *Library Administration and Management* 13, no. 1 (1999): 27–36; Shelley E. Phipps, "The System Design Approach to Organizational Development: The University of Arizona Model," *Library Trends* 53, no. 1 (2004), 68–111; Ricardo Andrade Raik Zaghloul, "Restructuring Liaison Librarian Teams at the University of Arizona Libraries, 2007–2009," *New Library World* 111, nos. 7–8 (2010): 273–86.

39. Phipps, "System Design Approach," 74.

40. Diaz and Pintozzi, "Helping Teams Work," 27–36.

41. Ibid.; Zaghloul, "Restructuring Liaison Librarian Teams," 284.

42. Sara Bronner Baron, "Employee Perspectives of Library and Information Technology Mergers: The Recursiveness of Structure, Culture, and Agency," (EdD diss., University of Massachusetts Boston, 2010), 1–21, 299–300; Mary K. Bolin, "The Library and the Computer Center: Organizational Patterns at Land Grant Universities," *Journal of Academic Librarianship* 31, no. 1 (2005): 3–11; Stephanie DeClue, "Measurement of Perceived Conflict between Members in American Higher Education Merged Library and Information Technology Departments" (EdD diss., University of Missouri–Columbia, 2013), 3–4, 20, 26–27; Quinlan and McHarg, "Emerging Library," 147–61.

43. Quinlan and McHarg, "Emerging Library," 147–61; Bolin, "Library and the Computer Center," 3–11.

44. Crumpton and Bird, *Handbook*, 7–20.

45. Bolin, "Library and the Computer Center," 3–11.

46. Quinlan and McHarg, "Emerging Library," 147–61.

47. Baron, "Employee Perspectives," 55–58, 340–41; DeClue, "Measurement of Perceived Conflict," 22–25; Sharon K. Kenan, "Perceptions of Personnel at Selected Texas Community Colleges Regarding the Impact of Technology on Their Libraries" (EdD diss., University of Nebraska–Lincoln, 2012), 219.

48. Robert E. Renaud, "Shaping a New Profession: The Role of Librarians When the Library and Computer Center Merge," *Library Administration and Management* 20, no. 2 (2006): 65–74; John K. Stemmer, "The Perception of Effectiveness of Merged Information Services Organizations," *Reference Services Review* 35, no. 3 (2007): 348–50.

49. Robin Wagner, "The Gettysburg Experience," in *Books, Bytes, and Bridges: Libraries and Computer Centers in Academic Institutions*, edited by Larry L. Hardesty, 164–77 (Chicago: American Library Association, 2000), 164–66.

50. Stemmer, "Perception of Effectiveness," 348–50.

51. Arnold, "Community College Conundrum," 220–36; Crumpton and Bird, *Handbook*, 7–20.

52. Douglas Kaylor, "Library/IT Mergers in Ohio's Public Two-Year Colleges: An Exploratory Study" (EdS diss., Wright State University, 2007), 36–53, https://etd.ohiolink.edu.

53. Joseph R. Matthews, *Strategic Planning and Management for Library Managers* (Westport, CT: Libraries Unlimited, 2005), 57–58.

54. Walter A. Brown and Barbara A. Blake Gonzalez, "Should Strategic Planning Be Renewed?" *Technical Services Quarterly* 24, no. 3 (2007): 1–14, doi:10.1300/J124v24n03_01.

55. This SMART model was first developed in management literature before its adoption in libraries; see George T. Doran, Arthur F. Miller, and James A. Cunningham, "There's a S.M.A.R.T. Way to Write Management's Goals and Objectives," *Management Review* 70, no. 11 (1981): 35–36.

56. For more on creating goals that measure the library's impact on its parent institution, see Megan Oakleaf, *The Value of Academic Libraries: A Comprehensive Research Review and Report* (Chicago: Association of College and Research Libraries, 2010).

Bibliography

Applegate, Rachel. "Who Benefits? Unionization and Academic Libraries and Librarians." *The Library* 79, no. 4 (2009): 443–63.

Arnold, Jennifer. "The Community College Conundrum: Workforce Issues in Community College Libraries." *Library Trends* 59, no. 1 (2010): 220–36.

Atkins, Stephen E. *The Academic Library in the American University*. Chicago: American Library Association, 1991.

Baron, Sara Bronner. "Employee Perspectives of Library and Information Technology Mergers: The Recursiveness of Structure, Culture, and Agency." EdD diss., University of Massachusetts, Boston, 2010.

Baughman, M. Sue. "Assessment of Teams and Teamwork in the University of Maryland Libraries." *portal: Libraries and the Academy* 8, no. 3 (2008): 293–312.

Birnbaum, Robert. *How Colleges Work: The Cybernetics of Academic Organization and Leadership*. San Francisco: Jossey-Bass, 1988.

Bolin, Mary K. "The Library and the Computer Center: Organizational Patterns at Land Grant Universities." *Journal of Academic Librarianship* 31, no. 1 (2005): 3–11.

———. "Librarian Status at US Research Universities: Extending the Typology." *Journal of Academic Librarianship* 34, no. 5 (2008): 416–24.

———. "A Typology of Librarian Status at Land Grant Universities." *Journal of Academic Librarianship* 34, no. 3 (2008): 220–30.

Born, Judy, Sue Clayton, and Aggie Balash, eds. *Community College Library Job Descriptions and Organizational Charts*. CJCLS Guide 4. Chicago: American Library Association, 2000.

Brown II, M. Christopher. *Organization and Governance in Higher Education*. 5th ed. ASHE Reader Series. Boston: Pearson Custom, 2000.

Brown, Walter A., and Barbara A. Blake Gonzalez. "Should Strategic Planning Be Renewed?" *Technical Services Quarterly* 24, no. 3 (2007): 1–14. doi:10.1300/J124v24n03_01.

Budd, John. *The Changing Academic Library: Operations, Culture, Environments*. No. 56. Chicago: Association of College and Research Libraries, 2005.

Coatsworth, John. "Libraries Update: University Librarian Search and Faculty Advisory Committee." *Columbia University: Office of the Provost*. November 17, 2014. https://provost.columbia.edu/node/180.

Crumpton, Michael A., and Nora J. Bird. *Handbook for Community College Librarians*. Santa Barbara, CA: Libraries Unlimited, 2013.

Curzon, Susan Carol, and Jennie Quiñónez-Skinner. "Academic Libraries." In *Encyclopedia of Library and Information Sciences*, 3rd ed., edited by Marcia J. Bates and Mary Niles Mack, 11–22. New York: CRC Press, 2010.

DeClue, Stephanie. "Measurement of Perceived Conflict between Members in American Higher Education Merged Library and Information Technology Departments." EdD diss., University of Missouri–Columbia, 2013.

Diaz, Joseph R., and Chestalene Pintozzi. "Helping Teams Work: Lessons Learned from the University of Arizona Library Reorganization." *Library Administration and Management* 13, no. 1 (1999): 27–36.

Doran, George T., Arthur F. Miller, and James A. Cunningham. "There's a S.M.A.R.T. Way to Write Management's Goals and Objectives." *Management Review* 70, no. 11 (1981): 35–36.

Downey, Annie, and Starr Hoffman. "The Value of the PhD for Academic Librarians." Paper number 2009-262. Presented at the annual conference of the Association for the Study of Higher Education, Vancouver, BC, Canada, November 2009.

Eden, Bradford L. *The Associate University Librarian Handbook*. Lanham, MD: Scarecrow Press, 2012.

Ellis, Erin L., Brian Rosenblum, John M. Stratton, and Kathleen Ames-Stratton. "Positioning Academic Libraries for the Future: A Process and Strategy for Organizational Transformation." *Proceedings of the IATUL Conferences*. Paper 13. 2014. http://docs.lib.purdue.edu/iatul/2014/plenaries/13.

Gilman, Todd. "Academic Librarians and Rank." *Chronicle of Higher Education*. January 4, 2008.

———. "A Matter of Degrees." *Chronicle of Higher Education*. May 18, 2005.

Gilman, Todd, and Thea Lindquist. "Academic/Research Librarians with Subject Doctorates: Experiences and Perceptions, 1965–2006." *portal: Libraries and the Academy* 10, no. 4 (2010): 399–412.

Herring, Mark Y., and Michael Gorman. "Conference Call: Do Librarians with Tenure Get More Respect?" *American Libraries* 34, no. 6 (2003): 70–72.

Herubel, Jean-Pierre V. M. "Doctoral Degrees and the Academic Librarian, or, 'Is There a Doctor in the House?'" *Indiana Libraries* 25, no. 3 (2006): 42–44.

Hoffman, Starr. "The Preparation of Academic Library Administrators." PhD diss.. University of North Texas, 2012.

Huling, Nancy. "Paraprofessionals at the Reference Desk: Not 'Whether,' but 'How.'" *Alki: WLA Journal* 12, no. 2 (July 1996): 19–20.

Johnson, Mary D. "Turning Ph.D.'s into Librarians." *Chronicle of Higher Education*. October 16, 2003.

Kaylor, Douglas. "Library/IT Mergers in Ohio's Public Two-Year Colleges: An Exploratory Study." EdS diss., Wright State University, 2007. https://etd.ohiolink.edu/.

Keller, George. *Academic Strategy: The Management Revolution in American Higher Education*. Baltimore: Johns Hopkins University Press, 1983.

Kenan, Sharon K. "Perceptions of Personnel at Selected Texas Community Colleges Regarding the Impact of Technology on Their Libraries." EdD diss., University of Nebraska–Lincoln, 2012.

KU Libraries. *User-Focused Organization Structure* (organizational chart). https://lib.ku.edu/sites/lib.ku.edu/files/images/general/KULibraries-org-structure-jan-2016.pdf.

Lee, Deborah. "Faculty Status, Tenure, and Compensating Wage Differentials among Members of the Association of Research Libraries." In *Advances in Library Administration and Organization* (Advances in Library Administration and Organization, vol. 26), edited by Edward D. Garten, Delmus E. Williams, James M. Nyce, and Janine Golden, 151–208. Bingley, UK: Emerald Group, 2008.

Lin, Chih-Feng P. "Changes in Stated Job Requirements of Director Positions of Academic Libraries in the U.S.: A Content Analysis of Qualifications and Job Expectations as Advertised in Selected Professional Periodicals." PhD diss., Simmons College, 2000.

Lindquist, Thea, and Todd Gilman. "Academic/Research Librarians with Subject Doctorates: Data and Trends 1965-2006." *portal: Libraries and the Academy* 8, no. 1 (2008): 31–52.

Lyle, Guy R. *The Administration of the College Library*. 4th ed. New York: H. W. Wilson, 1974.

Matthews, Joseph R. *Strategic Planning and Management for Library Managers*. Westport, CT: Libraries Unlimited, 2005.

Mayer, Jennifer, and Lori J. Terrill. "Academic Librarians' Attitudes about Advanced-Subject Degrees." *College and Research Libraries* 66, no. 1 (2005): 59–73.

McCook, Kathleen de la Peña. "There Is Power in a Union—2008–2009." *Progressive Librarian* 32 (2009): 55.

——. "Unions in Public and Academic Libraries." School of Information Faculty Publications, Paper 108. 2010. http://scholarcommons.usf.edu/si_facpub/108.

Mech, Terrence F. "Academic Library Directors: A Managerial Role Profile." *College and Research Libraries* 51, no. 5 (1990): 415–28.

"Mission and History of the Madden Library." *Fresno State*, August 2010. https://library.fresnostate.edu/info/mission-history.

Moran, Barbara B., and Elisabeth Leonard. "Academic Librarianship." In *Encyclopedia of Library and Information Sciences*, 3rd ed., edited by Marcia J. Bates and Mary Niles Mack, 1–10. New York: CRC Press, 2010.

Neal, James G. "Raised by Wolves: Integrating the New Generation of Feral Professionals into the Academic Library." *Library Journal* 131, no. 3 (2006): 42–44.

Nelson, Bryce. *The Academic Library Administrator's Field Guide.* Chicago: American Library Association, 2014.

Oakleaf, Megan. *The Value of Academic Libraries: A Comprehensive Research Review and Report.* Chicago: Association of College and Research Libraries, 2010.

Phipps, Shelley E. "The System Design Approach to Organizational Development: The University of Arizona Model." *Library Trends* 53, no. 1 (2004): 68–111.

Quinlan, Catherine, and Hugh McHarg. "The Emerging Library: Structure, Culture, and Lessons Learned from the Dissolution of a Combined Libraries–IT Organization." *Journal of Library Administration* 52, no. 2 (2012): 147–61.

"Reading Titles." *Confessions of a Community College Dean* (blog). April 6, 2010. https://www.insidehighered.com/blogs/confessions_of_a_community_college_dean/reading_titles.

Renaud, Robert E. "Shaping a New Profession: The Role of Librarians When the Library and Computer Center Merge." *Library Administration and Management* 20, no. 2 (2006): 65–74.

Schvaneveldt, Nena. "What Makes You a Librarian?" *INALJ.* September 27, 2013. http://inalj.com/?p=40581.

Stemmer, John K. "The Perception of Effectiveness of Merged Information Services Organizations." *Reference Services Review* 35, no. 3 (2007): 344–59.

Sweeney, Richard T. "Leadership in the Post-Hierarchical Library." *Library Trends* 43, no. 1 (1994): 62–94.

Thompson, James. *An Introduction to University Library Administration.* 2nd ed. Hamden, CT: Linnet Books, 1975.

——. *University Library History: An International Review.* New York: C. Bingley, 1980.

Wagner, Robin. "The Gettysburg Experience." In *Books, Bytes, and Bridges: Libraries and Computer Centers in Academic Institutions*, edited by Larry L. Hardesty, 164–77. Chicago: American Library Association, 2000.

Walters, William H. "Faculty Status of Librarians at U.S. Research Universities." *Journal of Academic Librarianship* 42 (2016): 161–71.

Weiner, Sharon Gray. "Leadership of Academic Libraries: A Literature Review." *Education Libraries* 26, no. 2 (2003): 5–18.

"What Is a Librarian?" *Annoyed Librarian, Library Journal.* June 17, 2009. http://lj.libraryjournal.com/blogs/annoyedlibrarian/2009/06/17/what-is-a-librarian.

Wilson, Louis Round, and Maurice F. Tauber. *The University Library: The Organization, Administration, and Functions of Academic Libraries.* New York: Columbia University Press, 1956.

Zaghloul, Ricardo Andrade Raik. "Restructuring Liaison Librarian Teams at the University of Arizona Libraries, 2007–2009." *New Library World* 111, nos. 7/8 (2010): 273–86.

4

Funding and Budgeting

Tahir Rauf

Introduction

Economic model theory addresses a fundamental question of how scarce resources should best be deployed to generate maximum benefits. An economic model includes financial forecasting, budget planning, proper resource allocation, growth predictions, and risk evaluation. This model is applicable in academic libraries because there is a strong relationship between the academic library and its economic efficiency in budget performance and use of limited funds.

This chapter provides a variety of financial management techniques and emphasizes the importance of various sources of funding. The management of funds is necessary to create appropriate budgets, to control expenditures, to make cost-effective decisions, to ensure adequate operational efficiency of information technology, and to plan for facility needs. Reduction in endowments and sharp declines in state funding have resulted in budget cutbacks, hiring freezes, and less capital spending. Allocation of funds for operating and collection development in a changing environment requires leveraging library resources.

Most academic libraries' funding comes from their institutions to support their operations. All state-affiliated colleges and universities receive funding from state sources. However, states have been cutting their support for higher education for more than a decade. For example, the higher education share of general fund spending fell from 14.6 percent in 1990 to 9.4 percent in 2014. One of the reasons for cutting states' support to higher education is that colleges and universities have built their revenue sources, such as tuition.[1] Gifts and grants comprise another source of income for academic libraries. One out of every five libraries seeks gifts and donations to provide their services. Eight percent of libraries receive grants as a substantial portion of their income stream from state government and private foundations. Many libraries are turning to fund-raising events outside their institutional funding.[2] Thus, entrepreneurship in academic libraries constitutes a new trend, promoted as a center of creativity with new services and innovative ways of exploring funding sources.

Financial Management Practices

Financial accounting is a set of accounting standards and guidelines to follow when reporting one of three financial statements: (1) the balance sheet, (2) the income statement, and (3) the statement of cash flows. The central finance unit of colleges and universities generally prepares these statements. The common set of generally accepted accounting principles (GAAP) are specified rules for institutional reporting in higher education in the United States.[3] Colleges' and universities' accounting systems work on an accrual basis and operate under the accounting standards set by the Financial Accounting Standards Board (FASB) used for not-for-profit organizations. Under the accrual-based accounting system, revenue is recognized when goods are received or services are performed and expenses are matched to related revenues at the time the transaction occurs rather than when payment is made. The accrual-based accounting system is effective in controlling financials over resources and cost of operation. This system also makes it possible to record accurate total costs for the periods in which these costs are actually incurred.[4] The academic library's finances work in the shadow of the central finance system of the institution using an accrual-based accounting system.

Another accounting practice is known as cash basis accounting. Under cash basis accounting, cash is recorded when received and when cash has been paid out. A few small academic libraries, mostly those affiliated with public institutions, use cash basis accounting. However, the auditor often uses modified cash basis accounting for government funds, cash receipts, assets, and liabilities. Cash basis accounting yields less accurate results than accrual-based accounting. The timing of cash flow does not necessarily reflect the proper timing of changes in the financial condition of a library. Because the results of cash basis financial statements can be inaccurate, management reports show an inaccurate picture of financial status.

Management accounting involves the interpretation of accounting information designed to aid the administration in running the library business. Management accounting is financial in nature, but it has been devised to assist in the decision-making process. Managerial accounting applies to all types of businesses. Both not-for-profit entities and for-profit enterprises need managerial accounting. In the past, managerial accounting was primarily engaged in cost accounting and reporting costs to management. Recently that role has changed significantly to automated methods to determine costs and strategic cost management. Business technology software is used for the preparation of financial records. Dissemination of digital information data is used for processing of the budget, analysis, and financial predictions. Managerial accounting is also involved in the strategic management process, where accounting information is used to support strategic decisions.[5]

The fund accounting system is another system used by institutions of higher education to support their boards of trustees and administrators in fulfilling their legal obligations regarding the use of various funds according to the guidelines set by the institution. Beyond allocations from the host institution, colleges and universities rely on nonrevenue sources of gifts, endowments, and donations. In a for-profit business, capital expenditures are funded through retained earnings or long-term debts and maintained in a special capital fund through financial planning. However, nonprofit college and university capital expenditures are funded through appropriation or capital fund drive campaigns. Colleges and universities rely on operating funds and surpluses rather than external loans. Endowment funds are pooled in an investment portfolio. Thus, fund accounting provides the administration control over the institution's total available assets to be used for a particular purpose.

Sources of Funding

Library managers make difficult choices regarding funding for their libraries' operations. Funding models for academic libraries vary depending on whether the institution is private or public, a state's budgetary regulations, funding formulas for higher education, and the overall budgetary situation of each college and university. However, securing funding from internal and external sources can be difficult, as discussed later.

Operating Budget

The academic library receives its operating and collection development budget from the central budget office based on allocations. National statistics reports on academic libraries do not show sources of revenue. There is no uniform approach for every small or large college or university library's budgeting. For the large private universities, operating and collection development budgets come from the college based on allocations. Because the academic library is a service center for different units on the campus, such as the college of arts and sciences, business school, education school, and so on, its budget allocation is based on how much it costs the library to provide services to its campus constituencies.

The budget request for library materials is prepared based on review of the previous year's budget, and information is built into the library requirements for the coming year. Taking account of trends and changes is crucial when planning for the future. Factors, including anticipated goals of the library, vendors' price increases, and inflation, must all be accounted for in the plan document. Users' needs are also an essential part of the budget plan. College libraries serve students and faculty, and the budget document has to accommodate the college's academic programs. Research and teaching libraries include research- and teaching-oriented materials, including books, databases, and journals in this document. An increase or decrease in the budget will directly affect the library's collection strategy.

The organizational structure of each institution affects the budget allocation. Many large private universities have constituent institutions, such as medical, law, or engineering schools; their libraries get their budgets from the parent institutions rather than from the central budget offices. These affiliated academic units of universities function as independent revenue centers and must absorb the cost of their own libraries.

Public universities and small community college libraries receive a fixed percentage of the education and general (E&G) budget their institution receives. There is no hard and fast rule for library funding. Many libraries are funded according to how much money is available rather than what it costs them to provide their services. Academic libraries are experiencing significant financial pressures as the demand for their offerings increases. These pressures include growth in volumes acquired, quality of services, ever higher personnel costs (salaries and benefits), and the rising price of other library materials. Academic libraries are increasingly concerned about costs incurred and value delivered by the services and resources offered to their users. New technologies are changing the services that libraries provide; for example, online reference and instruction, document delivery, user-initiated interlibrary loan, direct borrowing, and self-checkout. Moreover, converting historical books and journals into digital format requires additional funds. The pricing of journals is a focal point of university libraries and scholarly communication. Community college libraries have much smaller budgets, in keeping with their focus on teaching and learning rather than materials for scholarly research.

In general, library operating budgets are almost flat, and annual salary increases are minimal and unusually below the cost of living index. Benefit rates are determined and revised by the institution based on costs. Operating nonsalary budgets, which include lines for supplies, postage, telecommunications, travel, and equipment, are also fixed. However, postage rates have doubled, and average shipping costs have increased about 38 percent between 2001 and 2016. This has a substantial impact on the cost of interlibrary loans. Most often, computers and software are funded through one-time appropriation. One-time funding requests are not in the best interest of the institution because changes in higher education are likely to place new demands on the library. Norms of the academy make it difficult to retire programs and services unless they diminish over time. However, the academy tends to have an "add-on" environment for services, which often requires additional funds for libraries.

Community colleges and public universities receive revenue based on E&G expenditures, state appropriations, property taxes, and tuition and associated fees. Sharp declines in state funding and reduced endowments have produced budget cuts, hiring freezes, and a reduction in capital spending in US colleges and universities. Even though institutions' enrollments are at an all-time high, academic libraries are still assigned a fixed percentage of the E&G budget.

An ALA (American Library Association) study[6] on library funding found that cuts at the state level were often compounded by cuts at the local level. Some state and local budget cuts hit state-affiliated institutions and their libraries especially hard because they are seen as easy targets. The library loses

Table 4.1 Total revenue sources of private or public nonprofit degree-granting postsecondary institutions, 2012–2013

	Total Revenue of Public 2- to 4-Year Institutions (%)	Total Revenue of Private 2- to 4-Year Institutions (%)
Tuition and Fees	21	32
Operating Revenue (Grants and Sales)	27	8
Sales and Service of Hospitals	11	9
Appropriation (Federal, State, and Local)	22	13
Nonoperating Revenue (Grants)	8	2
Gifts	2	9
Investment	3	19
Others	2	0
Educational Activities	0	3
Other Revenue (Capital Appropriation, Capital Grants, Gifts, Endowments)	4	5
Total	**100**	**100**

Source: National Center for Education Statistics

each year as the E&G percentage declines and feels the impact in decreases in total expenditures. Currently, we have no commonly accepted standard for the budget appropriation a library should receive from university or college administrators. Public institutions receive funding through state appropriations. Table 4.1 shows how public and private two- and four-year institutions incorporate different funding streams.

The structure of the state budget system is different in higher education funding. Often, public institutions compete with each other for available funds. Administrators' personalities, party politics, and state priorities and interests can all affect funding decisions. State boards often operate in an awkward relationship with state legislatures, and they sometimes penalize administrators from a particular institution with whom they disagree. In such cases, funding to the institution is certainly affected.[7]

An American Association of Community Colleges (AACC) report shows that community colleges' revenue sources in 2013–2014 consisted of tuition (30 percent), allocations from the federal government (14.1 percent), state funding (29.8 percent), and local governments (18.1 percent). Other sources accounted for 8 percent. However, state funding decreased six percentage points from 2008–2009 to 2013–2014. Therefore, community colleges have become more reliant on tuition. Over the same period, tuition as part of total revenue jumped from 24 percent to 30 percent.[8] Thus, decreases in state funding for community colleges affect the level of funding for their libraries.

Endowments

The fiscal support from endowments is a longstanding tradition in many colleges and universities. Academic libraries rely on nonrevenue sources of endowment income and gifts. Endowment funds provide a significant level of financial stability for library collections. The endowment is built from such sources as cash gifts or income from real estate. These assets are invested on the market, and income earned from the investment is used to support library activities.

Endowment funds hold fund assets that earn additional income. The institution is allowed to use the additional income generated by the fund assets but is not allowed to touch the principal balance. Endowment income may be restricted or unrestricted, depending on donors' instructions. In some cases, income may be added back in to the endowment principal in order to earn interest for a certain number of years or to generate a certain amount of money to use for another purpose once the requirements have been met.

Large academic libraries use a risk management approach to diversify investment portfolios. Endowment investment in a widely diversified portfolio of stocks, alternative investments, private equity, hedge funds, and real estate is considered a balanced approach. Liquidity remains the primary consideration. Small community college libraries with limited endowments must be careful to gauge their tolerance for interest rate risk. There are several bonds that have either low interest or a significant income component. In fact, fixed income investment is an effective way to hedge inflation risks.

Gift Funds for Capital Improvement

Most academic libraries spend a significant amount of money on space, capital equipment, and infrastructure for the library. Academic libraries of private colleges and universities are often especially successful in obtaining donations for buildings and special facilities. Their donors typically have a special interest in the institution and are eager to support library services and programs. Library gifts are usually the result of various fund drives. Library web pages are often used to solicit gifts. "Friends of the Library" groups can also be valuable fund-raisers. Academic libraries also at times receive substantial gifts from private philanthropies. Moreover, academic libraries are introducing new service models tied to strategic planning that make a compelling case for additional financial support. The deans of academic libraries are assuming new roles as entrepreneurs to run development programs and become involved in fund-raising efforts for capital campaigns. The development office usually runs an annual campaign, and often, the large unrestricted gifts generated will be used for facility maintenance, renovations of library spaces, and new technology.

Funds through Grants

A grant is usually awarded for a specific project. Many state programs have strengthened library digitization and preservation projects. Many private and corporate foundations are receptive to library grant proposals and will provide funding for research libraries for digitization, preservation, purchase of materials, and technology upgrades. Library faculty grants are awarded for the librarians to attend workshops, conferences, seminars and symposia, and other professional development initiatives.

Program development grants are used as general operating funds to acquire resources. These awards might be used to create institutional repositories, collaborative learning spaces, technology centers in the library building, reading and writing support centers, or other library-specific initiatives. These types of grants easily match the needs of libraries. The New York State Foundation for Education Association (NYSFEA) offers a number of program development awards. The Andrew W. Mellon Foundation awards money for program development that supports new collaboration models, book publishing, and increased building capacity. Collection acquisitions grants usually account for a small percentage of the total grants disbursed by private philanthropies. However, New York State and California are leading the way in distributing their awards to different library programs.[9]

In preparing a successful fund-raising grant proposal, before submitting a request for funding for a specific project, the grant seeker must be sure to choose the right agency by conducting thorough research. Data shows that only about 35 percent of the approved funding requests were closely associated with the programs and services objectives of the agency.[10] Therefore, librarians should track down those private or public agencies that will likely welcome a request for support.

The central element of most grants is quality research. Therefore, academic research institutions receive research grants for their academic libraries. The fundamental mission of community colleges is to offer affordable access to higher education, not only to individual students, but also to the whole community, regardless of the vagaries of the economy. Community colleges receive grants based on their mission of teaching and learning. All incoming grant funds should support the core objectives of the library. Small libraries may not have a written mission and vision statement, but a library's core values revolve around its parent institution.

The Institutional Budget Allocation Process

The development of general budgets and resource allocations for all major units within the university and college is based on principles that ensure a strategic and sustainable budget process. The academic library's budget is based on central administration allocations. Most colleges and universities operate under a decentralized management structure, as revenue and expenses for each division are assigned to the respective unit or cost center. The costs that cannot be directly assigned to a division, such as central administration, student services, auxiliary operations, and campus libraries, are distributed to cost centers on an allocation basis. The allocation methodology for the campus library budget is based on providing services to school types by estimating the level of effort expended for each service line. The level of effort is measured based on usage statistics available in the institution's annual statistics book. Not every university or college follows a uniform budget allocation process. Most have developed their own processes depending on size, nature, and structure of the institution.

An effort study looks at past performance in order to gauge future needs. The study requires developing formulas, and this in itself is a complex process. Formulas are developed based on principles of need and objectivity. Allocation formulas include such elements as the number of faculty, student enrollments, majors, credit hours, and salary and wages expenditure. All statistical data are weighted according to these formulas. The effort study approach is valid for a large university in a situation in which the central library is funded by the university's college and other academic units, such as education or business schools, as part of the campus. Therefore, all the arms of the campus have to contribute to the central library budget based on the level of effort provided. There are many constituent institutions of the university, such as the medical and dental schools, engineering institute, or school of music, that operate as revenue centers of their own. The constituent units of the university fund their specialized libraries through their own resources; such libraries do not seek budget funding from central college administration.

Many private and most public academic libraries receive a fixed percentage of their institutions' E&G expenditures. E&G expenditures include a major category of "instruction" (to students), including teaching faculty salaries and wages, research, public service, academic support (including libraries), student services, institutional support, operation and maintenance of the physical plant, and scholarships and fellowships. The National Center for Education Statistics (2003) indicates that funding for "instruction" declined from 35.1 percent in 1980–1981 to 30.4 percent in 2000–2001 at public degree-granting institutions.[11]

Association of Research Libraries (ARL) members' expenditures as a percentage of total university (private and public) expenditure decreased from 3.7 percent in 1982 to 1.8 percent in 2011. Private university libraries' spending decreased from 3.77 percent in 1982 to 1.89 percent in 2011, while public university libraries' spending decreased from 3.63 percent to 1.75 percent between 1982 and 2011.[12] When two of the highest academic priorities, instruction and libraries, are pitted against each other in a competition for more funding, the goals of the institution are put at risk.

Budgeting for small college and community college libraries is quite different. A common method is simply to use the preceding year's budget plus or minus a certain percentage. Some institutions allocate funding to libraries based on FTE or increases or decreases in enrollment. In a nutshell, there is no one single approach for all academic libraries' budget allocations.

The community college budget sets the principles and policies for how best to manage college resources. Using a formal resource allocation model promotes transparency and equity across the college and reduces ambiguity. A root cause analysis identifies gaps between current levels of performance and desired future goals. The budget process is evaluated and resources adjusted accordingly based on institutional goals. A well-crafted budget document prioritizes directing limited resources toward the expenses of the college. A best practice when developing such a budget is to align resources with student needs. The budget document should focus on optimizing student achievement with available resources.

Academic library budgeting practices differ based on the size of the institution or its affiliated library, budgeting resources, administrative practices, and campus priorities or politics. For example, a small community college library with two or three full-time librarians and limited fixed resources may not need a formal budgeting process. Librarians in such libraries play multiple roles, and their budget numbers are at their fingertips, so they have the option to use cash basis accounting practices. In addition, the academic library theoretically serves everyone in the campus community. E&G expenditure is one of the main sources of institutional funding, so it makes sense that the central administration budget should provide funding for campus-wide library services. Library budgets and funding levels should be linked to other campus expenditures: academic departments, new programs, information technology, telecommunications, and wireless. Within the context of library funding today, knowledge management (KM) has become increasingly important. *Knowledge management* refers to a multidisciplinary approach to achieving organizational objectives by making the best use of knowledge.[13] It helps libraries to improve effectiveness for both themselves and their parent institutions. Knowledge management activities are intended to improve access to knowledge, share resources, network, facilitate the development of information technology, establish virtual libraries, install collaborative software or groupware, and partner with faculty in curriculum development. Thus, the technology push model of knowledge management requires institutions to invest more in library operations and their capital needs.

Developing Budget Systems

Academic libraries use a variety of management techniques borrowed from the corporate world. Management innovation concepts are being applied in academic libraries in order to improve core organizational processes and functions. These practices include line-item budgeting, zero-based budgeting, program budgeting, performance budgeting, activity-based budgeting, capital budgeting, benchmarking, and strategic planning. These new management practices have been integrated into North American library culture in such a way that each library differentiates itself from others by leveraging intellectual assets and facilitating knowledge creation. There are many budgeting techniques. The following are six budget models or budget-related practices utilized in colleges and universities:

- *Line-item budgeting*: Each category of activity is recorded as a separate line. The library mostly uses the institution's accounting structure. The challenge here is that it can be difficult to match each item with the goals of the library. Moreover, matching the current year's line-item expenses with the previous year's budget is complex because there are many variables not accounted for within each line of the budget.
- *Zero-based budgeting:* An appropriate technique to build the budget every year with a base of zero. It is assumed at the outset that no program is necessary and no money needs to be spent. For a program to be accepted, an interested administrator has to prove that it is financially sound in terms of revenue and expense. The objective is to reexamine all costs periodically with the assumption that certain costs will be reduced or eliminated. All expenditures must be justified regardless of allocations received in previous years. The cost of each activity is determined and compared with the cost of a similar activity that might adequately meet the needs of the patron or library. All library activities are ranked according to their level of importance.[14]

- *Program budgeting:* An extension of the line-item budget. The budget sheet has all programs listed across the top and all line items listed down the side so that one can easily compare line items with programs. This type of budget focuses on services the library provides to its patrons. Therefore, the program budget can be related to the overall goals and objectives of the library. A program budget requires that a program manager carefully think through all program objectives. In this way, each manager assumes personal responsibility for achieving the financial goals of his or her program.

- *Performance budgeting:* Shares many features with program budgeting. The main focus here is on different functions performed in the library; for example, acquisitions, technical services, facilities, and human resources. Functions are listed along the top of the budget sheet, with the nature of expenses listed down the side in line-item format. This technique measures the quantity of activities performed in the library rather than their quality.

- *Activity-based budgeting (ABB):* This approach focuses on the cost of the activities necessary to offer services in every functional area of the library (e.g., acquisitions or technical services). The administration identifies the specific cost driver for each cost pool. All activities are recorded, and their relationships are defined and analyzed. Activities are then tied to strategic goals, after which the projected cost of the activities is used to create a budget. ABB provides opportunities to align activities with objectives and to streamline costs and improve existing practices. It helps academic libraries to create accurate financial forecasts. The ABB approach is considered an expenditure control technique. The ABB process determines patrons' needs, forecasts the library staff's workload, establishes specific activity levels, coordinates interdepartmental projects to eliminate duplication of effort, defines and evaluates each activity in order to ensure continuous improvement, and finally specifies the budgeted activities and workload for the upcoming year. The ABB accounts for staff members allocating their efforts to the necessary activities within each department. Therefore, the ABB develops a comprehensive budget that shows a clear relationship between workload and costs.[15]

- *Capital budgeting:* This is the process of planning and evaluating proposals for capital expenditures. Capital budgeting might take account of a decision to purchase new equipment, to build a new facility, or to renovate an existing building. Expenditures for purchases or expansion of the physical plant are called "capital expenditures" and are recorded in the asset account of the institution's books.

Cost-Effective Collection Allocation Strategy

Collection development is both an art and a science. It requires a combination of knowledge, experience, and intuition. It is not realistic for any single library to collect everything that is published in a given year. Library collections and finance are interrelated. Library collection may be the single largest financial investment in a college and university library. Each library must balance the need to collect materials that support the mission of its parent institution with its own financial strengths and weaknesses.

Library management should develop a rationale for the collection allocation process. Most often libraries, especially small libraries, do not have a written collection development policy but instead rely on historical precedent. Budgeting based on historical precedent or yearly incremental increases is likely to lead to an unbalanced collection because this practice rewards those academic departments that were more active in the past and penalizes those that may deserve more materials in the present and future. Policies for collection development, whether in formally written documents or simple statements or ideas of resource allocation, help in formulating the budget request and allocating money for collections and other library purchases.

A 2012 survey of a total of twenty-two ARL libraries' chief collection development officers (CCDOs) reported that twelve (55 percent) of the libraries set their budgets based on historical allocation patterns, only two used a formula or a formula with additional money available through request, and the other seven employed a "combination of methods, usually based on historical allocation with other methods used to allocate specific parts of the budget, such as at the discretion of the CCDO."[16] No one method prevails for collection allocation. Seven libraries reported "that they use a combination of individual subject funds and larger aggregated funds such as those based on colleges or schools within their universities."[17] In other words, these libraries use a combination of several methods.

The ultimate goal is that the budget should be allocated based on the principle of equity. Any academic department with the same characteristics should receive the same allocations. The formula-based allocation minimizes the potential for arbitrary and political decisions. A formula should be considered based on demand, cost, and supply factors with respect to the budget. The collections budget should align with the academic structure of the university, such as the colleges and schools. In addition, the collections budget should reflect the changing mission of the university.

College libraries are inherently distinct from university libraries because their parent institutions have different missions. Universities support graduate and professional programs and major research initiatives. Their libraries, in response, seek to develop comprehensive collections that would support both current and future programs and research. But college libraries focus on supporting undergraduate teaching programs and the needs of undergraduates, so they do not attempt to build the comprehensive collections that have come to characterize university libraries.

ARL members' data show that serial expenditures increased 456 percent, bibliographic records and external network utilities expenditures increased 349 percent, and library materials expenditures increased 322 percent from 1986 to 2012.[18] The availability of countless materials and ever-increasing demands of users in a variety of disciplines may represent a set of conflicting goals for a collection development officer; purchase requests for materials that may broaden the scope of the collection typically get top priority. Moreover, the growing importance of supporting electronic resources while maintaining traditional collections requires a new strategy for collection development.

Percentage-Based Allocation (PBA) for Collections

Percentage-based allocation determines the fund allocation process by reflecting university curriculum and support for different programs. As a general guideline, PBA follows these steps:[19]

1. Obtain the instructional and research budget, broken out by academic departments on the spreadsheet, from the budget office.
2. Divide each department budget by all the departments, excluding the library, which will give a percentage representative of the total.
3. Divide the library materials budget into nondepartmental/general and departmental funds.
4. Set aside the nondepartmental budget portion for general collection needs, such as special collections and electronic resources (analogous with print reference materials). These costs are projected based on the previous year's spending pattern.
5. The projected cost of the nondepartmental budget is subtracted from the total library budget.
6. Five percent of the departmental budget is set aside as a contingency fund (used for inflation factors).
7. The remaining departmental funds are allocated among academic departments using PBA percentages from step 2.
8. Compare the past three years of materials spending for all disciplines.
9. For subject areas in which the past three years' average was higher than PBA, reduce the allocation derived from this average by not more than 10 percent. If the past three years' average spending was lower than PBA, then increase this average by no more than 10 percent. All continuations, monographs, and nonprint costs are included in each subject area.
10. Grants and gifts are not included and are considered part of the department's overall support.

The PBA allocation method works well for the university administration as well as for academic departments that have not raised objections to the fund allocation process.[20]

Data-Based Demand-Driven Collections

A demand-driven acquisitions (DDA) or patron driven acquisitions (PDA) system is an alternative to conventional library acquisitions of books. DDA is an economic model of collection development. The 80/20 rule suggests 20 percent of the library's collection circulates with patrons and 80 percent remains on library shelves.[21] It is reasonable to argue that resources spent on noncirculating materials are a complete waste. The DDA model offers new opportunities because the library will only pay for what is used. A demand-driven model offers many opportunities. Patrons are exposed to many more books than they would otherwise have in print, and DDA allows the library to buy all those books when patrons need them. The library imports all bibliographic records into its catalogs at no cost. For each book, the library pays a small transaction fee, a small percentage of list price, and automatically buys the book. The major providers (ProQuest, Ebrary, EBSCO) of DDA service offer libraries the opportunity to create a collection of titles of their choice in real time based on usage. Thus, DDA collection is more efficient and cost-effective for libraries to acquire e-books.

Consortial Programs

Academic libraries transitioning into the digital environment are mindful of the costs of storage. Thus, they often take the opportunity to engage in collaborative collection development with partner libraries in regional consortia whenever possible. Consortial programs' potential for expanding collection purchases at reduced rates are a boon to overcrowded libraries.[22] While consortia do not directly provide cost savings, they can engage in renegotiation of licenses for electronic resources and provide budget management for their members. Consortial membership and borrowing agreements brokered through such organizations as the Center for Research Libraries (CRL), OCLC, The Information Delivery Services Project (IDS), and GreenGlass can provide information about which collections are unique to each institution and what is available in the vicinity in order to reduce duplication.[23]

Universal Collaborative Library

Academic libraries are facing budgetary shortfalls and increasing pressures from their readers to provide a broader range of collections. Digital technology has dramatically enhanced library access and services from proprietary to digital collections through collaborative resource sharing. HathiTrust constitutes one of the largest collaborative library initiatives in the world. Participating libraries pay for initial software implementation and an annual membership fee.[24] The collaboration provides a cost–benefit edge to library collections budgets. Another strategic option is cost-sharing among participating institutions' libraries, such as campus medical libraries. Academic libraries have also considered canceling subscriptions to low-use and high-cost journals.

HathiTrust is an international community of research libraries. Therefore, most research institutions are members of this consortium. State community colleges' libraries mostly use state consortia for shared resources. Community college libraries' needs are quite different from those of large research academic libraries. For example, the Community College Library Consortium (CCLC) also provides a variety of collaborative services to community college libraries of California.[25] The CCLC program provides electronic databases and other online programs via the Internet to libraries at all 112 colleges and many off-campus centers around the state. The program negotiates significant price discounts on more than one hundred different databases covering nearly every discipline in a college's curriculum for purchase by the library. Similarly, Community College Libraries in North Carolina (CCLINC) is a consortium of community college libraries in North Carolina that has a shared catalog with more than one million learning resources. The e-Library online catalog gives access to the collections at each of the libraries to allow for searching the collection and placing items on hold. The catalog circulates approximately 500,000 items per year, and sends and receives more than 7,500 items annually to and from member libraries.[26]

Management planning tools allow each institution to assess the cost of interlibrary borrowing and lending operations. Academic libraries make their preliminary cost comparison between traditional services and alternative methods of obtaining and lending materials. Unit cost analysis is the best solution. Libraries rely on interlibrary services for cost-saving ideas. Many publishers offer a pay-per-view (PPV) alternative as another cost-saving option for libraries. With PPV, publishers are able to deliver articles more quickly than interlibrary loan services can.

Electronic resource management systems (ERMS) are tools that help librarians manage licenses to electronic resources, store administrative information, and generate usage statistics without duplication of effort. ERMS tools optimize access to data and electronic library collections in the physical and digital libraries. Thus, they maximize buying power through data management. The usage data obtained for electronic resources are used to make acquisitions decisions and serve as a basis for budget preparation. Any time a user views or downloads the full text of an article or book, this action is recorded and counts as a single use. The library uses this data to calculate average cost per search or full-text document retrieval by users. Equipped with user reports, librarians can make fiscally responsible acquisitions decisions, such as canceling low-use e-resources.[27]

As print collections shrink, the number of staff managing book stacks is reduced. Staff formerly devoted to shelving now assist faculty with electronic course reserves and learning management systems (LMS). The rapid increase in electronic resources also means less need of staff for the binding, sorting, and physical processing of materials associated with traditional print acquisitions.

The Wildcard: Managing Resources

Academic libraries consume a significant percentage of the colleges' and universities' resources. Yet even as library budgets have shrunk, administrators are devoting significant attention to redefining resources allocation models. They focus on continuously reviewing expenditure patterns within individual operation areas in order to make the most efficient use of resources. The bulk of any academic library budget goes to paying for personnel and materials costs. Therefore, it makes sense to recognize the complexities of expenses in these two categories. In 2013–2014, ARL member libraries' expenditures in salaries were 43.23 percent, library materials were 44.74 percent, and other operating expenses were 12.03 percent.[28] Moreover, ARL members' data shows that the total cost of salaries and benefits increased 146 percent, and operating expenses increased 134 percent in the quarter century between 1986 and 2012.[29]

Certain aspects of personnel expenditures can be somewhat complicated. The US National Center for Education Statistics survey data on FTEs[30] in academic libraries during the twelve years from 2000 to 2012 show that, while librarian staff increased to 31 percent from 26.3 percent and professional staff (such as those in information technology) rose from 6.1 percent to 9.1 percent, other staff (library assistants) decreased from 39.6 percent to 35.9 percent, and student workers fell from 27.7 percent to 23.9 percent.[31] We have witnessed an obvious shift toward more librarian and professional personnel than support staff. Moreover, we should note that the line between professional staff and librarians has become blurred because both groups are involved in all library operations at all levels. Both engage in routine activities or supervise and direct other staff; they also manage operations and contribute highly specialized skills to the organization. Data show that the creation of new positions results from administrators' analyses of the library's strategic goals as they relate to the parent institution. The growth of goal-driven programs and services in recent years has led to an increased need for specialist librarians and information technology professionals but not for paraprofessionals.

The demographic changes in academic librarianship have become a significant cause for concern because of the so-called graying of the profession. The proportion of librarians who were forty-five years of age and above increased from 42 percent in 1986 to 65 percent in 2000. Most senior librarians reached retirement age by 2015. New entrants to the profession require new skills and expertise to replace retirees.[32] In addition, academic libraries face the challenges of rigorous staffing and recruitment requirements. Many libraries will hire only those with a completed master's in library and information sciences (MLS or MLIS) for most positions and increasingly prefer to hire PhDs in a variety of disciplines to fill subject specialist positions.[33]

However, teaching pervades all aspects of academic librarianship. Small and medium-size community college libraries' mission is assisting users in both accessing information and teaching information literacy. Information technology is used as a better means of doing what we used to do. Most of these small libraries have limited staff, and their goal is to make students and faculty independent learners. Community college libraries have increased their use of databases. While the traditional librarian credential is the MLS, the day-to-day operations of these libraries are managed by paraprofessional or support staff who lack MLS training. The trend is for these paraprofessionals to attend many skill development programs run by the local councils or regional organizations of computer literacy, reference work, monitoring, continuing education, and other hands-on learning. By contrast, librarians devote most of their time to collection development, administration, and strategic planning.

Indeed, the academic librarians of today and tomorrow need to provide a higher level of expertise than ever before: They have to possess an in-depth understanding of emerging trends, from new models of scholarly communications to data curation to instructional design and other technologies.[34] Academic libraries making the transition to adopting these new, more sophisticated roles consequently have the financial responsibility to fund these programs adequately and hire the desired highly skilled staff at higher salaries than their predecessors were paid.

Moreover, the number of individuals working in technical services jobs dropped 35 percent between 1985 and 2000 because of a gradual reduction in hiring for cataloging expertise.[35] Technical services departments are being consolidated and shrunk because the nature of this work has been changing from general cataloging to implementing specialized metadata.[36] In many cases, technical services functions are outsourced because this is less expensive than training and paying local library staff to perform them. Licensing and copyright functions are also being consolidated. At some institutions, a single librarian is engaged in multiple roles in licensing, collection development, and assessment of technology services. For example, reference librarians serve as outreach librarians and participate in collection development or campus printing teams. Therefore, the demand for specialized and IT-related professionals is increasing in libraries, and salaries are much higher than those of average catalogers.

A benchmark study on academic library funding and priorities in 2011[37] shows that 79 percent of academic libraries are affiliated with four-year or graduate-level colleges and universities, while only 21 percent are affiliated with two-year colleges or technical schools. The data show that budget cuts were severe for larger libraries but that there were fewer cuts for smaller libraries. Still, four out of five academic libraries had budget cuts in one or more areas over the preceding year. The study confirms that a large portion of the libraries' funding goes to staffing and collections. On average, 43 percent of the budget is spent on salary and wages and another 34 percent goes to collection development, while only about 11 percent is spent on information technology and media equipment and only 6 percent is dedicated to operation and facilities. These percentages are quite consistent across all sizes of academic libraries.

Larger academic libraries are often able to exert pressure on vendors to get them to offer their publications on more favorable terms. Large to midsize libraries are moving toward e-book subscriptions, but smaller institutions (those with a student population of 5,000 to 10,000) have been able to increase e-books subscriptions up to 19 percent,[38] and overall, academic libraries increased their holdings to 52.7 million e-book volumes, or about 57 percent of total collections in 2012.[39]

Outsourcing

Outsourcing is a business strategy that moves some of an organization's functions, processes, activities, and decision-making responsibility to outside providers. Outsourcing generates better services and savings because specialized firms enjoy the benefits of economies of scale, division of labor, and a good balance of onsite support for employees. In an attempt to reduce costs and improve services, colleges and universities have outsourced much of their business. Libraries can realize significant cost savings in such areas as employee compensation and office space, which helps free up resources for other purposes. In some cases, the savings achieved have been used to acquire much-needed new technological equipment.

Libraries may employ service-level agreements (SLAs) with university IT for staff e-mail service, desktop support, software updates, and server maintenance to save staffing costs. Academic libraries are also strategically implementing other radical changes in order to achieve greater fiscal agility. Many have been able to bundle needed library materials through consortial purchasing, cease print journal subscriptions in favor of electronic surrogates, outsource cataloging, and employ students to do the work of traditional staff.

Leasing versus Purchasing

Academic libraries have learned from private business organizations how to deal with uncertainties. In a complex and unstable environment, administrators attempt to implement decisions that minimize the likelihood of failure. These libraries are leasing equipment instead of buying it because technology changes so rapidly today.[40]

Self-Generated Revenue Sources

Entrepreneurial development in the academic library is creating new income streams by leveraging assets. This strategy includes leasing special collections space for campus or other external parties' social events, providing library space to coffee carts (Starbucks) in the central library building, sharing resources with local libraries, launching publishing projects, and setting up instructional technology services including usability and digital humanities (DH) labs. Refurbished library building spaces, especially conference rooms equipped with modern audio, video, and wireless systems, increasingly serve as attractive venues for campus community meetings; and the library is allowed to charge fees for the use of such spaces in order to generate supplementary income. This income can be used for room renovations, new furniture, or technology upgrades for these spaces. Many librarians are providing consulting services to other libraries for evaluation of their technological infrastructure and managing library space. Moreover, library consulting provides a direct avenue for personal contact between industry and academia that prevents organizational rigidity for both parties.

Monitoring and Evaluation

Managerial accounting systems or decision support systems are designed to provide needed information to the internal administration at different organizational levels and for different functional specializations. Academic libraries' decision support systems combine two worlds: financial accounting and management accounting. The institution accounting system works on an accrual basis, so it cannot clearly show a library department head that income is earned and expenses are accrued in financial reports. Financial accounting systems do not record encumbrances formally in financial statements for commitments for services. Therefore, libraries' internal management reports include all liabilities, even those not yet recorded in the financial report of the institution.

A line-item report constitutes a simple snapshot that compares the budget with actual performance variances and indicates administrative decisions' effectiveness. All the libraries are part of the institution's systems and use university payroll systems for paychecks, university finance for vendor payments, and university purchasing for vendor purchase orders. All institutional business systems are consolidated under the university finance system for monthly ledgers.

Libraries must develop rigorous costing studies. Acquisitions, cataloging, and reference services need thorough cost scrutiny. The analogy between collection growth and circulation has seldom been investigated from a cost point of view.[41] The library's problem is that its products are distributed rather than concentrated. Library budget models should therefore be linked to the cost of activities.

Activity-Based Costing (ABC) Reports

This is one of the strategic management tools designed to break down the costs of all activities in the library. ABC is a unique approach that involves looking back at the cost of the services the library provides. ABC analyzes the activities of different departments within an academic library in order to provide focused information for decision-making. The goal of ABC is to understand all cost behaviors within the library. It is a process of linking operations costs in such a way that the library administration can identify the factors that drive expenditures and thereby manage these costs more effectively. The initial objectives are to understand the activities performed in the organization and estimate their cost. When the costs of the activities are identified with causes (cost drivers), more relevant data can be generated, and this in turn helps library administrators make better-informed decisions.[42]

The ABC reports help financial officers to understand changes in expenditure patterns, such as staffing costs, collection development, inflation in serials pricing, and metadata costs. These reports attempt to clarify how the various costs are incurred and thus how funds should be allocated to support departments' services or products.[43]

The closing of the library budget means tying up loose ends, making sure that all invoices are processed and central accounting will be able to send checks, and that transactions will appear in the library books. As soon as the fiscal year closes, the year-end reports are produced. These reports are checked for accuracy and serve as the basis for the next year's budget plan. Finance plays an active role in formulating a budget that reflects the library's goals and priorities. But to monitor the budget to see whether these goals and objectives have been met remains important.

Facility Planning

Remote Storage Facility

It makes good sense to keep books in the campus library that remain in current circulation and move any volumes that have not been used for several years to an offsite facility. According to one CLIR study, the cost of keeping a book in the open stacks for ten years was found to be $141.89, while the cost of keeping a book in high-density storage was found to be only $28.77.[44] Thus, high-density storage has proven to be an effective solution to minimize onsite storage space, but it involves transportation costs and remote storage, which risks inconveniencing the campus population. However, there is always a tradeoff between cost and storage space. Many university libraries use their discretionary funds beyond their operating budgets to purchase electronic backfiles. Backfile purchases are integrated with current online journals, online books, and databases and offer the same flexible search, retrieval, and printing capabilities. This option is also available for community colleges' libraries to access backfiles of more than sixty Wiley-Blackwell journals available through JSTOR. As noted earlier, community colleges negotiate significant price discounts on databases through JSTOR. Again, different options are available for libraries depending on their size, financial health, and the cost-benefits of the opportunity.

In most libraries, bibliographers and curators have the responsibility for building and collection maintenance. Campus libraries have to come up with cost-effective solutions to increasingly overcrowded book stacks.[45] Expenditure categories for such offsite facilities include the cost of leasing the space. Building, equipment, and administration costs are fixed, while utilities and retrieval costs are variable. To offset costs, a library can rent shelving space to other libraries on a square-footage basis (assuming the library can realistically spare the space). The information and library inventory is a unique asset. In a business setting, financial asset management permits physical assets to be depreciated and obsoleted overtime. Thus, information and knowledge life cycles work on the same principle in academic libraries, which must weed their collections over time while ensuring that relevant materials are available to their readers. The scarcity of resources necessitates consideration of priorities, interests, and choices. Libraries must strike a balance between these factors and the need to house their physical collections.

There is always a need to accommodate the students in community college libraries. Noise travels quickly, and library staff circulate to shush people with kindness and sometimes with good humor. Small libraries often have poorly designed buildings to control the noise and do not offer separate quiet study areas to their students. Students must hold group meetings in many other places on campus.

Every academic library has its own approach to collection development management. Large university libraries review and negotiate contracts to acquire or access e-resources, find new storage spaces, and preserve their holdings. Small libraries manage the collection through informed weeding or cancellation of materials. These decisions require cost-benefit assessments on a micro or macro level depending on the size of the library.

Key to the success of library facility planning are fund-raising efforts. Many institutions have run successful capital campaigns. Public institutions have been less successful in the fund-raising arena (table 4.1). However, that does not mean that they cannot achieve donation levels comparable to private institutions. In private institutions' libraries, every public space that is named for a donor reveals that administrators have formally planned every building and every corner of the library with an eye to generating revenue. Even outside the library staff or development office, other academic departments can generate dollars for the library. For example, the physics department might raise money for a special library to be located in their department's building.

Functions of the central university library have been supplemented by new functions and structures. Special or departmental libraries often operate under the central library of the university. Special libraries are created for many reasons. Some important schools or departments of the universities are engaged in capital campaigns and major gift programs because they want to have their own research materials for unique subjects in their department space. Resource management of academic libraries inevitably encompasses a political dimension. Some academic departments are located at a distance from the central library, and it becomes convenient for students and faculty to have readily available materials closer to their academic buildings. Departmental or branch libraries are mostly administered by a central library. Budgeting and collection development functions remain with the central library. However, decentralizing library operations increases efficiency and effectiveness.

Conclusion

The idea of economic value was promoted by the Scottish economist Adam Smith (1723–1790). Smith discussed the functioning of micro-macroeconomic systems under free markets. Finance and accounting are concerned with the economic problems resulting from scarcity of resources among competing opportunities within free and competitive markets. Academic libraries operate on the general principle that they are motivated by self-interest, are goal oriented, and engage in utility maximization.

Academic libraries are resource-intensive organizations and receive budgets from their parent institutions. Many academic libraries are facing funding constraints and budget cutbacks with declining support and increasing costs, posing serious threats to their continued viability. Cuts to higher education in general also impact academic libraries' staffing, collections, and ability to keep current with technology. Developing a whole new funding model for academic libraries constitutes a huge challenge, one that requires innovative thinking. Library administrators need to look beyond the traditional library business model and develop multiple strategies to maximize the efficiency and effectiveness of current resources and make the most cost-effective decisions.

Budgeting is a systematic method of allocating financial, physical, and human resources to achieve strategic goals. Budget processes are linked to costs. They must accommodate changes in tandem with the need for high-quality services. Therefore, the challenge is to map out the future. Procedures are designed to allocate resources strategically. Cost measurements and cost accounting constitute the primary concerns of budget development. Financial and physical resource management (technology, human resources, and collections) are inextricably bound. Business models are designed to define structures, processes, and means of achieving goals.

Many academic libraries receive substantial gifts and grants. Still, they must pay special attention to pursuing alternative sources of funding. This often entails the preparation of grant proposals and determining appropriate investment strategies.

Sustainable collection services highlights the current trends toward low use of print collections, the life cycle cost of managing print, and data-driven deselection of monographs. Consortial partnerships among peer libraries determine which titles are held in each library and can be shared. Dramatic changes in technology will continue to influence libraries over the coming decades. Indeed, academic libraries generally are experiencing a natural progression toward providing richer and better services.

Library buildings have become the center of campus, inviting a broad community of learners who anticipate a future with the institution. Library space matters because it includes the institutional mission of learning. Libraries have to deal with the financial ramifications of either maintenance or upgrades (air conditioning, heating, and lighting) through current budgets or through capital budgets for facilities, which are also tight. The goal is to establish and maintain an efficient and cost-effective physical learning environment over the long term. Operating budgets fund regular building maintenance, and gifts from private philanthropies facilitate planning for capital projects.

In a nutshell, the budget of the academic library may increase or, what's more likely, stay the same from year to year. The funding process is ever-changing, and vendors' prices will continue to rise. As a result, most academic libraries need to offer the same services and resources to their patrons, if not more, with their existing budgets.

Discussion Questions

1. List important differences between financial accounting and managerial accounting.
2. Would you prefer a traditional costing system or an activity-based costing system? Discuss both systems, and justify your selection.
3. Explain how academic libraries are entrepreneurial organizations. What initiatives might they undertake to generate income for themselves and explore private funding?
4. How and why are budgeted financial statements prepared at the end of the budgeting process?
5. Explain flexible budgeting as a managerial tool. How can it be used most efficiently to allocate resources and control budgets?
6. Describe the techniques that academic libraries should employ to account for the cost of their activities.
7. How have digital technologies dramatically enhanced libraries' ability to pool their resources by collaborating and gain access to a broader range of collections? Explain in detail with current examples.
8. Explain how the library building can serve as a marketing tool for the campus. What are some of the possible uses of the library building to generate additional revenue?

Assignment

Ms. Kathy Cox is dean of the academic library. She has asked a financial analyst to help her collection development officer develop a cost matrix of different purchasing models. An activity-based cost matrix will help track the cost of different activities in the process. The purchasing models to investigate are YBP/DDA; PDA via ILL; auto-ship; interlibrary loan; YBP Promptcat; rush orders; and nonrush, non-Promptcat orders.

Three library departments—acquisitions, technical services, and interlibrary loan—are involved in either the purchase process or acquiring materials.

Directions:

1. Prepare a work flow diagram for each of the processes and products, and determine who does which activity.
2. Calculate the direct cost of personnel based on their wage rates and average time for each activity they must complete.
3. Calculate employee cost (based on hourly rate and benefits), broken down to the minute to complete each activity. Formula: number of minutes per activity multiplied by per-minute staffing cost.
4. As you calculate direct cost per unit, add an institutional indirect overhead rate. You will have cost per title based on activities to acquire these materials.
5. Prepare all modes of the collection matrix, and compare them side by side, and then explain to the administration your strategy for collecting materials in the most cost-effective way possible.

Notes

1. American Academy of Art and Sciences, *Public Research Universities: Changes in State Funding* (Cambridge, MA: American Academy of Arts and Sciences, 2015), https://www.amacad.org/content/publications/publication.aspx?d=21942.
2. Joseph McKendrick, *Funding and Priorities: Academic Libraries: The Library Resource Guide Benchmarking Study on 2011 Library-Spending Plans* (Chatham, NJ: Unisphere Research, 2011), http://conan.lib.muohio.edu/ebooks/Fundingandpriorities.pdf.
3. Not-for-profits, such as colleges and universities, follow and prepare financial statements under prescribed guidelines of the Financial Accounting Standards Board (FASB). The boards for the FASB establish accounting principles for external reporting. Academic libraries also follow such principles for consolidated reporting of their central finance units. Therefore, financial accounting puts restrictions on academic libraries to provide the information to the central business office of the institution for external reporting.
4. Some small institutions use "cash basis accounting," a process of accounting whereby revenue and expense are recognized when cash is either received (revenue) or paid (expense).
5. Management accounting is the process of identification, measurement, accumulation, analysis, preparation, interpretation, and communication of financial data and advice to assist administrators in fulfilling organizational objectives.
6. See American Library Association, "Library Funding," *The State of America's Libraries*, http://www.ala.org/news/mediapresscenter/americaslibraries/libraryfunding.
7. John M. Budd, *The Changing Academic Library: Operations, Culture, Environments* (Chicago: American Library Association, 2005), 160–78.
8. American Association of Community Colleges, "Where the Revenue Comes From," *Data Points* 4, no. 7 (March 2016), http://www.aacc.nche.edu/Publications/datapoints/Documents/DP_CollegeRevenue.pdf.
9. The biggest grant-making states during the five-year period of 2003–2007 were New York and California. Grant-makers from the two states awarded 148 and 103 grants, respectively. New York and California grant-makers awarded $40 million and $37 million, respectively. California academic libraries received

the most awards, with 103 grants, for a total of $26 million received in these years. New York academic libraries came in second, with 51 awards given and a total of $10 million. However, the grant-makers from North Carolina awarded the highest number of grant dollars at $51,168,632, with most of these monies coming from the Duke Endowment Fund and targeted for Duke University. Luis J. Gonzalez, "Major Gifts Funding for Academic Libraries, 2003 to 2007," *Library Leadership and Management* 24, no. 3 (Summer 2010): 64–69, https://journals.tdl.org/llm/index.php/llm/article/download/1843/1116.

10. "Knowledge Base," *GrantSpace*, 2016, http://grantspace.org/tools/knowledge-base/Funding-Research/Statistics/Percentage-of-funded-grant-proposals.

11. National Center for Education Statistics, *Digest of Education Statistics 2003* (Washington, DC: US Department of Education, Office of Educational Research and Improvement, December 2004), http://nces.ed.gov/pubs2005/2005025.pdf.

12. Martha Kyrillidou, Gary Roebuck, and Shaneka Morris, eds., *ARL Statistics 2013–2014* (Washington, DC: Association of Research Libraries, 2015), http://publications.arl.org/ARL-Statistics-2013-2014/6.

13. Peter F. Drucker pointed out that "knowledge" would replace land, labor, capital, machines, and so on to become the chief source of production. While the business world is changing in the new knowledge economy and digital age, libraries of all types are undergoing drastic changes also. The new role of libraries in the twenty-first century needs to be as a learning and knowledge center for their users. Peter F. Drucker, *Harvard Business Review on Knowledge Management* (Boston: Harvard Business School Press, 1998).

14. Diane L. Velasquez, "Financial Management," in *Library Management 101: A Practical Guide*, edited by Diane L. Velasquez, 161–76 (Chicago: ALA Editions, 2013).

15. James A. Brimson and John Antos, *Driving Value Using Activity-Based Budgeting* (New York: John Wiley and Sons, 1998), 51–151.

16. University Libraries of the Pennsylvania State University, "Appendix 3: Summary of Survey of ARL Collection Development Officers, Examination of the University Libraries of the Pennsylvania State University (December 5, 2012)," *Report of the Collections Allocations Team* (August 1, 2013), 22–23, http://www.libraries.psu.edu/psul/groups/csag/coll_allocation.html.

17. Ibid.

18. "Expenditure Trends in ARL Libraries, 1986–2012," *ARL Statistics 2009–11* (Washington, DC: Association of Research Libraries), http://arl.nonprofitsoapbox.com/storage/documents/expenditure-trends.pdf.

19. Debbi A. Smith, "Percentage Based Allocation of an Academic Library Materials Budget," *Collection Building* 27, no. 1 (2008): 30–34, doi:http://dx.doi.org/10.1108/01604950810846224.

20. Anne Kaay and Peter Zimmerman, "The Development and Application of a Unique Percentage-Based Allocations Formula at the University of Windsor," *Library Collections, Acquisitions, and Technical Services* 32, no. 2 (2008): 92–96, doi:10.1080/14649055.2008.10766200.

21. William A. Britten, "A Use Statistic for Collection Management: The 80/20 Rule Revisited," *Library Acquisitions: Practice and Theory* 14, no. 2 (1990): 183–89.

22. WALDO is comprised of membership consortial organizations that support the procurement and administration of electronic information services for libraries.

23. OCLC's Sustainable Collection Services (SCS) supports shared-print projects through its GreenGlass application. The new GreenGlass group feature extends collection visualization and interactivity to consortial or regional collections, enabling participating libraries to better understand and manage their shared collections.

24. HathiTrust Digital Library is a digital library that has 11 million volumes, with more than 3.6 million in the public domain. Ninety-two academic and research institutions contribute material in more than 400 languages, medieval to present. *HathiTrust Digital Library*, n.d., https://www.hathitrust.org.

25. *Community College League of California*, 2014, http://www.ccleague.org/i4a/pages/index.cfm?pageid=1; *Community College Library Consortium*, 2016, http://www.cclibraries.org/index.html.

26. *Community College Libraries in North Carolina (CCLINC) Catalog*, 2016, http://www.nccommunitycolleges.edu/library-services/community-college-libraries-north-carolina-cclinc-catalog.

27. "Services for Academic and Research Libraries," *EBSCO Information Services*, n.d., http://www2.ebsco.com/en-us/Documents/prodServices/19198-academic-factsheet-web.pdf.

28. Kyrillidou, Roebuck, and Morris, *ARL Statistics*.

29. "Expenditure Trends."
30. Full-time equivalent (FTE) is a unit that indicates the workload of an employee. An FTE of 1.0 is equivalent to a full-time worker, while an FTE of 0.5 equals a half-time worker.
31. National Center for Education Statistics, *Digest of Education Statistics, 2012* (Washington. DC: US Department of Education, February 2014), https://nces.ed.gov/pubsearch/pubsinfo.asp?pubid=2014038.
32. Stanley J. Wilder, *Demographic Changes in Academic Librarianship* (Washington, DC: Association of Research Libraries, 2003).
33. Marta L. Brunner, "PhD Holders in the Academic Library: The CLIR Postdoctoral Fellowship Program," in *The Expert Library: Staffing, Sustaining and Advancing the Academic Library in the 21st Century*, edited by Scott Walter and Karen Williams, 158–88 (Chicago: Association of College and Research Libraries, 2010).
34. The Council on Library and Information Resources (CLIR) Postdoctoral Fellowship Program is systematically creating the future of librarianship by recruiting and training PhDs. The CLIR Postdoctoral Fellowship Program offers PhDs from various academic disciplines the opportunity to perform library work at a high level, such as data curation for sciences, social sciences, and medieval studies. CLIR, *CLIR Postdoctoral Fellowship Program*, http://www.clir.org/fellowships/postdoc.
35. Wilder, *Demographic Changes*, 30.
36. Ibid., 29–32.
37. McKendrick, *Funding and Priorities*. McKendrick's survey data show that budget crises are sweeping across the library world.
38. Ibid.
39. National Center for Education Statistics, *Digest of Education Statistics, 2012*.
40. A lease is a contract between the owner of an asset, called the lessor, and another party, called the lessee, who makes periodic payments to the owner for the right to use the asset. When a library buys an asset, it obtains the right to the services of that asset over the period it is owned plus the right to sell the asset at any future date. With a lease, the library acquires only the right to the asset's services for a period specified in the contract.
41. S. C. Kao, H. C. Chang, and C. H. Lin, "Decision Support for the Academic Library Acquisition Budget Allocation via Circulation Database Mining," *Information Processing and Management* 39, no. 1 (January 2003): 133–47, doi:10.1016/S0306-4573(02)00019-5.
42. Jerry J. Weygandt, Paul D. Kimmel, and Donald E. Kieso, *Managerial Accounting: Tools for Business Decision Making*, 5th ed. (Hoboken, NJ: John Wiley and Sons, 2010), 297–311, 441–49.
43. Julie Mabberley, *The Price Waterhouse Guide to Activity-Based Costing for Financial Institutions* (Chicago: Irwin Professional, 1996).
44. Paul N. Courant and Matthew "Buzzy" Nielsen, "On the Cost of Keeping a Book," in *The Idea of Order: Transforming Research Collections for 21st Century Scholarship*, CLIR publication no. 147 (Washington, DC: Council on Library and Information Resources, 2010), 96, http://www.clir.org.
45. Offsite facilities serve as storage units but are not warehouses. Some libraries call them "shelving facilities."

Bibliography

American Academy of Art and Sciences. *Public Research Universities: Changes in State Funding.* Cambridge, MA: American Academy of Arts and Sciences, 2015. https://www.amacad.org/content/publications/publication.aspx?d=21942.

American Association of Community Colleges. "Where the Revenue Comes From." *Data Points* 4, no. 7 (March 2016). http://www.aacc.nche.edu/Publications/datapoints/Documents/DP_CollegeRevenue.pdf.

American Library Association. "Library Funding." *The State of the America's Libraries.* http://www.ala.org/news/mediapresscenter/americaslibraries/libraryfunding.

Brimson, James A., and John Antos. *Driving Value Using Activity-Based Budgeting.* New York: John Wiley and Sons, 1998.

Britten, William A. "A Use Statistics for Collection Management: The 80/20 Rule Revisited." *Library Acquisitions: Practice and Theory* 14, no. 2 (1990): 183–89.

Brunner, Marta L. "PhD Holders in the Academic Library." In *The Expert Library: Staffing, Sustaining and Advancing the Academic Library in the 21st Century*, edited by Scott Walter and Karen Williams, 159–89. Chicago: Association of College and Research Libraries, 2010.

Budd, John M. *Changing Academic Library, Operations, Culture, Environments*. Chicago: American Library Association, 2005.

Community College League of California. 2014. http://www.ccleague.org/i4a/pages/index.cfm?pageid=1.

Community College Libraries in North Carolina (CCLINC) Catalog. 2016. http://www.nccommunitycol leges.edu/library-services/community-college-libraries-north-carolina-cclinc-catalog.

Community College Library Consortium. 2016. http://www.cclibraries.org/index.html.

Council on Library and Information (CLIR). *CLIR Postdoctoral Fellowship Program*. http://www.clir.org/fellowships/postdoc.

Courant, Paul, and Matthew "Buzzy" Nielsen. "On the Cost of Keeping a Book." In *The Idea of Order: Transforming Research Collections for 21st Century Scholarship*, 81–105. CLIR publication no. 147. Washington, DC: Council on Information Resources, 2010.

Drucker, Peter F. *Harvard Business Review on Knowledge Management*. Boston: Harvard Business School Press, 1998.

"Expenditure Trends in ARL Libraries, 1986–2012." *ARL Statistics 2009–11*. Washington, DC: Association of Research Libraries. http://arl.nonprofitsoapbox.com/storage/documents/expenditure-trends.pdf.

Gonzalez, Luis J. "Major Gifts Funding for Academic Libraries, 2003 to 2007." *Library Leadership and Management* 24, no. 3 (Summer 2010): 64–69. https://journals.tdl.org/llm/index.php/llm/article/download/1843/1116.

HathiTrust Digital Library. n.d. https://www.hathitrust.org.

Horngren, Charles T. *Introduction to Management Accounting*. 6th ed. Englewood Cliffs, NJ: Prentice-Hall, 1984.

Kaay, Anne, and Peter Zimmerman. "The Development and Application of a Unique Percentage-Based Allocations Formula at the University of Windsor." *Library Collections, Acquisitions, and Technical Services* 32, no. 2 (2008): 92–96. doi:10.1080/14649055.2008.10766200.

Kao, S. C., H. C. Chang, and C. H. Lin. "Decision Support for the Academic Library Acquisition Budget Allocation via Circulation Database Mining." *Information Processing and Management* 39, no. 1 (January 2003): 133–47. doi:10.1016/S0306-4573(02)00019-5.

"Knowledge Base." *GrantSpace*. 2016. http://grantspace.org/tools/knowledge-base/Funding-Research/Statistics/Percentage-of-funded-grant-proposals.

Kyrillidou, Martha, Gary Roebuck, and Shaneka Morris, eds. *ARL Statistics 2013–2014*. Washington, DC: Association of Research Libraries, 2015. http://publications.arl.org/ARL-Statistics-2013-2014/6.

Mabberley, Julie. *The Price Waterhouse Guide to Activity-Based Costing for Financial Institutions*. Chicago: Irwin Professional, 1996.

McKendrick, Joseph. *Funding and Priorities: Academic Libraries: The Library Resource Guide Benchmarking Study on 2011 Library-Spending Plans.* Chatham, NJ: Unisphere Research, 2011. http://conan.lib.mu ohio.edu/ebooks/Fundingandpriorities.pdf.

National Center for Education Statistics. *Digest of Education Statistics 2003.* Washington, DC: US Department of Education, Office of Educational Research and Improvement, December 2004. http:// nces.ed.gov/pubs2005/2005025.pdf.

———. *Digest of Education Statistics, 2012.* Washington, DC: US Department of Education, February 2014. https://nces.ed.gov/pubsearch/pubsinfo.asp?pubid=2014038.

———. *Digest of Education Statistics, 2014.* 50th ed. Washington, DC: US Department of Education, April 2016. http://nces.ed.gov/pubs2016/2016006.pdf.

"Services for Academic and Research Libraries." *EBSCO Information Services.* n.d. http://www2.ebsco .com/en-us/Documents/prodServices/19198-academic-factsheet-web.pdf.

Smith, Debbi A. "Percentage Based Allocation of an Academic Library Materials Budget." *Collection Building* 27, no. 1 (2007): 30–34.

University Libraries of the Pennsylvania State University. "Appendix 3: Summary of Survey of ARL Collection Development Officers, Examination of the University of Pennsylvania State University (December 5, 2012)." *Report of the Collections Allocations Team* (August 1, 2013), 22–23. http:// www.libraries.psu.edu/psul/groups/csag/coll_allocation.html.

Velasquez, Diane L. "Financial Management." In *Library Management 101: A Practical Guide,* edited by Diane L. Velasquez, 161–76. Chicago: ALA Editions, 2013.

Weygandt, Jerry J., Paul D. Kimmel, and Donald E. Kieso. *Managerial Accounting, Tools for Business Decision Making.* 5th ed. Hoboken, NJ: John Wiley and Sons, 2010.

Wilder, Stanley J. *Demographic Changes in Academic Librarianship.* Washington, DC: Association of Research Libraries, 2003.

5

Faculty Research and Scholarly Communication

Sarah K. Lippincott and Joan K. Lippincott

Introduction

The production and dissemination of knowledge lie at the heart of the university mission. Scholars in all disciplines conduct and communicate research in order to advance knowledge in their fields, to contribute to solving society's challenges, and to further their own intellectual curiosity and career aspirations. We commonly refer to the set of activities involved in this process of creation, evaluation, and sharing of scholarly research outputs as scholarly communication.[1] Libraries and librarians are integral to this process. They act as curators and stewards of the scholarly record, as advisors to faculty and students on the publishing process, and as advocates for systemic changes that improve access to the products of research.

As information curators and collection developers, librarians must be attuned to publishing trends as well as the research needs of the scholars at their institutions. As scholars produce and publish more and more content through informal and formal channels, librarians play an even greater role in assisting scholars with perceived information overload, helping to identify and make available relevant, high-quality content. Indeed, as the Association of College and Research Libraries (ACRL) notes, the "history of the library and the principles of librarianship is the history of the development of strategies to cope with the economics of and increasing noise in the scholarly communication system, in the interest of ensuring selectivity within, by, and for this system."[2] The economics of publishing has an equally acute influence on collection development. Escalating journal prices have far-reaching implications for libraries, many of which cannot afford to purchase or subscribe to all the content their researchers require.

While librarians' roles in scholarly communication may be most prominent in research universities, all higher education institutions have interests in the scholarly communications system. For example, the economics of that system have an impact on what types of readings may be made readily and freely available for courses. In addition, many librarians believe that an understanding of such concepts as the nature of scholarship as a conversation or the ways in which the value of information is construed from various sectors and perspectives should be part of the education of undergraduate and graduate students in all types of institutions; these precepts are reflected in the ACRL's *Framework for*

Information Literacy.[3] Faculty in some four-year institutions and community colleges may not face the same pressure to publish as those in research universities, but expectations may vary greatly among such institutions. In many of the highly selective liberal arts colleges, faculty are expected to have a publications record for tenure review and promotion.

Given the profound technological and economic changes disrupting the publishing system, librarians have become increasingly invested in transforming the scholarly communication system to better serve the needs of researchers and the academy. Librarians working in the field of scholarly communications advise faculty on authors' rights and publishing options, advocate for more open and accessible scholarship, and have even adopted the role of publisher in their own right. Librarians' roles with respect to scholarly communication are consequently manifold, "making sure [scholars] have robust online collections; creating research environments (e.g., collections and tools) that will help faculty and graduate students create the scholarship of the future; finding ways for the institution to take back more control and lower the cost of scholarship; and developing infrastructure and tools to enable multimedia."[4] In addition, many academic librarians conduct research themselves and publish in their field, whether in librarianship or in other disciplines related to their subject expertise.

This chapter explores in detail how scholarly communication shapes librarians' roles as collection developers, advisors, and advocates. Specifically, readers will learn about the relationship of scholarly communication to research expectations of faculty in university, college, and community college settings and to library collection development priorities. Readers will also be introduced to the history, purposes, and processes of scholarly publishing and its discontents, with special attention to the current debates in research evaluation, peer review, and authors' rights.

Scholarly Communication: Origins and Functions

When we talk about scholarly communication, we are fundamentally talking about scholarly *publishing*, the business of making scholarship public.[5] Scholarly publishing serves a dual function. First, it facilitates the dissemination and advancement of knowledge within a scholarly community and the broader public. Second, it serves as a way to evaluate the contributions of individual scholars to their fields.

Our modern concept of scholarly communication finds its roots in the seventeenth century, when Francis Bacon envisioned a "single [scientific] project that could be carried out only by a community of observers and experimenters who were conscious of their common goals."[6] These scientists developed a network of communication, relaying their individual findings within a network of scholars in order to advance common knowledge of scientific phenomena. Letters written between individual researchers eventually gave way to the first journals, published by early scholarly societies.[7] In the nineteenth century, the monograph emerged as a vehicle for publishing long-form scholarship. Though modern scholars benefit from a wide range of formal and informal channels for sharing their work, journals and monographs (i.e., scholarly books covering a small area of a field of learning) remain the primary modes of scholarly communication.

Indeed, while technology has transformed many aspects of modern publishing, the fundamental model of scholarly communication remains largely unchanged from its origins. The network of scholars Bacon envisioned closely resembles our modern concept of the invisible college, a "set of interacting scholars or scientists who share similar research interests concerning a subject specialty, who often produce publications relevant to this subject and who communicate both formally and informally with one another to work towards important goals in the subject, even though they may belong to geographically distant research affiliates."[8] These informal networks facilitate communication among colleagues in a discipline and contribute to the advancement of knowledge within a specific field. Meanwhile, formal publication in peer-reviewed journals (for the sciences, social sciences, and the humanities) and publication of a monograph from a highly regarded press (for the humanities and some social sciences) remain exceedingly important for advancing scholars' careers and for communicating knowledge to a broader public.

When a scholar is ready to formally share her work, she will submit a manuscript to an appropriate publisher, typically seeking out a prestigious and well-known journal or press. Publishers fall into two general categories: commercial publishers and nonprofit publishers. Large corporations dominate the scholarly publishing marketplace. Some of the most influential, such as Elsevier, Springer, Taylor and Francis, and Wiley-Blackwell, control a large and increasing share of the scholarly publishing market.[9] Nonprofit publishers, often referred to as "mission-driven" publishers, include university presses,[10] scholarly societies,[11] and libraries.[12]

Scholarly publishers carry out three primary functions: vetting, improvement, and discovery.[13] Vetting refers to the process of determining a manuscript's quality, validity, and impact. Editors serve as the first gatekeepers in this process. Authors submit manuscripts (or proposals for manuscripts) based on a publisher's prestige and expertise in the author's subject area or in response to a specific call for papers. Editors may also solicit content directly from authors on specific topics. Editors select content to publish based on its scholarly merit, its relevance to the publisher's specialization, and its potential market, among other factors. Once an editor determines that a manuscript or proposal has merit, she immediately sends it out for peer review. Peer reviewers, typically other faculty members with expertise in the discipline, ensure that the research methodologies employed are sound and assess the significance of the new research to the field. They may make specific or general recommendations to the author to improve the work. We discuss the process of peer review in more detail in the following section. After peer review, the author and editor ready the manuscript for publication. Especially in monograph publishing, editors may work with authors before and after peer review to improve structure and language. When the author and editor have finalized the manuscript, it enters the production phase, wherein it is prepared for printing or electronic publication. First, copyeditors ensure that the work contains no errors. Next, the content is typeset; that is, prepared for printing or for conversion to its final electronic format. Finally, publishers distribute and market the content, ensuring that it reaches its audience.

Formal publication remains imperative to a successful academic career in a research institution, whence the dictum "publish or perish." However, scholars also benefit from an increasingly diverse array of channels for making their work public, including blogs, social media (including general-interest microblogging services like Twitter as well as specialized social networks for academics like Academia.edu), preprint repositories, and e-mail lists and forums. In recent years, technology and the scholarly communication system have evolved to the extent that the "boundary between formal and informal communications may be blurring in some areas (for instance, un-refereed authors' original manuscripts . . . are increasingly cited in formal publications, while journal articles are becoming more informal and blog-like with the addition of reader comment)."[14] Librarians have joined faculty and others as advocates for and leaders of changes to scholarly publishing that reflect this evolution. They envision a future for scholarly publishing that effectively leverages the latest technologies, that espouses sustainable economic models, and that creates a more equitable environment for both producers and consumers of scholarship.

Peer Review

Peer review is a cornerstone of scholarly publication.[15] Through a peer review process, a journal or book editor seeks comments on a manuscript, often through a structured form that may solicit evaluations on such criteria as the quality of the literature review, the suitability of the methodology used, the quality of the writing, and the importance of the research to the field. Journal editors and monograph publishers usually maintain a list of potential reviewers who are qualified to evaluate manuscripts on specific topics. In the traditional scholarly publication review process, the author of the manuscript will receive the reviewers' comments, but the reviewers will remain anonymous to the author. In many cases, the reviewers will not know the identity of the author whose manuscript they are evaluating either; this type of double-blind peer review is intended to protect authors from preconceptions by the reviewers. However, in some fields, there are such a small number of specialists, each of whom may have a signature viewpoint, that an author may be able to guess the identity of a reviewer of her or his manuscript. In a single-blind form of peer review, the reviewers know the identity of the author whose manuscript they are reviewing, but the author will not be provided with the identities of the reviewers. At times, an author may believe that a reviewer's critique is biased and unfair, and the author will usually have an opportunity to respond to the critique, and an editor will make a final decision on acceptance of the manuscript. In the case of monographs, both the author and editor may know each other's identities. Studies have demonstrated that, when reviews are not blind and a reviewer's name is given with her or his review, it does not dilute the quality of the reviews. Some see that unblinding the review process may lead to increased accountability, fairness, and transparency.[16]

While the peer review process seeks to ensure the quality and validity of published literature in academic fields, it does not always meet the expectations of the scholarly community. In recent years, there have been a number of retractions of articles or statements in articles that have resulted from investigations into scientific fraud; in these cases, the deception was not caught through the initial peer review process prior to the publication of the articles.[17]

Another concern with the traditional peer review process is that it can significantly delay the publication of articles and books. Writing reviews can be a time-consuming process, involving reading the manuscript, possibly checking related work, reviewing methodologies and conclusions, and then writing a clear critique. The system relies on researcher volunteers for the reviews (usually multiple reviews for each article or monograph), and it can be difficult to enforce deadlines for submission of reviews. Some researchers, such as Paul Ginsparg, a faculty member at Cornell University and a founder of the arXiv preprint repository, a highly regarded site where scientists post papers for comment by their peers prior to submitting them to a journal for formal peer review, suggest that a two-tier peer review model, in which the initial stage would quickly weed out low-quality papers, leaving a smaller number for full peer review, would make the process more efficient.[18]

In today's digital environment, a number of scholars and scholarly societies have called for rethinking the nature and the role of peer review. One proposed innovation is crowdsourced peer review, by which authors would post papers for anyone to comment on, and some indication of quality would then be available to readers prior to a full peer review process. Stevan Harnad, a well-known writer on digital publishing, notes that, for the premise of crowdsourced peer review to work, authors would have to be willing to post their articles openly, there would need to be sufficient response from knowledgeable reviewers, and the resulting efforts would need to be sustainable and navigable to be of use to the community of scholars. In his view, "crowdsourcing will provide an excellent supplement to classical peer review but not a substitute for it."[19]

Expectations of Research

In research universities, selective liberal arts colleges, and medium-sized universities aspiring to higher ratings in various ranking systems, the output of faculty research, specifically in peer-reviewed publications, is the coin of the realm, particularly when it comes to promotion and tenure. However, specific research and publication needs and practices vary significantly across disciplines.[20]

Faculty, especially those in the sciences, are expected to both bring in grant funds and publish, ideally in prestigious journals. Humanities faculty rely on a small number of public agencies, such as the National Endowment for the Humanities (NEH), the National Historical Publications and Records Commission (NHPRC), and the Institute for Museum and Library Services (IMLS), and such private funders as the Andrew W. Mellon Foundation to assist with their research costs, such as trips abroad to consult primary sources, interview individuals, or visit historic sites. While research and development expenditures on academic humanities research increased a remarkable 75 percent between

2005 and 2014, the total amount spent was only a paltry .06 percent of the research and development expenditures for the sciences.[21] While humanities faculty may publish in journals, many of their disciplines still view monograph publication as the desirable goal for faculty. In the social sciences, both article and monograph publication are standard. Social scientists utilize a variety of funding sources, from local government to private agencies to international organizations. However, US federal funding has not been centralized in a small number of agencies as it has been for the sciences and humanities. Libraries often offer workshops or personalized consultations to assist faculty in identifying sources of funding in their disciplines.

In community college settings, publishing is typically not as important for faculty to achieve promotion and tenure. The rationale generally seems to be that these faculty specialize in teaching and have higher teaching loads than their four-year college and university counterparts. However, many faculty may be conducting applied research in their fields and some may perform research based on interest rather than requirement. An example of applied research could be an English faculty member who studies various pedagogical methods for enhancing student achievement in a composition course, as compared to an English faculty member in a research university who would typically conduct highly specialized studies in literary history, literary theory, or a particular era (e.g., the Renaissance or Victorian) or genre of literature (e.g., poetry, drama, or fiction).

Expectations for publishing vary among small and liberal arts colleges. Some of the highly selective liberal arts colleges have similar publication expectations of their faculty as research universities. Others may be more similar to community colleges in their emphasis on demonstrated effectiveness in teaching as carrying more weight in promotion and tenure decisions than publication records.

The expectations of how much to publish and in what types of publications are set by both the institution with which the faculty member is affiliated and the norms of the academic discipline. Many scientific and social science fields require their scholars to publish a number of journal articles in the years prior to tenure review. In the humanities, it is widely perceived that a junior faculty member on the tenure track must publish a monograph by a reputable press in order to achieve tenure, and this is also the case in some social science fields.

In addition to the number of publications by an author, many promotion and tenure committees, particularly in the sciences, use other metrics to evaluate the significance of the contribution of authors to the literature. For example, the number of times an article has been cited by others can serve as a measure of the article's influence in the discipline, and a journal whose articles are cited more than others can be viewed as having more influence or prestige than others in the field. The journal impact factor, developed by the Institute for Scientific Information (ISI), now Thomson Reuters, constitutes a "measure of the frequency with which the 'average' article of a journal has been cited in a particular year or period."[22] When faculty members submit a portfolio of information for tenure or promotion review, they will often cite the journal impact factor of the journals in which they have published to demonstrate the importance of their contributions.

At least two other systems of measuring impact have gained traction in the scholarly community. One is the h-index, developed by J. E. Hirsch, which provides a formula for calculating citations of articles by an author over time, yielding an index number.[23] The Eigenfactor constitutes another measure, using an algorithm to rank journals within an academic network of citations.[24]

The emerging field of altmetrics has also garnered attention among librarians and researchers. Proponents of altmetrics—new forms of measuring the impact of scholarly output—contend that these measures allow one to gauge more quickly the influence of a publication, take into account citation of publications in a wide variety of digital contexts, legitimize all types of scholarly output, and encourage a focus on public engagement.[25]

As librarians encourage faculty to publish their articles under the open access model, they may wish to guide faculty on that path by pointing to such studies as one demonstrating that open access articles have higher citation numbers than non–open access articles published in the same journal.[26] However, a subset of open access journals do not have much stature in their fields,[27] and librarians can advise junior faculty on legitimate places to publish their work.

Coauthorship can also affect how review committees evaluate a publication. When we look at issues related to coauthorship, we see striking disciplinary differences. Much of the scientific journal literature is coauthored. In some fields, this has gone to an extreme: The 2016 article announcing confirmation of a prediction regarding gravitational waves in Einstein's theory of relativity listed more than one thousand coauthors.[28] Individuals in the library and publishing fields are working on a taxonomy for identifying the specific role an author played in such a massively multiauthored article.[29] In the social sciences, coauthorship on a much smaller scale is common; however, a recent study by a Harvard graduate student found that, when a woman coauthors an article in economics, the benefit to her career prospects will be less than half that accorded to men.[30] Single authorship is still considered standard in the humanities and may be one of the problems in the acceptance of new forms of digital scholarship in those fields. Because teams develop almost all digital projects, works produced in digital humanities generally have multiple authors.

A variety of new forms of scholarly output take advantage of the affordances of new technologies. For example, researchers in the fields of art history, history, and archaeology now create digital representations of a variety of buildings and excavation sites, sometimes in 3-D.[31] In the sciences, the human genome project[32] and the Sloan Sky Survey,[33] whose underlying data can be used to create 3-D maps of the universe, exemplify large data collections to which many scientists have contributed. Researchers who develop these data representations as well as others can employ the data to examine new sorts of research questions. Faculty working on digital projects have expressed concern that promotion and tenure committees will not give their outputs due consideration compared to outputs in traditional forms. Some scholarly societies have taken up this issue, and the Modern Language Association (MLA), the highly regarded membership society for scholars in language and literature disciplines, has published guidelines for the evaluation of digital projects.[34] The question of earning credit for new forms of scholarship manifests itself in the sciences in relationship to such products as data sets, tools, or software, which may not be given the same weight as journal articles.

Implications for Libraries

In connection with their research, faculty may have contact with academic librarians with a variety of specialties, including subject liaisons, special collections, data and GIS services, reference, and access services. Many academic research libraries and those in highly selective liberal arts colleges now employ one or more scholarly communications librarians who offer consultations on intellectual property, repositories, and a variety of issues related to publication in the print and digital environments.[35]

Use of publications owned and licensed by the library continues to be a central concern of libraries in support of the research activities of faculty. The nature of publications most used in different disciplines impacts the types and quantity of purchases of and licenses for materials. Most academic research libraries spend the majority of their acquisitions budget on licenses for or subscriptions to journals, primarily e-journals. As journal prices rise and acquisitions budgets remain relatively flat, the proportion of the budget spent on monographs, particularly in the humanities, diminishes. The Association of Research Libraries (ARL) reported that, for its members, while monograph expenditures increased 71 percent during the period 1986–2011, serials expenditures increased 402 percent.[36]At this point, there seems to be general acceptance of digital versions of materials for journal content; faculty in the sciences, who rely most heavily on the journal literature, often access this content remotely and seldom enter the physical facility of the library. Many research universities have closed their branch science libraries in response, integrating collections into the main library. Faculty in the sciences also rate preprint versions of articles that will appear in peer-reviewed journals to be crucial to their research; preprints allow them early access to the latest findings.[37] In the humanities, faculty may express a strong preference for print monographs over e-book versions of the same titles but not necessarily, as demonstrated in a study at Florida State University: When asked their preference, many replied, "it depends."[38] A recent Ithaka S+R faculty survey also demonstrated that 70 percent of faculty consult e-books often or occasionally and believe that e-books play an important role in their research and teaching.[39] Also, in the same study, many faculty noted their heavy use of images, audiovisual materials, and artifacts. In the social sciences, in addition to books and journals, many faculty need access to standard data sets, such as those supplied through the US government or institutions like the Inter-university Consortium for Political and Social Research (ICPSR). Professional programs like business and engineering may require specialized databases; for example, for industry trends or patents.

Interlibrary loan and consortial access to materials not owned by the institution's library remain key services for faculty: 80 percent of respondents in the Ithaka faculty survey noted that they had used interlibrary loan or document delivery services often or occasionally.[40]

The increasing variety of formats of the output of scholarship has been the focus of a team of OCLC researchers. They suggest that we should understand the impact of the digital environment on the "evolving scholarly record." They state that "while in the past we might have thought of the scholarly record as consisting primarily of text-based materials like journals and monographs, today the cohort of materials over which the scholarly record can potentially extend has expanded dramatically, to include research data sets, computer models, interactive programs, complex visualizations, lab notebooks, and a host of other materials."[41] Also, these records of research then can become the data for future research by the authors or by other scholars. The research library community now grapples with its perceived responsibility to collect and curate this record, but clear processes and norms continue to develop. In addition, the costs of collection and curation of a broad array of complex digital content remain unknown.

The research interests of faculty can also lead to the development of various types of library services targeted to faculty. Librarians show increasing interest in partnering with faculty on new types of digital scholarship that will result in new forms of scholarly communication. While much of this activity has focused on the digital humanities (DH), a number of libraries have mounted efforts, often described through services offered by means of a digital scholarship center, that also encompass the social sciences and sciences.[42] Librarians may advise researchers on how to access existing large data sets, work with them to use tools to analyze data, and assist them with developing graphic representations of their data (data visualizations), which can often assist audiences in understanding findings in a deeper way than is possible using only text. Data visualization representations may assist in understanding cancer trends, analyzing growth patterns in a city, or exploring biodiversity in a region, for example. Librarians may also work with researchers creating data sets as products of their research, advising them on metadata issues (defining fields for tagging records) and development of data plans to address future access and preservation needs. Equally important, they may play a key role in working with faculty to ensure compliance with federal agency guidelines for openness of both publications and data, if federal funding has supported the research.[43] We should note that a minority of faculty in all disciplines currently find it crucial to participate in activities associated with digital scholarship, such as using models, simulations, or GIS tools; developing software; or engaging in text mining.[44] However, it seems likely that the number of researchers using new methodologies and tools will increase in coming years. In fact, many researchers indicated that they would be interested in learning more about digital research activities and methodologies if they had more technical support, time to learn about new methodologies, and assistance in understanding how to integrate those methodologies into their research.[45] Libraries now train existing staff to be able to provide this type of support to faculty and hire individuals with strong digital research skills to develop programs that allow libraries to both partner with and support new types of faculty research interests. Using these new tools for research enables researchers to ask new kinds of questions that were not possible in earlier eras, often because techniques were not available to analyze the vast amounts of data that are available in some fields, such as astronomy, and also provides opportunities to combine disparate sets of data in new ways to find new patterns, such as combining health data with environmental data.

Finally, many libraries offer services that advise their faculty about publication and intellectual property issues. They may offer workshops to junior scholars and graduate students that walk them through the publishing process. They may also advise faculty about their rights as authors. When a work is accepted for publication, the publisher typically requires the author to sign a publication agreement that transfers some or all of the copyright to the publisher. This transfer of rights has many implications for scholars. They may be prohibited from including the work in course packs, posting it to their personal websites, or depositing it in their institutional repositories. Scholarly communications librarians help scholars to negotiate the retention of some of their rights and also advocate on a national scale for less restrictive publishing contracts.

Scholarly Publishing and Its Discontents: Crises and Responses

The scholarly publishing system faces major disruptions due to changing economic realities and the increasing move to digital publication. These changes have implications for libraries, continuously tasked with maintaining robust collections in the face of shrinking budgets and rising costs. These changes also affect publishers, especially university presses, who must endeavor to survive and flourish in a new economic and technological environment. The gravity of these disruptions has led to a discourse of so-called crisis in the scholarly publishing world. This section provides an overview of the scholarly publishing crises, as well as contemporary debates that preoccupy scholars, publishers, and librarians.

The serials crisis, a term that refers to the skyrocketing cost of many commercially published academic journals, particularly in the sciences, over the last several decades, has caused many libraries to cut journal subscriptions and even call for boycotts of publishers of the most expensive journals.[46] Consolidation within the publishing sector has compounded the problem, resulting in decreasing diversity and competition among large commercial publishers.

Meanwhile, library budgets have not kept pace with rapidly rising prices. Libraries at institutions of all sizes have faced flat or falling collections budgets over the last decade due to a variety of factors, including the global financial crisis. Libraries, therefore, spend more than ever to acquire less content. Despite having larger overall budgets, research-intensive universities, especially those that focus on science, technology, engineering, and mathematics (the so-called STEM fields) are often hard-hit by this crisis because their faculty require subscriptions to many of the costliest journals. Libraries must often make difficult compromises, such as cutting important journals they can no longer afford and diverting money from their monograph collections budget to journal subscriptions.[47]

This state of affairs has generated no small amount of consternation and protest from librarians. Along with scholars, librarians have questioned not only the high prices of journals but also the premise of a scholarly publishing system in which the "faculty gives its research to the publishers for free; [and] the publishers sell it back to the university library at high prices."[48] The extent to which commercial publishers have driven up the cost of their products has even led some to suggest that the academy "reclaim" the scholarly publishing system from profit-driven commercial publishers.[49] The monograph publishing system, especially for the humanities, can also be said to be in a state of crisis, given the financial and existential pressures on university presses.[50] University presses, which have historically operated with subsidies, face decreasing investment from their parent institutions.[51] These presses thus find themselves caught between a mandate to publish niche scholarship with little market potential while producing enough revenue to remain financially viable.[52] Many have noted the urgency of sustaining humanities monograph publishing given the centrality of these publications to the careers of junior scholars.[53]

New economic models, facilitated by new technologies and new types of content, now challenge conventional assumptions about publishing and address concerns about sustainability and fairness in pricing.[54] Open access, so-called freemium models, and other alternative approaches to funding will make more sense than subscription-based models for some types of publications. New projects like Knowledge Unlatched[55] and the Open Library of Humanities,[56] for example, are flipping the payment system. They coordinate libraries and other funders to invest in the publication of books and journals up front (before publication) rather than through purchasing them. Upon publication, these works become open access.

Libraries and university presses are also heeding the call to create a more equitable and effective publishing system by actively experimenting with new publishing models. Collaboration between libraries and university presses has become increasingly common,[57] especially as university administrative structures change. As of 2013, twenty members of the Association of American University Presses (AAUP) had an administrative relationship with their university library.[58] Collaborations often leverage the prestige, disciplinary expertise, and editorial acumen of the press and the libraries' strengths in digital technologies, metadata, and organization of information to create innovative, technology-enhanced publications. Libraries are also independently taking on the role of publisher, primarily publishing open access journals.[59] Some university presses are part of the library system.

Conclusion

For almost all sectors of higher education (with the possible exception of community and some small colleges), faculty continue to be judged on their publication records during promotion and tenure reviews. Librarians should not underestimate the centrality of a faculty member's research to her or his career. Librarians who demonstrate knowledge of the scholarly communications environment of the disciplines of faculty with whom they work will have more credibility with those faculty. Being able to advise junior faculty on such issues as selection of publications to which to submit manuscripts, journal impact factors, intellectual property issues, and data curation requirements related to federal or other grants can lead to relationships in which faculty begin to understand the depth of librarians' knowledge and skill set. The traditions of scholarly communication are inherent to the culture of each discipline and to higher education as a whole. Changing those traditions and the perspectives faculty bring to them, as a result of the opportunities and challenges of the digital environment, continues and will take place at a different pace for each discipline.

Academic libraries of all types face the challenge of meeting faculty expectations, which often prioritize maintaining traditional collections and services, while simultaneously developing new infrastructure and support services for digital scholarship. Few academic libraries have the financial resources to expand their staff, which means examining priorities for the work of librarians, participating in training for new skills, and reconfiguring positions for new types of responsibilities when filling vacancies. Librarians may find that, contrary to expectations, senior faculty are most likely to create new forms of digital scholarship because junior faculty tend to create traditional works and publish in standard venues as a result of promotion and tenure pressures.[60] The new role of librarians includes librarians as publishers, working with faculty to address the need to provide both more affordable and accessible venues for publishing and an infrastructure for the publication of new forms of scholarship.

Discussion Questions

1. Are the current methods of evaluating faculty research output fair? What are the promises (and potential pitfalls) of alternatives, such as altmetrics?
2. Should data sets, digital humanities projects, and other new forms of scholarship count in faculty tenure and promotion decisions? Why or why not?
3. Many have questioned the efficacy and value of current methods of peer review. What do you see as the strengths and weaknesses of blind peer review? What about open or so-called crowd-sourced peer review?

4. Libraries are increasingly adopting the role of publisher. Why do libraries choose this role? What skills might librarians bring to publishing, and what skills might they lack?

Assignment

You are a librarian at a large research institution, and a junior faculty member approaches you for advice on where to publish an article. What factors do you suggest to him to examine in the selection of a target journal? Identify and expand on at least three factors he should consider.

Further Reading

Journals

Journal of Electronic Publishing, http://www.journalofelectronicpublishing.org.

Journal of Librarianship and Scholarly Communication, http://jlsc-pub.org.

Learned Publishing, http://www.alpsp.org/Learned-Publishing.

Monographs and Reports

Bonn, Maria, and Mike Furlough, eds. *Getting the Word Out: Academic Libraries as Scholarly Publishers*.

Davis-Kahl, Stephanie, and Merinda Kaye Hensley. *Common Ground at the Nexus of Information Literacy and Scholarly Communication*.

Fitzpatrick, Kathleen. *Planned Obsolescence*.

Gilman, Isaac. *Library Scholarly Communication Programs: Legal and Ethical Considerations*.

Ithaka S+R. *US Faculty Survey 2012*.

Morrison, Heather. *Scholarly Communication for Librarians*.

Regazzi, John J. *Scholarly Communications*: *A History from Content as King to Content as Kingmaker*.

Blogs and Websites

ACRL Scholarly Communication Toolkit. http://acrl.ala.org/scholcomm.

Digital Scholarship. http://www.digital-scholarship.org.

Scholarly Communication Lab at Dartmouth. http://sites.dartmouth.edu/scholarly-communication-lab.

Scholarly Communications @ Duke. http://blogs.library.duke.edu/scholcomm.

The Scholarly Kitchen. http://scholarlykitchen.sspnet.org.

SPARC. http://sparcopen.org.

Notes

1. "Principles and Strategies for the Reform of Scholarly Communication 1," *Association of College and Research Libraries*, 2016, http://www.ala.org/acrl/publications/whitepapers/principlesstrategies.
2. Charles B. Osburn, "The Structuring of the Scholarly Communication System," *College and Research Libraries* 50, no. 3 (May 1989): 286, http://crl.acrl.org/content/50/3/277.full.pdf.
3. "Framework for Information Literacy for Higher Education," *Association of College and Research Libraries*, January 11, 2016, http://www.ala.org/acrl/standards/ilframework.
4. Laura Brown, Rebecca Griffiths, and Matthew Rascoff, "University Publishing in a Digital Age," *Ithaka Report*, July 26, 2007, 15, http://www.sr.ithaka.org/wp-content/uploads/2015/08/4.13.1.pdf.

5. Paul Courant, "Why I Hate the Phrase 'Scholarly Communication,'" *Au Courant*, November 23, 2007, http://paulcourant.net/2007/11/23/why-i-hate-the-phrase-scholarly-communication/.

6. Stanley Chodorow, "Scholarship and Scholarly Communication in the Electronic Age," *EduCause Review* (January/February 2000): 86–92, https://net.educause.edu/ir/library/pdf/ERM001B.pdf.

7. Osburn, "Structuring," 277–86.

8. A. Zuccala, "Modeling the Invisible College," *Journal of the American Society for Information Science and Technology* 57, no. 2 (2006): 152–68, doi:10.1002/asi.20256.

9. Vincent Larivière, Stefanie Haustein, and Philippe Mongeon, "The Oligopoly of Academic Publishers in the Digital Era," *PLOS One*, June 10, 2015, http://journals.plos.org/plosone/article?id=10.1371/journal.pone.0127502#pone-0127502-g001.

10. "About University Presses," *Association of American University Presses*, 2016, http://www.aaupnet.org/about-aaup/about-university-presses.

11. Robert Harington, "The Role of Scholarly Societies," *Scholarly Kitchen* (blog), September 24, 2014, http://scholarlykitchen.sspnet.org/2014/09/24/the-role-of-scholarly-societies.

12. "Library Publishing Directory 2016," *Library Publishing Coalition*, 2016, http://www.librarypublishing.org/resources/directory/lpd2016.

13. Kent Anderson describes nearly one hundred specific activities that publishers undertake in "96 Things Publishers Do," *Scholarly Kitchen* (blog), February 1, 2016, http://scholarlykitchen.sspnet.org/2016/02/01/guest-post-kent-anderson-updated-96-things-publishers-do-2016-edition.

14. Mark Ware and Michael Mabe, *The STM Report: An Overview of Scientific and Scholarly Journal Publishing*, 4th ed. (The Hague: International Association of Scientific, Technical, and Medical Publishers, 2015), http://www.stm-assoc.org/2015_02_20_STM_Report_2015.pdf.

15. A useful overview of the history of peer review can be found in Ann C. Weller, *Editorial Peer Review: Its Strengths and Weaknesses*, ASIST Monograph Series (Medford, NJ: Information Today, 2001).

16. Susan van Rooyen, Fiona Godlee, Stephen Evans, Nick Black, and Richard Smith, "Effect of Open Peer Review on Quality of Reviews and on Reviewers' Recommendations: A Randomised Trial," *BMJ* 318 (January 2, 1999): 26, doi:http://dx.doi.org/10.1136/bmj.318.7175.23.

17. Retraction Watch, "The Top Ten Retractions of 2015," *Scientist*, December 23, 2015, http://www.the-scientist.com/?articles.view/articleNo/44895/title/The-Top-10-Retractions-of-2015.

18. Paul Ginsparg, "Can Peer Review Be Better Focused?" *Cornell University Department of Computer Science*, March 13, 2003, http://www.cs.cornell.edu/~ginsparg/physics/blurb/pg02pr.html.

19. S. Harnad, "Crowd-Sourced Peer Review: Substitute or Supplement for the Current Outdated System?" *LSE Impact Blog* (blog), August 21, 2014, http://openaccess.eprints.org/index.php?/archives/1121-Crowd-Sourced-Peer-Review-Substitute-or-Supplement.html.

20. For an in-depth examination of differences and commonalities of research across disciplines, see Diane Harley et al., *Assessing the Future Landscape of Scholarly Communication: An Exploration of Faculty Values and Needs in Seven Disciplines—Executive Summary* (Berkeley: University of California, Berkeley, Center for Studies in Higher Education, 2010), http://escholarship.org/uc/item/0kr8s78v.

21. "Research and Development Expenditures at Colleges and Universities," *Humanities Indicators*, last updated January, 2016, http://humanitiesindicators.org/content/indicatordoc.aspx?i=86.

22. "The Thomson Reuters Impact Factor," *Current Contents* (June 20, 1994), http://wokinfo.com/essays/impact-factor.

23. J. E. Hirsch, "An Index to Quantify an Individual's Scientific Research Output," *Proceedings of the National Academy of Science USA* 102, no. 46 (November 15, 2005): 16569–72, http://www.ncbi.nlm.nih.gov/pmc/articles/PMC1283832.

24. Carl T. Bergstrom, Jevin D. West, and Marc A. Wiseman, "The Eigenfactor™ Metrics," *Journal of Neuroscience* 28, no. 45 (November 5, 2008):11433–34, http://www.jneurosci.org/content/28/45/11433.short.

25. Heather Piwowar and Jason Priem, "Altmetrics: What, Why, and Where?" *Bulletin of the Association for Information Science and Technology*, Special Section 39, no. 4 (April/May 2013): 8–9, http://www.arl.org/focus-areas/scholarly-communication/scholarly-impact#.VsyvLykZ1w4. Note: This special section contains a number of useful articles on the topic of altmetrics.

26. Gunther Eysenbach, "Citation Advantage of Open Access Articles," *PLOS Biology* 4, no. 5 (2006): e157, doi:10.1371/journal.pbio.0040157.

27. Jeffrey Beall publishes a list of "potential, possible, or probable scholarly open-access publishers" on his website *Scholarly Open Access*, last updated April 16, 2016, https://scholarlyoa.com/publishers; his list has sparked some controversy but raises legitimate issues about predatory publishers.

28. B. P. Abbott et al., "Observation of Gravitational Waves from a Binary Black Hole Merger," *Physical Review Letters* 116, no. 061102 (February 12, 2016), doi:10.1103/PhysRevLett.116.061102.

29. Amy Brand, Liz Allen, Micah Altman, Marjorie Hlava, and Jo Scott, "Beyond Authorship: Attribution, Contribution, Collaboration, and Credit," *Learned Publishing* 28 (April 2015): 151–55, doi:10.1087/20150211.

30. Heather Sarsons, "Gender Differences in Recognition for Group Work" (working paper, Harvard University, Cambridge, December 3, 2015), http://scholar.harvard.edu/sarsons/publications.

31. For example, see Columbia University, *Real? Virtual: Representing Architectural Time and Space*, n.d., http://www.learn.columbia.edu/ha/html/medieval.html.

32. US National Institutes of Health, "All about the Human Genome Project (HGP)," *National Human Genome Research Institute*, last updated October 1, 2015, https://www.genome.gov/10001772.

33. *The Sloan Digital Sky Survey: Mapping the Universe*, accessed February 23, 2016, http://www.sdss.org/.

34. Committee on Information Technology, "Guidelines for Evaluating Work in Digital Humanities and Digital Media," *Modern Language Association*, revised January 2012, https://www.mla.org/About-Us/Governance/Committees/Committee-Listings/Professional-Issues/Committee-on-Information-Technology/Guidelines-for-Evaluating-Work-in-Digital-Humanities-and-Digital-Media.

35. Scholarly communications librarians typically have an MLIS with coursework and field experience that focuses on copyright, intellectual property, institutional repositories, and open access, among other areas. Some scholarly communications librarians have a JD instead of or in addition to their MLIS, reflecting deeper expertise in copyright and intellectual property.

36. Martha Kyrillidou et al., "Monograph and Serial Costs in ARL Libraries, 1986–2011," *ARL Statistics 2010–11* (Washington, DC: Association of Research Libraries, 2012), http://www.arl.org/focus-areas/statistics-assessment/statistical-trends#.Vt2bfykZ1w4.

37. Ross Housewright, Roger C. Schonfeld, and Kate Wulfson, *Ithaka S+R US Faculty Survey 2012*, April 2013, http://www.sr.ithaka.org/publications/us-faculty-survey-2012/.

38. Sarah Buck Kachaluba, Jessica Evans Brady, and Jessica Critten, "Developing Humanities Collections in the Digital Age: Exploring Humanities Faculty Engagement with Electronic and Print Resources," *College and Research Libraries* 75, no. 1 (January 2014): 91–108.

39. Housewright, Schonfeld, and Wulfson, *Faculty Survey 2012*, 31. The survey also provides insight into the particular ways that faculty use e-books and their preferences for one format over another based on the intended use.

40. Ibid., 36.

41. Brian Lavoie, Eric Childress, Ricky Erway, Ixchel Faniel, Constance Malpas, Jennifer Schaffner, and Titia van der Werf, *The Evolving Scholarly Record* (Dublin, OH: OCLC Research, 2014), http://www.oclc.org/content/dam/research/publications/library/2014/oclcresearch-evolving-scholarly-record-2014.pdf. An earlier work focusing on the sciences also discussed some of these issues, including the notion that the scholarly record itself could become a source of computation; see Clifford A. Lynch, "Jim Gray's Fourth Paradigm and the Construction of the Scientific Record," in *The Fourth Paradigm: Data-Intensive Scientific Discovery*, edited by Tony Hey, Stewart Tansley, and Kristin Tolle, 177–83 (Redmond, WA: Microsoft Research, 2009), http://research.microsoft.com/en-us/collaboration/fourthparadigm.

42. Joan K. Lippincott and Diane Goldenberg-Hart, *Digital Scholarship Centers: Trends and Good Practice*, December 2014, https://www.cni.org/events/cni-workshops/digital-scholarship-centers-cni-workshop.

43. In the memorandum "Expanding Public Access to the Results of Federally Funded Research," issued on February 22, 2013, the White House mandated that publications and data that are the results of federally funded research needed to be available to the public, generally within one year of publication. A helpful overview can be found on the SPARC website, http://sparcopen.org/our-work/2013-executive-directive.

44. Housewright, Schonfeld, and Wulfson, *Faculty Survey 2012*, 42.

45. Ibid., 44.

46. Ian Sample, "Harvard University Says It Can't Afford Journal Publishers' Prices," *Guardian*, April 24, 2012, https://www.theguardian.com/science/2012/apr/24/harvard-university-journal-publishers-prices.

47. MLA Ad Hoc Committee on the Future of Scholarly Publishing, "The Future of Scholarly Publishing," *Profession* (2002): 172–86, https://apps.mla.org/pdf/schlrlypblshng.pdf; Judith M. Panitch and Sarah Michalak, "The Serials Crisis: A White Paper for the UNC–Chapel Hill Scholarly Communications Convocation," January 2005, http://www.unc.edu/scholcomdig/whitepapers/panitch-michalak.html.

48. Chodorow, "Scholarship and Scholarly Communication," 89.

49. Kathleen Fitzpatrick, "Profit, Publishing, and the University Mission," in *Planned Obsolescence: Publishing, Technology, and the Future of the Academy*, 44 (New York: New York University Press, 2011), http://mcpress.media-commons.org/plannedobsolescence/five-the-university/profit-publishing-and-the-university-mission.

50. Colin Steele, "Scholarly Monograph Publishing in the 21st Century: The Future More than Ever Should Be an Open Book," *Journal of Electronic Publishing* 11, no. 2 (2008): 1–14, doi:10.3998/3336451.0011.201.

51. Paul Courant identifies the tension between universities' interest in the public good and in advancing scholarship generally and their local financial interests. Most university presses expressly avoid publishing scholarship authored by faculty on their campuses. University presses may therefore have difficulty convincing campus administrators of the press's value to the campus mission. Furthermore, given that most universities do not operate presses, those that do may feel they contribute disproportionately to supporting scholarly communications. University presses frequently refer to this as the free-rider problem. For more, see Paul Courant, "What Might Be in Store for Universities' Presses," *Journal of Electronic Publishing* 13, no. 2 (2010), doi:http://dx.doi.org/10.3998/3336451.0013.206.

52. Steele, "Scholarly Monograph Publishing."

53. For a thorough analysis of the state of affairs in humanities publishing, see Fitzpatrick, "Undead," in *Planned Obsolescence*, 7, http://mcpress.media-commons.org/plannedobsolescence/introduction/undead.

54. Brown, Griffiths, and Rascoff, "University Publishing in a Digital Age," 14.

55. *Knowledge Unlatched*, n.d., http://www.knowledgeunlatched.org.

56. *Open Library of Humanities*, 2016, https://www.openlibhums.org.

57. The Association of American University Presses, "Press and Library Collaboration Survey," 2013, http://www.aaupnet.org/images/stories/data/librarypresscollaboration_report_corrected.pdf.

58. Charlotte Roh, "Library–Press Collaborations: A Study Taken on Behalf of the University of Arizona," *Journal of Librarianship and Scholarly Communication* 2, no. 4 (2014): eP1102, http://dx.doi.org/10.7710/2162-3309.1102.

59. See, for example, the 115 libraries listed in "Library Publishing Directory 2016."

60. Diane Harley, Sophia Krzys Acord, Sarah Earl-Novell, Shannon Lawrence, and C. Judson King, *Assessing the Future Landscape of Scholarly Communication: An Exploration of Faculty Values and Needs in Seven Disciplines* (Berkeley: University of California, Berkeley, Center for Studies in Higher Education, January 2010), http://escholarship.org/uc/cshe_fsc.

Part II

Academic Librarians and Services Today

This section begins with the topic of public services, which spans two chapters: one devoted to reference, instruction, outreach to faculty and students, and faculty–librarian collaboration; the other, to collection development, circulation, and resource sharing. The former, by Carrie Forbes and Peggy Keeran, engages with recent library science literature to detail current thinking on best practices, including service models, such as traditional versus newer ways of providing general reference assistance, library liaisons to academic departments, embedded librarianship, ACRL's Information Literacy Competency Standards versus the newer Framework for Information Literacy for Higher Education, and so-called critical information literacy. These authors also introduce pedagogic methods and instructional technology designed both to improve students' information literacy by emphasizing critical thinking and active learning and to accommodate different learning styles. Finally, they consider the importance of assessment as a means of continuously monitoring and improving all these services.

The latter chapter, by Lidia Uziel, concerns collection development for general collections as well as special collections and archives and both print and electronic formats. Uziel lays out how collection development is currently accomplished in various sizes of North American academic libraries as well as how collecting priorities differ depending on the size of the parent institution and its library and on the students and faculty served. She also addresses recent and future consortial lending partnerships among the largest libraries, how these libraries must now emphasize access over ownership of library materials, and how they need to find ways to share new and emergent types and formats of scholarly resources as the production and consumption of scholarship continuously proliferate and change.

Uziel's chapter leads naturally to Autumn Faulkner's chapter on technical services, which examines current challenges facing cataloging, metadata, systems, electronic resource management, resource discoverability, and the changing roles of professionals. Faulkner emphasizes technical services for general collections but also touches on issues unique to rare book and manuscripts specialists and archivists. She notes that all technical service tasks will soon undergo a sea change because catalog records in MARC (MAchine Readable Cataloging) format no longer meet the needs of many library users, especially those accustomed to surfing the web to satisfy all their information needs. With the advent of the semantic web—as the Internet slowly evolves from a web of documents into a web of links (or linked data)—library materials will become discoverable in ways never possible before. A likely successor to MARC is Bibliographic Framework (BIBFRAME), a structured vocabulary initiated by the Library of Congress. If BIBFRAME were to be widely adopted, then the focus of cataloging would shift from describing one resource at a time—as we currently do—to creating unique identifiers for entities, such as works and their creators, and tracing the relationships between them in a structured way. As Faulkner puts it, "[c]atalogers will establish many nodes of data and build a network of connections between them, rather than create individual records comprising mostly text strings." We hope eventually to be able to offer our readers one single point of access for all library materials and provide them far more sophisticated tools than we now have to isolate specific resources they seek.

So as not to overemphasize large university libraries, Zoe Fisher and Kim Read devote a whole chapter to librarians, programs, and services in four-year college and community college libraries. Fisher and Read describe how they seek to meet the needs of many different types of students—all of them undergraduates—as well as other readers who may be unaffiliated with the college, and face other unique professional challenges as well as enjoy unique opportunities. As the authors observe, "in contrast to university librarians, college and community college librarians are committed to a broader array of tasks and a wider scope of focus in their work." Much smaller than major research university libraries, college and community college libraries also have different organizational models (fewer departments) and governance structures. They may also have fewer financial resources than their research library counterparts, which means that employees might serve in multiple and quite disparate roles, such as reference and instruction librarian, collection development librarian, and library director all rolled into one. At community colleges in particular, which many students choose for their affordability, librarians are constantly seeking ways of saving students money; thus, they have become staunch advocates of providing access to open educational resources as a replacement for costly textbooks and strive to maintain current and diverse book and journal collections along with essential library databases.

6

Reference, Instruction, and Outreach
CURRENT METHODS AND MODELS

Carrie Forbes and Peggy Keeran

Introduction

Library reference services, information literacy instruction (ILI), and outreach have been transformed by technological advances, social changes, and educational developments. The reference desk has gained mobility and ubiquity, reaching out to users in new territories, both physical and virtual. Information literacy has infiltrated the educational curriculum, moving beyond the library and the classroom to the policy and strategy arena, locally and globally. Changes in the higher education environment in particular have enabled library reference services and information literacy programs to develop and diversify in a dynamic, networked world. Reference services, instruction, and outreach are central to meeting the needs of users in this era of great change, and this chapter provides an overview of the issues and trends while also offering justifications concerning how and why librarians will continue to remain essential in the future academic library. In addition, various sections detail the current thinking on best practices and service models in three major areas: liaison services, reference work, and information literacy instruction. Throughout we provide detailed discussions of how information technology has affected services, how academic librarians need to show their value to their institutions and communities, and how changes in service can elevate the nature of academic librarianship.

The Role of the Liaison in Reference, Instruction, and Outreach

In order to fulfill the teaching, learning, and research missions of institutions of higher education, academic librarians provide a number of services to the public (i.e., the academic community). Public services in academic libraries tend to encompass reference and research services and library instruction, as well as outreach to the campus community. In essence, public service librarians are responsible for all library functions that involve direct contact with library users. One of the most common models for delivering reference, instruction, and outreach services in an academic library is the liaison model. Through a traditional liaison program, librarians are assigned as liaisons to provide services for collections, reference, and instruction for specific academic departments. Academic librarians assigned as liaisons may have a number of different job titles, including reference librarian, instruction librarian, or research and instructional services librarian.

Whatever the title, the liaison role in academic libraries has evolved rapidly, and liaisons now play two essential new roles, those of advocate and consultant, both with an emphasis on campus engagement. As advocates, they have become integral to an academic library's outreach plan, speaking on a wide range of topics and trends in higher education, influencing and persuading campus stakeholders on important issues, and serving as ambassadors to student and faculty organizations. As consultants, liaisons identify faculty and student needs, provide in-depth reference and instruction services, and often make referrals to colleagues with more specialized, often technical, expertise. Different models of liaison services are discussed later in this chapter, including embedded and personal librarianship, within the context of both reference and instruction. While the liaison role looks slightly different depending on the service being provided, the main goal remains the same. Liaisons serve as the bridge between the higher education community and the services and resources of the library.

Outreach is intricately tied to the liaison services of an academic library because the purpose of outreach is to "reach out" to a library's clientele to actively educate them about the services a library may offer as opposed to passively waiting for them to come to the library. Large events, such as first-year student orientations and recruitment fairs, still feature at most academic libraries, but smaller, more focused occasions with specific affinity groups, composed of individuals who share backgrounds, interests, or goals, have become increasingly widespread.[1] Specialty groups, such as graduate students, international students, student athletes, and participants in summer scholar and study abroad programs, increasingly prevail on reference and instruction librarians for specialized assistance and education. As the need to promote library services continues to expand, some libraries have redesigned traditional reference and instruction positions to become student outreach librarians tasked with making connections between the library and student governance, organizations, and affinity groups.

Reference Services

Reference librarians at any type of academic library will have a teaching mission, whether at the reference desk or virtually, ensuring that members of their community are taught to develop the lifelong skills necessary to navigate a complex, information-rich world. Any interactions with students can be teaching opportunities.[2] In the networked environment, the reference librarian's role as a liaison to an external unit, department, or group has grown in importance, for in order to communicate with and instruct constituents beyond the library walls, they must engage in outreach. Collaboration with faculty and other campus service centers offers occasions to become integrated into the curriculum and into the continuum of the scholarly research process, from inquiry to expression. Activities, such as answering in-person and virtual research questions and collaborating inside and outside the physical library building, while remaining true to the library teaching mission, offer opportunities and challenges to reference librarians. The choices we make concerning the services we offer in order to meet the needs of the academic community and the collaborative partnerships we establish indicate how the profession continuously adjusts to and incorporates changes in a dynamic environment.

Reference Desk Models

The traditional reference desk emerged as a feature in libraries at the end of the nineteenth century, when the role of the librarian shifted from custodial to service-oriented, and involved a central, physical location where librarians helped patrons with their queries. This model remained the most prevalent until the end of the twentieth century and the advent of the Internet.[3] With the web and mega search engines, individuals were no longer dependent on librarians to help locate facts and conduct research, and another shift started to occur in the role of the librarian. The Internet made it possible for institutions of all sizes and missions to offer online courses. Remote access to library collections became a reality, with databases followed by full-text journal collections, followed by e-books gaining prominence, and reference models evolved to reach patrons beyond the library building. As technology developed, academic reference librarians began to reexamine some of the job skills required, to experiment with different delivery models in order to meet the changing needs of their communities, and to question assumptions about how they interact with patrons. With the shift from collections toward a collaborative, outward focus, new reference positions with such titles as distance education, outreach, data management, and digital humanities librarian came into being. In today's reference service, we see a wide variety of options for meeting the needs of specific academic communities.

During the transition period of integrating technology into the library, the staple of the reference department—the reference desk—came under scrutiny, for to some it symbolized the passive nature of traditional reference service, with the reference librarian waiting (not so eagerly, critics complained) for patrons to approach him or her with questions. Although some academic libraries have either removed the reference desk altogether or merged it with allied services, such as circulation and information technology (IT), others have extended the physical location outward by enhancing the service at the desk to include virtual reference, which can incorporate a variety of online communication methods to respond to inquiries: e-mail, web-based request forms, chat, text, video, and social media (e.g., Facebook, YouTube, Twitter, blogs, wikis). Members of the profession question the need for the desk itself in this networked world, yet there remain advocates both for and against it. Those opposed to keeping the reference desk call it inefficient and ineffective, a place where 89 percent of the questions are directional or peripheral to research rather than substantive, thus wasting the valuable time of librarians.[4] Librarians who believe that every interaction at the reference desk can be an important teachable moment resist the call to stop serving at the desk. Small college and community college libraries, where reference service often comprises just one piece of a librarian's job description (i.e., he or she might also be responsible for access services or cataloging or even be the director of the library), may determine that the reference desk, including its virtual component, remains an invaluable central point of contact with their readers.

The American Library Association, which collects data on reference questions, provided statistics showing that a 50 percent drop in reference transactions occurred between 1994 and 2008.[5] Because the type of ready reference questions asked in the past generally could be answered independently via an online search in mega search engines, reference questions at the desk have become more in-depth, and interactions have become longer. This trend has prompted some institutions to move to an on-call or consultation reference model. Hazel McClure and Patricia Bravender found that the number of true reference questions that came through referrals from a shared desk remained steady, which alleviated the anxiety of the librarians at their institution.[6] But Dennis B. Miles questions whether this drop in reference statistics pertains across all libraries and suggests that his findings show little or no drop in reference statistics at the midsize academic libraries he surveyed that have small to medium MA programs. In these smaller settings, the community values the personal contact with professionals, so such libraries will be less likely to stop staffing the reference desk with librarians, although they do incorporate other virtual models to reach out beyond the library building. Overall, the best advice remains that library administration should evaluate and assess the needs of the community served and listen closely in order to respond to what patrons indicate they want as components of their reference service. What users require will differ, from large research libraries that serve undergraduate, masters, and PhD programs to college libraries for undergraduates where personal interactions with professionals are expected to community colleges serving diverse populations where students may have limited experience with libraries and technology. At some places eliminating or merging the reference desk might be the right choice given either the makeup of the student body or budget and staffing levels (or both), while at others keeping the desk staffed with librarians may be essential because of the culture of the institution.

In the networked environment, most academic reference librarians offer at least one method, and typically more, to communicate and interact with patrons virtually—e-mail, request forms, chat, and text being most common. Sharon Q. Yang and Heather A. Dalal found that academic institutions with large undergraduate populations or that offered higher degrees were most likely to provide chat and that public institutions were more likely to offer chat than private.[7] The authors speculate that larger institutions and those offering advanced degrees have more librarians who can add chat to their other responsibilities, while smaller or private institutions may not have the budget or the technological expertise to implement chat. Over time, chat software has become easier to implement so that those not currently using it might be able to do so. Barbara Blummer and Jeffrey M. Kenton found that large community colleges tend to use chat and online subject guides, such as those created using Springshare's LibGuides (http://www.springshare.com), to reach as many as possible of their mainly nontraditional students; technology has become essential for their communities.[8] Depending on the physical desk model, the librarians and staff at the reference or shared desk can multitask, helping patrons in person and virtually, thus more effectively meeting the needs of their communities.

The shared and the tiered desk models allow libraries to offer help at a physical location in the library, but this might not be staffed with librarians. In the shared or merged model, libraries combine staff from different departments (e.g., circulation/access, reference, IT) so that questions that do not require a librarian's expertise can be answered at a single location. In the tiered model, the reference desk remains in place, but paraprofessionals or students staff it. On the one hand, these models may be more cost-effective, either because the staff already works at that location, such as the circulation desk, or because paraprofessionals and students are not as highly paid as librarians;[9] on the other, training staff to ensure both high-quality answers and correct referrals to reference librarians is crucial. The logistics of bringing staff together to train can be difficult and the varied skill levels challenging. Libraries using this model may also extend their hours late into the evening when librarians are not there, so librarians considering these options must assess the resources required to teach staff and monitor interactions with patrons. The librarians at Radford University used the READ scale, which rates the difficulty level of reference questions, to assess the quality of referrals and responses and then to follow up with enhanced training for student staff.[10] Software packages, such as LibAnswers, another Springshare product, offer online solutions for tracking questions and answers so that all interactions and responses including in-person, phone, e-mail, chat, and other types of communication can be monitored and evaluated, thus helping to ensure quality control. In addition, when the content entered into such software packages can be searched, the written responses to questions become a knowledge base able to be mined for information; some packages can generate and even post the most common questions to the library website's FAQ section. In both the shared and tiered models, the reference librarians make themselves available for in-depth consultations, either by appointment or on call, and can interact in person, over the phone, or by means of video chat. Reference librarians can be scheduled to be present in a consultation room adjacent to the reference desk, making them highly visible, but other librarians may hold consultations in their offices or at public workstations.[11]

Liaison Librarians in Reference Work

The removal of the reference desk altogether or the merged or tiered models all provide free time for reference librarians to engage and collaborate with faculty on their research and integrating instruction into the curriculum. The profession recognizes that we have witnessed a shift from subject specialists who build collections to subject liaison librarians who build connections with faculty and students in particular academic departments. It is through liaison programs that reference librarians, generally those with a BA or MA degree or knowledge of the discipline, establish long-term connections with faculty in their assigned areas. To build successful relationships with faculty, notes Isabel D. Silver, the "importance of personal contact, communication, and visibility cannot be overstated."[12] By making personal connections, reference librarians learn about faculty research and teaching interests

Carrie Forbes and Peggy Keeran

and needs and become part of the conversations on campus related to other aspects of scholarship, such as data management and visualization, open access, and creating digital content. Faculty also serve as essential partners because librarians rely on them to refer students to us for research help.[13] Rather than engage in formal public relations activities, faculty librarians can make connections at informal events, departmental meetings, and visits to faculty offices; Silver proposes a variety of ways to reach out to faculty and students, from hallway conversations to holding office hours in the academic department to welcoming new faculty to meeting for coffee.[14] Formal liaison programs may have a library advisory group comprised of librarians and a designated faculty member from each department to facilitate communication between the library and its communities and to meet as a group on a regular basis to share information and solicit feedback in person. A librarian at a large institution may serve as a liaison to two or three departments, while those at small to midsize institutions or community colleges may cover whole divisions, such as business, arts and humanities, or social sciences. For students, librarians focus on building personal connections by meeting them wherever they may be and employing technologies they themselves use to communicate. Some liaison librarians also experiment with other reference models designed to reach out to faculty and students, such as the embedded librarian, the personal librarian, and the roving librarian.

Embedded, Personal, and Roving Reference Models

The embedded librarian will generally be a subject specialist who collaborates closely with teaching faculty to become integrated virtually into a course or physically in an academic department in order to provide personal contact with faculty and their students. The librarians working in traditional branch libraries located in the same buildings as the communities they serve (e.g., art and architecture, business, music, law, engineering, or science) can be considered embedded librarians, too, but we typically find such satellite libraries only at large institutions. Depending on the goals for this model, the embedded librarian could collaborate with a faculty member to become part of the virtual community, whether the class meets on campus or online, in order to be available to respond to questions during online sessions in real time or to contribute to conversations that take place in a learning management system, such as Blackboard, D2L, or Canvas. A more ambitious (because it's more time-consuming) goal would be to interact directly with each student in the class. Embedded librarians might request physical spaces in their liaison departments to hold office hours to answer questions. As embedded librarians learn more about the workings of their departments and the assignments students must complete, they can help to increase traffic to the reference desk.[15] Although the type of embedded librarian will vary by institution, the best core practices are to lay the groundwork (establish that there is a need, be realistic about what can be offered, and get support from the library administration and department), to prepare (be proactive, learn what types of help will be needed and what technologies and spaces will be required, and plan for the various interactions, taking time into account), and to execute the plan (establish good avenues of communication and outreach, be flexible, anticipate problems, and resolve any that arise).[16]

The personal librarian program can be seen as an extension of the embedded librarian because both offer subject-specific research help to every faculty member and student in the librarian's liaison area; however, personal librarians most often see their role as designed to alleviate anxiety in new students and help to keep them on track. Each student new to an institution is paired with a specific librarian in order to develop a personal relationship that offers the student research support and guidance over time. For example, Yale's first-year student program, which many libraries follow, matches first- and second-year students with personal librarians, and then the students move on to subject specialists once they declare majors.[17] The *Yale Personal Librarian* webpage (which also includes links to their graduate Divinity and Medical Personal Librarian Programs), explains the role of the personal librarian: The librarian will send e-mail updates about the library, answer library questions, assist with locating resources, and help with research.[18] This model can be scaled to fit various types of traditional four-year academic institutions but would be challenging for community colleges with large populations ranging from students with little knowledge of libraries or technology (who may require more remedial measures) to the growing population of adult learners returning as students (who may be comfortable with reference desks but not with library technology). This type of library would need to access the different ways of serving its constituents, such as a combination of the physical reference desk, virtual reference, and the roving librarian.

In the roving model, the librarian identifies places in the library or on campus where individuals congregate and appears there in person to reach out to students and faculty; mobile devices have made such programs more effective, for questions can generally be answered on the spot. To make this type of program successful, Ruth M. Mirtz recommends designing it for the specific institution as a so-called niche form of reference, asking when, where, and why this service would be helpful.[19] Librarians are frequently asked to attend student orientations, but a librarian who intentionally goes out on campus during the first week of classes to attract the attention of and help those who appear to be lost or confused or establish a presence in spaces where students meet (e.g., cafés, student centers, residence halls), can generate goodwill for and raise awareness of the library. The librarians at Tunxis Community College Library in Farmington, Connecticut, took advantage of the renovation of the library to establish a roving librarian program: They applied for and were awarded a $6,000 grant to purchase high-quality portable hardware that allowed them to successfully establish themselves in spaces where students congregated.[20] Several libraries advertise the roving reference service within the library on their websites and offer the service at various locations during specific hours. The University of Mississippi librarians roam the library stacks during busy times,[21] taking iPads to help answer questions, while the University of California at Merced offers a student roaming reference program to provide help on the go, each roamer equipped with a laptop.[22] These proactive programs, however, can be difficult to staff, which is why limiting them to certain times of the academic year, times of day, and locations allows librarians to manage them more easily. Technological issues, such as the awkwardness of using laptops without a hard surface on which to place them or poor Internet access outside of buildings, can also be challenges that dictate location. Tablets and iPads can help with the former problem, but they require investment. When considering any of the aforementioned models, librarians should determine the needs of the various populations of the academic community, open conversations with potential partners, choose a sustainable and affordable model, start with a pilot project and assess it periodically, and be flexible in both planning and implementation.

Services in a Library "Commons"

As more content becomes available online, academic libraries evolve from a space housing physical books into a "commons" (most often referred to as information, knowledge, learning, or academic commons), where faculty and students enjoy redesigned space and robust opportunities for collaboration. A commons brings together under the library's roof a variety of services from across campus, such as tutoring, writing, teaching and learning, data visualization, digital media, and technology service centers. These commons are intended to create a central learning and collaborative environment where students and faculty can seek opportunities and expert help for the continuum of their scholarly and learning needs. Reference librarians, too, can collaborate with these partners in order, for example, to integrate research into the writing program courses, design workshops that teach faculty and students new skills related to incorporating digital media or data visualization into projects, or work closely with the teaching and learning center to integrate research into course development. Because research and writing are iterative processes, reference librarians could be embedded in the writing center to help with research questions. Some libraries have successfully experimented with combining the research and writing center and have found that this model can alleviate student anxiety and lead to their success, for, according to Norma Estela Palomino and Paula Ferreira Gouveia, the partnership "reflects the fact that thinking, researching and writing are interwoven and recursive processes that are further enhanced when supported by their physical collocation."[23] Libraries undergoing renovation on a large scale can more easily incorporate such changes, but those libraries that are not can still think strategically about how to redesign portions of the space to bring in collaborative partners. Disadvantages of reinventing the library space as a commons include the possibility that the library could lose its identity and the fact that freeing up space often means storing parts of the collections or reducing student study spaces. Communicating clear and thoughtful reasons for becoming a commons is essential for the library to ensure that the academic community understands and will be comfortable with the changes.

Information Literacy Instruction

Changes to the academic curriculum, the demographics of the college student body, and the place of information technology in higher education have all contributed to a sharper focus on the role of the librarian as a teacher. As a result, academic librarians increasingly assume responsibility for a variety of activities directly related to teaching and learning, and the scope of those responsibilities has expanded in recent years to encompass instruction delivered in the library, across campus, and in online learning environments.[24] Academic librarians working in public services primarily conduct information literacy workshops for students, but in smaller libraries, such as those in community colleges, all librarians may actively participate in educating readers.

The term *information literacy* has encompassed many meanings over the past thirty years, and while debate continues over its appropriate use and exact meaning,[25] it is most commonly understood to refer to an individual's ability to "recognize when information is needed and . . . to locate, evaluate, and use effectively the needed information."[26] Information literacy instruction (ILI) refers to any formal instructional program housed in an academic library designed to foster the development of skills related to the identification, acquisition, evaluation, use, and management of information to meet a specific need.[27] Information literacy instruction may be either conducted by an academic librarian directly with students or designed in collaboration with a member of the classroom faculty as an integral part of a course. Information literacy instruction may also be referred to in the literature and on campuses as "bibliographic instruction," "library instruction," "research education," or "user education."[28]

Approaches to ILI in Academic Settings

Over the past two decades, information literacy instruction has become an established feature of the higher education curriculum. As a result, academic librarians have developed a number of models or approaches for offering instructional services. As noted previously, in larger college and university libraries the librarian may have specialized knowledge of specific subject areas and serve as a subject expert teaching advanced research methods classes to students in specific disciplines. Larger, research-intensive universities often have research and instruction librarians assigned to narrowly defined disciplines (e.g., anthropology librarian) while more midsize colleges and universities tend to have librarians who specialize in broad disciplinary areas (e.g., social sciences librarian).

With the increased focus on teaching activities, many academic libraries now also hire instruction librarians with expertise in pedagogy, curriculum, and assessment. Instruction librarians will often be assigned to develop curriculum and programming for specific populations in higher education, such as freshmen, first-generation college students, students of color, or adult learners. In many academic libraries, instruction librarians also serve as coordinators of instructional services and as instructional leaders in their organizations. Rather than focus on a specific population or discipline, they implement broad-reaching, curriculum-integrated information literacy programs and assess the impact of the library's instructional services on student learning.[29] Librarians have also assumed leadership roles in developing instructional activities related to broader campus initiatives, such as instruction in critical thinking,[30] first-year-experience programs,[31] and Writing across the Curriculum.[32]

While some universities offer required credit-bearing information literacy courses taught by librarians, the majority of library instruction takes place in guest lectures or workshops during regular class time or through scheduled workshops outside class (sometimes called cocurricular workshops) on such topics as how to locate information on a given subject or use a particular software application. Many academic librarians offer presentations as part of campus-wide faculty development programs and also provide a series of one-on-one tutorials through daily interactions with students, staff, faculty, and members of the local community at the reference desk (and, increasingly, online). In order to be successful, instruction librarians need to engage in a high level of collaboration with faculty, other academic support units on campus, and administrators.

Models of faculty–librarian collaboration feature prominently in the literature and have been recognized as an essential component of any information literacy program.[33] A national survey of higher education faculty by Ithaka S+R, a not-for-profit organization that conducts research on the impact of technology on higher education and libraries, shows that faculty increasingly worry about their students' research skills and look to librarians as teaching partners to address this issue.[34] While faculty are beginning to embrace coteaching with librarians, it can still be a struggle for librarians to become fully integrated into courses. Teaching faculty are frequently concerned about having enough time to cover the content of their subject areas and may worry about spending too much time on information literacy skills. Political issues may also come into play because some faculty may resent giving up control of their classrooms to librarians, perhaps especially to librarians without faculty status, whom they may not consider to be their peers. Ultimately, it takes time and patience to build strong relationships with faculty in order to be successful at collaborations for information literacy teaching, but the results are well worth the efforts.

Models, Standards, and Best Practices

Models play an important role in helping academic librarians to implement and promote information literacy. They also provide practitioners a starting point to build and assess their educational offerings. The traditional information literacy standards define the most common professional job expectations. The standards reflect how those in the field of library and information science generally understand information literacy. They also continue to inform the learning outcomes mandated by accrediting agencies and developed by course instructors.

Professional and educational organizations, such as the American Library Association (ALA), the Association of College and Research Libraries (ACRL), and the Middle States Commission on Higher Education (MSCHE), have developed definitions of *information literacy* and outlined characteristics of

---

TEXTBOX 6.1.

The Association of College and Research Libraries (ACRL) Five Information Literacy Standards

1. Determine the extent of information needed.
2. Access the needed information effectively and efficiently.
3. Evaluate information and its sources critically.
4. Use information effectively to accomplish a specific purpose.
5. Understand the economic, legal, and social issues surrounding the use of information, and access and use information ethically and legally.

Source: Association of College and Research Libraries 2000

Carrie Forbes and Peggy Keeran

information-literate individuals. MSCHE is one of a number of higher education accreditation agencies that have mandated that the institutions they accredit include information literacy in the curriculum across disciplines, particularly in general education components.[35] In addition, many academic libraries have adopted the recommendations of ACRL to inform their information literacy practices. ACRL defines five information literacy standards; these skills must be mastered for an individual to be considered information literate. Each ACRL standard is subdivided into several performance indicators, and these are further divided into outcomes. The standards outline competencies, skills, and outcomes that students will need to achieve in order to be considered information literate.[36]

In contrast, the new "Framework for Information Literacy in Higher Education" presents six frames, each centered on a *threshold concept* determined to be an integral component of information literacy.[37] *Threshold knowledge* is a term from the study of higher education used to describe core concepts that, once understood, transform perception of a given subject.[38] For many librarians, threshold concepts are unfamiliar constructs; represent a new, more contemporary way of thinking about instruction and assessment; and will require a concerted effort to integrate into practice.

TEXTBOX 6.2.

Framework for Information Literacy in Higher Education
1. Authority is constructed and contextual.
2. Information creation is a process.
3. Information has value.
4. Research is inquiry.
5. Scholarship is conversation.
6. Searching is strategic exploration.

Adopted by ACRL in January 2016

A reoccurring concern regarding the previous ACRL standards was the linear, check-the-box structure of the model, which many librarians believe does not fully recognize the lived experiences of the students.[39] Information literacy development can be unpredictable and not as straightforward as the original ACRL standards suggest. Models with competency-based structures frequently assume that there are right and wrong ways to complete information literacy tasks. Many scholars argue that such models implicitly depict learners as passive recipients of information; students come to us as blank slates waiting for librarians to "fill" them with information. This viewpoint does not fully appreciate the literacy skills that students may already possess and can cause learners to feel that their nonacademic information experiences have no relevance to academic and college life.[40] Advocates of new critical and relational approaches to information literacy (such as the approach found in the ARCL framework) recommend creating guidelines that embrace, enhance, and challenge an individual's understanding of information.[41] Debate as to whether the new framework adequately addresses these issues continues.

Information Literacy Pedagogy

ILI in an academic setting often consists of a variety of instructional approaches and active learning strategies, such as course-related library instruction sessions, online tutorials and guides, stand-alone courses, and specialized sessions on the use of archival and other primary source materials.[42] Over the last several years, librarians have sought to develop more dynamic and diverse approaches to ILI. Recent research indicates that many students genuinely believe that they already know how to conduct research on the web.[43] Librarians must employ engaged pedagogical approaches to ensure that students begin to understand the differences between search engines versus academic article indexes, web resources versus online journals, and freely available versus subscription databases. To better elucidate these concepts, ILI practices today have shifted in focus from teaching specific information resources to teaching a set of critical thinking skills involving the ethics and use of information.[44] As a result, most instructional service models in academic libraries today emphasize the importance of incorporating active learning strategies, providing instruction for different learning styles, and engaging students with larger issues of information ethics. Depending on the size of the university and the demographics of the student population, instruction librarians may need to adjust their techniques to match student needs. For example, in community college libraries, where there may be significant populations of students requiring remediation, librarians often need to help students develop basic information literacy skills before progressing to more advanced concepts.

Active learning refers to a process whereby students engage in such tasks as reading, writing, discussion, or problem-solving that promote analysis, synthesis, and evaluation of class content. Individual strategies to promote active learning in the classroom abound and include a wide range of lessons and applications across different disciplines, from class discussion to hands-on activities to group exercises to problem-based learning to peer teaching and simulations to interaction with new technology. Active learning emphasizes maximizing the classroom learning experience and environment while deemphasizing the traditional lecture format.[45]

The phrase *learning styles* refers to a range of competing and contested theories that aim to account for differences in the ways individuals learn best. These theories propose that all people can be classified according to their style of learning, although the various theories present differing views of how we should define and categorize the styles. One common contention is that individuals differ in how they learn, and therefore librarians should provide content in different formats (online, print) to aid the learning of all students. Incorporating approaches to different learning styles proved to be a popular method of library instruction in the past and still frequently features in discussions of best practices. In recent years, however, the idea of learning styles has come under more scrutiny, with some librarians arguing that the whole notion of "learning styles" has no sound scientific evidence to support it. In either case, learning styles can be useful to information literacy in several ways. For one thing, some of the advice associated with learning theories, particularly active learning strategies, is practical and sound. Knowing more about how people learn can help librarians to increase their sensitivity to diversity within the student body and motivate students. For their part, students who themselves develop an awareness of how people learn can also benefit: They can cultivate a more reflective, self-aware approach to their learning and take more control of it by developing strategies for a range of learning situations.[46]

Critical information literacy (CIL) has recently emerged as another approach or alternative channel through which IL can be taught to students. Drawing on critical pedagogy, critical literacy, and critical information theories, CIL resists easy definition but constitutes a departure from typical library instruction practice. According to Allan Luke and Cushla Kapitzke, when using critical information literacy in the classroom, librarians need to focus on the "social construction and cultural authority of knowledge; the political economies of knowledge ownership and control; and the development of local communities' and cultures' capacities to critique and construct knowledge."[47] James K. Elmborg further suggests that critical information literacy pedagogy attempts to teach students to critique the very nature of information itself.[48] For example, instruction librarians can teach students to ask questions about information access and cost. Why do scholarly journal articles cost money, and how does this affect who has access to the information? Why is peer-reviewed research valued in higher education? What role should indigenous knowledge play in academic research? Essentially, CIL helps students to begin to deconstruct how information is organized, shared, and communicated and what values are emphasized (or not) through these processes.

Professional Development for Teaching Practices

To work as an instruction librarian today requires not only an understanding of library science and information literacy but also a significant background in established educational practices and theories, as well as emerging pedagogies. Instruction librarians need to know not only what to teach but also how to teach, which methods to use, how to adapt to different student populations, how to develop a lesson plan, and how to assess learning. Recognizing these expanded requirements, academic libraries, as well as library professional organizations, have developed training seminars and conferences to help librarians to master these skills.

The Association of College and Research Libraries (ACRL) Information Literacy Immersion Program offers multiday training sessions for instruction librarians that provides an opportunity for them to work intensively on various aspects of information literacy teaching. Different tracks cater to the expertise and needs of each librarian. Immersion Program offerings include tracks on managing instruction programs, developing an instructional program, learning how to teach, enhancing teaching skills, designing assessment measures, and teaching with technology.[49] Another popular professional development opportunity for instruction librarians is LOEX (Library Orientation Exchange), a self-supporting, nonprofit educational clearinghouse for library instruction and information literacy information. Founded in 1971 at Eastern Michigan University, LOEX has grown from a lending repository of library instruction materials and host of an annual conference on the subject to an internationally recognized organization that serves many of those working in the field.[50]

Impact of Technology

Often, advances or changes in technology make more information available to more people, empowering those already able to find and use information effectively but also overwhelming those who have few or no skills and limited time to filter and evaluate masses of information appearing in various formats. Technology literacy is often inseparable from information literacy. In order to find information today, users also need to be able to use the online databases and websites that contain that information. Instruction librarians strive to strike a balance between teaching a particular tool and teaching the broader concepts and theories related to the use of information. While there may be no single defined way to balance these priorities, many scholars of education believe that devoting the majority of teaching time to broad conceptual issues achieves the best results.[51]

With the development of information commons in many academic libraries, instruction librarians enjoy new and exciting opportunities to use technology in their teaching. Instruction librarians have developed websites, online tutorials and research guides, blogs and wikis, as well as mash-ups, podcasts, and RSS feeds to help students learn to use information effectively and ethically. Social networking tools also present unique challenges and opportunities to discuss and analyze how information is created, shared, and repurposed in the digital age.

Assessment

Instruction librarians should also be aware of the current philosophies and movements in higher education assessment because these employees increasingly need to demonstrate that the information literacy instruction they provide has a positive impact on student learning.[52] There are various assessment tools available, and the choice of assessment will depend on the purpose of the assessment together with the capabilities of the various assessment methods. Instruction librarians use assessment to improve instructional classes, to justify programs to administrators, and to help institutions to meet regional and professional organizations' accreditation standards. Academic librarians running formal ILI programs must also consider university curricular objectives and student learning outcomes.[53]

Librarians engaged with assessment can choose to use standardized assessment tests, create their own assessments, and work with teaching faculty to create assignments and rubrics for the assessment of IL within a particular course. Popular standardized assessment tests include the Project SAILS Information Literacy Assessment, iSkills, and Information Literacy Test.[54] Standardized assessments allow librarians to test a large segment of their student population and compare scores across institutions, but the tests have been criticized for not being applicable to real-life situations and not allowing for differences in disciplinary research practices.[55] Because much information literacy instruction takes place in one-shot sessions, classroom assessment techniques (CATs) have also become popular tools for measuring student learning.[56] CATs are generally simple, nongraded, anonymous in-class activities designed to give the instructor and students useful feedback on the teaching-learning process as it is happening.[57]

Key Issues and Challenges

Teaching and outreach are the hallmarks of the library profession today, as more and more people confront the challenges of accessing, retrieving, evaluating, and managing information from an ever-increasing variety of resources. The possible methods for academic reference librarians to reach out to and collaborate with members of their academic communities continue to evolve and grow as new technologies emerge, but each academic library must decide which skills its reference and instruction librarians require in order to develop realistic, sustainable service models that meet the needs of their specific communities. Librarians must also work to integrate information literacy and research services into the overall curriculum in order to improve student learning and demonstrate the value of library services. Librarians need to be willing to experiment with pilot projects to test new services. Finally, they should identify underserved populations in the academic community and explore ways to reach out to them to offer reference and instruction services that will help them to succeed.

Conclusion

Blossoming student populations, increasing expectations for accountability and assessment measures, and changes in technology have ultimately shifted the nature of public services in academic libraries of all sizes. The association with academic institutions has ensured academic libraries access to better technological networks and support than many other types of libraries enjoy, creating an environment in which innovation is held in high regard.[58] Contrary to popular expectations, the rise of the Internet and new technologies have made reference and instruction services more, not less, necessary. Service remains central to library functions; it is only *the way* we provide such service that has changed.

Discussion Questions

1. In today's networked environment, librarians and administrators question whether a reference librarian scheduled to work at a traditional reference desk is passively waiting for patrons to come ask for help. Which side are you on? What are your arguments for moving the reference librarians off the desk? Alternatively, why might the reference librarian at the reference desk still be important?
2. Do technological developments, which offer new ways to provide services, change the nature of academic reference work? If yes, then how? If no, then why does the nature of reference work remain unchanged?
3. What are three to five strategies instruction librarians might use to form collaborative relationships with faculty to integrate information literacy into the curriculum?
4. What types of specific active learning activities could be used to engage student audiences with varying skill levels and learning styles: community college students with little knowledge of librar-

ies, first-year students at a four-year institution, advanced undergraduate majors, nontraditional adult students with limited technical skills, and graduate students?

5. When librarians assess reference and instruction services, which types of data and feedback would be useful to meet each of the following challenges: Determine which changes and adjustments to the services need to be made, and determine which models would be most helpful to the academic community and most effectively demonstrate to the administration and wider community the impact and relevance of library services for students?

6. Taking into account constraints on numbers of librarians, budgets, and time, which opportunities and challenges do the various types of reference and information models offer: large public universities, small to midsize private universities and colleges, and community colleges?

Assignment

Students will work in groups, and each group will be assigned a type of academic institution. The group will choose a library that fits the type of academic institution they were given. The goal of this assignment is to learn about a specific library's reference and instructional service models. Students will gather information (e.g., examine institution and library websites, interview librarians, ask for the library's annual reports) about the institution's and library's missions, the academic community (including demographics of student population), and existing reference and instructional models. Then they will analyze why the library offers those services, describe how the library's services align or do not align with the mission, and offer suggestions for modifications or additional services. Students will present their findings in class. Students should consider the following areas and questions as they gather and analyze information.

1. The library's mission, objectives, and governance: What is your library's mission and what does the mission statement say? How does your library's mission relate to the parent institution? How is the institutional mission reflected in the library's goals, objectives, and strategic plan? How is your library organized? Discuss the organizational structure of your library and the governance structure under which your library operates.

2. Reference and instruction models and staffing: Within the reference and instruction department, describe the composition of your library's staff and the role of student assistants. Which reference models are in place (is there a reference desk, who staffs it, are one-on-one consultations offered)? Which, if any, virtual reference services do they offer? Are the librarians liaisons to departments, and how large are their areas of responsibility? Do they offer embedded, personal, or roving services? Which types of data do they collect to assess their services?

3. Library instruction and information literacy (IL): How does your library contribute to teaching on your campus? How do librarians and faculty work together on IL programs? What does your library do for IL and library instruction? Who's in charge? Does it have a curriculum for IL? What are the details of the program? Does it offer workshops to the general public? How does the library assess the impact of library instruction?

4. The library as a place: Does it have a learning or academic commons? Which other service centers are located in the library (e.g., writing, academic tutoring, teaching and learning, technology support)?

5. Library website: Which access points and services does the library website offer? Does it offer virtual tours and online guides? How well does the website represent reference and instruction?

6. Outreach services and programs: How does your library market itself among faculty and students? Which innovative programs are being offered to make the library an essential part of the college community?

7. Challenges and opportunities: What is happening in the library and university as a whole that might be affecting reference and instruction services?

Notes

1. Erin E. Meyer, "Low-Hanging Fruit: Leveraging Short-Term Partnerships to Advance Academic Library Outreach Goals," *Collaborative Librarianship* 6, no. 3 (2014): 112–20.
2. Although generally true, "community college library reference services . . . tend to be a blend between the typical academic perspective (teach the student to find the information) and the traditional public library (provide the patron with the information)." Jennifer Arnold, "The Community College Conundrum: Workforce Issues in Community College Libraries," *Library Trends* 59, nos. 1–2 (2010): 230, doi:10.1353/lib.2010.0033.
3. Dennis B. Miles, "Shall We Get Rid of the Reference Desk?" *Reference and User Services Quarterly* 52, no. 4 (2013): 320–33.
4. Susan M. Ryan, "Reference Transactions Analysis: The Cost-Effectiveness of Staffing a Traditional Academic Reference Desk," *Journal of Academic Librarianship* 34, no. 5 (2008): 389–99, doi:10.1016/j.acalib.2008.06.002.
5. Miles, "Reference Desk," 321.
6. Hazel McClure and Patricia Bravender, "Regarding Reference in an Academic Library: Does the Desk Make a Difference?" *Reference and User Services Quarterly* 52, no. 4 (2013): 302–8.
7. Sharon Q. Yang and Heather A. Dalal, "Delivering Virtual Reference Services on the Web: An Investigation into the Current Practice by Academic Libraries," *Journal of Academic Librarianship* 41, no. 1 (2015): 68–86, doi:10.1016/j.acalib.2014.10.003.
8. Barbara Blummer and Jeffrey M. Kenton, "The Availability of Web 2.0 Tools from Community College Libraries' Websites Serving Large Student Bodies," *Community and Junior College Libraries* 20, nos. 3–4 (2014): 75–104, doi:10.1080/02763915.2015.1056703.
9. Ronald Martin Solorzano, "Adding Value at the Desk: How Technology and User Expectations Are Changing Reference Work," *Reference Librarian* 54, no. 2 (2013): 89–102, doi:10.1080/02763877.2013.755398.
10. Lisa Vassady, Alyssa Archer, and Eric Ackermann, "READ-ing Our Way to Success: Using the READ Scale to Successfully Train Reference Student Assistants in the Referral Model," *Journal of Library Administration* 55, no. 7 (2015): 535–48, doi:10.1080/01930826.2015.1076309.
11. Erin Meyer, Carrie Forbes, and Jennifer Bowers, "The Research Center: Creating an Environment for Interactive Research Consultations," *Reference Services Review* 38, no. 1 (2010): 57–70, doi:10.1108/00907321011020725.
12. Isabel D. Silver, "Outreach Activities for Librarian Liaisons," *Reference and User Services Quarterly* 54, no. 2 (2014): 9.
13. Krista M. Soria, Jan Fransen, and Shane Nackerud, "Library Use and Undergraduate Student Outcomes: New Evidence for Students' Retention and Academic Success," *portal: Libraries and the Academy* 13, no. 2 (2013): 147–64, doi:10.1353/pla.2013.0010.
14. Silver, "Outreach Activities," 10–14.
15. Valerie Freeman, "Embedded Librarianship and the Personal Librarian," in *The Personal Librarian: Enhancing the Student Experience*, edited by Richard J. Moniz Jr. and Jean Moats, 39–55 (Chicago: ALA Editions, 2014).
16. Ibid., 47–48.
17. Jean Moats, "Development and Implementation of the Personal Librarian Concept," in *The Personal Librarian: Enhancing the Student Experience*, edited by Richard J. Moniz Jr. and Jean Moats, 13–24 (Chicago: ALA Editions, 2014).
18. "Yale College Personal Librarian Program," *Yale University Library*, last modified August 28, 2016, http://web.library.yale.edu/pl.
19. Ruth M. Mirtz, "The Second Half of Reference: An Analysis of Point-of-Need Roving Reference Questions," in *Imagine, Innovate, Inspire: Proceedings of the ACRL 2013 Conference*, 518–24 (Chicago: Association of College and Research Libraries, 2013), http://www.ala.org/acrl/acrl/conferences/2013/papers.
20. Lisa Lavoie, "Roving Librarians: Taking It to the Streets," *Urban Library Journal* 15, no. 1 (2008), http://ojs.gc.cuny.edu/index.php/urbanlibrary/article/view/1271/1365.

21. "Roving Reference Services," *University of Mississippi Libraries*, 2014, http://www.libraries.olemiss.edu/uml/story/learning/roving-reference-service.
22. "Roving Reference," *UC Merced Libraries*, n.d., http://library.ucmerced.edu/research/students/improve/roving-reference.
23. Norma Estela Palomino and Paula Ferreira Gouveia, "Righting the Academic Paper: A Collaboration between Library Services and the Writing Centre in a Canadian Academic Setting," *New Library World* 112, nos. 3-4 (2011): 131, doi:10.1108/03074801111117032.
24. Sharon A. Weiner, "Institutionalizing Information Literacy," *Journal of Academic Librarianship* 38, no. 5 (2012): 287-93, doi:10.1016/j.acalib.2012.05.004.
25. Maria Pinto, José Antonio Cordón, and Raquel Gómez Diaz, "Thirty Years of Information Literacy (1977-2007): A Terminological, Conceptual and Statistical Analysis," *Journal of Librarianship and Information Science* 42, no. 1 (2010): 3-19, doi:10.1177/0961000609345091.
26. "Information Literacy Competency Standards for Higher Education," *Association of College and Research Libraries (ACRL)*, 2000, http://www.ala.org/acrl/standards/informationliteracycompetency.
27. Fiona Salisbury and Linda Sheridan, "Mapping the Journey: Developing an Information Literacy Strategy as Part of Curriculum Reform," *Journal of Librarianship and Information Science* 43, no. 3 (2011): 185-93, doi:10.1177/0961000611411961.
28. Esther S. Grassian and Joan R. Kaplowitz, *Information Literacy Instruction: Theory and Practice*, 2nd ed. (New York: Neal-Schuman, 2009).
29. Judith A. Wolfe, Ted Naylor, and Jeanetta Drueke, "The Role of the Academic Reference Librarian in the Learning Commons," *Reference and User Services Quarterly* 50, no. 2 (2010): 108-13.
30. Brenda Refaei, Rita Kumar, and Stephena Harmony, "Working Collaboratively to Improve Students' Application of Critical Thinking to Information Literacy Skills," *Writing and Pedagogy* 7, no. 1 (2015): 117-37, doi:10.1558/wap.v7i1.17232.
31. M. Sara Lowe, Char Booth, Sean Stone, and Natalie Tagge, "Impacting Information Literacy Learning in First-Year Seminars: A Rubric-Based Evaluation," *portal: Libraries and the Academy* 15, no. 3 (2015): 489-512, doi:10.1353/pla.2015.0030.
32. James K. Elmborg, "Information Literacy and Writing across the Curriculum: Sharing the Vision," *Reference Services Review* 31, no. 1 (2003): 68-80, doi:10.1108/00907320310460933.
33. Meggan D. Smith and Amy B. Dailey, "Improving and Assessing Information Literacy Skills through Faculty-Librarian Collaboration," *College and Undergraduate Libraries* 20, no. 3-4 (2013): 314-26, doi:10.1108/00907321311326246.
34. Christine Wolff, Alisa B. Rod, and Roger C. Schonfeld, "Ithaka S+R US Faculty Survey 2015," last modified April 4, 2016, http://sr.ithaka.org/?p=277685.
35. Laura Saunders, "Regional Accreditation Organizations' Treatment of Information Literacy: Definitions, Collaboration, and Assessment," *Journal of Academic Librarianship* 33, no. 3 (2007): 317-26, doi:10.1016/j.acalib.2007.01.009.
36. "Information Literacy Competency Standards."
37. "Framework for Information Literacy for Higher Education," *Association of College and Research Libraries (ACRL)*, accessed on January 30, 2016, http://www.ala.org/acrl/standards/ilframework.
38. Jan H. F. Meyer and Ray Land, "Threshold Concepts and Troublesome Knowledge (2): Epistemological Considerations and a Conceptual Framework for Teaching and Learning," *Higher Education* 49, no. 3 (2005): 373-88, doi:10.1007/s10734-004-6779-5.
39. Laurie Kutner and Alison Armstrong, "Rethinking Information Literacy in a Globalized World," *Communications in Information Literacy* 6, no. 1 (2012): 25-33.
40. James K. Elmborg, "Critical Information Literacy: Implications for Instructional Practice," *Journal of Academic Librarianship* 32, no. 2 (2006): 192-99, doi:10.1016/j.acalib.2005.12.004.
41. Ibid.
42. Kelly E. Miller, "Imagine! On the Future of Teaching and Learning and the Academic Research Library," *portal: Libraries and the Academy* 14, no. 3 (2014): 329-51, doi:10.1353/pla.2014.0018.
43. Alison J. Head, "Learning the Ropes: How Freshman Conduct Research Once They Enter College," last modified December 5, 2013, http://projectinfolit.org/images/pdfs/pil_2013_freshmenstudy_fullreport.pdf.

44. Thomas P. Mackey and Trudi E. Jacobson, "Reframing Information Literacy as a Metaliteracy," *College and Research Libraries* 72, no. 1 (2011): 62–78, doi:10.5860/crl-76r1.

45. Brian Detlor, Lorne Booker, Alexander Serenko, and Heidi Julien, "Student Perceptions of Information Literacy Instruction: The Importance of Active Learning," *Education for Information* 29, no. 2 (2012): 147–61, doi:10.3233/EFI-2012-0924.

46. Rae-Anne Diehm and Mandy Lupton, "Approaches to Learning Information Literacy: A Phenomenographic Study," *Journal of Academic Librarianship* 38, no. 4 (2012): 217–25, doi:10.1016/j .acalib.2012.05.003.

47. Allan Luke and Cushla Kapitzke, "Literacies and Libraries: Archives and Cybraries," *Pedagogy, Culture and Society* 7, no. 3 (1999): 483–84, doi:10.1080/14681369900200066.

48. Elmborg, "Critical Information Literacy."

49. "Immersion Program," *Association of College and Research Libraries*, 2016, http://www.ala.org/acrl/ immersion.

50. "About LOEX," *Library Orientation Exchange (LOEX)*, 2016, http://www.loex.org/about.php.

51. Wan Ng, "Can We Teach Digital Natives Digital Literacy?" *Computers and Education* 59, no. 3 (2012): 1065–78, doi:10.1016/j.compedu.2012.04.016.

52. For a discussion on the effect of library services on student learning outcomes, see "Documented Library Contributions to Student Learning and Success: Building Evidence with Team-Based Assessment in Action Campus Projects," *Association of College and Research Libraries*, last modified April 2016, http:// www.acrl.ala.org/value.

53. Catherine Fraser Riehle and Sharon A. Weiner, "High-Impact Educational Practices: An Exploration of the Role of Information Literacy," *College and Undergraduate Libraries* 20, no. 2 (2013): 127–43, doi:10.1 080/10691316.2013.789658.

54. For a complete list of assessment tests for information literacy, see Cheryl L. Blevens, "Catching Up with Information Literacy Assessment: Resources for Program Evaluation," *College and Research Libraries News* 73, no. 4 (2012): 202–6, http://crln.acrl.org/content/73/4/202.full.

55. Melissa Gross, Don Latham, and Bonnie Armstrong, "Improving Below-Proficient Information Literacy Skills: Designing an Evidence-Based Educational Intervention," *College Teaching* 60, no. 3 (2012): 104–11, doi:10.1080/87567555.2011.645257.

56. For a list of classroom assessment techniques useful for library instruction, see Thomas A. Angelo and K. Patricia Cross, *Classroom Assessment Techniques: A Handbook for College Teachers*, 2nd ed., 18th print (San Francisco: Jossey-Bass, 2008).

57. Toni M. Carter, "Use What You Have: Authentic Assessment of In-Class Activities," *Reference Services Review* 41, no. 1 (2013): 49–61, doi:10.1108/00907321311300875.

58. Ronald C. Jantz, "Innovation in Academic Libraries: An Analysis of University Librarians' Perspectives," *Library and Information Science Research* 34, no. 1 (2012): 3–12, doi:10.1016/j.lisr.2011.07.008.

7

Collection Development

GENERAL AND SPECIAL, PRINT AND DIGITAL, AND RESOURCE SHARING

Lidia Uziel

Introduction

This chapter begins with a broad view of collection development in North American academic libraries. While some attention is given to the basics of collection development in academic libraries generally and to small college libraries and community college libraries, the main focus is on the evolution of collaborative collection development initiatives for general and special collections in certain large North American public and private academic research libraries and library systems in the context of changes observed during the last decade in research, teaching, and learning. It suggests some future directions for interinstitutional resource sharing in such libraries based on various models of consortial lending partnerships and cooperative acquisition agreements. I look at the changing dynamics of print and digital collections; at greater engagement with research and learning behaviors; and at trends in scholarly communication, including open access. The chapter emphasizes a new paradigm for managing shared collections in a consortial environment: a paradigm defined as a progressive transition from a traditional model of institutionally organized stewardship toward a holistically defined, group-scaled collection and content stewardship model. As the current environment in North American research institutions becomes increasingly collaborative and scholarship fundamentally shifts due to the globalization of academia and ongoing technological change, we will be seeing important innovations in how large library collections are managed in the coming years: changes in focus, priorities, and boundaries.

This chapter considers the ways in which many large academic libraries' approaches to collections and content stewardship broadly understood—including general and special collections, print and digital resources—are rapidly advancing in an evolving network environment. I address these developments by looking at some core aspects of shared collection development and management initiatives and at the larger context of continuous change in the scholarly communication and publishing industry. The treatment is discursive and not at all comprehensive; it focuses on several areas that I believe to be especially interesting and important to understand the ongoing shifts in twenty-first-century collection building. The chapter presents some specific themes that may facilitate discussion about future directions in collection development for general and special collections, including print and digital materials, in a variety of academic libraries. These selected themes are presented by means of three fundamental concepts of change that library collections face: change in focus, priorities, and boundaries.

The Variety of Academic Libraries in North America

There are many types of libraries throughout North America. Most libraries can be classified into several categories: academic libraries, public libraries, school media centers, law libraries, federal depository libraries, special libraries, and medical libraries. According to the Association of College and Research Libraries,[1]

> Library systems at universities generally consist of a main university library plus several branch or special libraries. The large campus environment often defines the quality of the library in terms of the strengths and size of the research collection. Concentration of the main and branch libraries is frequently on the needs of specific fields or departments of study at a research level.[2]

Academic libraries are also classified via many institutional characteristics, such as: control (public versus private), level (total four-year and above: doctorates, master's, bachelor's, and less than four-year), size (FTE enrollment: less than 1,000; 1,000 to 2,999; 3,000 to 4,999; 10,000 to 19,999; and 20,000 or more), and Carnegie classification[3] (doctoral/research, master's I and II, baccalaureate/associate's, associate's, specialized, and not classified).[4] The needs of academic library users fall on a spectrum, with use of introductory research materials and instruction in the research process at one end and primary source materials and highly specialized research services at the opposite end. Accordingly, and depending on the institution and its type, collection development in academic libraries can be done on six different levels, including: 0 (out of scope), 1 (minimal level), 2 (basic information), 3 (instructional support), 4 (research level), and 5 (comprehensive level). This approach is based on the conspectus methodology[5] originating with the Research Libraries Group (RLG) in the United States in 1979 and that was adopted by the Association of Research Libraries (ARL)[6] in the early 1980s as a means of providing a map of library collections and collecting policies within individual libraries or among a group of libraries. It was also adopted in Canada, where the National Library of Canada organized a number of regional conspectus projects.

Means of Collection Development

Collection development in academic libraries (also known as collection management or information resources management) involves the identification, selection, acquisition, and evaluation of library resources (e.g., print materials, audiovisual materials, and electronic resources) for a community of users. Collection development is the means by which the library provides high-quality information resources of print and nonprint materials and provides access to electronic resources that will meet institutional needs. It is an ongoing process undertaken by librarians and library services staff with input from faculty, administrators, staff, and students. Large research libraries, such as those affiliated with doctorate-granting universities, enjoy the largest budgets for collections. Within the Carnegie classification framework, their universities are classified according to their level of research activity (highest, higher, or moderate; or R1, R2, and R3, respectively), and these libraries seek to build their collections accordingly. R1 doctoral universities include such institutions as most of the Ivy League universities, as well as such big state schools as the University of California system, the University of North Carolina at Chapel Hill, and the University of Michigan–Ann Arbor. R2 doctoral universities include such regional public universities as Cleveland State University and Florida Atlantic University, along with such private schools as Drexel University and Marquette University. R3 doctoral universities include such smaller private schools as Adelphi University and DePaul University; such smaller public schools as Eastern Michigan University and Georgia Southern University; and many for-profit schools, such as the University of Phoenix, Capella University, and Argosy University. Master's colleges and universities are classified according to the size of their programs (large, medium, smaller; or M1, M2, M3), and their libraries collect accordingly. By contrast, liberal arts college libraries, other baccalaureate-granting college libraries, and community college libraries have the mission to provide a select set of resources to meet the needs of their users. Such resources often include only a limited focus on research. These libraries seek to provide only the best and most immediately relevant materials and most often weed items that are no longer current or that do not have continuing value. They focus on undergraduate students rather than on doctoral or master's students' and faculty research. That said, all libraries engage in the following methods of acquisition:[7]

- *Standing orders*: open orders for all titles that fit a particular category or subject. For example, these are usually developed for serials; additionally, the library knows that it will want any book published in a particular series, such as Oxford University Press's International Policy Exchange series or Routledge's Second Language Acquisition series. The great benefit to this style of ordering is that it is automatic: Collection development librarians do not have to continuously order the next title in the series.

- *Approval plans*: similar to standing orders, except that they cover quite a few topic areas, are sent from the vendor, and the library is only charged for the specific titles that it accepts into its collection. Under these circumstances, the library is free to return anything that it does not wish to add to its collection. A collection development librarian works closely with the materials vendor to craft a profile of specifications, such as publisher and author lists; subject parameters; and other criteria governing academic level, edition, language, and price. As new titles are published, the vendor reviews them to make selections on the library's behalf, following the terms of the library's profile. Approval plans serve as helpful tools to ensure that the library acquires core materials as soon after publication as possible. For many academic libraries, it is important to buy high-demand titles, even those that may also be acquired by the library's peers, in order to support immediate research and teaching needs on campus. Moreover, approval plans are designed to reduce the selection burden for easy-to-obtain commercial and mainstream publishing output, leaving bibliographers time to concentrate on more specific, elusive, and difficult-to-obtain titles. In addition to time savings, approval plans often reduce the cost of acquiring materials by providing a significant discount on titles purchased through the plans. Libraries work with approval plan vendors who specialize in specific publishing output areas delimited geographically or linguistically. Vendors that many North American academic libraries use include YBP (US/UK imprints), Harrassowitz (German), Benelux Union (Belgium, the Netherlands, and Luxembourg), Erasmus (Benelux and Scandinavian imprints), Casalini (Italian, Spanish, and Portuguese imprints), Iberoamericana (Spanish and Portuguese imprints), Amalivre (formerly Aux Amateurs de Livres International and Librairie Internationale Touzot; Francophone materials), Coutts (North American, especially Canadian, and Scandinavian titles), and East View (Russian, Eurasian, and Middle Eastern imprints).

- *Blanket orders*: largely a combination of both a firm order and an approval plan. Blanket orders represent the library's commitment to purchase all of a certain class of materials. For example, a library makes a contract with a certain publisher or vendor and will purchase everything that this publisher or vendor has available on a given topic. A great advantage of this style of ordering is the automatic acquisition of materials for a particular field, which can be especially beneficial to specialized or academic libraries.

- *Subscriptions*: to individual titles, leases of so-called big deal packages or bundles of serials. Individual subscriptions are generally adopted for journals, newspapers, or other serials that a library wishes to acquire. As in the case of standing and blanket orders, with a subscription, a library only has to develop a contract once with a vendor or publisher, and the items are automatically delivered when published. Subscriptions are often designated for a specific length of time and must be renewed at the end of the contract. Leases of so-called big deal packages or bundles of serials are most commonly adopted with electronic resources, such as databases, journals, and web-based materials. The library pays for access to the material versus ownership. This acquisition method has been predominantly used in the STEM fields (Elsevier, Springer, and Wiley are key vendors), and it is constantly causing significant controversies surrounding the escalating costs of scholarly materials. Several vendors and content providers (such as ProQuest, Lexis-Nexis, EBSCO, Alexander Street Press, Adam Matthew and Adam Matthew Digital, and Gale Cengage), from which academic libraries typically license or buy large databases, are offering an array of new content acquisition models, ranging from purchase to subscription to demand-driven (see more later) and various hybrid models (e.g., the video streaming service offered by Kanopy) and many other types of digital content distribution services (e.g., OverDrive for downloadable e-books, audiobooks, and music).

- *Gifts and exchanges*: in some cases, libraries may allow adding to the collection the gifts that people give to the library and exchange unwanted or duplicate gifts with other libraries. A library's collection development policy usually states whether the library accepts gifts and exchanges. Institutions that have a process for this type of acquiring are usually larger academic or research libraries.

- *Firm orders*: orders that are determined by their bibliographical information specifically. For example, a collection development librarian orders a specific book, textbook, or journal that the library wants using a vendor platform (e.g., YBP, Harrassowitz, or Casalini). Area studies librarians, subject specialist librarians, and curators use this and many different selection methods, often working with small shop dealers in countries where there are no large content suppliers or sophisticated technological infrastructure that would allow various levels of automation of collection-building activities. Finally, special collections librarians acquire materials in many different ways, including at auction, from rare book and manuscript dealers' catalogs, through donated personal and institutional papers (which require archival processing within the library before readers can work with them), and with other gifts.

- *Patron-driven acquisitions (PDA) or data- (or demand-) driven acquisitions (DDA)*: one of the most dramatic changes in contemporary collection development. Records for book titles supplied by a vendor get loaded into an institution's library catalog so that readers can discover them as though they were already part of the collection. Readers can then trigger a purchase by their library by requesting a particular book that they have found among these records. In the case of e-books, the vendor merely has to enable a link to the book within the catalog record itself and then bill the library, a convenience that significantly streamlines the acquisition process. Print copies, of course, must be mailed, but even this offers welcome efficiency: Many such titles arrive so-called shelf ready, meaning they have been cataloged and labeled by the vendor and so can be shelved immediately on arrival. This way, the reader enjoys the speediest possible access to them.[8] Rick Anderson, the main proponent of this strategy for collection development, applied it at the University of Utah, an R1 doctoral university. Another R1, Wayne State University, has also adopted it, as have many others, and the trend continues.

Change in Collection Focus in Large North American Academic Research Libraries

Until the early 1990s, the major large North American public and private academic libraries were configured as quite complex and large collections of predominantly print and tangible materials supported by libraries and archives that acquired and curated them locally on an institutional level. The main focus of existing collection-building policies was to grow largely autonomous and highly comprehensive collections of local resources designed to satisfy the past and future research and teaching needs on campus. A library was measured by its wealth of locally collected and curated materials and by the expertise of its staff, who provided the necessary care for institutional collections housed locally. Building highly autonomous local collections that were as comprehensive as possible for *just in time* current needs and *just in case* future research, supported by the required technical services and preservation infrastructure, were crucial strengths to the scholarly endeavor and to a successful library enterprise of the time.

The focus on building autonomous institutional collections has started to change significantly during the last few decades. Ubiquitous networks of library infrastructure have progressively developed at regional levels, allowing libraries to collaborate around large-scale, consciously planned, and distributed collective collections of printed materials. Numerous studies, writings, and research findings demonstrate one unifying theme and trend underlying the last twenty-five years of collection development in North American research institutions: the constantly growing need for deeper interinstitutional collection development collaboration. Studies show that libraries are progressively moving from so-called institutionally contained collections, built locally as individual and institutional collections, to distributed so-called collective collections, built at the network level and via interinstitutional collaborative arrangements.[9] Print collections are being coordinated at regional levels; the geography of their distribution is used as a main framework for deduplication of mainstream library holdings, allowing libraries to progressively focus on other areas of their collection-building activities, including primary and distinctive materials, curation of data, and many other activities. The current shift in collection development focus toward collaborative collection development arises from change factors that are affecting the academic library both internally[10] and externally. This part of the chapter focuses on external change factors to library collection building that are causing a shift toward collaborative collection building on a mega regional or national scale.

The constantly changing patterns of research and learning in academia are an important factor exerting significant pressures on collection development activities in academic libraries. Libraries are not ends in themselves but serve the needs of their constituencies; this is their primary mission. As those needs develop, so do the requirements placed on the library. Advances in the way research and learning are done—the ways in which scholarship is produced, consumed, and disseminated—are important drivers for collaboration. Therefore, the most important reason for libraries to change their collection-building focus and to engage in interinstitutional collaboration is to effectively respond to rapidly evolving users' expectations; research behaviors; and developments in scholarship, research, and learning. Twenty-first-century scholarship, research, and learning grow in many unconventional ways, supported by constantly progressing technological infrastructure and increased content accessibility via sophisticated open and global networks. We need to understand several important parameters in concert in order to fully grasp the importance of external change factors influencing the philosophical and methodological framework of academic library collection-building.

In the past, when academic libraries operated in a predominantly print world, the library's exposure to the scholarly record and its life cycle was limited. The library collected only the final products of scholarship and organized them intellectually as collections of thematic and interrelated sets of materials. In the current digital environment, the library is being directly exposed to the whole life cycle of the scholarly record. This requires a deeper engagement with the research and learning behaviors of the institution and of individual researchers. To stay relevant in this research context, libraries must now provide support for current and emerging activities that they did not have to before: curation of working papers, preprints, and research data; facilitation and funding of data mining and visualization; assistance with copyright compliance, new forms of scholarly publishing, bibliometrics,[11] and research profiling;[12] and many others.[13] The creation of the scholarly record transcends its existing boundaries as it becomes a collective interinstitutional research enterprise around the collection and interpretation of data, documents, and other resources, which vary by discipline. Researchers increasingly rely on new cross-disciplinary methodologies, experiment with new research models, and constantly annotate their observations. Scholarly output is recorded in, and dependent on, the complex infrastructures where the research is produced, analyzed, and distributed. In the print environment, the scholarly record had simply one notification stream that the library collected, while in the digital environment, its notification streams multiply continuously. To remain relevant and provide value to researchers and library users, academic library collecting efforts of the twenty-first century will need to embrace and support multiple streams of scholarly output.

Due to continuous changes in scholarship and the scholarly record, academic libraries must now collect not only new types of publishing and scholarly output but also different types of materials than they did before. They need to provide access to comprehensive global collections due to the globalization of research and academia; collect new transdisciplinary content and materials in emerging areas of research; collect new types of content, including data sets and so-called born digital materials produced and disseminated in unconventional ways; and effectively support digital humanities and text and data mining projects and research.[14] Finally, they must increasingly collect distinctive, unique, and difficult-to-find primary source materials that are now directly incorporated into the core of the research process.[15] Traditional collection-building will not be sufficient to respond to rapidly shifting attitudes toward data-gathering and analysis in this constantly evolving meta-information environment, an environment featuring continuous technological advances, reliance on cross-disciplinary methodologies, and an emphasis on nontraditional research and learning inquiries. Libraries will need to significantly expand their collecting in these areas to support the research and scholarship of the twenty-first century. If successfully implemented, then these initiatives will help to alleviate some significant pressures, such as a growing need for library collection services to take on new roles and responsibilities to support shifts in research and in the academy overall.

Change in Collections Priorities in Large North American Academic Research Libraries

The constantly growing need for deeper interinstitutional collection development collaboration in North American research institutions also results from important change factors that are internal to the academic library enterprise. With a shifting focus and the redefinition of collection-building directions in twenty-first-century research institutions, the value of interinstitutional collaboration is becoming a standard of excellence for many institutional collections. Given the fact that we cannot achieve the goal of satisfying existing institutional research and teaching needs entirely at the local level, interinstitutional collaboration becomes an important prerequisite for any successful collection-building operation in North American research institutions. A carefully planned and holistic coordination of library acquisitions via interinstitutional partnerships organized at regional or national levels can effectively accommodate the crucial challenges that academic libraries increasingly face: stagnating library budgets, rising costs of library materials, the constant and steady increase in the number of publications globally, and the transition from analog to digital format.

Even if library budgets in North American research institutions have been growing steadily during the past few decades, they have shrunk compared to university budgets by more than 20 percent during the last decade.[16] Universities have been investing a declining proportion of funds in libraries, and it has become common knowledge that library budgets are unsustainable. The cost of library materials has risen at a rate exceeding inflation for well over two decades. This is the case for all disciplines, including humanities, social sciences, and STEM disciplines, and particularly for serials and electronic databases.[17] For example, the overall effective publisher price increase for English-language humanities and social science serials in 2015 was in the range of 5 percent to 7 percent, before taking relative currency values into account.[18] No library can maintain its existing coverage without a significant increase in its collection budget. For instance, I estimated that, to maintain longstanding extensive collections coverage at Harvard in humanities and social science materials published in Western European and English-speaking countries, the existing collections budget will need to increase by

Lidia Uziel

around 10 percent to 40 percent, depending on the specific area, and will need to increase every year thereafter on average by 5 percent to 7 percent.

The constant and steady increase in the number of print publications in the various major publishing markets has become another important reason for collaboration. This is particularly true for the North American and European (EU) publishing markets. According to the Federation of European Publishers,[19] statistically over the last five years, new print title output has increased steadily on average by 1 percent to 3 percent per year, depending on the EU country. This represents up to ten thousand additional new titles available to acquire per fiscal year for the EU zone alone. No single library or library system can achieve comprehensive coverage to capture this constantly expanding collections universe. Some recent studies, such as Cornell University's review of purchases in German language,[20] revealed that BorrowDirect (BD)[21] institutions collectively acquired only approximately 60 percent to 70 percent of the content available in the German vendor database; therefore, a large percentage of content never reaches the stacks of any of these institutions. The percentage of the overall publishing output acquired in any given fiscal year varies by institution: For instance, in 2011, it was 53 percent for Harvard, 35 percent for Columbia, and 26 percent Cornell.[22] BD members duplicated a large proportion of this acquired content.

In addition, library purchasing power is diminishing due to the continuous transition to the digital medium. The number of formats libraries now acquire has increased, with greater attention now paid to e-books, databases, visual materials, data sets, and other digital publications. Library patrons count on instantly available electronic information for their coursework and projects, often in addition to the print materials that the library holds. Therefore, in many cases, libraries acquire the same content in both print and digital formats, and some institutions do not consider this to be duplication per se.[23] Instead, they see it as offering an alternative means of access that will allow their patrons to use the same content in different ways and for completely different purposes: discovery and full text searching versus traditional reading and learning. This collecting practice exerts an additional pressure on library budgets because these libraries are technically paying twice for the same content. Libraries are trying to negotiate reduced pricing with publishers and content providers for e-books that duplicate their print holdings; however, these acquisitions remain an additional and important burden on their budgets. To solve this problem, academic libraries are constantly seeking and trying new approaches to digital resources, including a continued focus on collaborative licensing arrangements, closer scrutiny of so-called big deals, experimentation with just-in-time article delivery models, and support and advocacy for both open access and changing scholarly communications models and (as noted earlier) new PDA/DDA models. Of course, significant barriers to sharing persist. Because e-books are typically licensed rather than purchased, research libraries may not be able to share resources easily. This becomes especially important now that much scholarship is published only as e-books, the sharing of which is not automatically protected by fair use. Unfortunately, there is no obvious solution to this problem.

Emerging shared print initiatives in North America[24] are making it possible for libraries to manage local collections in a collaborative environment. An interinstitutional collection-building consciously coordinated on a mega scale allows maintaining historically existing collection-building levels, lowers the operational and collections costs, and eliminates the unwanted duplication of materials that will be rarely used in the future. It allows libraries to stay relevant as they can continue providing important benefits to academic research and scholarship by satisfying their users' needs. As a result, collaborative collection development initiatives make the distinction between what *is* considered to be part of the collection and what *is not* less clear, as many academic libraries now emphasize access over ownership as a new important value of their collection-building enterprise.

Change in Collections Boundaries in Large North American Academic Research Libraries

The fundamental changes that, as noted previously, academic library collections are facing—changes in collection-building focus and priorities—have a significant impact on redefining collection-building boundaries. They force research libraries to redefine their boundaries in collecting, including general collections, special collections, and research and learning materials. The redefinition of these boundaries can be described as an important future imperative in collection-building in research libraries: a progressive move from purchasing materials to curating content. It will allow North American research libraries to transcend their existing boundaries and increasingly move to deeper engagement with faculty research and learning.

I believe that curating digital content will be one of the most important and robustly growing collection-building activities in academic libraries during the next ten years and beyond. An explosion of digital content that is now available to users and that they increasingly need, including born digital resources and many new forms of digital communication, will require ever greater curatorial attention from libraries. An academic research library will no longer be measured by its wealth of locally collected materials but by its capacity to adapt its collecting boundaries to existing research needs: enlarging it from merely purchasing materials to curating digital content. While taking on additional activities and associated costs, libraries will need to invest in new infrastructure and redefine existing technical services and preservation work flows as they embark on new activities, including everything from identifying all these new types of content to storing them to describing them to devising various innovative means of document delivery or fulfillment in order to share them as easily and as widely as possible with others. This undertaking will require major shifts in the patterns of operational support for different types of resources in academic libraries, such as the creation of the necessary technological infrastructure to support and enable the collaborative transitions taking place at the regional, national, and international levels. Several important drivers of collaborative collection-building initiatives will need to be redefined to achieve these ambitions, including operational and transaction costs and new infrastructure requirements. I believe that this shift is one of the most important challenges that academic libraries currently face, at both the methodological and practical levels. A successful enlargement of collection-building boundaries toward curatorial pursuit of digital content promises to help users and will define the future of the largest and wealthiest academic libraries' collection development.

Interinstitutional collection development collaboration on a network scale will redefine how twenty-first-century collections will look in the future. Instead of providing access to local or available collections at other institutions,[25] large academic libraries will provide discovery and access to comprehensive global collections built on a regional or national network level, including digital collections that are licensed by the library for the user, open access materials that are freely available on the web,[26] and global collections available from other institutions. Consequently, twenty-first-century collection-building will be an era of what some have labeled "facilitated collections."[27] In a network environment, access is dispersed across many network resources, such as disciplinary or institutional repositories, services for social discovery and scholarly reputation management, and many data storage and manipulation tools.[28] Such dispersal will significantly diminish the importance of traditional library access points and physical gates, such as library catalogs and library stacks. Therefore, by changing their collection-building boundaries and embracing their new curatorial activities, large academic libraries will be able to thrive successfully and meet research and learning needs in the best ways available. These libraries will not just collect and assemble materials locally as they did in the past but will also provide an important library service by organizing their collection-building activities according to network logic, whereby they assemble a consciously planned and coordinated mix of local, external, and collaborative services around user needs.

This important change factor in library collection development—increasingly moving toward facilitated access to materials and redefining collection-building as a service—will be operationally possible if academic libraries fully realize ongoing changes in collection-building on a holistic level—changes in its focus, values, and boundaries—and if they fully integrate them into their collection-building philosophical and methodological framework.

A New Paradigm for Collection-Building in Large North American Academic Research Libraries

By changing their collection-building focus, priorities, and boundaries, academic libraries in North America can move from what Lorcan Dempsey, Constance Malpas, and Brian Lavoie[29] have called the "outside-in" model, whereby "materials are purchased or licensed from external sources and made available to a local audience," to an "inside-out" model, whereby institutional materials (e.g., digitized special collections, research data sets, teaching and learning materials) are shared with external audiences in new ways. Consequently, a new methodology and conceptual framework for collection-building operations in academic research libraries based on interinstitutional collaboration can be defined as an effort to provide wider access to a collective collection and shared content by leveraging existing resources—financial, human, and infrastructural—on a network level:

- Achieve larger coverage by leveraging collective purchasing power and alleviating some of the financial constraints.
- Lower storage costs and alleviate space constraints. It is becoming more and more expensive to house print materials. The academic library space is a highly competitive asset as its use shifts progressively from housing content to providing new spaces for creative and innovative activities for users.
- Solve some human resources problems: a shortage of staff with traditional and new cutting-edge collections skills. While traditional collection development expertise is still crucial to collection-building operations, we need to hire staff with new skills and expertise to effectively respond to the ongoing shift in scholarship, publishing, and academia, including assessment, data expertise, and licensing skills. By empowering collaboration—sharing traditional expertise and new staff expertise—libraries can invest in staff with new skills.
- Leverage the collective infrastructure to realize the promise of *doing more with less*: The need for constant innovation to keep up with technological change and to remain competitive is constantly growing. Libraries need to streamline redundant library operations and achieve scale and network effect in library operations through aggregation of existing activities on a network level.

A new paradigm for managing shared collections in a consortial environment can be defined as a progressive transition from a traditional model of institutionally organized stewardship toward a holistically defined and group-scaled collection and content stewardship model.

Conclusion

As noted earlier, collection development in academic libraries entails the identification, selection, acquisition, and evaluation of library resources for a community of readers. Collection development practices used in certain large North American public and private academic and research libraries and library systems are constantly evolving, allowing academic and research libraries to take on new roles and responsibilities and responding to changes happening in research, teaching, and learning. As the current environment in North American research institutions becomes increasingly collaborative and technologically driven, we will be seeing important innovations in how library collections are managed in the coming years and how collection-building activities are done at both the practical and methodological levels. Collection-building at the vast majority of academic libraries, including nearly all small college libraries and community college libraries, will continue with librarians using the traditional methods of collecting detailed at the outset of this chapter. However, for many of the largest institutions, the collection and content stewardship model for library materials in North American research institutions will be fundamentally reconfigured in the twenty-first century as collections focus, priorities, and boundaries evolve in a network environment. Research collections will transcend their local identities as they become increasingly embedded in networks of collaboration and cooperation. The consolidation of collecting will fundamentally change the ways in which collections-related infrastructures are developed and managed. Building shared collection management operations will be challenging due to the unavoidably increasing need for operational efficiencies and more intelligent and data-driven work flows. Moreover, significant limitations on libraries' ability to share e-books due to licensing restrictions will increasingly hinder cooperation.

The shift toward the holistically defined and group-scaled collaborative collection and content stewardship model will generate important benefits. Library patrons will be operating in a network environment that will be rich in instantly available resources. By reducing the centrality of local library collections, libraries will be able to focus on related infrastructure alongside the life cycle of creation, curation, and access. The library staff will be able to engage more deeply with broader research and learning activities, including more effective management, exposure, and dissemination of institutional research and learning materials. Academic libraries will have the opportunity to become more involved in supporting the content creation of their researchers and scholars.

Discussion Questions

1. What challenges do libraries face at the organizational level (e.g., technological infrastructure and human and financial resources) as they transition from an institutionally organized stewardship model toward a holistically defined and group-scaled collection and content stewardship model?
2. What will be the impact of this new collection-building model on library teaching, research, and outreach services?
3. What opportunities will result from this shift? How will it affect the traditional roles of both collection development librarians and research services/reference librarians? What impact will it have on libraries overall?
4. What impact will it have on library preservation and access services over the long term?
5. How will it affect the existing boundaries between the general collections and special collections? How will primary sources and unique and distinctive collections (PS&UDCs) fit into this larger picture?

Assignment

Collection development policy for two interinstitutional consortia in North America: a response paper.

Objectives

- Students will evaluate two collection development policies for strengths and weaknesses.
- Students will practice professional communication skills in writing a concise analytical response paper.

This paper will be based on responses to two collection development policies that students compare in terms of content, usefulness, and suggestions for improvement.

Notes

1. According to their website, the Association of College and Research Libraries (ACRL) is the "higher education association for librarians. Representing more than 11,000 academic and research librarians and interested individuals, ACRL develops programs, products and services to help academic and research librarians learn, innovate and lead within the academic community. Founded in 1940, ACRL is committed to advancing learning and transforming scholarship." For more information, see "About ACRL," *Association of College and Research Libraries*, 2016, http://www.ala.org/acrl/aboutacrl.

2. "Guidelines for University Library Services to Undergraduate Students," *Association of College and Research Libraries*, 2013, http://www.ala.org/acrl/standards/ulsundergraduate. Approved by the ACRL Board of Directors at ALA annual conference, June 2005. Revision approved October 2013.

3. The Carnegie Classification of Institutions of Higher Education is a framework for classifying colleges and universities in the United States. The framework primarily serves educational and research purposes, where it is often important to identify groups of roughly comparable institutions. Used as a framework for recognizing and describing institutional diversity in US higher education for the past four and a half decades, it has been widely employed in the study of higher education, both as a way to represent and control for institutional differences and also in the design of research studies to ensure adequate representation of sampled institutions, students, or faculty. By selecting and tracking peer institutions on selected benchmarks, Carnegie classification data assists enrollment professionals and the administration in understanding how their institutions compare to peers on strategic enrollment indicators.

4. Tai Phan, Laura Hardesty, Jamie Hug, and Cindy Sheckells, *Academic Libraries: 2010: First Look* (NECES 2012-365) (Washington, DC: US Department of Education, National Center for Education Statistics, 2011), 11, https://nces.ed.gov/pubs2012/2012365.pdf.

5. For more information, please see "Collecting Levels," *Library of Congress*, n.d., https://www.loc.gov/acq/devpol/cpc.html.

6. A nonprofit organization of 124 research libraries in the United States and Canada that share similar research missions, aspirations, and achievements. For more information, please see "About," *Association of Research Libraries*, n.d., http://www.arl.org/about.

7. G. Edward Evans and Margaret Zarnosky Saponaro, *Collection Management Basics*, 6th ed. (Oxford: Libraries Unlimited, 2012), 103–30.

8. Edward A. Goedeken and Karen Lawson, "The Past, Present, and Future of Demand Driven Acquisitions in Academic Libraries," *College and Research Libraries*, preprint, accepted March 28, 2014, http://crl.acrl.org/content/early/2014/03/31/crl14-579.short.

9. Brian Lavoie, Constance Malpas, and J. D. Shipengrover, *Print Management at "Megascale": A Regional Perspective on Print Book Collections in North America* (Dublin, OH: OCLC Research, 2012), http://www.oclc.org/research/publications/library/2012/2012-05.pdf.

10. I examine internal factors in the next part of this chapter.

11. Bibliometrics is the statistical analysis of bibliographic data, commonly focusing on citation analysis of research outputs and publications; that is, how many times research outputs and publications are being cited. Bibliometric analysis is becoming an increasingly important way to measure and assess research impact of individuals, groups of individuals, or institutions.

12. Research profiling is an analysis method based on bibliometrics and text extraction tools, and it is used to broadly scan the contextual literature information with the objective of depicting the research context and research efforts.

13. Kristi Palmer, "New Models of Scholarship and Publishing," *ACRL Scholarly Communication Toolkit*, October 15, 2010, last updated September 16, 2015, http://acrl.ala.org/scholcomm/?page_id=19.

14. Jennifer Rutner and Roger C. Schonfeld, *Supporting the Changing Research Practices of Historians* (New York: Ithaka S+R, 2012), http://sr.ithaka.org/?p=22532.

15. Rick Anderson, "Can't Buy Us Love: The Declining Importance of Library Books and the Rising Importance of Special Collections," *Ithaka S+R* (August 1, 2013), http://sr.ithaka.org/?p=24613.

16. Martha Kyrillidou, Shaneka Morris, and Gary Roebuck, eds., *ARL Statistics 2013–2014* (Washington, DC: Association of Research Libraries, 2015), http://publications.arl.org/ARL-Statistics-2013-2014.

17. Glenn S. McGuigan and Robert D. Russell, "The Business of Academic Publishing: A Strategic Analysis of the Academic Journal Publishing Industry and Its Impact on the Future of Scholarly Publishing," *E-JASL: The Electronic Journal of Academic and Special Librarianship* 9, no. 3 (Winter 2008), http://southernlibrarianship.icaap.org/content/v09n03/mcguigan_g01.html.

18. "Serials Price Projections for 2015," *EBSCO*, September 25, 2014, https://www.ebscohost.com/promoMaterials/Serials_Price_Projections_for_2015.pdf.

19. "European Book Publishing Statistics 2014," *Federation of European Publishers*, November 13, 2015, https://www.fep-fee.eu/European-Book-Publishing-741.

20. Unpublished internal report distributed internally among BorrowDirect institutions in 2015. Cited in Sarah Thomas, "A Library and Collections in the 21st Century: Widener Library, the Materials Budget, and Monographic Acquisitions," internal report distributed at FAS Standing Committee on the Harvard Library, Thursday, December 10, 2015, Widener Library, Harvard University.
21. "BorrowDirect is an unmediated library resource sharing partnership encompassing twelve Ivies Plus academic institutions supplying over 250,000 books, music scores, and other returnable library items per year. BorrowDirect went live in the fall of 1999 after a four-year planning and development period during which the three founding institutions, Columbia University, the University of Pennsylvania, and Yale University, partnered with the Research Libraries Group (RLG) for project management and assessment. The BorrowDirect Partnership expanded to seven member libraries in 2002 with the addition of Brown University, Cornell University, Dartmouth College, and Princeton University. In 2004, the Partnership exceeded 100,000 transactions for the first time. The Partnership grew to include Harvard University and MIT in 2011. BorrowDirect added one library a year starting in 2013 with the University of Chicago followed by Johns Hopkins University and Duke University." For more information, see *BorrowDirect*, n.d., http://www.borrowdirect.org.
22. Unpublished internal report distributed internally among BorrowDirect institutions in 2015. Cited in Thomas, "Library and Collections."
23. For instance, this is still the case at Harvard University.
24. For more information about such shared print initiatives, please see, "Shared Print Repositories Fact Sheet," *Association of Research Libraries*, April 29, 2015, 1–7, http://www.arl.org/storage/documents/mm15sp_SharedPrint_FactSheet.pdf; Lorcan Dempsey, "The Emergence of the Collective Collection: Analyzing Aggregate Print Library Holdings," *OCLC Research*, December 2013, http://www.oclc.org/content/dam/research/publications/library/2013/2013-09intro.pdf; Lorcan Dempsey, Brian Lavoie, and Constance Malpas, with Lynn Silipigni Connaway, Roger C. Schonfeld, J. D. Shipengrover, and Günter Waibel, *Understanding the Collective Collection: Towards a System-wide Perspective on Library Print Collections* (Dublin, OH: OCLC Research, 2013), http://www.oclc.org/content/dam/research/publications/library/2013/2013-09.pdf.
25. As is the current practice via ILL or regional collection delivery networks, such as BorrowDirect.
26. Caren Milloy, Graham Stone, and Ellen Collins, "OAPEN-UK: An Open Access Business Model for Scholarly Monographs in the Humanities and Social Sciences," in *Social Shaping of Digital Publishing: Exploring the Interplay between Culture and Technology—Proceedings of the 16th International Conference on Electronic Publishing* (Amsterdam: IOS Press, 2012), n.p., http://elpub.scix.net/data/works/att/105_elpub2012.content.pdf.
27. See Lorcan Dempsey, "The Facilitated Collection," *Lorcan Dempsey's Weblog* (blog), January 31, 2016, http://orweblog.oclc.org/towards-the-facilitated-collection.
28. For instance, Google Scholar, arXiv, SSRN, RePEc, and PubMed Central (disciplinary repositories that have become important discovery hubs); Mendeley, Citavi, and ResearchGate (services for social discovery and scholarly reputation management); and Galaxy Zoo, figshare, and OpenRefine (data storage and manipulation tools).
29. Lorcan Dempsey, Constance Malpas, and Brian Lavoie, "Collection Directions: The Evolution of Library Collections and Collecting," *portal: Libraries and the Academy* 14, no. 3 (July 2014): 393–423, http://muse.jhu.edu/journals/portal_libraries_and_the_academy/summary/v014/14.3.dempsey.html.

Bibliography

Anderson, Rick. "Can't Buy Us Love: The Declining Importance of Library Books and the Rising Importance of Special Collections." *Ithaka S+R*. August 1, 2013. http://sr.ithaka.org/?p=24613.

Courant, Paul N., Charles Henry, Geneva Henry, Matthew "Buzzy" Nielsen, Roger C. Schonfeld, Kathlin Smith, and Lisa Spiro. *The Idea of Order: Transforming Research Collections for 21st Century Scholarship*. Washington, DC: Council on Library and Information Resources, 2010. http://www.clir.org/pubs/reports/pub147/pub147.pdf.

Dempsey, Lorcan. "The Emergence of the Collective Collection: Analyzing Aggregate Print Library Holdings." *OCLC Research*. December 2013. http://www.oclc.org/content/dam/research/publications/library/2013/2013-09intro.pdf.

———. "The Facilitated Collection." *Lorcan Dempsey's Weblog* (blog). January 31, 2016. http://orweblog.oclc.org/towards-the-facilitated-collection.

———. "Libraries and the Informational Future: Some Notes." *Information Services and Use* 32, no. 3 (2012): 203–14.

Dempsey, Lorcan, Brian Lavoie, and Constance Malpas, with Lynn Silipigni Connaway, Roger C. Schonfeld, J. D. Shipengrover, and Günter Waibel. *Understanding the Collective Collection: Towards a System-wide Perspective on Library Print Collections*. Dublin, OH: OCLC Research, 2013. http://www.oclc.org/content/dam/research/publications/library/2013/2013-09.pdf.

Dempsey, Lorcan, Constance Malpas, and Brian Lavoie. "Collection Directions: The Evolution of Library Collections and Collecting." *portal: Libraries and the Academy* 14, no. 3 (July 2014): 393–423. http://muse.jhu.edu/journals/portal_libraries_and_the_academy/summary/v014/14.3.dempsey.html.

"European Book Publishing Statistics 2014." *Federation of European Publishers*. November 13, 2015. https://www.fep-fee.eu/European-Book-Publishing-741.

Goedeken, Edward A., and Karen Lawson. "The Past, Present, and Future of Demand Driven Acquisitions in Academic Libraries." *College and Research Libraries*. Preprint. Accepted March 28, 2014. http://crl.acrl.org/content/early/2014/03/31/crl14-579.short.

"Guidelines for University Library Services to Undergraduate Students." *Association of College and Research Libraries*. 2013. http://www.ala.org/ala/mgrps/divs/acrl/standards/ulsundergraduate.cfm.

Kyrillidou, Martha, Shaneka Morris, and Gary Roebuck, eds. *ARL Statistics 2013–2014*. Washington, DC: Association of Research Libraries, 2015. http://publications.arl.org/ARL-Statistics-2013-2014.

McGuigan, Glenn S., and Robert D. Russell. "The Business of Academic Publishing: A Strategic Analysis of the Academic Journal Publishing Industry and Its Impact on the Future of Scholarly Publishing." *E-JASL: The Electronic Journal of Academic and Special Librarianship* 9, no. 3 (Winter 2008). http://southernlibrarianship.icaap.org/content/v09n03/mcguigan_g01.html.

Milloy, Caren, Graham Stone, and Ellen Collins. "OAPEN-UK: An Open Access Business Model for Scholarly Monographs in the Humanities and Social Sciences." In *Social Shaping of Digital Publishing: Exploring the Interplay between Culture and Technology—Proceedings of the 16th International Conference on Electronic Publishing*. Amsterdam: IOS Press, 2012. http://elpub.scix.net/data/works/att/105_elpub2012.content.pdf.

Lavoie, Brian, Eric Childress, Ricky Erway, Ixchel Faniel, Constance Malpas, Jennifer Schaffner, and Titia van der Werf. *The Evolving Scholarly Record*. Dublin, OH: OCLC Research, 2014. http://www.oclc.org/research/publications/library/2014/oclcresearch-evolving-scholarly-record-2014-overview.html.

Lavoie, Brian, Constance Malpas, and J. D. Shipengrover. *Print Management at "Megascale": A Regional Perspective on Print Book Collections in North America*. Dublin, OH: OCLC Research, 2012. http://www.oclc.org/research/publications/library/2012/2012-05.pdf.

Palmer, Kristi. "New Models of Scholarship and Publishing." *ACRL Scholarly Communication Toolkit*. October 15, 2010. Last updated September 16, 2015. http://acrl.ala.org/scholcomm/?page_id=19.

Phan, Tai, Laura Hardesty, Jamie Hug, and Cindy Sheckells. *Academic Libraries: 2010: First Look* (NECES 2012-365). Washington, DC: US Department of Education, National Center for Education Statistics, 2011. https://nces.ed.gov/pubs2012/2012365.pdf.

Rutner, Jennifer, and Roger C. Schonfeld. *Supporting the Changing Research Practices of Historians.* New York: Ithaka S+R, 2012. http://sr.ithaka.org/?p=22532.

"Serials Price Projections for 2015." *EBSCO.* September 25, 2014. https://www.ebscohost.com/promo Materials/Serials_Price_Projections_for_2015.pdf.

"Shared Print Repositories Fact Sheet." *Association of Research Libraries.* April 29, 2015. http://www.arl .org/storage/documents/mm15sp_SharedPrint_FactSheet.pdf.

8

Challenges Facing Technical Services

Autumn Faulkner

Introduction

Predicting the future can be a tricky business. Research and reading can support intelligent guesses, but as a well-respected clairvoyant[1] once said, "Books can take you only so far in the field" (Rowling 1999, p. 103). This is the precarious position in which technical services librarians now find ourselves—peering into a foggy crystal ball, trying to discern the exact shape of forthcoming changes, and wondering if we have the means to prepare for them.

The units within academic libraries traditionally known as technical services can vary widely between institutions: Some might only include the usual acquisitions and cataloging functions, while others may encompass database maintenance, circulation, collection development, copyright and licensing, digitization, interlibrary services, remote storage management, and more (Davis 2016). But those in the field generally agree that a technical services unit, whether given the conventional name or a more updated label, assumes primary responsibility for the many layers of processing that library resources require before they can be made available to patrons.

This work takes many forms. In small libraries, one or two (heroic) people might be responsible for ordering, cataloging, and labeling all the print books, as well as negotiating licenses for e-resource packages, loading batches of accompanying records, and tweaking displays in the public catalog. At big universities with large collections budgets, a technical services unit might have a team of people for each separate step on the processing path—purchasing, receiving, copy and original cataloging (retrieval or creation of catalog records for the database and for online display), authority work (retrieval or creation of established forms of names, topics, places, etc., and cross-references between variant forms), batch processing (making updates or revisions to many catalog or authority records at once), database maintenance, physical processing, and so on. In libraries with special collections units, technical services assists at least with the more special ordering procedures that are often necessary for rare or unusual items, and although some special collections staff do their own cataloging because it requires knowledge of conventions for describing archival or rare books, at other times, technical services might provide traditional cataloging for special collections resources.

Although the specifics are still in flux, we know that *all* of these types of tasks will undergo a sea change in the near future. Right now, all catalog and authority records that contain standardized and encoded description of our library resources (bibliographic data, or metadata, as it is often called) are stored in a sadly outdated format called MARC (MAchine Readable Cataloging). But as the Internet slowly evolves from a web of documents into a web of links—an evolution commonly referred to as the semantic web—we also expect bibliographic data to make the long-awaited leap out of our MARC silo and into the web, where search engines, applications, and any number of software programs can ingest, manipulate, and display it. This transition is long overdue and, if managed even partially successfully, will represent a big step forward for the discoverability of our resources and the presence of libraries in the public consciousness.

But the transition will also present steep challenges for every academic library, from community colleges to research institutions. Larger libraries will be tasked with converting their millions of records. Smaller libraries will have fewer records to transform, but they may struggle to find time and resources for training and implementation. We know we will have to learn to use new systems, adapt to new roles, and leave some comfortable conventions behind, but that is about all we know! Because the standards designed to carry us into this new era are still in flux, and because we have no dependable indication that library systems are being prepared for this transition, we cannot devise a surefire way to plan for the future. Instead, technical services librarians must keep a weather eye on the horizon during the next few years, researching and blueprinting for several possible scenarios while still finding ways to work efficiently with today's systems and standards. A comprehensive listing of every potential outcome may not be realistic, but I am a cataloger, after all. How can I resist the attempt? Let's examine three crucial areas of technical services work and the forces that may transform them in the near future.

Acquiring Library Resources

Acquisitions librarians have already seen a good deal of change in recent years, brought about by the shift in library collections from print to electronic resources. The advances in technology that have caused this shift have also allowed some improvements to the logistical work of purchasing library materials, including more efficient online ordering processes as well as collection development tools like more highly automated and customized approval plans (vendor-facilitated purchasing of resources such that items that fit a given library's collecting profile are automatically sent to the library; these plans have been implemented for about forty years) and demand-driven acquisitions (DDA, also referred to as patron-driven acquisitions, or PDA, the principle of which is waiting to purchase an item until a patron specifically requests it).

The increasing disruption in traditional publishing models and the call for open access resources could also change the landscape of acquisitions. Right now, if scholars wish to publish their research (and they do because publication is usually essential to attain tenure), they generally must do so in periodicals that charge very high subscription fees. Because scholarly literature lies at the heart of all academic library services, we are obliged to pay dearly for individual journal titles, packages of journals, and subscriptions to third-party databases like JSTOR or Web of Science that permit access to the indexed content of hundreds of academic journals. But demand for more equitable channels of publication and access is growing in the scholarly community. If we are lucky, journal articles will not always be extravagantly priced and hoarded in giant databases or behind high subscription paywalls; as publishing models change, so will collections budgets and the way we spend them.

What remains unchanged, however, is the eternal need for robust searching, tracking, and record-keeping. Right now, we accomplish all of this using modules or functions that are built into the same library systems we use for storing catalog data, managing circulation, running queries on the database, and so on. The biggest library systems on the market right now are those produced by Innovative Interfaces, Ex Libris, and SirsiDynex,[2] and most academic libraries are using the acquisitions functions of one of these systems as the primary tool for managing their purchasing work flows.

The upcoming transition to a semantic-web-friendly approach to describing library resources, though long anticipated, has not been thoroughly road-mapped. BIBFRAME, the Library of Congress's proposed replacement for MARC, has been developed and discussed enough to give technical services professionals some idea of how cataloging will change, even if BIBFRAME does not become the wholly embraced successor to MARC that many catalogers expect. But every function of the conventional vendor-supplied library system revolves around our MARC database—purchasing, labeling and barcoding, circulation, inventory, reporting, indexing, and public display. BIBFRAME, or any similar replacement to MARC that may emerge, is just one piece of the puzzle, and it is only a structured vocabulary after all, not a system. The move out of MARC will render our current platforms obsolete, but there is no clear picture yet of what will replace them.

Something must. So much of the acquisitions ordering process is intertwined with the catalog database: searching the library's holdings, generating order records to track fund use, bringing in placeholder bibliographic records to prevent duplicate orders,[3] recording payments once the item has been received, and more. Academic libraries' unique and complex logistical needs require a custom management tool. Our systems have been meticulously designed to accommodate and index fields that store financial data like fund codes (indicators—usually abbreviated names or strings of numbers—of the specific collections monies to be used for purchasing materials) and order numbers. If these functions disappeared tomorrow, then library purchasing would grind to a rather apocalyptic halt. Large or small, academic libraries are entrusted with a significant portion of an institution's funds, which are intended to support the research of our universities' faculty and students. A library's failure to adequately track and responsibly spend those funds could land it in academic and possibly even legal hot water.

Although we know that we have to leave our MARC-based systems, we do not know if future systems will be interdependent with a BIBFRAME database in the same way. First of all, leaving MARC also means leaving behind the idea of the bibliographic "record." The focus of cataloging will no longer be on describing one resource at a time; instead, the philosophy behind the semantic web's web of links (or linked data, to use the more popular term) is to create unique identifiers for entities, like works and their creators, and trace the relationships between them in a structured way. Catalogers will establish many nodes of data and build a network of connections between them rather than create individual records comprising mostly text strings.

This means the structure and functionality of our local databases will change on a fundamental level. For many years, individual catalog records were stored in a flat file and could be queried using the familiar Boolean logic we all learned in our college library orientations. In recent years, many libraries have moved their MARC data into relational databases, using query languages like SQL to manage them. To accommodate the move out of MARC, however, we will need to change yet again to a database structure called a triple store, which is built using an open data model called Resource Description Framework (RDF) and can be queried with languages like SPARQL. Although triple store database products are emerging in the commercial world ("List of Subject-Predicate-Object Databases"), no all-in-one management platforms have been developed yet that can accommodate a library's needs, and there's no certainty right now that they ever will be. There has been little activity or discussion among library vendors to indicate that such products are even being considered for development.

But given the differences between these types of databases in terms of structure and language, is it even realistic to expect that the same kind of interchange between ordering and bibliographic data could be achieved? The BIBFRAME vocabulary itself is not designed to accommodate the information like cost, fund codes, vendor codes, and date ordered, that we usually include in order records in our current systems, nor should it be. BIBFRAME is only concerned with the description of bibliographic entities and their attributes. Ordering and paying for resources is a completely separate and completely local work flow that we cannot expect to be included in any of the metadata schemas designed for cataloging (*metadata* is a term that describes data about data and is often used by catalogers to refer to bibliographic data; a *schema* is a set of rules for a certain type of metadata).

The second consideration for systems of the future is the growing complexity of acquisitions work. The management of electronic resources, for instance, has quickly become a thorny problem for academic libraries. Traditional methods of purchasing do not apply to packages of e-books, which must be leased and licensed instead. Finding efficient ways to track whether these materials have annual subscriptions, pay-per-use fees, or licensing restrictions that may affect patron access has become rather nightmarishly complicated (Walters 2013). These pain points are augmented by the remarkable volatility of e-book offerings. Items available in certain packages last year may disappear from our holdings this year, leaving behind outdated bibliographic records with dead links.

In addition, recent movements toward open access for scholarly resources indicate possible shake-ups in the publishing world. The entire industry of costly academic journals and proprietary article databases is a bubble that some experts expect will pop very soon.[4] In the future we may have entirely new work flows for acquiring peer-reviewed journals.

Given these rapidly developing areas of resource management along with the possible barriers to incorporating purchasing functions into the as-yet-unrealized platforms of the future, it may be that an acquisitions module stuck like a barnacle to the catalog database is no longer a realistic solution. Could any such module be robust enough to accommodate the wide range of purchasing work flows that academic libraries are increasingly obliged to maintain? Perhaps the advent of the post-MARC environment will force the splintering apart of the functions of the traditional library system. Perhaps we will use separate products and platforms for each.

This may not be as disruptive as it sounds. The MARC format is only readable and actionable (i.e., able to be processed and manipulated) by a few specially designed products, but once our data is housed in an open schema, it will be accessible to any application a developer can dream up. Even if we have different platforms for different functions, the whole point of semantic web technology is to allow such platforms to talk to each other with ease and efficiency. Perhaps library vendors will develop software clients that keep our acquisitions and circulation work flows private and local, while also being able to read and speak to the public-facing bibliographic data we put on the web. Or perhaps libraries will be obliged to create such products themselves. High-quality open-source solutions seem to be a much more realistic (if somewhat daunting) prospect in this future world of open data.

Of course, that magical world will never materialize until we finally free our catalog data from MARC. We are on our way, but we still have a long road ahead.

Describing Library Resources

For library resources to be discoverable, they must be described in consistent ways, and then that description must be encoded, or "marked up." This allows indexing and display in computer applications. For the better part of four decades, the Anglo-American Cataloging Rules, second edition (AACR2), and MAchine Readable Cataloging (MARC) were the cataloger's bedrock guides for description and encoding. AACR2 gave instructions for identifying and describing important elements in a resource, such as author, title, format, imprint, dimensions, and extent; MARC structured those AACR2-derived descriptions in a format that permitted library systems to interpret and display them. See figure 8.1 for an illustration of how these and other commonly used cataloging standards interoperate.

MARC was created in the '60s. Yes, the *1960s*. Back when the civil rights movement had reached its height and NASA was aiming for the moon and lots of people apparently wore really nice suits and drank cocktails every day and computer programming was still largely relegated to women (Henn 2014). Sponsored by the Library of Congress, built by a team of programmers led by Henriette Avram, and implemented on a historically enormous scale, MARC proved to be a brilliant solution for library automation needs (Avram 2003).

Autumn Faulkner

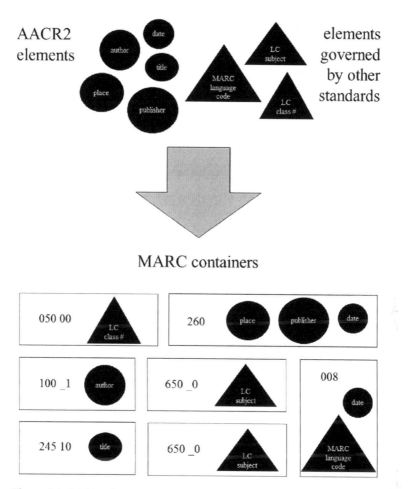

Figure 8.1 AACR2 elements, elements governed by other standards, and MARC containers

But today, when information does not really count unless it is actionable on the web, MARC has long outlived its usefulness. It might be best to think of MARC as a sort of ancestor of XML—a way of sticking bits of data into containers so they can be stored and shared. Those containers all have labels on them, with smaller containers within the large ones. An application built to read MARC knows how to store, use, and display those containers. But of course, the problem now is that only a handful of library applications designed by vendors like Innovative or Ex Libris can read MARC. No web technologies know or care about MARC containers. It is a completely arcane format. It was once the key that set our data free, yet it has become the prison that keeps millions of catalog records from joining the rest of the information world.

How is it possible that libraries still do not have their data on the web? We are well in to the twenty-first century already. Almost any information that would be free in print is also freely available on the web. A Google search can help me find out how many Elizabeths were christened in Canterbury in the 1500s,[5] but it cannot help me find a baby name book in my local library.

Although we are woefully behind, catalogers really are working on this. In 2013, most major academic libraries adopted the replacement for AACR2, called Resource Description and Access (RDA).

This is a descriptive standard like AACR2, but it was designed with several new principles in mind that will help us to move into a linked data environment.

The first of these principles is that we should be working from a well-drawn map of the bibliographic universe, much like the periodic table is a well-drawn map of the chemical universe. Every chemical element is there, defined and arranged in a logical, connected way. This arrangement supports scientists in their practical work with chemistry—it allows them to name and refer to and make use of all the substances listed there.

The Functional Requirements for Bibliographic Records (FRBR) along with their companion FRAD (Functional Requirements for Authority Data, usually just lumped in with FRBR in cataloging discussions) are mappings in the same spirit—a conceptual framework that attempts to name and place every entity in the "universe of discourse" (Riva and Žumer 2015, 4) and define the relationships between them. This conceptual framework forms the bones of RDA, as it were. It is behind all the instructions RDA gives us for describing resources.

The FRBR concepts are abstract and can be rather bewilderingly esoteric on first exploration, so I do not go into them in any depth here. Suffice it to say that FRBR tells us, for example, what a work is, how we can identify the creator of that work, and how that work may be expressed in a number of versions. For example, *Harry Potter and the Sorcerer's Stone* is a work. Its creator is J. K. Rowling, and it has been expressed as a book in English published by Arthur Levine in 1998. It has also been expressed as a book in Russian, translated by Matsuoka Yuko and published by Seizansha, and as an audiobook in English narrated by Jim Dale and released in 1999 by Listening Library. J. K. Rowling is the creator of all of these various expressions of her work, but each different version also involves other people whose noncreator roles should be defined and accounted for in bibliographic description: translator, publisher, narrator, and so on. FRBR gives us language and structure for identifying all these entities and the relationships between them.

Despite its initial abstruseness, FRBR makes sense as a foundation for bibliographic description. Libraries are entrusted with describing the entire "universe of discourse" for our patrons, so it is crucial for us to think about the types of resources that exist, which roles various agents play, how relationships between resources and agents should be defined and described, and so on. The ultimate goal of FRBR, after all, is to guide users to the information they want. The more we map out the universe of resources, the more our patrons can travel between works or formats or people, disambiguating between similar resources and discovering related works.

The second principle behind the formation of RDA is inclusiveness and extensibility. While AACR2 was a primarily monograph-focused standard with a notable bias toward Anglo-American descriptive language, RDA attempts to provide flexible guidelines that may be applied to a variety of formats in a variety of language environments.

In our current library work, we are dealing with electronic resources and Blu-Rays and streaming media and print items and kits for makerspaces. Who can predict which new media technologies will emerge in ten or twenty years, with resulting formats that libraries will want to collect? It is important that we have a descriptive standard that leaves room for new entities and relationships that will need to be described down the road.

For three years, academic libraries have been adjusting to the adoption of RDA. This has involved extensive changes to the routine practice of cataloging, including both the fundamental way we are asked to define different types of resources as well as the MARC coding used in describing those resources. We have found that MARC limits what we can accomplish with new areas and types of description called for by RDA, and we are also frustrated that our current systems impose even further constraints by failing to take full advantage of new RDA terms and fields.

The fact that FRBR will soon be thoroughly overhauled will surely be another source of upheaval. The group behind this proposed revision, called FRBR-LRM (Library Reference Model), believes that FRBR's definitions of entities needed some further refining to accurately reflect today's information world. They also wish to incorporate related but separate models FRAD and FRSAD (Functional Requirements for Subject Authority Data) into one unified model (Riva and Žumer 2015). There has been little formal response to the new FRBR-LRM model at the time of this writing, but it is bound to cause some discontent in the cataloging community because changes to FRBR will necessarily mean changes to RDA, our day-to-day cataloging instructions. No one will be thrilled when some of the new practices we have striven to implement start shifting ground beneath us.

Working with one eye constantly on the future, knowing that some work we are doing now may be undone by future updates, is not always satisfying. But we also know that some of the data we are creating now will be very meaningful one day. We trust that RDA will make a lot more sense to us and be a lot more effective for discovery when it does not have to be clumsily implemented through MARC. Although there have been and will be plenty of complaints at each new step, ultimately we are moving in the right direction. The philosophy behind these changes indicates an ever-growing concern with and an increasing intelligence about the needs of patrons, who can be better served by more explicit tracing of relationships between resources. As those of us who frequently fall down the Wikipedia rabbit hole can attest, more and more of our online discovery is guided by traveling links between related concepts and entities. RDA is the first step toward creating a catalog that can offer a similar experience.

Additionally, growing acclimated to a limbo state has some unintended benefits. Longstanding in-jokes in our field poke fun at catalogers for being finicky, rigid rule-followers who cannot see the forest for the trees. We are not as bad as all that, but stereotypes aside, it is true that the precise nature of cataloging work can make us steer away from risk-taking and messiness. But now ripples of excitement and exploration are disrupting the surface of our field. There's room now for experimentation and new ideas. As we learn more about the possibilities of the semantic web, we are realizing that the bibliographic data we have lovingly curated for so long has a chance to reach its full potential. We are also realizing that the semantic web can be an avenue for uniting traditional catalog data with the other types of metadata libraries use, like Dublin Core (often used to describe digital collections) and Encoded Archival Description (EAD, used to describe archival collections). The idea of the semantic web was proposed by Sir Tim Berners-Lee and outlined in a 2006 paper discussing the need to move from a web of documents to a web of links (Shadbolt, Hall, and Berners-Lee 2006). Although there have been some dissenting opinions,[6] expert communities generally agree that the semantic web will become the next iteration of the web as we know it.

It is easy to get very technical very fast when talking about the semantic web, but for the present purpose, we only need a high-level understanding of a content model called Resource Description Framework (RDF, not to be confused with RDA, described earlier) and the concept of linked data. Right now, the web is mostly constructed of textual and graphic information that has been encoded (or marked up) with HTML—that is, a series of instructions that tell the computer how to render that information so it can be accessible and human-readable online. Aside from the HTML markup, there is nothing on a web page that a machine can truly understand or use. RDF and linked data will change that. By encoding all of our data in structured ways and in a certain arrangement, we can actually create networked paths that allow machines to read and thereby act on the information we are putting on the web.

Here is how it works. Let's say we want to make a simple statement: "Charlotte Bronte wrote *Jane Eyre*." A normal HTML resource would only go this far with encoding:

```
<p>Charlotte Brontë wrote Jane Eyre.</p>
```

The <p> tag tells the browser how to display that string of text. But in a linked data environment, strings of text are verboten. Instead, each distinct element of this statement would be marked up with tags and linked to a Uniform Resource Identifier (URI), which functions as a unique web address and machine-readable definition of that element. It is easy to imagine URIs for Charlotte Brontë and *Jane Eyre*; those are both familiar types of entities that librarians deal with all the time and for which we are accustomed to creating authorized forms (the established versions of names, works, and concepts). But the truly revolutionary part of this structure is the URI representing the actual *relationship* between Charlotte Brontë and *Jane Eyre*: the relationship of author to work. By using the subject→predicate→object triple structure that RDF outlines and supporting each of those pieces with a URI, we can actually teach machines to recognize the connections between entities. Here's what that might look like:

> <subject:URI for Charlotte Brontë>
> <predicate:URI for author-work relationship>
> <object:URI for *Jane Eyre*>

Just think of the constellations of data waiting to be linked together! Applications reading these nodes of data could zip from URI to URI to read related statements, like "*Jane Eyre* was adapted as a 2006 miniseries" and "The 2006 miniseries starred Ruth Wilson" and "Ruth Wilson is a cast member in the BBC show *Luther*" and so on. That is the vision of the semantic web: a vast network of links, all expressed in organized URIs that connect them in machine-readable ways.

Even my cataloger powers will not allow me to enumerate all the positive changes such an environment would bring, but I can think of several that I feel hopeful about with regard to libraries. Consistent, flexible metadata means much more powerful and efficient batch processing for technical services. Such work is starting to dominate our work flows, and we are growing weary of correcting thousands of poor-quality e-book records, which have often been automatically generated in huge batches and lack proper coding and description. But there may also come a time when mass creation and maintenance of bibliographic description for all library materials becomes the norm. We need better standards and interoperability to produce high-quality data.

Even more exciting, though, is the prospect of unprecedented discovery for patrons. RDF's smaller bytes of encoded data will allow for much more robust indexing and searching on *any* attribute of a resource. We will also be able to reveal so many more relationships between resources, like *West Side Story* as an adaptation of *Romeo and Juliet* or the link between John Keats's poem "On First Looking into Chapman's Homer" and its repeated quotations in P. G. Wodehouse's Jeeves and Wooster novels. Imagine the sheer power of such search capabilities!

FRBR and RDA give us two of the three components we need to move into a semantic web environment: names for entities and the relationships between them and instructions for describing those entities and relationships, respectively. The last component we need is a way to encode our descriptions that permits semantic "reading" by computers. Right now, the front-runner for this replacement to MARC is called the Bibliographic Framework (BIBFRAME). This is a vocabulary that can work within XML and is structured according to RDF principles.

BIBFRAME was designed by a consulting firm hired by the Library of Congress and is currently undergoing final testing and revision by its catalogers. The arrangement of BIBFRAME's vocabulary will be crucial in the future, so many others from the cataloging community have had the opportunity to supply feedback and suggest changes. Finally, the Library of Congress has also developed a homegrown editor that will help catalogers create descriptions of resources in BIBFRAME, much like OCLC's desktop software called Connexion now provides an interface for creating and editing MARC records (McCallum 2016).

Although it is generally (though not unanimously) agreed to be the designated replacement for MARC, BIBFRAME is not really like MARC. Rather, it is a way of giving names to the bibliographic data elements we are interested in recording and organizing. Those named data elements and their URIs can then be stored in XML containers and arranged into RDF triples—all of which will permit applica-

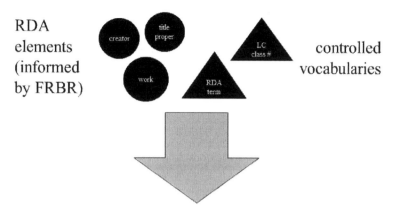

RDA
elements
(informed
by FRBR)

controlled
vocabularies

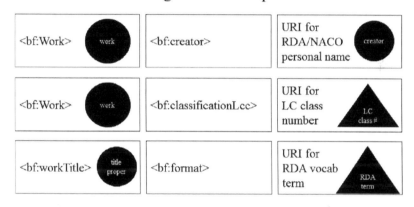

XML containers with BIBFRAME* names
arranged in RDF triples

*all BIBFRAME elements are supported by URIs as well

Figure 8.2 RDA elements, controlled vocabularies, and XML containers with
BIBFRAME names arranged in RDF triples

tions to understand and act on statements about the resource in question. Much alphabet soup here, but see figure 8.2 for a diagram of how all these standards fit together.

XML is not the only way to store and share BIBFRAME data. Other notations can also be used to render and arrange RDF triples, including the Turtle syntax and Notation3.[7] But because a growing number of cataloging and metadata professionals have been turning to XML for various MARC data transformation projects, I anticipate that XML/RDF will be the most accessible way for libraries to create and work with BIBFRAME data, at least at first.

Given that you as a reader have just survived a very condensed crash course in future bibliographic data standards, it will be easy for you to understand how moving from MARC to this new environment sometimes feels like an enormous cognitive leap. Plenty of seasoned catalogers will be no more likely to feel at home with these layers of specifications and standards than any library school student. For many of us, the demands of daily cataloging work prevent us from pursuing extensive reading in these new areas, and for most of us, early experimentation to gain hands-on experience is unrealistic.

Despite the fact that the work of catalogers is always mediated by software that produces the necessary raw code in the background, the more technical aspects discussed here cannot remain a total mystery to us if we are going to be effective in our descriptions of bibliographic resources, especially those of us who will be increasingly responsible for batch processing and large-scale data transformation. And unfortunately, it appears that we will be shouldering the combined weight of FRBR-LRM, an updated RDA, and BIBFRAME almost simultaneously. This could prove rather overwhelming for catalogers who have spent most of their careers working in the MARC environment and for libraries whose technical services units do not have the time or staff or resources to implement such sweeping changes all at once.

But in the end, by hook or by crook, we must take this cognitive leap. Our users are looking for information on the web, and we have to meet them there.

Improving Discoverability of Library Resources

Why is the vision of the semantic web so important? Are libraries really wise to pursue this dreamed-of future when we cannot be certain how it will come about? I believe so, for two reasons: serendipity and accessibility. In our print collections, libraries use classification by subject to create a serendipitous shelf-browsing experience for patrons. You may come to that shelf looking for one known title, but you are likely to discover other titles by the same author, or additional works on the topic you are interested in. We have all had this experience in public libraries especially; maybe you look up a book about Norse mythology because you really enjoyed Marvel's *Thor* and you wonder how much of that Asgard stuff people actually used to believe. On the same shelf, you find some books on Russian and Egyptian and African mythologies as well, and you decide to take them all home because you are pretty excited about the upcoming adaptation of Neil Gaiman's *American Gods* and you would like to get all your gods and goddesses straight before it airs. You did not know you wanted those books; they just happened across your path. That is serendipity. This joyful experience of curiosity and discovery is, in my opinion, one of the best parts of being human, and supporting that experience is the privilege and core mission of libraries everywhere.

The structure of the semantic web—all those URIs linked together in RDF statements, as we saw earlier—permits us to recreate this serendipitous experience for online searching. We can draw paths between works and people and topics and places, allowing users to follow a trail of links as far as their interest and energy can carry them. Serendipity may seem like an odd concept when applied to academic libraries. After all, some of us might argue, our mission is to support serious research and learning, not recreational reading or idle curiosity. I would vehemently counterargue that these things are not mutually exclusive, but it is true that academic libraries must make the former a priority and hope the latter comes about as a natural byproduct. But even those of us who believe academic libraries should be research-oriented only should be able to see that serendipity can be just as useful in an academic setting; why should we expect users to think of every possible keyword term that might apply to their topic of interest and then perform a search on each? Instead, we should be forming a network of structured connections that lead our patrons to the resources they don't know they need—the relevant but unknown topics, the indirectly related adaptions or reframings, the tenuously connected studies done by different institutions at different times.

Let's also examine the accessibility of our resources compared with other information available on the web. Right now we expect users to come to our library websites and learn how to navigate multiple search interfaces to find our resources—interfaces that do not behave like the web. Neither article databases nor the classic catalog nor recently developed discovery layer products that attempt to unite the two (like Primo, Summon, and WorldCat Discovery) can offer anything like normal web browsing.

The classic catalog does have some hyperlinks in it, but if you click one, it does not do what you expect from a link. For instance, if you click a link for *Sacagawea* in a record in the Michigan State University Libraries' catalog, you are not taken immediately to information about the Shoshone woman without whom the Lewis and Clark expedition would have failed. You are just directed to a "where" in our gigantic record database—a list of headings for *Sacagawea* and other nearby headings in alphabetical order. You have to click again on the heading you are interested in to see a list of resources. This is very disorienting. Web users expect a "what" at the end of their hyperlinks, not a "where."

Discovery layers have been developed by library system vendors in an attempt to unite some of our silos of information. To a certain extent, they can map to MARC data and some other metadata schemas (like EAD and Dublin Core), allowing libraries to include local digital or archival collections, article databases, and the catalog in one search box. These products do come a bit closer to the mark in terms of native web behavior but not close enough. This is less because of a flaw in their design and more a result of the fact that none of our collections data are encoded in ways that make a weblike experience possible. Too many elements of bibliographic description are not consistently structured or actionable as facets or limiters, meaning that searches are not as powerful or as intuitive as they should be.

It is already unforgivable that we are not on the web, but the sad fact is that we cannot even offer a passable imitation! Many academic librarians work hard developing effective instruction for library users so they know how to find our resources, and that is valuable work, but should we have to focus so much of that instruction on the array of systems that hold our resources? Wouldn't it be great if, instead, all of our resources—electronic and print, born digital and archival, physical or streaming— were united into one harmonized search? Then our instruction librarians could focus on helping users to develop their research skills rather than providing technical support for various clunky interfaces.

The semantic web could help us to accomplish this. It would not matter that some of our materials come from different content providers or repositories. Once we make our bibliographic descriptions web-ready and build or acquire systems that can query RDF data, the possibilities for interoperability are essentially endless. Ultimately, we could offer our users one single entry point for all of our materials and give them far more powerful tools than we have now for quickly isolating the subset of resources they seek.

Of course, we face some challenges in realizing this new era of discoverability. Building the network of connections the semantic web requires means catalogers will be spending far more time creating and curating URIs for entities on both local and national levels. As the world of information continues to expand exponentially, creating linked data to represent all the entities and concepts it contains sounds like a Herculean undertaking. It seems likely that many conventional cataloging roles and tasks will eventually disappear, to be replaced by this work and its ancillary responsibilities.

And although catalogers have always been committed to neutrality in their description of resources, our code of ethics needs fleshing out to fit the work we will be doing in the near future. Creating an authorized form for a name or a concept means making certain decisions about that entity. Is it really our responsibility to record the gender of an author, for instance? By doing so, are we not making an assumption and speaking on that person's behalf without his or her consent? The same concerns could apply to establishing the identity of places or the definitions of concepts or movements or political positions.

Another concern about this brave new world, and one that all web communities share, centers on privacy. Library vendors have begun to offer cloud-based solutions (software and data housed on remote servers instead of being downloaded to a library's local servers and individual computers) to their customers, in keeping with trends in the commercial sector. Thus, it should be only a matter of time before academic libraries begin contemplating the merits of hosting their enormous databases remotely rather than locally, especially within the linked data environment of the future. Bibliographic description will become much more hefty and robust, which means databases will need to be correspondingly huge. But relying on the cloud entails obvious risks. Possible data loss constitutes just the first of those risks; others include security breaches, malicious use, and corruption.

All these concerns will be compounded by the fact that library vendors may never come up to scratch in terms of moving out of the MARC environment. Open-source platforms seem more and more attractive as we contemplate the challenges of the future and the numerous needs unique to academic libraries. Perhaps we would do better to develop our own systems? But if so, then we must address concerns about storage and security even more rigorously and change technical services roles even more drastically by adding software development and maintenance responsibilities to them. Smaller libraries with fewer resources must find ways to ensure they are not left behind.

Libraries will need to tread cautiously as cloud-based and open-source systems become more and more common, but I think the possible benefits of both of these types of platforms far outweigh the risks. The ability to move, manipulate, and customize our data with ease will be essential to discovery in the future, and I would prefer that libraries relied on their own expertise to build the appropriate systems. Open-source systems especially would act as an equalizer, allowing institutions of any size to participate in the post-MARC environment and preventing some library patrons from being denied access to features that other, larger schools can offer.

Conclusion

In the end, all of the investigation into and planning for the possible scenarios discussed here will come to naught if we do not pay attention to how our patrons use the web for nonlibrary needs. How are commercial resources being published, discovered, and consumed? How are people finding and using information in their daily lives?

Libraries today increasingly invest in assessment of their services and interfaces, but historically, we have always remained behind the curve, and we just do not have the resources for the kind of research and development that would tell us exactly what the world needs from us. You know who does? Google, Apple, Amazon, and all the other giants of Internet technology. Libraries should pay close attention to their innovations. After all, libraries' survival depends on meeting users where they are and anticipating where they might wish to go.

We need to imitate Google and others like it. We should stop expecting patrons to learn the idiosyncratic systems and search behaviors of academic libraries and librarians. Our mission should not only be to make information available but also to deliver it in intuitive, web-informed ways. Otherwise, I fear all the naysayers will have been right all along, and libraries will drift into a sad irrelevance. This is not to say that we need to change our methods to fit every new trend, but cherishing traditional arrangements and expecting patrons to respect them seems foolish.

Over the next decade, technical services librarians will need to balance healthy caution with enthusiastic experimentation. The semantic web environment has been long in coming, and perhaps it may never arrive or at least not in the form we expect. But our only option is to try to prepare for it anyway; at least we will be taking steps to leave our current silos behind and will be that much more prepared to transform our data into whatever web-ready form it finally needs to assume.

Discussion Questions

1. What do you think is the most important aspect of the management of electronic resources? Pricing? Licensing? Record quality and discovery? To which problem should libraries give top priority?
2. In recent years, the library system industry has seen a good deal of consolidation. At this point, there are only a handful of viable vendors to provide libraries with the platforms they need. What do you see as the dangers of this lack of options? Are there corresponding benefits?
3. Cataloging and metadata professionals are working hard to advance their field using the principles of the as-yet-unrealized semantic web. But what if the commercial sector of the web ultimately takes a different course and the semantic web as it has been predicted never materializes? Based on current trends, does that seem likely? How concerned should libraries be about this possibility?

4. Libraries are increasingly investing in assessment of their services and interfaces. Which aspects of user discovery should we focus on to make our time and resources really count, especially when anticipating a linked data environment?
5. As a user, what would you like to see in a future library discovery system?

Assignment

Conduct a survey of currently available vendor-designed library systems like Sierra, Alma, and Symphony, as well as the growing number of open-source solutions like KualiOLE. Consult librarytechnology.org for a complete listing of major vendors. As far as possible, investigate and summarize the features of these platforms that accommodate acquisitions functions, electronic resource management, and public-facing discovery. Finally, choose the platform that appears to be most prepared for a smooth transition to the post-MARC environment, and explain your choice.

Notes

1. Professor Sybill Trelawney.
2. Marshall Breeding of librarytechnology.org maintains an informative annual listing and report on vendors in the library automation field: Marshall Breeding, "Perceptions 2015: An International Survey of Library Automation," *Library Technology Guides*, January 31, 2016, http://librarytechnology.org/perceptions/2015.
3. When a library resource is ordered, a placeholder catalog record is either brought in or hand-keyed for that resource, even though the library has not received the item yet. This is done to alert any patrons searching for the item that it will be available shortly.
4. For numerous arguments and perspectives, see *Create Change*, 2016, http://www.createchange.org/index.shtml.
5. Familysearch.org results obtained in under one minute: *Family Search*, 2016, https://goo.gl/b5isqL.
6. For a very candid and somewhat profane example, see ManuSporny, "JSON-LD and Why I Hate the Semantic Web," *Beautiful, Tormented Machine*, January 21, 2014, http://manu.sporny.org/2014/json-ld-origins-2.
7. For examples of N3/Turtle, see "Edition Statement—Property," *BIBFRAME.org*, n.d., http://bibframe.org/vocab/edition.html.

Bibliography

Avram, Henriette D. "Machine-Readable Cataloging (MARC) Program." In *Encyclopedia of Library and Information Sciences.* 2nd ed. Edited by Miriam A. Drake. 4 vols. 3: 1712–30. New York: Marcel Dekker, 2003. doi:10.1081/E-ELIS 120008993.

Davis, Jeehyun Yun. "Transforming Technical Services: Evolving Functions in Large Research University Libraries." *Library Resources and Technical Services* 60, no. 1 (2016): 52–65. http://dx.doi.org/10.5860/lrts.60n1.52.

Henn, Steve. "When Women Stopped Coding." *NPR Planet Money.* October 21, 2014. http://www.npr.org/sections/money/2014/10/21/357629765/when-women-stopped-coding.

"List of Subject-Predicate-Object Databases." *Wikipedia: The Free Encyclopedia.* https://en.wikipedia.org/wiki/List_of_subject-predicate-object_databases.

"List View, BIBFRAME Vocabulary." *BIBFRAME.org*. http://bibframe.org/vocab-list.

McCallum, Sally. "Update on BIBFRAME Vocabulary Development." Powerpoint presentation given at BIBFRAME Update Forum, ALA midwinter 2016. Boston: Network Development and MARC Standards Office, Library of Congress.

Riva, Pat, and Maja Žumer. "Introducing the FRBR Library Reference Model." Paper presented at the IFLA World Library and Information Congress, Cape Town, South Africa, August 2015. http://library.ifla.org/1084/1/207-riva-en.pdf.

Rowling, J. K. *Harry Potter and the Prisoner of Azkaban.* New York: Arthur A. Levine Books, 1999.

Shadbolt, Nigel, Wendy Hall, and Tim Berners-Lee. "The Semantic Web Revisited." *IEEE Intelligent Systems* 21, no. 3 (2006): 96–101. http://eprints.soton.ac.uk/262614/1/Semantic_Web_Revisted.pdf.

Walters, William H. "E-books in Academic Libraries: Challenges for Acquisition and Collection Management." *portal: Libraries and the Academy* 13, no. 2 (2013): 187–211.

Abbreviations

- AACR2: Anglo-American Cataloging Rules, second edition
- BIBFRAME: Bibliographic Framework
- FRBR: Functional Requirements of Bibliographic Records
- FRBR-LRM: Functional Requirements of Bibliographic Records, Library Reference Model
- MARC: MAchine Readable Cataloging
- RDA: Resource Description and Access
- RDF: Resource Description Framework
- URI: Uniform Resource Identifier
- XML: eXtensible Markup Language

9

Librarians and Services in College and Community College Libraries

Zoe Fisher and Kim Read

Introduction

College and community college libraries play a crucial role in providing resources and instruction for many different types of students, including working parents, high school diploma-seekers, traditional full-time undergraduates, and graduate students. Librarians working in these institutions enjoy unique responsibilities and opportunities but also face unique challenges. In contrast to university librarians, college and community college librarians are committed to a broader array of tasks and a wider scope of focus in their work.

In this chapter, we focus on distinguishing instruction, policies, and services at college and community college libraries from libraries at large research universities. We compare the roles of instruction librarians, staff, and student workers, and we also examine different structures of governance and organizational models. Academic libraries face many common issues, including the debate over whether librarians should be granted faculty status, student learning assessment, information literacy program coordination, patron privacy, collection development, and budgeting; accordingly, we discuss how these topics are addressed in college and community college libraries.

Definition of College Libraries

The term *college libraries* usually refers to libraries in smaller colleges and universities that offer a four-year degree, including liberal arts colleges. These libraries can be distinguished from those in larger universities by the smaller number of students enrolled and the lack of emphasis on supporting a large number of graduate-level researchers. While many smaller colleges and universities have graduate programs, they focus on meeting the needs of undergraduate students. Community colleges offer associate's degrees for students intending to transfer to a four-year institution as well as certificates and degrees in professional and technical programs for students who are preparing to enter the workforce. In some ways, small college libraries share more in common with their university counterparts than with community college libraries. In those areas, we distinguish community college libraries by calling them out specifically. Otherwise, in this chapter, we use the phrase *college libraries* to refer to college and community college libraries together.

Purpose of College Libraries

College libraries serve the research and information needs of faculty, staff, and students at their institutions. Policies, programs, services, and collections of the college library align with the overall goals and aims of the institution. College libraries typically provide specialized collections and services to support the different academic, professional, and technical programs offered. For example, a college with an early childhood education program would include picture books in its library collection to support the curriculum for teachers, while a college with a nursing program might circulate kits of plastic bones to students in anatomy and physiology classes.

The college library also provides support to faculty, most of whom are focused on teaching rather than conducting their own research, and to staff and administrators who may use the library to access materials for personal or professional use. Community college libraries often play a special role in providing services and resources to community patrons who may be unaffiliated with the college.

All college libraries share a strong focus on the undergraduate experience and developing information competency. For many students, the college library will be the first place they encounter subscription databases, find books in a catalog, and write citations to support academic work. It may also be the first place that students encounter critical and theoretical frameworks for the production, dissemination, and use of information. Librarians interested in critical pedagogy use library instruction to discuss the intersections of power, domination, oppression, and information literacy. In a popular monthly Twitter chat about critical librarianship (#critlib), past discussion topics have included anti-oppressive facilitation strategies, information services for incarcerated people, emotional labor, and digital preservation.

Roles of Librarians, Staff, and Student Workers

Librarians provide instruction in the library, both at service desks (typically called the reference desk, ask desk, or help desk) and in sessions provided to an entire class. In community college libraries, instruction focuses on preparing students for transfer and using libraries at universities or preparing students to use information in their future careers as nurses, dental hygienists, automotive mechanics, and chefs. Depending on the size of the library and the number of librarians, some librarians may specialize in particular areas, such as electronic resources or distance learning. However, college librarians consider themselves generalists and work with a variety of students in many different contexts.

In large research libraries, especially at institutions with graduate students studying library and information science, it is common practice to employ student workers to answer basic reference questions, while librarians make themselves available on call for more in-depth research consultations. Librarians at college libraries spend most of their time working with students directly as needed rather than make appointments with them. Student workers in college libraries most often provide circulation services. In some cases, there may be specific contracts in place that prevent librarians from doing classified staff work and vice versa. Classified staff, also known as paraprofessionals, are paid hourly wages and provide crucial services, including interlibrary loan, circulation, and copy cataloging and other technical services. Other staff positions may include so-called exempt employees, who are paid annual salaries and whose duties might include managing, supervising, and overseeing library operations.

Organizational Models and Governance Structures

There are a wide variety of organizational models and governance structures across academic libraries. Generally speaking, large university libraries are stand-alone organizations with many departments and complex reporting structures. They may even have their own foundations, endowments, and designated "Friends of the Library" nonprofit groups. By contrast, college libraries are much smaller and exist within the organizational structures of their institutions. In most colleges and community colleges, libraries have a dean or director who reports to an instructional division and administrator (e.g., the vice president of instruction or the dean of academic affairs) or a student affairs administrator (e.g., the vice president of student affairs or the dean of academic support services). Some librarians stress the importance of reporting to an instructional division so that they can be involved in faculty conversations concerning pedagogy, curriculum, course planning, and educational resources. At other institutions, libraries are viewed as an auxiliary support service for students. Libraries are expected to coordinate with other service areas, such as advising, tutoring, technology help, and student life programming, in colleges where libraries are part of student affairs. Within the college library, departments are generally divided into education and outreach activities (management of databases and the library website, information literacy instruction, the reference desk, collection development) and technical services (circulation, interlibrary loan, acquisitions processing, facilities management).

Faculty Status for Librarians

Both within and outside librarianship, academics have long debated the relevance, benefits, and drawbacks of faculty status for librarians. Some argue that librarians do not have training and education equivalent to teaching faculty in other disciplines. This point of view is strongest in university and four-year college library settings, where most faculty hold doctoral degrees. The opposing view argues that the master of library science should be considered a terminal degree in the same way the master of fine arts is a terminal degree for faculty who teach such subjects as creative writing.

In community colleges, members of the teaching faculty usually hold master's degrees in their fields; some faculty possess doctoral degrees, but most do not. Depending on the culture of the institution, librarians might be seen as peers at community colleges because they have the same level of formal education as other faculty (i.e., a master's degree) or even a higher level: Some teaching faculty in adult basic education or high school completion programs may have only bachelor's degrees.

At most institutions, teaching faculty (or "discipline faculty") see themselves primarily as teachers and researchers. These faculty hold many different views of academic librarians. Some faculty outside the library consider librarians' duties to be more administrative than pedagogical, and they approach librarians accordingly.

The definition of *teaching* is central to the question of whether librarians should be considered faculty. Some librarians teach courses for credit, but many only teach individual sessions for other courses as guest lecturers; these sessions are often referred to as one-shot instruction sessions or "one-shots" for short. Librarians also provide information literacy instruction in a variety of other ways that are not paralleled in other disciplines. For example, librarians provide one-on-one instruction in person, over the phone, or via online chat. They create virtual learning tutorials and online research guides. Some librarians may even be embedded in courses, physically or online, so they can be available to groups of students throughout the semester. Some have questioned the extent to which these activities should be deemed comparable to other faculty's teaching duties.

Those in favor of faculty status for librarians argue that other faculty members are more likely to respect faculty librarians and see them as peers. Other advantages of faculty status include

- participation in college governance and inclusion on faculty campus committees,
- faculty salary and benefits (including sabbatical and professional development opportunities),
- tenure and promotion equal to other faculty, and
- academic freedom and safety from censorship.

Academic freedom provides protection from job loss or discipline, and it applies to scholarship; teaching; and, for librarians, collection development. When librarians are granted faculty status, they generally must fulfill the same or equivalent requirements as others with faculty status, including instruction, scholarship (professional publications and conference presentations), and other conditions for tenure or faculty appointment. With this expectation comes support for research, publishing, and attending conferences that may exceed the support given to nonfaculty librarians.

For those who oppose faculty status for librarians (including many librarians working in academic libraries), the reasons are myriad. As mentioned previously, some do not believe that librarians can effectively meet the qualifications of tenured faculty, while others reject the contention that information literacy should be considered its own discipline. Many librarians feel grateful to be able to focus on their work without worrying about "proving" that they are the same as faculty; in fact, many librarians take pride in distinguishing the work they do as complex, interdisciplinary, and multifaceted—in contrast to expectations of traditional faculty roles. For librarians in nonteaching roles, such as technical services librarians, faculty status may be a hindrance rather than a help to their work. Other librarians report that being outside the realm of faculty allows them to work across departments more effectively without being bogged down by institutional politics.

Patron Privacy

College librarians maintain a commitment to the ethics of the profession, including a sensitivity to patron privacy. The value of patron privacy is challenged in different ways in academic settings. For example, it is common for an instructor to assign the same material to an entire course, which results in a glut of students at the library trying to share resources. A frustrated student who is unable to access the item because someone else has it checked out will ask, "Who has it?" Unfortunately, the library cannot provide this information, even if it would be practical in assisting students in completing their work.

The nature of academic librarianship also lends itself to bending patron privacy in ways that may strike readers as awkward or unfamiliar at first. At the reference desk, many academic librarians ask students how they intend to use the information (e.g., Is this for a research paper? A group presentation?). This is a reasonable question in the course of a reference interview, but public librarians are generally more sensitive in questioning how information will be used. (For example, an eighteen-year-old woman asking for information about abortion in a public library would probably have a different experience than an eighteen-year-old woman asking for information about abortion in a college library.) The librarian may also ask the student for details about the assignment and the course, including the name of the instructor. This might seem intrusive, but it can be necessary for academic librarians to monitor trends at the reference desk in order to provide better instructional experiences. If several of Professor Cooper's students come to the library asking how to find scholarly articles, the instruction librarian might contact the instructor and offer to conduct a session for the entire class.

Assessment

College libraries come under constant pressure to measure and evaluate their performance. Yet the energy and attention devoted to assessment varies by institution. At some colleges and community colleges, assessment may refer only to the work of measuring student learning outcomes in information literacy instruction. In other contexts, assessment programs might measure outcomes across the library as a whole, including circulation, technical services, and website usability. Accreditation standards require that libraries evaluate their programs and services to ensure that students' needs are met. College libraries gather assessment data in a variety of ways. Gate counts (how many people enter the facilities), circulation counts (how many items are browsed or borrowed), the number and kind of questions answered at the reference desk, and the number of instruction sessions offered are common types of quantitative data collected. College libraries also measure their effectiveness through surveys, focus groups, and comment cards. To evaluate the efficacy of information literacy programs, some college libraries use standard pre- and posttests for entering and exiting students.

Librarians also collect assessment data from instruction sessions and reference desk transactions by asking students to reflect on what they have learned. In some cases, librarians may partner with teaching faculty in evaluating completed assignments (research papers, annotated bibliographies, presentations, etc.) to determine the degree of information competency each student demonstrates. Assessment data can be used internally to improve programs and services. It may also be used externally to demonstrate the need for funding for library faculty, staff, facilities, and resources, as well as to prove that accreditation standards have been met. Some libraries are experimenting with collecting student data to tie library use to individual student outcomes. However, there remain concerns that collecting student data constitutes a violation of patron privacy.

New Technologies

Librarians in all types of libraries must keep up to date with new technologies. This involves staying informed about the latest devices, software, apps, and systems. Certain types of technology are particularly important to libraries, such as integrated library system (ILS) software, discovery and delivery systems, and content management systems. An ILS allows libraries to store and retrieve data related to their assets: acquisitions, cataloging, patron records, and such features as circulation analytics. Discovery and delivery systems control the functionality of library catalogs and databases and consequently how users search for and find library resources. Content management systems (CMS), such as Drupal and WordPress, are used to create, publish, and maintain a web presence. While some libraries have a dedicated librarian who designs, develops, and maintains the library website, college libraries without a librarian in this specialized role often depend on many librarians to possess the skills needed to update and manage their websites.

At some institutions, much of this web work is now done by IT or marketing departments. Yet library staff and teaching faculty do not always welcome such external control of the library website. In some college libraries, librarians need to assert their knowledge of web technologies because non-library faculty and staff may not realize how tech-savvy librarians really are. In other words, many on campus may not know that their colleagues in the library have been trained to design, develop, and maintain websites. Still others may not understand how important the library's web presence can be to student instruction.

Many college libraries choose to use LibGuides as the web platform for some or much of their library presence. LibGuides is a content management system and one in a suite of products developed by the company Springshare. Librarians use LibGuides to create tailored research guides for a variety of instructional topics, including disciplines, courses, subject matter, and specific information literacy skills. LibGuides facilitates the creation of web pages by providing easy-to-use templates specifically designed for libraries. In this way, LibGuides is a convenient "out-of-the-box" CMS. Some libraries with limited resources use LibGuides for their entire websites even though LibGuides cannot be customized to the same degree as other CMS options, including Drupal and WordPress.

In addition to websites, because of their focus on instruction, college librarians pay particular attention to other technology developments that affect pedagogy and assessment. As distance education grows and a significant amount of librarians' reference assistance and instruction is provided online, librarians are wise to keep abreast of eLearning technologies. According to the National Center for Education Statistics, 4.6 million undergraduate students took at least one online course in fall 2012, with almost half of these students taking online courses exclusively.[1] In the same time period, 867,000 graduate students took at least one online course, and 639,000 of those students took only online courses.[2] Those graduate students engaged exclusively in distance education represent 22 percent of all graduate students in 2012.[3] Some of the technologies that affect librarians' instruction include learning management systems, such as Canvas and Blackboard; digital tools, such as Articulate Storyline and Adobe Captivate for creating online tutorials that can be embedded in web pages; screen capture and screencasting tools, such as Jing for contributing images and brief video snapshots to virtual reference interactions; and online tools that support real-time virtual interactions, such as instant messaging "chat" software like LibraryH3lp, video and group chat like Skype and Google Hangouts, and web conferencing tools like GoToMeeting and WebEx.

Finally, digital repositories, also referred to as institutional repositories, constitute an important part of libraries' curatorial responsibilities, and technological advances affect this component of librarianship as well. Faculty and students use digital repositories to store and share their research, publications, projects, and papers and make them accessible online. They are also used to provide wider accessibility to items stored in a college's physical archive, such as historical photos. Because they archive local content, digital repositories reflect the scholarship and culture of a college and therefore contribute to a college's identity. Students, faculty, and other researchers also use digital repositories as a discovery tool to find and access the university's scholarly and cultural output. The content in digital repositories is varied. Content will differ in each library. Articles, books, images, maps, data sets, dissertations and theses, audio files, and videos are some of the types of resources that are managed and discoverable in a digital repository. Not all libraries have digital repositories, though, and as is the case with other library services, budgetary and staffing constraints can prevent smaller college libraries from establishing an institutional repository. If a college library does have an institutional repository, then budgets will again determine whether a single librarian must develop and maintain it or whether others share the responsibility.

Some college libraries have taken their scholarly communications endeavors one step further by developing publishing services. Similar to institutional repositories, publishing programs at colleges often reflect local interests and faculty teaching and learning curricula. While smaller libraries generally do not enjoy the level of funding available to university libraries for publishing services, this model of publishing may be more attractive to faculty in community colleges, where publishing requirements for tenure can be less demanding.

Libraries today see an increasing demand for their resources and services to be accessible through mobile platforms so that students can complete assignments using tablets, e-readers, and smartphones. Large research institutions have greater resources than smaller colleges and community colleges have to devote to supporting mobile access for students. As a result, many colleges and community colleges struggle to meet the needs of students who work exclusively on mobile devices. Students with more money have more devices and therefore more options for accessing resources and preparing their assignments: They can often choose between a desktop computer, a laptop, a tablet, and a phone. The others must complete all of their academic work on their phones or use campus resources because they lack access to adequate technology at home.

Policies

College library policies reflect the culture of the institution and the needs of the faculty, staff, and students. Policies cover a range of activities, from circulation and borrowing to collection development and facilities access and use. In these areas, libraries in small colleges and universities may share more in common with research university libraries than with community college libraries. With regard to access, most college libraries have some open stacks as well as policies for guests, including allowing visitors to use certain computers, browse the catalog, access databases, and use study spaces. Unlike college and research libraries, community colleges do not typically offer alumni borrowing privileges; instead, community users can purchase a library card on an annual basis. Community users tend to have greater access to community college libraries, and it is common for community college libraries to fulfill some of the functions of a public library, such as helping users with nonacademic information needs, navigating community and social welfare resources, and even registering as a new student at that institution. Community college library policies also tend to be more accommodating of students who juggle the responsibilities of family, work, and school. For example, some academic libraries do not allow any users under the age of fifteen (even when accompanied by an adult), while community college libraries may allow students to bring children with them as long as they are not disruptive. Because community colleges serve more diverse populations with different needs, they are more likely to have flexible and broad policies than college and research libraries.

OER

Open educational resources (OER) consist of such educational materials as textbooks, course packs, images, and other resources that are freely available and licensed to be remixed and shared. OER reduce educational costs for students, and their customizability allows instructors to design course materials specifically for a particular course. Librarians at all different types and sizes of academic libraries support OER in different ways, from collaborating with faculty on finding and selecting appropriate resources to administering programs that encourage the transition to OER as a replacement for costly textbooks.

While it is desirable to reduce costs for students at all types of colleges and universities, librarians in community colleges are particularly sensitive to working with less affluent students. Many students choose community colleges for their affordability. Textbooks that cost one hundred to two hundred dollars each are often prohibitively expensive for typical community college enrollees. In some areas, community college librarians participate in alliances to support OER in their institutions, such as Open Oregon and Open Washington. In these statewide organizations, community colleges share resources, including licensing and copyright guidelines, OER discovery tools, and the personal experiences of faculty who have developed or used OER.

Some faculty look to the library to provide required resources for their students. While libraries support the curriculum by purchasing relevant books, films, and databases for all students to use, they cannot purchase required texts for specific classes. Some instructors express frustration when the library refuses to purchase an expensive required text. Faculty who prefer to use traditional textbooks have the option of bringing an instructor's desk copy to the library to be placed on reserve, but reserve items rarely suffice for students who need to use a text regularly throughout the term. This issue has become increasingly complex as more faculty use online resources, including streaming films, because vendors intentionally make these resources difficult to catalog for broad access. Therefore, digital items with limited access (such as streaming films embedded in a learning management system) are analogous to expensive texts that can only be used by a small group of students, and libraries are unlikely to fund these resources.

Collection Development

Because smaller colleges often have limited numbers of graduate students and community colleges have no upper division or graduate students, collections place a greater emphasis on teaching and learning, while in larger universities, collections need to support advanced research as well. Alongside large research university libraries, college libraries are likely to be members of consortia that affect collection development practices. These reciprocal relationships have been fostered to increase efficiency, reduce costs, and widen access to resources. Collection development in community college libraries may also be similar to collection development in public libraries. Some students in community colleges may have lower-level reading skills and may need fiction options, such as young adult literature, for both assignments and pleasure reading. Many community colleges also offer courses for high school students. For this reason, their libraries may acquire popular young adult titles as well as academic resources suited to high school students.

In large research universities, public service librarians typically specialize in a single subject area, such as business or education. In smaller college libraries, the librarians often serve as liaisons for multiple subjects and consequently must collect resources for all of these. Some librarians might consider handling a variety of subject areas to be more interesting than handling just one. Others might prefer to dedicate their knowledge and collection development time to a single discipline, so it might be frustrating for them to have to divide their collection development efforts. Community college librarians often feel the heaviest burden of collection development. At small community colleges, all collection development decisions (acquisitions, weeding, policy changes, etc.) may be handled by just one or two librarians who provide all of the reference and instruction for the institution as well. Many college librarians have difficulty finding time for collection development given so many competing priorities.

Budgeting

Many factors influence a college library budget, including but not limited to institutional culture, funding sources and requirements, and whether an institution is public or private. Personnel and collections costs comprise the bulk of academic library budgets. Library administrators in all types of libraries need finance and management skills in order to make decisions about the library's budget. Staff and faculty librarians outside of library administration have varying degrees of involvement in budget management and accountability. Many smaller college libraries struggle to keep up with the increasing cost of subscription resources. Some college libraries have made the strategic decision to limit print acquisitions and focus their budgets on maintaining online resources. This is especially important for online learners and community college students, many of whom are not able to come to campus to use physical resources and rely heavily on online articles and e-books.

Conclusion

College libraries share many goals and services with libraries at large research universities. However, college libraries must meet the needs of diverse student populations, an increasing demand for open education resources, and the pressure to measure the library's impact—all with fewer resources and smaller departments than university libraries. Working at a college library can be fast-paced and dynamic, and it is a job best suited to librarians who are energized by problem-solving; close relationships with their coworkers; and interacting with students from diverse cultural, social, and economic backgrounds.

Discussion Questions

1. Do you see yourself working in a college or community college library some day? Why or why not? Which roles in these libraries are most and least appealing to you, based on their unique characteristics?
2. College and community college libraries serve diverse populations of students. How can library policies meet the needs of diverse populations? In what ways are libraries limited in their ability to meet students' needs?
3. What makes information literacy unique in colleges and community colleges, compared to other educational settings (high schools, large research universities, etc.)? How are the information literacy needs of students different now than they were ten years ago?
4. Is faculty status important to you? Do you aspire to a position as a librarian with faculty status? Why or why not?
5. Do you think that librarians in colleges and community colleges face more or fewer challenges than other librarians (e.g., public, special, etc.)? Why do you think that?
6. Based on what you read in this chapter, how do you anticipate college and community college libraries will change in the next few years? What should these libraries do now to prepare for those changes?

Assignments

Assignment A

Join the Community and Junior College Libraries Section LISTSERV or the INFOLIT (Information Literacy) LISTSERV (both available through the American Library Association website), and through the recent archives or through reading current discussions, find a hot topic being debated by members of the LISTSERV. Write a thorough summary of the issue being discussed, drawing special attention to the responses and contributions of librarians from community college and four-year college libraries. What are the different points of view expressed? What was the consensus reached, if any? Provide your own perspective on the topic as well.

Assignment B

Contact a librarian at a community college or small four-year college in your area for a brief informational interview, either by phone or in person. (E-mail is not recommended for this assignment.) In your interview, ask the librarian:

1. How did you become a librarian at your institution? From your perspective, what are some major differences between your role and the role of librarians at other major academic institutions in the area?
2. What are some of the most pressing issues facing your library today? If possible, can you share how you and your colleagues are approaching these issues?
3. Which courses or experiences in graduate school best prepared you for your role today?
4. Add one to two prepared questions of your choosing.

Write a detailed summary of the interview, including the librarian's responses and your reaction to what you learned. What was new or surprising for you? What will you do differently based on what you learned?

Notes

1. National Center for Education Statistics, *The Condition of Education 2014*, NCES 2014-083 (Washington, DC: US Department of Education, 2014), 62, http://files.eric.ed.gov/fulltext/ED545122.pdf.
2. Ibid., 67.
3. Ibid.

Suggestions for Further Reading

Accardi, Maria, Emily Drabinski, and Alana Kumbier. *Critical Library Instruction: Theories and Methods.* Duluth, MN: Library Juice Press, 2010.

Bailey, Thomas R., Shanna Smith Jaggers, and Davis Jenkins. *Redesigning America's Community Colleges.* Cambridge, MA: Harvard University Press, 2015.

Bonn, Maria, and Mike Furlough. *Getting the Word Out: Academic Libraries as Scholarly Publishers.* Chicago: Association of College and Research Libraries, 2015.

Coker, Catherine, Wyoma vanDuinkerken, and Stephen Bales. "Seeking Full Citizenship: A Defense of Tenure Faculty Status for Librarians." *College and Research Libraries* 71, no. 5 (2010): 406-20. doi:10.5860/crl-54r1.

Galbraith, Quinn, Melissa Garrison, and Whitney Hales. "Perceptions of Faculty Status among Academic Librarians." *College and Research Libraries.* Preprint, accepted October 13, 2015. http://crl.acrl.org/content/early/2015/11/05/crl15-825.full.pdf.

Turner, Christine N. "E-Resource Acquisitions in Academia Library Consortia." *Library Resources and Technical Services* 58, no. 1 (2014): 33–48. doi:10.5860/lrts.58n1.33.

Bibliography

National Center for Education Statistics. *The Condition of Education 2011*. NCES 2014-083. Washington, DC: U.S. Department of Education, 2014. http://files.eric.ed.gov/fulltext/ED545122.pdf.

Part III

Changing Priorities, New Directions

This section opens with Marta Brunner and Jennifer Osorio's chapter discussing the recruitment, retention, and supervision of academic library staff, especially appropriate educational requirements for professional and paraprofessional employees and the need for greater emphasis on diversity, mentorship, and professional development. They emphasize that previously standard academic librarian positions, such as many cataloger jobs, are quickly evolving into metadata librarian positions requiring expertise in a wide range of standards and schemas. Similarly, they note that outreach librarian positions have evolved into embedded librarian positions, such as research informationist or data management librarian. In short, calls for computer skills in job postings and descriptions increase with each passing year. And given that the profession remains overwhelmingly white and female, they observe a need for greater demographic heterogeneity to make librarian diversity more closely mirror that of the general population, "not just in terms of race, ethnicity, gender, and sexual orientation, but also in terms of work and communication styles." Brunner and Osorio also discuss the changing balance between librarian work and paraprofessional work, with more and more tasks formerly assigned to librarians now performed by library assistants, and the conflict this can create, especially in a union environment and in the context of the "sensitive question of the value of the terminal library degree." Related to this, they observe a trend toward greater educational attainments among librarians of all kinds, required or not, because the job market has become so competitive in recent years.

Then comes David W. Lewis's chapter on physical and virtual library spatial design. Lewis details how rethinking and reconfiguring library spaces, such as the learning commons and smart classrooms, actually and potentially affect teaching, learning, and research today and in the future. Lewis begins his chapter by noting that many academic libraries still in use today date from the second half of the twentieth century and some from before World War II, and he provides a brief history of "why these buildings were designed as they were and what goals the architects and librarians who planned them sought to accomplish." He proceeds to discuss the challenges librarians and architects face as they design and redesign library spaces, particularly the need for the flexibility to reconfigure and repurpose spaces and services as faculty and students' teaching, learning, and research priorities evolve over time and affect the perceived importance of large legacy print collections (with their concomitant high maintenance costs and safety issues) in these spaces. Along the way, he illustrates various solutions that new academic library buildings in the United States, such as the James B. Hunt Jr. Library at North Carolina State University, have offered and explores their relative strengths. Lewis concludes with a discussion of the most pressing issues we need to consider when planning new libraries or renovating existing ones.

Debbie Faires's chapter on serving both campus and remote users acknowledges the increasing need to accommodate people where they are, including students learning online who may be on campus or hundreds or thousands of miles away and the faculty who seek to reach them in technologically sophisticated ways. After defining and distinguishing the concepts of *distance education* and *online learning*, Faires observes that distance education enrollments continue to rise to the point that this form of education must now be considered mainstream. Moreover, she adduces evidence to demonstrate that online learning can be just as effective as face-to-face education, if not more so, for both subject-based courses and research education or information literacy classes. In fact, a majority of chief academic officers surveyed whose colleges and universities provide online learning have agreed that this mode of education has become crucial to the long-term strategy of their institutions. Faires then explores the phenomenon of massive open online courses (MOOCs), which entered the educational world between 2008 and 2013 and continue to attract enrollees at a steady pace. After explaining what MOOCs are and how they work, she details some of the issues currently facing institutions who wish to offer such courses, including difficulties of offering access to licensed databases, e-books, and e-journals for students unaffiliated with the college or university sponsoring the course and possible ways in which librarians might effectively assist such large numbers of enrollees with the help of technology.

In the next chapter, Brian Owen focuses on the newest means of access to and security of scholarship and raw data: open access, institutional repositories (IRs), e-science and digital curation (including digital humanities, or DH), and digital preservation. Opening with a brief history of the transformative technological innovations academic libraries and their collections and services witnessed beginning in the 1970s, Owen then takes us to the first decade of the twenty-first century, when, as he explains, libraries began inventing their own in-house solutions to technological problems that commercial vendors were slow to address. He describes how, simultaneously, regional and national library consortia emerged in an effort to combat the skyrocketing costs of scholarly materials, noting that soon "these consortia were largely responsible for flipping the content subscription model from a print to a digitally based one and substituting library-created model licenses for vendor-provided ones." Next comes a discussion of the recent open access (OA) movement, which, as Owen states, entails not only free public access to scholarly articles and related content but also "open source software, open data, open educational resources (OER), open government, and a still-growing array of 'open' concepts." Libraries continue to face many challenges surrounding OA publishing, the most fundamental of which is how to evolve a business model to sustain it. Owen observes, "Article processing charges (APCs), whereby the author pays a fee to have his or her article published and openly available immediately, are quickly gaining ascendancy." Yet because these fees can be prohibitively expensive for both individuals and institutions, we now see a growing interest in exploring a non-APC model for OA publications that will better serve the producers and purchasers of scholarship. Owen then proceeds to introduce IRs and efforts to create local digital collections in college and university libraries that IRs can store and make accessible, with caveats about potential copyright violations and suggestions for how to avoid them. This leads to an exploration of some libraries' recent efforts to publish their own journals. Owen concludes his chapter with a discussion of research and development in academic libraries, addressing current initiatives in DH and E-science, in which faculty and librarians across the disciplines employ their complementary knowledge and technical skills to collaborate on projects and produce entirely new forms of scholarship.

Nisa Bakkalbasi's chapter on assessment, promotion, and marketing of academic libraries acknowledges the need for these libraries to be accountable to their stakeholders in measurable ways as never before. She addresses key concepts, best practices, and tools in an effort to "help students develop critical thinking skills in identifying the appropriate uses of methods and tools essential to undertaking a rigorous assessment project." Central to her theme is the importance of developing a so-called culture of assessment within academic libraries in order to keep them relevant to their users. Simply put, this means creating an environment in which we base our decisions on hard evidence: facts, research, and analysis. She concludes with an exploration of promotion and marketing, arguing that "in order to establish and maintain a culture of assessment, assessment, evaluation, promotion, and marketing activities must join forces" and that "library services cannot be promoted effectively and efficiently without understanding users' needs and expectations."

The book ends with Ronald C. Jantz's consideration of a number of possible new roles for academic librarians of the future. As Jantz notes, his chapter "takes an approach in which new roles for academic librarians are extrapolated from emerging functions in the academic library and the author's observance of incongruities that suggest we in the profession should be doing something differently." He believes that academic libraries will witness a likely radical change in order to address the information needs of the university of the future. Jantz ties the new roles he foresees to a number of traditional library activities, such as research and marketing. Yet he also proposes roles that will offer support for newer activities. These include digital library architect, digital archivist, research data librarian, and publishing director. In all cases, the "skills and competencies embodied in these roles," Jantz argues, "emphasize the impact of the external world—technology, politics, and economics—highlighting the importance for each librarian to take a leadership role in the transformation of the academic library."

10

Recruitment, Retention, Diversity, and Professional Development

Marta Brunner and Jennifer Osorio

Introduction

Technological and social disruption are changing the nature of academic libraries, with significant implications for staffing and professional development. In this chapter, we discuss the current state of academic library work, what will continue to be true in the foreseeable future, which new priorities and practices will necessarily change the way our work is done, and which kinds of people will be doing it.

Literature Review

Some Things Stay the Same

As tempting as it may be to focus first on all the things that are changing in academic librarianship, we ought to be cautious about assuming that everything is changing, even though the work we do on a day-to-day basis may look very different from that of our counterparts in decades past. Andrew M. Cox and Sheila Corrall observe in a 2013 article that, despite a host of new developments, the core activities of academic librarianship remain constant.[1] Thus, it helps to understand new roles and priorities as responses to pressures rather than paradigm shifts.

For example, one of the biggest drivers of change in academic library work has been technology. However, technological innovation is actually more of a constant than a new development. In fact, some authors like Laura Saunders have argued that we should focus less on what lies ahead than on what is in front of us: She holds that libraries ought to focus more on resource allocation planning than on identifying new directions because libraries are not pushing sufficiently into important areas where they could be leaders in higher education, such as data management, student assessment, digital humanities, or mobile environments.[2] Likewise, Steven J. Bell maintains that, while user expectations may shift radically in light of technological changes, librarians' responses should conform to core professional values and practices.[3]

Regardless of the specific kinds of work academic librarians are doing, there are professional organizations producing guidelines or identifying competencies for the teams and individuals doing the work. Those professional organizations include the Association of College and Research Libraries (ACRL), the Society of American Archivists (SAA), the Medical Library Association (MLA), the Special Libraries Association (SLA), NASIG (formerly the North American Serials Interest Group), and the National Information Standards Organization (NISO).[4] The professional literature frequently discusses established and proposed competencies. For example, Emma Lawson, Roën Janyk, and Rachel A. Erb discuss the need for library school curricula to address the core competencies for electronic resources librarians put out by NASIG.[5] Clint Chamberlain and Derek Reece also refer to the NASIG core competencies, suggesting that these standards have a role to play in change management. Specifically, as libraries reorganize to create more cross-unit collaboration, they can use core competencies to ensure that team members share appropriate expertise.[6] Melissa L. Gold and Margaret G. Grotti observe that job postings do not always reflect core competencies, prompting concern that academic library recruitment efforts may not be aligned with professional standards.[7] Finally, there are standards for specific subject fields of academic librarianship, as illustrated in Kristin Motte and colleagues' discussion of the Association of Vision Science Librarians' revision of the "Standards for Vision Science Libraries."[8] It is worth noting, however, that some of these standards are not regularly updated. Given the rapid changes in the profession, more frequent revisiting of standards seems warranted.

Another constant in academic librarianship is professional identity, which is closely tied to structures for promotion and advancement, including job categories. In the United States, academic librarians tend to fall into one of four categories: (1) tenure-track faculty status, (2) non-tenure-track faculty status, (3) nonfaculty status (e.g., academic staff), and (4) nonfaculty status with something similar to tenure (sometimes referred to as "continuing appointment").[9] The question of whether academic librarians ought to have faculty status and tenure is still hotly debated and is explored at greater length in the discussion section that follows this literature review. ACRL's Committee on the Status of Academic Librarians produced a set of standards regarding faculty status, approved in 2007 and revised in 2011.[10] Shin Freedman's study of New England librarians explores the ways in which employment status relates to or is in tension with professional identity, ultimately concluding that the relationship is highly context-dependent.[11] There have been passionate appeals for faculty status or tenure in recent years.[12] In a short opinion piece called "No, It Can Hamper Their Roles," Deborah A. Carver makes an argument against tenure for academic librarians.[13] ACRL has also produced a "Guideline for the Appointment, Promotion and Tenure of Academic Librarians." This document was drafted in 1973 and has been updated twice since, most recently in 2010.[14]

Librarians at community colleges and smaller institutions, where tenure status is rare, face issues related to funding and professionalization. Jennifer Arnold reports that 60 percent of community colleges receive most or all of their funding from state and local sources, as opposed to 25 percent of four-year institutions,[15] leaving them much more vulnerable to funding cuts. Librarians at these institutions receive little support for professional development and often find themselves filling many roles at once with smaller staffs, where the line between professional librarians and paraprofessional staff is often blurry. While librarians at research institutions may be able to move up in rank without a change in responsibilities, due to the prescribed rules of the tenure system, this is usually not the case at smaller institutions, where promotion is tied to either taking on additional responsibilities or moving into managerial ranks. These librarians face additional pressures to diversify their skill sets in order to fill all the necessary roles in their libraries, often without much of a support system from their institutions.

Some Things Change

Though change is arguably a *constant* in academic libraries, specific developments are shaping current priorities and affecting the nature of academic library work going forward. Stephen Bell, Lorcan Dempsey, and Barbara Fister discuss many of them in *New Roles for the Road Ahead: Essays Commissioned for ACRL's 75th Anniversary*.[16] This book-length white paper takes stock of the current state of academic libraries, with recommendations for new priorities and opportunities. Fister points to emerging literacies that require academic librarians to devise novel approaches to instruction and research support, often calling on new skill sets and training. Likewise, economic pressures and intellectual property issues arising in the digital domain, along with consolidation and entrenchment of big for-profit database companies and publishers, have required librarians and paraprofessionals to educate themselves and others on open access and scholarly communication more generally.[17]

New approaches to teaching and learning in higher education are affecting the work of academic libraries. Kelly E. Miller has speculated on the ways that work in research libraries is changing to become more student-centered than ever before and offers seven strategies for achieving this. Miller's piece points to new skills needed in libraries: pedagogy, outreach, and assessment.[18]

Digital research and scholarship outside the sciences (a.k.a., digital humanities, or DH) and big data (a generic term for all sorts of large data sets used for research and decision-making) have significantly affected the work of academic libraries, especially at research institutions. Micah Vandegrift and Stewart Varner have written about the natural synergies between libraries and DH scholars and stress the importance for librarians to familiarize themselves with DH. They write, "The roles and responsibilities of research librarians are shifting to encompass the broadening scope of scholarship, especially involving digital archival and special collections, digital tools and progressive service models."[19] One effort to paint a fuller picture of what DH means for the work of academic librarians is Arianne Hartsell-Gundy, Laura Braunstein, and Liorah Golomb's recent edited volume, *Digital Humanities in the Library: Challenges and Opportunities for Subject Specialists*.[20] Miriam Posner, herself a DH scholar who has worked closely with research libraries, identifies common obstacles that, if overcome, will enable libraries to support digital research and scholarship more effectively.[21]

Digital projects and born-digital scholarship require metadata, data that itself describes other data and is necessary for description of digital assets. Metadata has been around for some time in libraries, but its current rise represents a shift for earlier generations of librarians who were primarily trained in MAchine Readable Cataloging (MARC), the standard format since the 1960s. Jeanne M. K. Boydston and Joan M. Leysen observe that technological innovations, as well as the adoption of Resource Description and Access (RDA),[22] Functional Requirements for Bibliographic Records (FRBR),[23] and non-MARC schemas, have driven the expansion of cataloger roles to include description of electronic acquisitions and digitized collections, batch loading records, and institutional repository work. In recent years, exposing hidden collections through digital projects has become a high priority for many libraries, calling upon the work of metadata specialists.[24] More recently, three external factors are playing a role in determining the future of cataloging and metadata librarianship, including financial pressures, competition from search engines (e.g., Google Scholar), and pressure to justify the need for cataloging positions in the face of automation and vendor-supplied records.[25] There are training implications in relation to the new activities, like working with linked data or semantic web[26] or RDA/FRBR. According to Myung-Ja Han and Patricia Hswe, the metadata librarian position is still evolving, which means the skills and competencies required for the role will change over time. Also, the position of the metadata librarian within the organizational structure of an academic library may be shifting. What is the relationship of the metadata librarian to the cataloging librarian? Do they have separate responsibilities, or are all cataloging librarians' roles eventually going to become those of metadata librarians? Han and Hswe suggest that the main difference between the two roles is that metadata librarians must be conversant in a wider variety of standards and schemas, as well as emerging technologies, than traditional cataloging librarians. Also, metadata librarians have, since 2004, been seen as straddling several library units (e.g., digital library, collection development, library IT) rather than wholly based in one unit (i.e., cataloging).[27]

Many libraries are now pursuing new methods for supporting research. For instance, we have seen increased attention in the literature devoted to embedded librarianship,[28] which takes librarians out of the library setting and places them on-site with researchers. A striking example of this is the research informationist (a form of embedded librarian mainly in the biological and health sciences) or the data management librarian.[29] Diane Zabel and colleagues define an *informationist* as a "librarian who searches the information resources and provides context for [the resulting content or data] through a strong consulting relationship with information consumers."[30] The research informationist role is not entirely unprecedented but has attracted renewed attention in the literature recently, thanks in part to more recent federal requirements for data management plans, which vary by agency but generally mandate that researchers develop plans to make federally funded data available to the public free of charge within twelve months of publication. Lisa Federer offers a case study to illustrate the impact of the research informationist role on health sciences research teams. She notes that the research informationist is involved with a research team "from project inception and grant seeking to final publication, providing expert guidance on data management and preservation, bibliometric analysis [statistical analysis of publications], expert searching, compliance with grant funder policies regarding data management and open access, and other information-related areas."[31] In order to succeed in this role, the research informationist needs a wide range of expertise, including data management, data preservation, funding compliance, and grant writing, in addition to more traditional librarian expertise.[32]

For librarians and archivists working in special collections, formats may change and require new work or new expertise, but the principles of preservation, stewardship, discoverability, and access remain the same. An article by Meredith R. Evans lays out a strategic agenda for twenty-first-century special collections. New knowledge and expertise will be needed, but "it is critical that we not throw aside the fundamentals of our profession."[33] For example, digital preservation includes the need to preserve hardware, or access to content will be impeded. That said, innovations like crowdsourcing—seeking funding, usually online, from large groups of people—have become increasingly important in order to get special collections work done. Evans suggests that "moving away from traditional curatorship of physical objects does not mean we ignore them; it means we think beyond how it's always been done."[34]

Job postings now reflect some of the changes described here. A recent study by Therese F. Triumph and Penny M. Beile found that, although the number of job postings has remained consistent—with a slight 6.3 percent increase indicating slow growth of the market—calls for foreign language skills have decreased, while calls for computer skills have increased. The MLS requirement also remained consistent among traditional jobs, but the degree is not required as often for jobs in electronic services or administrative jobs. Overall, the study found that academic librarian job titles are becoming increasingly specialized and many require new skills in such emerging technologies as mobile computing or data analysis and digital materials. Another significant new development is a trend toward jobs that work across divisions within an organization, such as librarians who work in the analog world of maps and the digital world of GIS (geographic information systems).[35]

In some respects, twenty-first-century professional development remains much the same as it always has been. Professionals learn and grow in formal and informal settings: in workshops, classes, conferences, and conversations. According to Bell, library leaders should have a strategic approach to professional development within their organizations but keep the structure flexible enough for individuals to take advantage of opportunities as they arise.[36] Ideally, professional development becomes a collective habit, like regular exercise, that everyone in a library organization contributes to and practices.[37] Mentoring also plays an important role, especially because information studies programs may not adequately prepare MLS students for tenure-track faculty positions, which can involve participating in shared governance, pursuing independent research, preparing for tenure review, advising students, and applying for grants. Yet even some mentoring programs themselves leave much to be desired. In their survey of academic librarians, Mandi Goodsett and Andrew Walsh found frustration with the matching process that pairs mentors and mentees and with the lack of support for mentoring programs within their institutions.[38] Marni R. Harrington and Elizabeth Marshall found a gap between the expectations of mentoring on the part of new librarians versus those of experienced administrative librarians.[39]

Finally, a persistent issue in academic libraries that is garnering renewed interest is diversity. For Anjali Gulati, the need for heterogeneity in staffing stems directly from diversity within user communities.[40] Articles by Emily Love and Teresa Y. Neely and Lorna Peterson discuss ways to recruit new library professionals from underrepresented backgrounds, beyond traditional categories of race, gender, and ethnicity.[41] Alexia Hudson-Ward argues in *American Libraries* that diversity initiatives need to move beyond demographics to a values-based model that takes into account a number of factors beyond race, ethnicity, gender, and sexuality, such as communication styles, generational differences, and work-life balance issues.[42] Similarly, a 2015 roundtable discussion titled "Why Diversity Matters," which grew out of an ACRL conference panel, asserts that the issue of inclusivity is much more complicated than simply responding to a more heterogeneous user base.[43] We describe the relationship of diversity to recruitment and retention in the academic librarian profession at greater length in the next section.

Discussion

What does this new context—the wider scope of scholarship, new digital tools and research methods, evolving collections, and a wider variety of service models—mean for academic libraries and their staffs? A nimble workforce that is well qualified to serve increasingly diverse communities becomes ever more important. Library leaders must have the vision and the skills to ensure that they provide academic library staff of all stripes with the skills and self-improvement opportunities to meet challenges and take advantage of new developments and trends. In this section, we discuss some of the issues the profession faces: the distinction between librarian work and paraprofessional work; necessary skills and professional development; and questions surrounding diversity, recruitment, and retention.

Librarian Work versus Paraprofessional Work

Library administrators, faced with tightened budgets and changing priorities, find themselves constantly renegotiating the distribution of tasks among their staff members. While expectations for professional librarians have expanded to include increased technical skills, knowledge of advanced research methods, and higher-level pedagogical skills, libraries still see demand for traditional skills, like doing reference and instruction. The master's degree in library science accredited by the American Library Association (ALA), the standard educational requirement for the field since 1975, is still required for the vast majority of professional jobs, but advanced subject degrees, technical certifications, and additional training are becoming increasingly necessary for library professionals to be competitive in the academic job market.[44] Professionals in academic libraries today demonstrate a wide range of skills and educational backgrounds, largely dependent on the context of their particular job titles and the skills necessary to carry out their duties.

The same can be said of nonprofessional staff. Duties that were traditionally performed by MLS-holding librarians are today routinely assigned to paraprofessionals. This is especially true at smaller institutions, where there are often fewer professional librarians relative to the number of staff members. Budgetary concerns and changing priorities, along with technological advances, have been the main drivers of this shift. The role of the paraprofessional—which historically demanded only "routine" tasks in libraries, such as copy cataloging, initial acquisitions work, and physical processing—has grown to include original cataloging, metadata creation, management of electronic resources, and other higher-level tasks. This trend extends even into the leadership ranks, with the management of technical services departments. But it also may be seen as a natural shift because librarians find their own duties changing to require more outreach, instruction, and assessment, all duties that increasingly take them out of the library and into the classroom and data lab.

Some say this development blurs the line between the two job categories and endangers the professional credential.[45] Because the question of paraprofessionals doing so-called professional work touches on the sensitive question of the value of the terminal library degree, there is unlikely to be consensus anytime soon. In the meantime, the opportunity exists to make the difference between professional and paraprofessional work more explicit by shifting the focus of library education toward addressing the areas where professional librarians can truly differentiate themselves, such as data management, pedagogy, and outreach.

A clearer differentiation and definition of what it means to be a librarian would go a long way toward settling the other major debate of the profession, that of faculty status and tenure. Current arguments for faculty status often center on the ways in which being faculty would help librarians do their job rather than how library faculty can contribute to their institutions. Although the American Association of University Professors (AAUP) has issued a joint statement with ACRL in support of faculty status for librarians,[46] the issue remains highly contested from campus to campus, and there may even be a trend away from granting librarians faculty status or tenure.[47] Professional identity is highly contextual and related in many cases to individual job titles and duties, but in general, MLS-holding librarians do work that requires higher-level planning, coordination, and judgment skills than work that paraprofessionals typically perform, even now. This can include administrative work; public-facing duties, such as engaging with faculty and students; and professional development work, such as serving on committees and involvement in professional associations. Academic librarians are frequently involved in governance at their institutions, serving on committees and contributing to service work similar to or even alongside teaching faculty.

Tenure status is more common but not consistent across large research libraries; it is rare at smaller institutions and at community colleges, where librarians are largely engaged in instructional roles, with little opportunity for independent research. Revising the standard MLS program curriculum to teach higher-level skills and knowledge, along with providing a strong basis in information theory, would strengthen librarians' argument for faculty status and tenure, given that the PhD is not standard for working librarians.[48] Higher-level skills would include, for example, course design, pedagogical theory and classroom teaching experience, fieldwork research experience, discipline-specific expertise, digital research, and scholarship skills.

Skills and Professional Development

While the degree itself remains the standard for professional positions, required by more than 95 percent of job listings, there is increased recognition that new professionals need more than just an MLS to be competitive.[49] Job listings may not require a second subject degree (master's or doctorate), but the reality of a competitive job market is that many candidates will have one regardless. With slow growth of the profession and the failure of the so-called retirement boom to materialize, new graduates are facing a lack of entry-level jobs.[50] Even when they do find entry-level postings, the positions often go to more experienced candidates.[51] In light of this situation, additional educational qualifications can help newly minted MLS graduates to compete on the job market. Along with the educational credentials, experience in the form of internships or previous work experience in nonprofessional roles has become increasingly important. Those looking to enter the field will be well served by choosing programs that recognize this need and have developed strong internship networks and career planning services. Postgraduate residency programs can also give new professionals the necessary training and on-the-job experience to be competitive.[52] These short-term appointments often seek to draw minority candidates to academic librarianship and improve their retention in the profession.

The importance of strong mentoring is also being recognized in the field, although not yet by most graduate programs. Most academic libraries do not yet offer formal mentoring either, although many do have informal programs through staff associations, or take advantage of mentoring programs offered by professional organizations. The tacit knowledge that is conveyed through conversations among colleagues on the job provides a valuable kind of informal mentoring.[53] That said, finding qual-

Marta Brunner and Jennifer Osorio

ified mentors who understand the importance of the process and how to make mentoring valuable beyond just being a sounding board can be invaluable, particularly to new professionals who often need guidance in understanding institutional culture or complicated tenure processes or both.

Aspiring library professionals need to understand the highly contextual field they are entering in terms of the kinds of skills and educational background they need to acquire in order to be competitive. As demonstrated in the literature review at the beginning of this chapter, many positions still require traditional reference and instruction skills, but solid technological skills are also necessary for all jobs. This goes beyond the basic knowledge of productivity software (such as Microsoft Office) to the ability to keep up with the latest innovations, work comfortably in increasingly networked environments, and adapt nimbly to constant technological change. Academic libraries are also cognizant of the need to continuously demonstrate their worth to their institutions, which naturally leads to a greater demand for librarians who can conduct a wide variety of outreach tasks and have the knowledge to assess these activities along with the skills to present information in ways that speak to how people learn today, whether they are inexperienced commuter students at community colleges, distance learners, or advanced graduate-level researchers. Because MLS programs that train new librarians cannot necessarily provide libraries with needed advanced skills and expertise, libraries have benefited from hiring non-MLS-holders who can. The Council on Library and Information Resources Postdoctoral Fellowship Program is an example of an effort to match libraries with doctorally trained individuals who can bring such advanced expertise as in-depth subject knowledge, cutting-edge pedagogy, data curation, and digital humanities experience.[54]

Professional development for librarians is a continuous process, one that libraries must support if they are to remain competitive in the future. A strategic, flexible approach to professional development can help libraries to take advantage of opportunities as they arise, while also ensuring that staff remain challenged and able to keep pace with trends and new developments. Beyond the original degree, such programs as the Harvard Institute for Academic Librarians, the Leading Change Institute (formerly the Frye Leadership Institute), and the ALA Leadership Institute can reinvigorate librarians, provide valuable networking opportunities, and bring new ideas back to the library. Librarians at institutions with little to no funding for professional development may be able to take advantage of workshops or webinars offered by professional organizations, especially through local or regional chapters. These librarians may feel isolated from their colleagues, either because of the size of their staff or because of their physical locations; networking through professional organizations or social media (or both) can mitigate some of this isolation and provide learning and development outlets. The ability to stay abreast of new and emerging literacies is absolutely vital to remaining competitive, both on a personal level for individual staff and also for libraries as a whole.

Aside from supporting the professional development activities of professional staff, libraries must also ensure that they support crucial paraprofessional staff who, as noted earlier, are increasingly assigned duties that require judgment and accountability. Supporting paraprofessional staff by providing better training opportunities, including resources to pursue a library degree, can not only assist in the day-to-day operations of the library but also help to build a pipeline of future librarians. Because the ranks of paraprofessional staff are often more diverse than those of professional librarians, this particular pipeline could help to diversify the profession. An important caveat, however, is that it may not always be possible for a paraprofessional to move into a professional position at her or his current institution without needing to apply outright for the position, even if that staff person has been doing what might be considered traditional librarian work. Funding lines for different job categories may be structurally bound in ways that make it difficult to reclassify a position from paraprofessional to professional. Also, administrators may operate according to a "grass is greener" mentality, assuming that an external search will yield a better candidate than the current, known employee, even in institutions that claim to prize so-called promotion from within. In some cases, union contracts may preclude or at least inhibit easy reclassification of positions.

Diversity, Recruitment, and Retention

The library world as a whole remains stubbornly homogeneous, with approximately 11 percent of credentialed librarians coming from underrepresented groups,[55] while the general population of the United States becomes increasingly diverse. From 1991 to 2001, the percentage of MLS degrees awarded to minorities went from 9 percent to 13 percent, while the number of minorities (i.e., other than non-Hispanic whites) in the general population during almost the same period (1990–2000) went from 25.5 percent to 36.25 percent.[56] There is wide acknowledgment in the field that this needs to change not only for the sake of the communities we serve but also for the strength of the profession. How to effect this change remains the question, especially when some elements of diversity—sexual orientation, for example—may not be visibly apparent during the recruitment process.

Recruitment and retention efforts by ALA and other professional organizations have done little to affect the numbers, and the reason remains unclear. Juleah Swanson and colleagues suggest that there are significant issues with current data collection related to diversity and organizational culture; the latter can remain stubbornly unchanged if issues of implicit bias among existing staff are not addressed. The authors call for initiatives that expose these biases and encourage critical inquiry into attitudes and behaviors.[57] Neely and Peterson recommend goals for recruiting academic librarians of color, including a comprehensive public awareness campaign, possibly modeled on one done by nurses. They also recommend a research agenda to gather membership data, identify realistic goals for assessment and analysis, prompt more study of retention strategies, and develop opportunities for and support of career advancement.[58] It is important to acknowledge that diversity is much more than just demographics, however. Academic libraries need to consider the whole candidate in order to ensure that the workforce represents variety, not just in terms of race, ethnicity, gender, and sexual orientation, but also in terms of work and communication styles. A well-represented generational range is another example of diversity that can help to strengthen library workforces. Cross-generational relationships among library staff can provide not just continuity but also a wider range of ideas and styles necessary to address problems. Similarly, building teams that include individuals with less traditional training and expertise can provide greater resilience across the library organization.

Recruitment of new librarians is a vital issue for a graying workforce. Besides recruiting a diverse workforce, academic libraries also have to ensure that they retain the workers they do successfully entice to the profession. Libraries need to provide new librarians with the tools they need to succeed. Bell, Dempsey, and Fister report on three different problems new hires often face: new hire messianism, by which new hires become responsible for bringing change to the organization; the coordinator syndrome, in which librarians are put into positions of responsibility without the authority and resources to accomplish their tasks; and the Bartholomew Cubbins effect, with librarians becoming responsible for too many areas (i.e., wearing a lot of hats) due to staffing shortages and an increasing array of duties.[59] All of these problems, along with a paucity of opportunities to advance, a lack of a succession planning, and weak administrative leadership, can contribute to attrition, driving talented librarians from the profession.

Conclusion

Our chapter discusses how the work of academic libraries is changing and what that means for the skills, experience, and workforce composition of the field. We have observed a shift away from rigid professional roles or tracks (cataloging, reference, bibliography, digital libraries) toward a more functional orientation of staffing models that address organizational needs. We have also observed that MLS programs may not be preparing their graduate students adequately for faculty positions or providing them with advanced skills that would be needed to enable these new librarians to thrive in twenty-first-century academic libraries. These observations notwithstanding, Damon E. Jaggars offers this important counsel:

Marta Brunner and Jennifer Osorio

While what an individual staff member, or an organization for that matter, knows is critical to success, the ability to effectively create the futures we imagine will be less about specific operational or technical skill sets (data, coding, constructivist pedagogy) and more about the metacognitive capacities that enable the individual and collective growth that fuel organizational change.[60]

These metacognitive capacities—the ability to engage in self-reflection and understand and perhaps change one's ways of thinking and feeling in particular situations—promote creativity and resilience, which in turn help the entire organization to flourish through change. But, Jaggars continues, "While there is no end to the ideas about what should be done operationally to create a vital future, there is little discussion about how to develop a workforce equipped with the metacognitive tools needed to work through difficult change processes in constructive, thoughtful, and effective ways."[61] In other words, the academic library profession and the library schools that train its workforce have a crucial professional development puzzle to think through in coming years. How do we recruit, prepare, and retain librarians who can adapt creatively to a rapidly changing academic landscape? Rather than focus on traditional or even emerging skills, library leadership may be better off finding ways to increase their staff's ability to continuously change and adapt.

Discussion Questions

1. Ken Haycock, a longtime library and information science program director, has offered these three criteria for defining professional librarians: (1) "Librarians manage and lead," (2) "Librarians develop and train staff," and (3) "Librarians understand deeply the principles and theories of the discipline."[62] Is this a sufficient rubric for deciding which tasks and duties ought to be done by librarians and which ought to be done by nonlibrarian staff in an academic library setting? In other words, should academic librarians be defined by the work they do or the skills or training they have or some combination thereof? What are the potential ramifications of the approach you propose for a library organization? Take into account professional development needs as well as the larger context of the campus in which the library resides.

2. In academic libraries and other organizations, innovations over time lead to a situation in which the volume of work to be done eventually outstrips the capacity of the workforce within the organization. In some cases, technology can produce efficiencies that increase capacity; in other cases, managers and administrators are forced to consider which tasks and practices will be jettisoned in order to make room for new ones. Can you come up with examples of academic library work that is no longer done? Given what you know about trends in teaching, learning, and research in higher education, as well as such technological trends as cloud computing, which activities could academic librarians and paraprofessionals stop doing?

3. Despite numerous attempts to diversify the profession through recruitment of minorities, targeted fellowships, and leadership programs aimed at underrepresented groups, the library profession remains stubbornly and overwhelmingly white and female, especially in academic libraries. Discuss the reasons these programs have failed and what, if anything, libraries should be doing instead. How should they measure success, especially the success of difficult-to-quantify variables, like organizational culture?

4. Do you see faculty status as a benefit or an obstacle to the work of academic librarians? For instance, if you were offered two nearly identical jobs, the only difference being that one has tenure-track faculty status and the other does not, which would you choose to accept and why? To what extent does faculty status for librarians, or the lack thereof, affect the academic library profession?

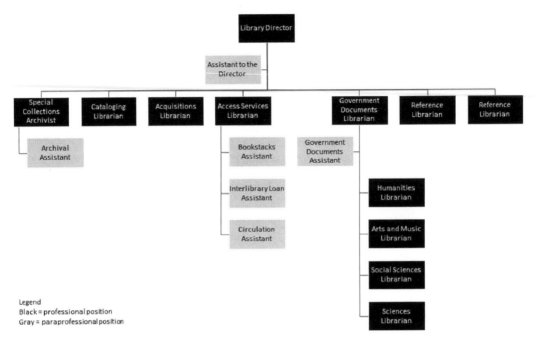

Figure 10.1 Library organizational chart

Assignments

Reorganization Assignment

You are a new library director at Small University in an urban community with a large immigrant population. Your library is currently staffed according to the following organizational chart (figure 10.1), referred to colloquially as an org chart.

Despite the diversity of the surrounding community, 100 percent of your librarians and 70 percent of nonprofessional staff identify as white. The cataloging librarian just got a new job at a nearby college, and the government documents librarian is retiring in six months. Considering the future needs of SU faculty and students, as well as the health of your library organization, propose your next two hires, and reorganize the org chart as needed. Explain your rationale in a two- to three-page brief to your provost, briefly describing the process you took to arrive at these proposed changes. Your brief may address such things as stakeholder input; an environmental scan; future trends; conversations within your organization; and advice from anyone in particular, such as an outside consultant or a published work. Be sure to include mention of your timeline for the recruitments and the reorganization process, if applicable. Attach one- to two-paragraph job descriptions for each position, making sure to include required and desired qualifications.

Rubric: org chart 10 percent, brief 60 percent, job descriptions 30 percent.

Mentoring Program Assignment

Design a mentoring program for an academic library. How would you pair mentors and mentees? What kind of training would you provide for mentors? Which goals would you set for mentor relationships, and how would you assess the success of both individual match-ups and the program overall? Which kinds of resources would you provide for mentors and mentees? In your paper, develop goals and an action plan for the program, and create a ten-week formal mentoring program with weekly

Marta Brunner and Jennifer Osorio

assignments that mentors and mentees must complete together. Make sure to establish metrics and checkpoints during the program that participants can use to check progress and that can be used to assess the program upon completion.

Rubric: goals and action plan 40 percent, weekly assignments 30 percent, assessment 30 percent.

Notes

1. Andrew M. Cox and Sheila Corrall, "Evolving Academic Library Specialties," *Journal of the Association for Information Science and Technology* 64, no. 8 (August 2013): 1526–42, doi:10.1002/asi.22847.
2. Laura Saunders, "Academic Libraries' Strategic Plans: Top Trends and Under-Recognized Areas," *Journal of Academic Librarianship* 41, no. 3 (May 2015): 290.
3. Steven J. Bell, "Staying True to the Core: Designing the Future Academic Library Experience," *portal: Libraries and the Academy* 14, no. 3 (2014): 369–82, http://dx.doi.org/10.1353/pla.2014.0021. See also Elizabeth Leonard and Maureen J. Morasch, "If You Can Make It There, You Can Make It Anywhere: Providing Reference and Instructional Library Services in the Virtual Environment," *Journal of Electronic Resources Librarianship* 24, no. 4 (October 2012): 257–67, doi:10.1080/1941126X.2012.731946.
4. See "Competencies for Information Professionals," *Special Libraries Association*, April 13, 2016, https://www.sla.org/about-sla/competencies; "Core Competencies," *NASIG (Formerly the North American Serials Interest Group)*, 2016, http://www.nasig.org/site_page.cfm?pk_association_webpage_menu=310&pk_association_webpage=1225; "Guidelines, Standards, and Frameworks," *Association of College and Research Libraries*, 2016, http://www.ala.org/acrl/standards; "Professional Competencies," *Medical Library Association (MLA)*, 2016, http://www.mlanet.org/p/cm/ld/fid=39; "Standards Portal," *Society of American Archivists (SAA)*, 2016, http://www2.archivists.org/standards; and "Welcome to NISO," *National Information Standards Organization (NISO)*, 2016, www.niso.org.
5. Emma Lawson, Roën Janyk, and Rachel A. Erb, "Getting to the Core of the Matter: Competencies for New E-Resources Librarians," *Serials Librarian* 66, nos. 1–4 (January 2014): 153–60.
6. Clint Chamberlain and Derek Reece, "Library Reorganization, Chaos, and Using the Core Competencies as a Guide," *Serials Librarian* 66, nos. 1–4 (January 2014): 248–52.
7. Melissa L. Gold and Margaret G. Grotti, "Do Job Advertisements Reflect ACRL's Standards for Proficiencies for Instruction Librarians and Coordinators? A Content Analysis," *Journal of Academic Librarianship* 39, no. 6 (November 2013): 558–65, doi:10.1016/j.acalib.2013.05.013.
8. Kristin Motte, C. Brooke Caldwell, Karen S. Lamson, Suzanne Ferimer, and J. Chris Nims, "Standards for Vision Science Libraries: 2014 Revision," *Journal of the Medical Library Association* 102, no. 4 (October 2014): 288–91.
9. See the "Academic Librarian Status: A Guide to the Professional Status of Academic Librarians in the United States (and Other Places)," *Wikispaces*, n.d., http://academic-librarian-status.wikispaces.com/home, for a listing of college and universities by librarian status. This wiki includes a fifth category: mixed status.
10. ACRL Committee on the Status of Academic Librarians, "Association of College and Research Libraries Standards for Faculty Status for Academic Librarians," June 2007, revised October 2011, http://www.ala.org/acrl/standards/standardsfaculty.
11. Shin Freedman, "Faculty Status, Tenure, and Professional Identity: A Pilot Study of Academic Librarians in New England," *portal: Libraries and the Academy* 14, no. 4 (October 2014): 533–65. See also Nathan Hosburgh, "Librarian Faculty Status: What Does It Mean in Academia?" *Library Philosophy and Practice* (June 2011): 1–7, http://digitalcommons.unl.edu/cgi/viewcontent.cgi?article=1603&context=libphilprac.
12. Catherine Coker, Wyoma vanDuinkerken, and Stephen Bales, "Seeking Full Citizenship: A Defense of Tenure Faculty Status for Librarians," *College and Research Libraries* 71, no. 5 (September 2010): 406-20; Shalu Gillum, "The True Benefit of Faculty Status for Academic Reference Librarians," *Reference Librarian* 51, no. 4 (October 2010): 321–28, doi:10.1080/02763877.2010.501419.
13. Deborah A. Carver, "No, It Can Hamper Their Roles," *Chronicle of Higher Education* 52, no. 6 (September 30, 2005): B10–11.
14. "A Guideline for the Appointment, Promotion and Tenure of Academic Librarians," *College and Research Libraries News* 71, no. 10 (2010): 552–60, http://staffweb.lib.washington.edu/committees/aluw/status/reading/a-guideline-for-the-appointment-promotion-and-tenure-of-academic-librarians-acrl.

15. Jennifer Arnold, "The Community College Conundrum: Workforce Issues in Community College Librar-ies," *Library Trends*, 59, nos. 1–2 (2010): 220–36.
16. Steven Bell, Lorcan Dempsey, and Barbara Fister, *New Roles for the Road Ahead: Essays Commissioned for ACRL's 75th Anniversary*, edited by Nancy Allen (Chicago: Association of College and Research Libraries, 2015), http://www.ala.org/acrl/sites/ala.org.acrl/files/content/publications/whitepapers/new_roles_75th.pdf.
17. See also James M. Matarazzo and Toby Pearlstein, "Academic Libraries: A Soft Analysis, a Warning and the Road Ahead," *IFLA Journal* 41, no. 1 (2015): 5–12.
18. Kelly E. Miller, "Imagine! On the Future of Teaching and Learning and the Academic Research Library," *portal: Libraries and the Academy* 14, no. 3 (2014): 329–51, http://dx.doi.org/10.1353/pla.2014.0018.
19. Micah Vandegrift and Stewart Varner, "Evolving in Common: Creating Mutually Supportive Relation-ships between Libraries and the Digital Humanities," *Journal of Library Administration* 53, no. 1 (2013): 68, doi:10.1080/01930826.2013.756699.
20. Arianne Hartsell-Gundy, Laura Braunstein, and Liorah Golomb, *Digital Humanities in the Library: Chal-lenges and Opportunities for Subject Specialists* (Chicago: Association of College and Research Libraries, 2015).
21. Miriam Posner, "No Half Measures: Overcoming Common Challenges to Doing Digital Humanities in the Library," *Journal of Library Administration* 53, no. 1 (January 2013): 43–52, doi:10.1080/01930826.2013.756694.
22. Eric Miller, "An Introduction to the Resource Description Framework," *Bulletin of the American Society for Information Science and Technology* 25, no. 1 (October–November 1998): 15–19.
23. IFLA Study Group on the Functional Requirements of Bibliographic Records, "Functional Requirements of Bibliographic Records: Final Report," Munich: K. G. Saur, 1998, http://www.ifla.org/VII/s13/frbr/frbr.pdf.
24. Jeanne M. K. Boydston and Joan M. Leysen, "ARL Cataloger Librarian Roles and Responsibilities Now and in the Future," *Cataloging and Classification Quarterly* 52, no. 2 (2014): 233, doi:10.1080/01639374.2013.859199. For a list of funded projects by the Council on Library and Information Resources Hidden Collections initiative, see "Funded Projects," *Council on Library and Information Resources*, 2014, http://www.clir.org/hiddencollections/awards.
25. Boydston and Leysen, "ARL Cataloger Librarian Roles," 241.
26. For an explanation of linked data and the semantic web, see Autumn Faulkner's chapter on technical services in this volume (chapter 8) and "Semantic Web," *World Wide Web Consortium*, 2015 https://www.w3.org/standards/semanticweb.
27. Myung-Ja Han and Patricia Hswe, "The Evolving Role of the Metadata Librarian," *Library Resources and Technical Services* 54, no. 3 (July 2010): 129–41.
28. Carrie Forbes and Peggy Keeran describe this role in greater detail in chapter 6 of this volume, on reference, instruction, and outreach. See also Mary Talley, "Success and the Embedded Librarian," *Information Outlook* 15, no. 3 (May 4, 2011): 25–28.
29. See, for example, Diane Cooper and Janet A. Crum, "New Activities and Changing Roles of Health Sciences Librarians: A Systematic Review, 1990–2012," *Journal of the Medical Library Association* 101, no. 4 (October 2013): 268–77; Michelynn McKnight, "Librarians, Informaticists, Informationists, and Other Information Professionals in Biomedicine and the Health Sciences: What Do They Do?" *Journal of Hospital Librarianship* 5, no. 1 (March 2005): 13–29.
30. Diane Zabel, Elizabeth A. Thomas, Nora Bird, and Richard J. Moniz Jr., "Informationists in a Small Uni-versity Library," *Reference and User Services Quarterly* 51, no. 3 (Spring 2012): 223.
31. Lisa Federer, "The Librarian as Research Informationist: A Case Study," *Journal of the Medical Library Association* 101, no. 4 (October 2013): 298.
32. Ibid., 301.
33. Meredith R. Evans, "Modern Special Collections: Embracing the Future while Taking Care of the Past," *New Review of Academic Librarianship* 21, no. 2 (2015): 118.
34. Ibid., 123.
35. Therese F. Triumph and Penny M. Beile, "The Trending Academic Library Job Market: An Analysis of Library Position Announcements from 2011 with Comparisons to 1996 and 1988," *College and Research Libraries* 76, no. 6 (2015): 716–39, doi:10.5860/crl.76.6.716.

36. Bell, Dempsey, and Fister, *New Roles*, 87.
37. Ibid., 91.
38. Mandi Goodsett and Andrew Walsh, "Building a Strong Foundation: Mentoring Programs for Novice Tenure-Track Librarians in Academic Libraries," *College and Research Libraries* 76, no. 7 (2015): 914–33, doi:10.5860/crl.76.7.914.
39. Marni R. Harrington and Elizabeth Marshall, "Analyses of Mentoring Expectations, Activities, and Support in Canadian Academic Libraries," *College and Research Libraries* 75, no. 6 (2014): 763–90.
40. Anjali Gulati, "Diversity in Librarianship: The United States Perspective," *IFLA Journal* 36, no. 4 (2010): 288–93.
41. Emily Love, "Generation Next: Recruiting Minority Students to Librarianship," *Reference Services Review* 38, no. 3 (August 2010): 482–92; Teresa Y. Neely and Lorna Peterson, "Achieving Racial and Ethnic Diversity among Academic and Research Librarians: The Recruitment, Retention, and Advancement of Librarians of Color—A White Paper," *College and Research Libraries News* 68, no. 9 (2007): 562–65.
42. Alexia Hudson-Ward, "Eyeing the New Diversity," *American Libraries* 45, nos. 7–8 (2014): 32–35.
43. Juleah Swanson, Ione Damasco, Isabel Gonzalez-Smith, Dracine Hodges, Todd Honma, and Azusa Tanaka, "Why Diversity Matters: A Roundtable Discussion on Racial and Ethnic Diversity in Librarianship," *In the Library with the Lead Pipe*, July 29, 2015, http://www.inthelibrarywiththeleadpipe.org/2015/why-diversity-matters-a-roundtable-discussion-on-racial-and-ethnic-diversity-in-librarianship.
44. Phillip J. Jones, "Academic Graduate Work in Academic Librarianship: Historicizing ACRL's Terminal Degree Statement," *Journal of Academic Librarianship* 24, no. 6 (1998): 437.
45. See, for example, John B. Harer, "The Economic Crisis and the Decline of the Academic Librarian Professional," *New Review of Academic Librarianship* (November 2011): 151–54.
46. Joint Committee on College Library Problems, "Association of College and Research Libraries Joint Statement on Faculty Status of College and University Librarians," *Association of College and Research Libraries*, 2012, http://www.ala.org/acrl/standards/jointstatementfaculty.
47. William H. Walters, "Faculty Status of Librarians at U.S. Research Universities," *Journal of Academic Librarianship* 42, no. 2 (March 2016): 163, doi:10.1016/j.acalib.2015.11.002.
48. See Todd Gilman and Thea Lindquist, "Academic/Research Librarians with Subject Doctorates: Experiences and Perceptions, 1965–2006," *portal: Libraries and the Academy* 10, no. 4 (2010): 399–412, doi:10.1353/pla.2010.0007; Thea Lindquist and Todd Gilman, "Academic/Research Librarians with Subject Doctorates: Data and Trends 1965–2006," *portal: Libraries and the Academy* 8, no. 1 (2008): 31–52, doi:10.1353/pla.2008.0008.
49. Triumph and Beile, "Trending Academic Library Job Market," 733–35.
50. See two articles by Rachel Holt and Adrienne L. Strock: "The Entry-Level Gap," *Library Journal* 130, no. 8 (2005): 36–38; "The Entry-Level Gap, Revisited." *Library Journal* 132, no. 16 (2007): 44.
51. Sojourna J. Cunningham and Ingrid J. Ruffin, "Experience Mandatory: Assessing the Impact of Previous Career and Educational Experience on LIS Education and the Academic Library Job Hunt," *Southeastern Librarian* 62, no. 4 (Winter 2015): 12.
52. See, for example, Teresa Y. Neely and Megan K. Beard, "Recruiting and Retaining Academic Research Librarians," *College and Research Libraries News* 69, no. 6 (June 2008): 314–15.
53. Mónica Colón-Aguirre, "Organizational Storytelling among Academic Reference Librarians," *portal: Libraries and the Academy* 15, no. 2 (April 2015): 233–50.
54. For more information, see "CLIR Postdoctoral Fellowship Program," *Council on Library and Information Resources*, 2014, http://www.clir.org/fellowships/postdoc.
55. Gulati, "Diversity in Librarianship," 290.
56. Jenifer Grady and Tracie Hall, "The World Is Changing: Why Aren't We? Recruiting Minorities to Librarianship," *Library Worklife* 1, no. 4 (April 2004), http://ala-apa.org/newsletter/2004/04/16/the-world-is-changing-why-arent-we.
57. Swanson et al., "Why Diversity Matters."
58. Neely and Peterson, "Achieving Racial and Ethnic Diversity."
59. Bell, Dempsey, and Fister, *New Roles*, 70.

60. Damon E. Jaggars, "We Can Imagine the Future, but Are We Equipped to Create It?" *portal: Libraries and the Academy* 14, no. 3 (2014): 321, http://dx.doi.org/10.1353/pla.2014.0014.
61. Ibid., 322.
62. Ken Haycock, "Three Role Features of Professional Librarians," *Ken Haycock and Associates Blog*, June 13, 2011, http://kenhaycock.com/three-role-features-of-professional-librarians.

Bibliography

"Academic Librarian Status: A Guide to the Professional Status of Academic Librarians in the United States (and Other Places)." *Wikispaces*. n.d. http://academic-librarian-status.wikispaces.com/home.

ACRL Committee on the Status of Academic Librarians. "Association of College and Research Libraries Standards for Faculty Status for Academic Librarians." *Association of College and Research Libraries.* June 2007. Revised October 2011. http://www.ala.org/acrl/standards/standardsfaculty.

Arnold, Jennifer. "The Community College Conundrum: Workforce Issues in Community College Libraries." *Library Trends* 59, nos. 1–2 (2010): 220–36.

Bell, Steven, Lorcan Dempsey, and Barbara Fister. *New Roles for the Road Ahead: Essays Commissioned for ACRL's 75th Anniversary.* Edited by Nancy Allen. Chicago: Association of College and Research Libraries, 2015. http://www.ala.org/acrl/sites/ala.org.acrl/files/content/publications/whitepapers/new_roles_75th.pdf.

Bell, Steven J. "Staying True to the Core: Designing the Future Academic Library Experience." *portal: Libraries and the Academy* 14, no. 3 (2014): 369–82. http://dx.doi.org/10.1353/pla.2014.0021.

Boydston, Jeanne M. K., and Joan M. Leysen. "ARL Cataloger Librarian Roles and Responsibilities Now and in the Future." *Cataloging and Classification Quarterly* 52, no. 2 (February 2014): 229–50. doi:10.1080/01639374.2013.859199.

Carver, Deborah A. "No, It Can Hamper Their Roles." *Chronicle of Higher Education* 52, no. 6 (September 30, 2005): B10–11.

Chamberlain, Clint, and Derek Reece. "Library Reorganization, Chaos, and Using the Core Competencies as a Guide." *Serials Librarian* 66, nos. 1–4 (January 2014): 248–52. doi:10.1080/0361526X.2014.881162.

"CLIR Postdoctoral Fellowship Program." *Council on Library and Information Resources.* 2014. http://www.clir.org/fellowships/postdoc.

Coker, Catherine, Wyoma vanDuinkerken, and Stephen Bales. "Seeking Full Citizenship: A Defense of Tenure Faculty Status for Librarians." *College and Research Libraries* 71, no. 5 (September 2010): 406–20.

Colón-Aguirre, Mónica. "Organizational Storytelling among Academic Reference Librarians." *portal: Libraries and the Academy* 15, no. 2 (April 2015): 233–50.

"Competencies for Information Professionals." *Special Libraries Association.* April 13, 2016. https://www.sla.org/about-sla/competencies.

Cooper, Diane, and Janet A. Crum. "New Activities and Changing Roles of Health Sciences Librarians: A Systematic Review, 1990–2012." *Journal of the Medical Library Association* 101, no. 4 (October 2013): 268–77.

"Core Competencies." *NASIG (Formerly the North American Serials Interest Group).* 2016. http://www.nasig.org/site_page.cfm?pk_association_webpage_menu=310&pk_association_webpage=1225.

Cox, Andrew M., and Sheila Corrall. "Evolving Academic Library Specialties." *Journal of the Association for Information Science and Technology* 64, no. 8 (August 2013): 1526–42. doi:10.1002/asi.22847.

Cunningham, Sojourna J., and Ingrid J. Ruffin. "Experience Mandatory: Assessing the Impact of Previous Career and Educational Experience on LIS Education and the Academic Library Job Hunt." *Southeastern Librarian* 62, no. 4 (Winter 2015): 12–20.

Evans, Meredith R. "Modern Special Collections: Embracing the Future while Taking Care of the Past." *New Review of Academic Librarianship* 21, no. 2 (2015): 116–28. http://dx.doi.org/10.1080/13614533.2015.1040926.

Federer, Lisa. "The Librarian as Research Informationist: A Case Study." *Journal of the Medical Library Association* 101, no. 4 (October 2013): 298–302.

Freedman, Shin. "Faculty Status, Tenure, and Professional Identity: A Pilot Study of Academic Librarians in New England." *portal: Libraries and the Academy* 14, no. 4 (October 2014): 533–65.

"Funded Projects." *Council on Library and Information Resources.* 2014. http://www.clir.org/hiddencollections/awards.

Gillum, Shalu. "The True Benefit of Faculty Status for Academic Reference Librarians." *Reference Librarian* 51, no. 4 (October 2010): 321–28. doi:10.1080/02763877.2010.501419.

Gilman, Todd, and Thea Lindquist. "Academic/Research Librarians with Subject Doctorates: Experiences and Perceptions, 1965–2006." *portal: Libraries and the Academy* 10, no. 4 (2010): 399–412. doi:10.1353/pla.2010.0007.

Gold, Melissa L., and Margaret G. Grotti. "Do Job Advertisements Reflect ACRL's Standards for Proficiencies for Instruction Librarians and Coordinators? A Content Analysis." *Journal of Academic Librarianship* 39, no. 6 (November 2013): 558–65. doi:10.1016/j.acalib.2013.05.013.

Goodsett, Mandi, and Andrew Walsh. "Building a Strong Foundation: Mentoring Programs for Novice Tenure-Track Librarians in Academic Libraries." *College and Research Libraries* 76, no. 7 (2015): 914–33. doi:10.5860/crl.76.7.914.

Grady, Jenifer, and Tracie Hall. "The World Is Changing: Why Aren't We? Recruiting Minorities to Librarianship." *Library Worklife* 1, no. 4 (April 2004). http://ala-apa.org/newsletter/2004/04/16/the-world-is-changing-why-arent-we.

"A Guideline for the Appointment, Promotion and Tenure of Academic Librarians." *College and Research Libraries News* 71, no. 10 (November 2010): 552–60.

"Guidelines, Standards, and Frameworks." *Association of College and Research Libraries.* 2016. http://www.ala.org/acrl/standards.

Gulati, Anjali. "Diversity in Librarianship: The United States Perspective." *IFLA Journal* 36, no. 4 (2010): 288–93.

Han, Myung-Ja, and Patricia Hswe. "The Evolving Role of the Metadata Librarian." *Library Resources and Technical Services* 54, no. 3 (July 2010): 129–41.

Harer, John B. "The Economic Crisis and the Decline of the Academic Librarian Professional." *New Review of Academic Librarianship* (November 2011): 151–54.

Harrington, Marni R., and Elizabeth Marshall. "Analyses of Mentoring Expectations, Activities, and Support in Canadian Academic Libraries." *College and Research Libraries* 75, no. 6 (2014): 763–90.

Hartsell-Gundy, Arianne, Laura Braunstein, and Liorah Golomb. *Digital Humanities in the Library: Challenges and Opportunities for Subject Specialists*. Chicago: Association of College and Research Libraries, 2015.

Haycock, Ken. "Three Role Features of Professional Librarians." *Ken Haycock and Associates Blog*. June 13, 2011. http://kenhaycock.com/three-role features of professional-librarians.

Holt, Rachel, and Adrienne L. Strock. "The Entry-Level Gap." *Library Journal* 130, no. 8 (2005): 36–38.

———. "The Entry-Level Gap, Revisited." *Library Journal* 132, no. 16 (2007): 44.

Hosburgh, Nathan. "Librarian Faculty Status: What Does It Mean in Academia?" *Library Philosophy and Practice* (June 2011): 1–7.

Hudson-Ward, Alexia. "Eyeing the New Diversity." *American Libraries* 45, nos. 7–8 (August 7, 2014): 32–35.

IFLA Study Group on the Functional Requirements for Bibliographic Records. "Functional Requirements of Bibliographic Records: Final Report." Munich: K. G. Saur, 1998. http://www.ifla.org/VII/s13/frbr/frbr.pdf.

Jaggars, Damon E. "We Can Imagine the Future, but Are We Equipped to Create It?" *portal: Libraries and the Academy* 14, no. 3 (2014): 319–23. http://dx.doi.org/10.1353/pla.2014.0014.

Joint Committee on College Library Problems. "Association of College and Research Libraries Joint Statement on Faculty Status of College and University Librarians." *Association of College and Research Libraries*. 2012. http://www.ala.org/acrl/standards/jointstatementfaculty.

Jones, Phillip J. "Academic Graduate Work in Academic Librarianship: Historicizing ACRL's Terminal Degree Statement." *Journal of Academic Librarianship* 24, no. 6 (1998): 437–43.

Lawson, Emma, Roën Janyk, and Rachel A. Erb. "Getting to the Core of the Matter: Competencies for New E-Resources Librarians." *Serials Librarian* 66, nos. 1–4 (January 2014): 153–60. doi:10.1080/0361526X.2014.879639.

Leonard, Elizabeth, and Maureen J. Morasch. "If You Can Make It There, You Can Make It Anywhere: Providing Reference and Instructional Library Services in the Virtual Environment." *Journal of Electronic Resources Librarianship* 24, no. 4 (October 2012): 257–67. doi:10.1080/1941126X.2012.731946.

Lindquist, Thea, and Todd Gilman. "Academic/Research Librarians with Subject Doctorates: Data and Trends 1965–2006." *portal: Libraries and the Academy* 8, no. 1 (2008): 31–52. doi:10.1353/pla.2008.0008.

Love, Emily. "Generation Next: Recruiting Minority Students to Librarianship." *Reference Services Review* 38, no. 3 (August 2010): 482–92.

Matarazzo, James M., and Toby Pearlstein. "Academic Libraries: A Soft Analysis, a Warning and the Road Ahead." *IFLA Journal* 41, no. 1 (2015): 5–12. http://dx.doi.org/10.1177/0340035215571356.

McKnight, Michelynn. "Librarians, Informaticists, Informationists, and Other Information Professionals in Biomedicine and the Health Sciences: What Do They Do?" *Journal of Hospital Librarianship* 5, no. 1 (March 2005): 13–29.

Miller, Eric. "An Introduction to the Resource Description Framework." *Bulletin of the American Society for Information Science and Technology* 25, no. 1 (October–November 1998): 15–19.

Miller, Kelly E. "Imagine! On the Future of Teaching and Learning and the Academic Research Library." *portal: Libraries and the Academy* 14, no. 3 (2014): 329–51. http://dx.doi.org/10.1353/pla.2014.0018.

Motte, Kristin, C. Brooke Caldwell, Karen S. Lamson, Suzanne Ferimer, and J. Chris Nims. "Standards for Vision Science Libraries: 2014 Revision." *Journal of the Medical Library Association* 102, no. 4 (October 2014): 288–91. doi:10.3163/1536-5050.102.4.010.

Neely, Teresa Y., and Megan K. Beard. "Recruiting and Retaining Academic Research Librarians." *College and Research Libraries News* 69, no. 6 (June 2008): 314–15.

Neely, Teresa Y., and Lorna Peterson. "Achieving Racial and Ethnic Diversity among Academic and Research Librarians: The Recruitment, Retention, and Advancement of Librarians of Color—A White Paper." *College and Research Libraries News* 68, no. 9 (October 2007): 562–65.

Posner, Miriam. "No Half Measures: Overcoming Common Challenges to Doing Digital Humanities in the Library." *Journal of Library Administration* 53, no. 1 (January 2013): 43–52. doi:10.1080/01930826.2013.756694.

"Professional Competencies." *Medical Library Association (MLA).* 2016. http://www.mlanet.org/p/cm/ld/fid=39.

Saunders, Laura. "Academic Libraries' Strategic Plans: Top Trends and Under-Recognized Areas." *Journal of Academic Librarianship* 41, no. 3 (May 2015): 285–91. doi:10.1016/j.acalib.2015.03.011.

"Semantic Web." *World Wide Web Consortium.* 2015. https://www.w3.org/standards/semanticweb.

"Standards Portal." *Society of American Archivists (SAA).* 2016. http://www2.archivists.org/standards.

Swanson, Juleah, Ione Damasco, Isabel Gonzalez-Smith, Dracine Hodges, Todd Honma, and Azusa Tanaka. "Why Diversity Matters: A Roundtable Discussion on Racial and Ethnic Diversity in Librarianship." *In the Library with the Lead Pipe.* July 29, 2015. http://www.inthelibrarywiththeleadpipe.org/2015/why-diversity-matters-a-roundtable-discussion-on-racial-and-ethnic-diversity-in-librarianship.

Talley, Mary. "Success and the Embedded Librarian." *Information Outlook* 15, no. 3 (May 4, 2011): 25–28.

Triumph, Therese F., and Penny M. Beile. "The Trending Academic Library Job Market: An Analysis of Library Position Announcements from 2011 with Comparisons to 1996 and 1988." *College and Research Libraries* 76, no. 6 (September 2015): 716–39. doi:10.5860/crl.76.6.716.

Vandegrift, Micah, and Stewart Varner. "Evolving in Common: Creating Mutually Supportive Relationships between Libraries and the Digital Humanities." *Journal of Library Administration* 53, no. 1 (January 2013): 67–78. doi:10.1080/01930826.2013.756699.

Walters, William H. "Faculty Status of Librarians at U.S. Research Universities." *Journal of Academic Librarianship* 42, no. 2 (March 2016): 161–71. doi:10.1016/j.acalib.2015.11.002.

"Welcome to NISO." *National Information Standards Organization (NISO).* 2016. www.niso.org.

Zabel, Diane, Elizabeth A. Thomas, Nora Bird, and Richard J. Moniz Jr. "Informationists in a Small University Library." *Reference and User Services Quarterly* 51, no. 3 (Spring 2012): 223–25.

11

Library as Place[1]

David W. Lewis

"The academic library as place holds a unique position on campus. No other building can so symbolically and physically represent the academic heart of an institution."

—Geoffrey T. Freeman[2]

Introduction

Today, the academic library building should be the place on campus reserved for nonclassroom academic work. It should provide a variety of spaces that match the variety of ways students and faculty do their work—quietly and privately, in groups, with their own technology, and with technology supplied by the library. The library should create spaces to match each and should aspire to be at once a sacred and comfortable "third place." Beyond simply being study space, the library should house other functions that support academic success and provide opportunities for faculty and students from different disciplines to mingle and mix. The particulars will differ from campus to campus, but the basic framework will be the same. Missing from this description is the notion that libraries should be a place to store books, as they have always been in the past.

Libraries as buildings, for most of their history, have served as the places where books and people came together. They were about safely storing and protecting books and providing spaces for people to use them. Preserving paper books remains important, but today most library resources are digital and available from anywhere there is a network connection, which for all practical purposes means everywhere. This begs the question, "Why do we need a physical space called a library?" Colleges and universities will continue to need to store their legacy book collections and special materials, but is a special and dedicated space for the interaction of students and faculty with digital content still required? Good question. The answer should be yes, but the change in the medium of scholarship from paper to bits changes what a library building—the library as place—needs to be. As Deanna Marcum puts it, the "local library is no longer a collection, but a set of services that connects the user to all information everywhere."[3]

Many of the academic libraries now in use date from the second half of the twentieth century and a few from before World War II. These buildings were constructed in times very different from those we live in today. The first lesson to take from this should be that library buildings last a long time. A twenty-year-old library building might often still be considered "new." In beginning our consideration of the library as space and place, we find it useful to look at why these buildings were designed as they were and which goals the architects and librarians who planned them sought to accomplish. We consider three periods and three design frameworks. The first is the period until World War II, which featured a central weight-bearing stack core surrounded by reader and staff spaces. The second period began in the 1950s and featured an open or modular design, with stacks and reader spaces intermingled, usually on the upper floors, and services points and staff space on the main and lower levels. While there were many quite imaginative variations, library buildings from this period generally had three to five stories and were rectangular. Beginning in the 1990s, technology was inserted into this style of building, but it retained its basic configuration. In about 2010, automated book storage systems—often called BookBots—replaced stacks as an option for book storage, and what will likely be the model for most buildings for at least a decade or two was born. In this design, books are primarily stored in the BookBot, and the architect enjoys the freedom to create reader spaces without the constraints imposed by the need to store books in public spaces. These libraries inevitably include a coffee shop front and center and usually incorporate other academic units that support student academic success, such as writing and tutoring centers.

In all of these cases, the designers needed to address several key questions. The first was, How will the books be stored? Central to answering this question is the balance between security and access. The manner in which the book collection will be stored frames the possibilities for the design of the rest of the building. Once designers have answered the central book storage question, they must consider how they will configure reader space and which other services and functions they should include in the library. This requires determining the mix of individual and group study, tables versus carrels versus soft seating, and the nature and extent of technology to be deployed. Designing these spaces will be important because providing nonclassroom academic space has become a priority on many campuses. In earlier periods, the design of many staff spaces hinged on workflow because optimizing the way materials traveled from the loading dock to the stacks mattered. This is much less important today; instead, service strategies will more likely determine the arrangement of space for staff and the location and layout of service points.

One issue of central concern in academic library design for some time has been flexibility. This began as a desire to be able to reconfigure space and became one of the reasons for moving to modular design in the 1950s. Today this remains an issue, but flexibility for both power and data and other building infrastructure have become equally important. One difficulty is that libraries tend to be iconic rather than utilitarian buildings. This fact often leads to grand and sweeping spaces that are by their nature not very flexible. This creates an inevitable tension in library design.

This chapter reviews the history of academic library buildings and then considers the issues librarians and architects face in designing and redesigning library space. The chapter does not deal in any depth with the details of construction, such as lighting and HVAC. Should you become involved in a building project, your role will not be designer or engineer. Your first priority will be to articulate to these professionals the needs the library will fill for students and faculty. You must have a sense of where library services are going in the future and where flexibility will matter. Which physical collections should remain, and how will they be stored or weeded? To the best of your ability, you should bring evidence to this process. Design is by its nature a process that balances competing priorities. Not everything that should be on the main floor will fit. The desire to have space that serves both symbolic and utilitarian purposes will create conflicts. The best projects result from imaginative compromise.

Being involved in a building project can be challenging, but it will often prove to be the most rewarding undertaking of your career. In the end, you will have helped to create something tangible and lasting.

The final consideration by way of introduction is that we face a large backlog of library construction. In the sixteen years between 2000 and 2015, *Library Journal*, in their "Architecture Year in Review," documented 157 new library buildings and 275 more renovations or additions, for a total of 432 projects. However, only 52 of these were large projects involving more than 150,000 square feet, or more than $50 million.[4] This level of construction comes nowhere near what will be needed to keep up with the aging of library buildings. The National Center for Educational Statistics reports that, in 2012, there were 3,793 academic libraries in the United States.[5] If the *Library Journal* figures have captured most of the construction projects, then this means that only about 10 percent of the academic libraries in the United States have been replaced or significantly renovated since the turn of the century. This in combination with the rapid changes in the way libraries are being used means that we will likely see many more library construction projects in the next decade or two. How library space should and will be developed will become part of many academic librarians' portfolio.

The History and Future of Library Buildings[6]

Pre–World War II: Weight-Bearing Stacks

Surprisingly, we find buildings of this type still in use, though many have been renovated or added to; for example, Butler Library at Columbia, the Alderman Library at the University of Virginia, Widener Library at Harvard, or maybe most notably the cathedral-like Sterling Memorial Library at Yale. In this

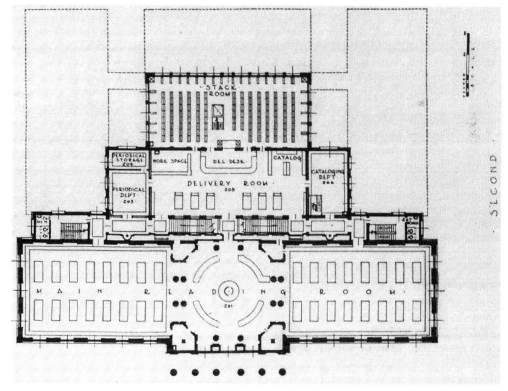

Figure 11.1 University of North Carolina, Chapel Hill, 1929. *Source: Edna Ruth Hanley,* College and University Library Buildings *(Chicago: American Library Association, 1939), 35; courtesy of the Libraries, University of North Carolina at Chapel Hill.*

Figure 11.2 Weight-bearing stacks, Widener Library, Harvard University.
Source: https://en.wikipedia.org/wiki/Widener_Library.

design, a weight-bearing stack core was surrounded by reading rooms and rooms containing staff and services. In a weight-bearing stack core, the stack uprights serve structural purposes and carry the weight of the books and the rest of the building (see figures 11.1 and 11.2). These stack cores could support ten stack levels or more; for example, the book tower of Sterling Memorial Library at Yale comprises seven stories and sixteen stack levels. In such libraries, the standard ceiling height from deck to deck measured seven feet six inches. This meant the stack core really constituted a building inside the surrounding structure. This configuration resulted in highly efficient storage largely because of the low ceiling heights. In addition, it provided security for the collection by allowing controlled access to the stacks, which were often closed. Edna Ruth Hanley in her 1939 book on academic library buildings outlines the functions these structures needed to accommodate. They included efficient processing and managing of collections and the "provision of quiet, comfortable, and attractive rooms for reading and study;" to these she added "assistance with developing the reading habit" and stimulating users "to read for culture and for pleasure."[7] The design was intended to accommodate individual study and interaction with books. Libraries built in this period were often meant to be architecturally significant.

Because the weight-bearing stack cores cannot be easily repurposed, the only reasonable way to renovate buildings from this period would be to remove the stack structure. This is expensive, but because of the architectural quality of many of the libraries from this period, with a sufficient budget, we can create striking renovated and expanded buildings. While not an academic library, Indianapolis Public Central Library demonstrates the possibilities.

1950 to 2000: Open or Modular Design

In the early 1950s, limits of the prewar approach to library buildings became clear, and a new design, at the time called "modular," was developed. Central to this proposition was a concern for how libraries were actually used and for librarian engagement in the planning and design process.[8] As Ralph E. Ellsworth, a champion of this approach, puts it, "Proof of the adaptability of the modular idea lies no longer on claims but in the operation of existing buildings."[9] By the 1960s, a building boom for academic libraries was underway. In his comprehensive book on library architecture, published in 1965, Keyes D. Metcalf reports that 504 academic libraries were built in the United States between 1960 and 1965.[10] Ellsworth opens his 1973 version of the complete guide by saying, "Indeed, the past five years alone could qualify as the Golden Age of library-building."[11] David Kaser documents library construction from 1840 to 1994. It peaked in 1967, when 71 new libraries were opened.[12]

Metcalf focuses on one truth about libraries at the time—they grew. Collections were at the time growing at rates of 4 percent to 5 percent per year, leading to a doubling of collection size in sixteen or seventeen years. Space required for students and faculty grew as colleges and universities expanded to accommodate the baby boom. It also became clear that technology would affect library operations. These forces changed the way people viewed library architecture. Utility and flexibility became much more important. Metcalf poses several telling questions in his chapter on library objectives:

1. "It can readily be agreed that the library should not be ugly. But how important is its architectural style?"
2. "Should the construction be of such high quality that the structure will be sound after a hundred years, or should its life be thought of in terms of a limited period . . . for instance, twenty-five years?"[13]

Metcalf defines *flexibility* as follows: "As large a percentage of the floor space as possible should be useable for any of the primary functions of the library: reader accommodations, service to readers, space for staff activities, and housing for collections."[14] Ellsworth echoes Metcalf, saying, "everyone knows that a modular library is one in which most of the floor space, except core service areas, can be used to support free standing book stacks, or subdivide into rooms."[15] The views of Metcalf and Ellsworth guided much of the library construction for the next fifty years. A second edition of Metcalf's book, published in 1986, as the preface states, "retains all of Mr. Metcalf's principles."[16] This led to a half-century of library buildings, usually rectangular and three to five stories high, with open plans and without weight-bearing interior walls. Modular shelving and seating became the norm. Book security systems made it possible to locate collections in open public areas. The resulting buildings were rarely architecturally distinguished. Air conditioning was usually required, which was sometimes a concern early on. But these buildings proved easy and relatively inexpensive to renovate, add on to, or repurpose. Later in the period, technology infrastructure in buildings became more important, and group spaces in part replaced a sole focus on the individual user. In a trend that Kaser bemoans, the "unadorned modular simplicity" of the 1960s gave way to more architecturally inventive but less functional and less flexible buildings (see figure 11.3).[17] Examples of such buildings include the Geisel Library at the University of California, San Diego, or the Main Library at Northwestern University, with three towers containing shelving arranged like the spokes of a wheel.

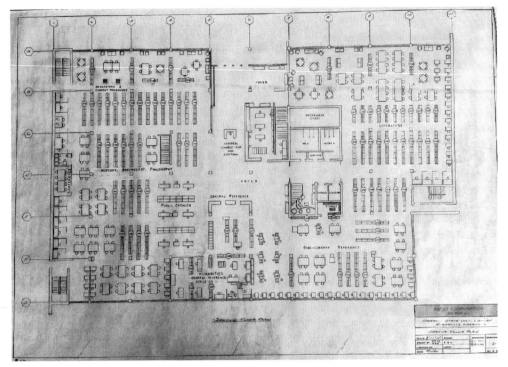

Figure 11.3 Kerr Library, Oregon State University, 1963. *Source: Oregon State University Libraries Special Collections and Archives Research Center;* from Planning Library Buildings for Service, Proceedings of a Library Buildings and Equipment Institute, Kent State University, July 6–8, 1961 *(Chicago: American Library Association, 1964), 85.*

As more library resources became digital, many grew concerned that libraries might become deserted. One response was to look to bookstores, then in their heyday, as models.[18] Barbara Fister describes this period as follows:

> Throughout the next decade [2000 to 2010], the "library as place" was a hot topic as librarians reconsidered how the library as a physical facility could shed its functional identity as a warehouse for collections and better facilitate student learning. Library cafés replaced prohibitions against food. Stacks were moved to make room for information commons, which in turn became learning commons as a technology focus gave way to partnerships with learning support offices such as writing centers, advising, tutoring, and (yes) tech support.[19]

Christopher Stewart provides a good summary of academic library construction in the first decade of the twenty-first century. He notes an increased focus on undergraduates and their use of libraries and a decline in concern for faculty spaces.[20]

Remote Storage Facilities, the Collective Print Collection, and BookBots

Beginning in the mid-1980s, several major universities began developing remote storage facilities. These facilities provided for less expensive storage of little-used materials. In 1986, Harvard University opened its facility in Southborough, MA, which became the standard model for efficient, high-density library storage. Typically, these facilities are located off campus on less expensive land. They provide climate control to maximize the long-term preservation of paper, a stable temperature of 50° Fahrenheit and relative humidity of 35 percent, and feature high-density shelving, with fifteen to twenty times the capacity of traditional library shelving. As Lizanne Payne says, "Harvard-model facilities are designed to achieve maximum space efficiency at the lowest cost of construction. They are not designed for rapid retrieval, and most often house materials specifically identified as 'low use.'"[21] Payne reports that, by 2007, there were at least 68 remote storage facilities in the United States and Canada, with a combined capacity of 70 million volumes.[22]

As digital content became more important, the use of print materials declined. The number of general and reserve circulations in academic libraries in the United States as reported by the National Centers for Education Statistics declined by a third, or more than 77 million circulations, in the eighteen years between 1996 and 2014.[23] As the use of print materials declined, the costs of managing them became more apparent. Paul N. Courant and Matthew "Buzzy" Nielson calculate the cost of the perpetual storage of a print book in open stacks to be $141.89, with an annual average (in 2009 US dollars) of $4.26.[24] They admonish us that "it is important to recognize that the costs associated with a print-based world, often assumed to be small, are actually large."[25] Courant and Nielson document the fact that, even in high-density storage, the annual cost to keep a print volume comes to $0.69.[26]

The recognition of the high cost of storing print books and the decline in their use has led to a rethinking of the role of print collections on local campuses and a move toward multi-institution or national-level collaboration on a "collective collection."[27] The collections housed in remote storage facilities can provide the basis for such a collection, and using such tools as those provided by the consulting firm Sustainable Collection Services, libraries can identify books to be weeded because they are little used and held where they can be borrowed when needed. This, in combination with large-scale digitization of print books by Google Books and the HathiTrust Digital Library,[28] means that individual libraries can reasonably expect to reduce their print collections significantly over the next decade.

The final development in the storage of print books are BookBots, or—as they are sometimes referred to—automatic (or automated) storage and retrieval systems (ASRS or AS/RS). The first such system was installed in 1991 in the Oviatt Library at California State University Northridge, but they were not generally considered a reasonable option until twenty years later. Based on the technology used in automated warehouses, these systems have long, high aisles with robotic arms that retrieve metal boxes in which books are stored. A computer inventory system tracks the location of individual books and their locations. These systems can store books in one-ninth the space required by traditional open stacks, and like remote storage facilities, the temperature and humidity can be kept at levels conducive to the long-term preservation of paper. BookBots are generally part of new construction and provide the means of storing large quantities of print items securely while at the same time making them quickly available. The decline in the importance of print books and the new strategies for storing them allow the focus of library design to shift. Focus now can be nearly exclusively on the user.

The New Library Model

The James B. Hunt Jr. Library at North Carolina State University boasts the distinction of being the most widely recognized library today.[29] In winning the Stanford Prize for Innovation in Research Libraries, it was cited for offering an "integrated technology environment, and a suite of services [that make] the Hunt Library . . . an innovative model for the research library as a high-technology research platform."[30] In reviewing the building, *Library Journal* quotes Susan Nutter, the library director at North Carolina State, as saying it was intended to "create spaces that encourage collaboration, reflection, creativity, and awe."[31] Designed by international firm Snøhetta and opened in 2013, the 221,000-square-foot LEED silver building[32] was constructed at a cost of $115.2 million. While the Hunt Library garners the most attention, the model it uses is not unique. The Mary Idema Pew Library Learning and Information Commons at Grand Valley State University, also opened in 2013, employs the same model.[33] Collectively, these two buildings represent the template for new library construction that can be expected to dominate for the next decade or two.

The Hunt and Pew Libraries are both built around BookBots as the primary means of storing books and contain varied user spaces, including many group studies, rich technology, service points reminiscent of the Genius Bar at an Apple Store, a coffee shop, meeting rooms, and space for other campus units. While they share this template, each has implemented it very differently. As Nutter's quote suggests, Hunt constitutes a grand piece of architecture. The only books not housed in the BookBot line reading rooms, primarily to create ambiance. While striking, the Hunt Library cannot be considered flexible (see figure 11.4). One small detail of Hunt strikes me as telling in this regard. The Maker Space, containing several 3-D printers, is located in what was obviously once a very small office or storage room. What clearly happened is that the Maker Space was a late addition for the program or was added after the building was completed, and the planners had nowhere else to put it. The Pew Library building on the other hand, aside from the BookBot, is one that Metcalf and Ellsworth would appreciate—rectangular, five stories, and few weight-bearing interior walls. Pew also houses 100,000 volumes of its 750,000-volume collection on traditional library stacks. Over the long haul, I believe that Pew will prove a more successful, if less architecturally distinguished, building because it will be less expensive to renovate and the space that now holds traditional library stacks can be repurposed when books get withdrawn or moved to the BookBot. The growing importance of energy efficiency and sustainability has become an additional factor to consider in the new model. This shows in the pride universities take when a new building earns a high LEED rating.[34]

While Hunt and Pew will likely serve as the template for new construction, we can see an equally interesting set of developments in renovations. The William Oxley Thompson Memorial Library at Ohio State University represents a good example of this. Originally constructed in 1913, the library was expanded in the 1950s and again in the 1970s. The square footage of the building did not increase in the renovation, but collections shrank and moved to remote storage, and the reader space expanded.

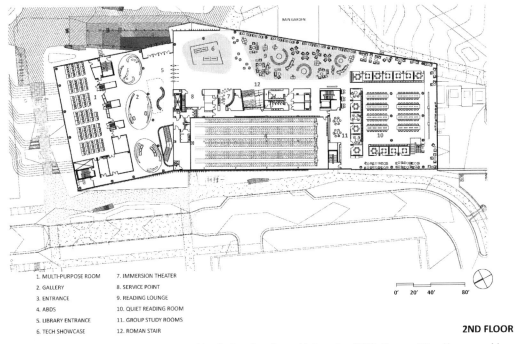

1. MULTI-PURPOSE ROOM	7. IMMERSION THEATER
2. GALLERY	8. SERVICE POINT
3. ENTRANCE	9. READING LOUNGE
4. ABDS	10. QUIET READING ROOM
5. LIBRARY ENTRANCE	11. GROUP STUDY ROOMS
6. TECH SHOWCASE	12. ROMAN STAIR

0' 20' 40' 80'

2ND FLOOR

Figure 11.4 James B. Hunt Jr. Library at North Carolina State University, 2013. *Source: http://www.world-architects.com/en/projects/42358_James_B_Hunt_Jr_Library.*

Much of the 1950 and 1977 additions were demolished, and a new window wall brought in light and matched the scale of the original Beaux Arts building. Glass walls exposed the 1950s closed-stack core so that the books became a dominant feature of the interior space.[35] Interestingly, in planning for a similar renovation at the University of Maryland, "Books as Heart" featured as one of the two themes explored in depth.[36] So while we see a trend to place books out of sight either in remote storage facilities or in BookBots, we can also see a countertrend to make books the focus of the building design.

Creating the Library as Place

Clearly, academic libraries as physical places are still much in demand, especially among students. The *Chronicle of Higher Education* reports a study by the research firm Student Monitor that found that 64 percent of students reported being more satisfied with their libraries than they were with any other spaces on campus.[37] In a September 2014 *Ubiquitous Librarian* blog post, Brian Mathews asks the question, "Why do people who love libraries love libraries?" Mathews is not asking about people who like libraries in the general sense but rather about people who come to libraries and who spend their time in them. In answering the question, he quotes a student who says in part, "There's just kind of a library community of library people doing library things." Mathews then goes on to argue for the importance of creating this library community because it makes the library a place that is, as he concludes, "different from anywhere else on campus."[38]

Libraries serve as special places on campus. Using methods drawn from the psychology of religion, Heather Lea Jackson and Trudi Bellardo Hahn make a case for the library as sacred space. As they put it,

> This empirical study affirmed our hypothesis that spaces deemed as "sacred" or "sanctified" produce affective benefits for people that extend beyond attitudes and into the realm of behavior (projected library use). Circulation statistics do not measure these benefits; students may not actually use the books on the shelves, but they "sanctify" the books—being around the books makes them feel more scholarly and connected to the institution's educational mission.[39]

This quotation echoes the words of the architect Geoffrey T. Freeman, designer of many academic libraries, who says, "While students are intensely engaged in using new technologies, they also want to enjoy the library as a contemplative oasis. Interestingly, a significant majority of students still considers the traditional reading room their favorite area of the library—the great, vaulted, light-filled space, whose walls are lined with books they may never pull off the shelf."[40]

Others have argued that libraries should be what are sometimes called "third places" or "third spaces." This concept comes from the work of Ray Oldenburg and his classic book *The Great Good Place: Cafés, Coffee Shops, Community Centers, Beauty Parlors, General Stores, Bars, Hangouts, and How They Get You through the Day*.[41] Oldenburg looks broadly at space in the United States and argues that, in post–World War II America, what he calls the first two spaces, home and work, had expanded to the exclusion of spaces for informal public life. He argues for the "third place" between work and home as being crucial for a healthy society. Translating this concept to a campus, we can identify a variety of third places, places beyond the classroom or dorm room. Many of Oldenburg's characteristics for third space fit academic libraries:

1. *On Neutral Ground.* Libraries are neutral ground. Most of the other space on a campus belongs to a department and is thus part of a silo. One of its great strengths as a place is that people from all parts of the campus and all disciplines can mix in the library.
2. *Leveler.* Third places do not restrict who can use them. Oldenburg also suggests that the third place is upbeat, cheerful, and a place to enjoy the company of others. It might be a stretch to call the library upbeat and cheerful, but it does function as a place to be in the company of others.

3. *Accessibility and Accommodation.* Anyone can go to a third place at almost any time of day and find acquaintances. Third places keep long hours. They accommodate activities that are, as Oldenburg puts it, "largely unplanned, unscheduled, unorganized, and unstructured."[42] These are prime characteristics of libraries.

4. *The Regulars.* The regulars set the tone for the space but generally welcome others. Libraries have regulars who always study in the same place at regular times, and in many cases, these regulars set the tone of the space they use.

5. *Low Profile.* Third places tend to be plain. They do not intend to be flashy, to be places to be seen in; rather, they are modest, easy places to be comfortable in. Most library buildings begin their lives with high ambitions, but in many cases, over time, they slip into being a bit shabby in an agreeable way.

6. *The Mood Is Playful.* The third place is a place of play. We often witness a sense of playfulness in libraries, especially in the evening, when the adults have left campus and the library becomes truly student space.

7. *Home Away from Home.* The third place roots people in a space where they can feel belonging, ease, and warmth. For many students, the library becomes their second home.

So while the library hardly resembles the neighborhood tavern, it clearly serves, at least in the context of a college campus, as the kind of space that Oldenburg would identify as a third place. Oldenburg's third place criteria also provide a useful guide to what we should be striving for as we build and renovate library space.

If the library strives to be the primary third place on campus and the primary place for non-classroom learning, then we need to understand what this really means. Scott Bennett has looked at learning and the spaces outside the classroom that campuses provide to encourage it and concludes, "[W]hen one looks at much of non-classroom campus space, its design is more likely to respond to the concerns of service providers—in residence and dining halls and in computer laboratories—than to the needs of students as learners. This has been demonstrably the case in libraries."[43] Bennett suggests that, if we hope to design space to support learning, then we need to be clear about which type of learning behaviors we wish to encourage and how the space we design will advance this goal. He uses the term *intentional learning* as a frame for discussing nonclassroom spaces, arguing that, when students move beyond the classroom, they take responsibility for and control of their own learning. He then develops a set of behaviors, mostly drawn from the National Survey of Student Engagement (NSSE).[44] In a study that spanned six institutions, Bennett used this framework and asked questions of both students and faculty. His findings show that there is consensus on which behaviors these groups consider important. They include collaborative learning, studying alone, and discussing material with other students. At most of the institutions, both students and faculty felt that some of the behaviors were supported and the library was the most likely place where this happened. Bennett concludes that campuses could make better investments in space if they were more consciously aware of which learning behaviors they wished to cultivate. He also argues that too often librarians, when they design space, start with a services perspective rather than a learning perspective.

Fister suggests that, at least to some extent, librarians have begun to do this. She says, "Librarians began to seriously consider the library in the life of the user rather than the user in the life of the library."[45] The most tangible example of this is the use of ethnographic research methods to explore how students use space at different times for different purposes. The initial work was done at the University of Rochester and has been followed by the ERIAL Project at a number of Illinois institutions and most recently at the University of Maryland, where the work was part of a building design project.[46] John K. Stemmer and David M. Mahan studied how student use of library space correlated with measures of academic success. Their analysis shows different impacts of library use at different points of a student's career and the academic impact of different kinds of library spaces and services.[47]

One important consideration is the type of spaces that should be provided to users. One way to think about this is what the furniture company Steelcase, which has done considerable research in this area, calls a "palette of place."[48] They propose a two-by-two grid, with one axis being public–private and the other axis being alone–together. There are in this model four types of space. Private/alone spaces are for individually focused work, and they provide visual and acoustical accommodations and include "study enclaves," small breakout rooms, and old-fashioned library carrels. Public/alone spaces are for individual work in the presence of others, providing social connections while studying alone. The easiest way to provide this kind of space is with tables. Private/together spaces are for group work in areas with visual and acoustical accommodations. Group study rooms are probably the best way to provide this kind of space, but they are expensive. Public/together spaces are open for impromptu collaboration. These spaces are best when they are flexible and the furniture is moveable. Libraries need to provide all of these spaces, but doing so is a design challenge. Noise is an especially challenging issue. It is important not to underestimate the need for private/alone and public/alone space, as it is the kind of space that most students need most often. A study of the daily rhythm of library use done by Gensler Research finds that individual focused work outranked other uses of academic libraries by a factor of 3:1.[49] The lesson according to Gensler is to focus on pragmatic individual student needs and not to sacrifice quiet in pursuit of collaboration.[50]

At the beginning of their book on designing library spaces, Brian Mathews and Leigh Ann Soistmann say, "As libraries shape-shift in response to digital migration and other seismic changes, our spaces have emerged as experimental landscapes fostering personal growth and multimodal expression. Our buildings are active laboratories for human progress."[51]

Considerations for Library Building Projects

In concluding, we look at a number of issues we need to consider when building new library buildings or renovating existing library space. It is important to understand that designing space is a puzzle, sometimes complex and often one that needs to be solved in the face of significant constraints. Projects generally start with a program; that is, a statement of the functions to be included in the new or redesigned space, usually down to the number of square feet required, and the relationships of spaces and required adjacencies between these functions. Creating organizational agreement on the program is the first challenge. Not everyone will agree on what is important or where it should be located. The program is often the first time financial constraints enter the picture. At this stage, even a simple per-square-foot calculation might indicate that there is not enough money to accomplish what is desired. Difference of opinion about the importance of creating an architecturally distinguished building at the cost of additional square feet for desired services or space will arise. The opinion of the president or members of the board of trustees may trump even the best arguments the library puts forward. With this understanding, these are the major issues that need to be considered in a building project:

1. Where do the print books go? Large university libraries will have remote storage facilities. New libraries will have BookBots. In both cases, print books will be stored in secure, climate-controlled environments. Some books will inevitably remain in public spaces for political reasons or to create "sacred" space with a scholarly feel. In many cases libraries will be downsizing their print book collections. As they do so, the items they continue to keep will likely be heavily used or relatively rare. This will mean that security and long-term preservation will become more important. The open design of most academic libraries is not well suited to do this. Creating closed storage space for print books could become the preferred option. A related issue concerns special collections space. Going forward, academic libraries will find what they hold that is unique or special is the basis for their reputation. Space must be considered the most important asset in developing physical special collections. Adding space for special collections will provide an advantage.

2. Which service points do we need, and how will they be staffed? Reference services have changed significantly in the last decade, and circulation desks change as readers check out print items less often. Managing building access and security changes as print books are secured by removing them from public areas. Technology support might be reduced if users increasingly bring their technology with them. We might anticipate that traditional-looking desks will remain to some extent, but the Apple Store Genius Bar approach used in the Hunt Library and the collaboration counters in the Pew Library provide interesting alternatives. Whatever we do, we should probably be able to undo and rebuild because service patterns will inevitably remain in flux.

3. Which types of user spaces do we desire? The easy answer to this question would be to accommodate all possibilities. Do not underestimate the need for enclosed group spaces, and quiet spaces are a surprising priority for many. We should ask students what they want and, equally important, watch what they do. Ethnographic studies provide powerful evidence and should be pursued where possible. Finally, do not forget that some grand and inspiring space is a good thing.

4. Where will staff be located? Situating staff adjacent to service points seems less important today than it might have been in the past, as are concerns about arranging staff space to accommodate the flow of print materials. It remains important to cluster staff to the greatest extent possible to encourage interaction and collaboration. Contemporary approaches to office design and university standards will likely dictate the office options.

5. Which other functions or units should be invited into the library? A coffee shop will likely prove to be a required feature. Using it as part of a larger casual user space in the spirit of a bookstore coffee shop seems like a good idea. Other units that support student academic success should be welcomed, as should units that support cross-disciplinary research or facilities like Maker Spaces that provide common resources to users from different academic units. We should give consideration to meeting spaces of various sorts, as well as event space, including provision for catering. Not all libraries will want to regularly host wedding receptions, but accommodating alumni or donor events would be a plus.

Regardless of individual circumstances, every academic library should have a strategy for how it wishes to develop its space. Whether the library wants to do so or not, it will come under pressure to reduce print collections and reallocate this space to other campus priorities. If the library fails to devise a plan, then it faces the danger that space reallocation will proceed in a piecemeal fashion, and the result will be suboptimal. Library administrators should also impress on campus constituents that, while they see the potential to reallocate some library space by reducing print collections, this space remains the most valuable space on campus and should be used carefully. It likely stands in the center of campus, it stays open long hours, and it will probably be relatively inexpensive to repurpose. It should be used for what really matters.

Discussion Questions

1. What is the best way to store printed books? Why? Is this change based on campus characteristics or other factors?

2. What are the best ways to define the kinds of spaces students want and need for their nonclassroom academic work? How do you develop evidence to support your answer?

3. In planning for new or renovated library space, how long should the new space be expected to last before the next renovation? Ten years or twenty-five or more? Why?

4. What is the best way to build flexibility into a newly constructed library? Does flexibility still matter? If so, where?

Assignment

You are a librarian in a public master's-level university with 18,000 students. The library on your campus was built in 1974 and has had no significant renovations since then. It is a classic building from the period, with three stories and a basement that houses mechanical and staff space. Each floor is 125 feet by 200 feet. It is a reinforced concrete building with columns on 25-foot centers. Each floor is five by eight bays (see figure 11.5). The university has just funded the renovation of the main floor that currently houses the entrance and lobby, the circulation desk with staff and processing space, the reference desk and collection with a cluster of thirty computers, reference staff offices, and the current periodicals room. Space has been created on the other floors to house all of the print items now on the main floor. Library staff can be housed on other floors if necessary. The floor is entirely open for redevelopment. The university president has said publicly that she wants the renovated library to inspire learning and to be the crossroad of ideas for the campus. Your team has been asked to conceptualize this renovation. Specifically, you are to do the following:

1. Develop a vision for the renovation that articulates its goals and creates excitement about the project. This should be no more than a sentence or two and should include a graphic.
2. Develop a program for the main floor that defines which functions will be on the floor and their size and relation to each other, including library and nonlibrary functions as appropriate. Provide a short justification for why each function should be included and how it fits into the vision.

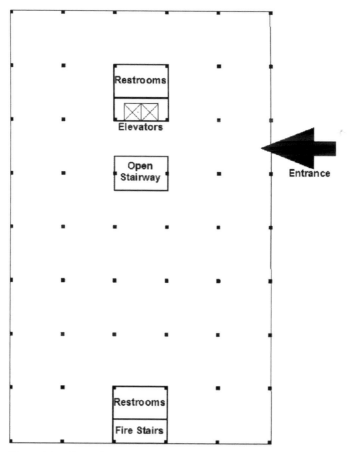

Figure 11.5 Floor plan for assignment

3. If service points are to be located on the floor, describe how they will be staffed, and develop a preliminary design for them.
4. Develop a conceptual design of the floor that defines the functions and their locations and sizes. Indicate traffic patterns. Include general characteristics of the space for each function, including number of users it will accommodate, expected noise level, technology needs, and type of furnishings.

Notes

1. This chapter draws in part on David W. Lewis, "Step Two: Creating the Library as Place" in *Reimagining the Academic Library* (Lanham, MD: Rowman and Littlefield, 2016), 93–102.
2. Geoffrey T. Freeman, "The Library as Place: Changes in Learning Patterns, Collections, Technology, and Use," in *Library as Place: Rethinking Roles, Rethinking Space* (Washington, DC: Council on Library and Information Resources, February 2005), 9, http://www.clir.org/pubs/reports/pub129/pub129.pdf.
3. Deanna Marcum, *Issue Brief: Library Leadership for the Digital Age* (New York: Ithaka S+R, March 28, 2016), 4, http://www.sr.ithaka.org/publications/library-leadership-for-the-digital-age.
4. See the *Library Journal* "Architecture Year in Review" issues published annually in November or December.
5. Tai Phan, Laura Hardesty, and Jamie Hug, *Academic Libraries: 2012 First Look.* (Washington, DC: National Center for Education Statistics, January 2014), table 1, http://nces.ed.gov/pubs2014/2014038.pdf.
6. The best history of the academic library in the United States to the end of the twentieth century is David Kaser, *The Evolution of the American Academic Library Building* (Lanham, MD: Scarecrow Press, 1997).
7. Edna Ruth Hanley, *College and University Library Buildings* (Chicago: American Library Association, 1939), 11.
8. A good description of the change in approach can be found in Ralph E. Ellsworth, "Library Architecture and Buildings," *Library Quarterly* 25 no. 1 (January 1955): 66–75, http://www.jstor.org/stable/4304384.
9. Ralph E. Ellsworth, "Determining Factors in the Evaluation of the Modular Plan for Libraries," *College and Research Libraries* 14, no. 3 (April 1953): 125, doi:10.5860/crl_14_02_125.
10. Keyes D. Metcalf, *Planning Academic and Research Library Buildings* (New York: McGraw-Hill, 1965), vii.
11. Ralph E. Ellsworth, *Academic Library Buildings: A Guide to Architectural Issues and Solutions* (Boulder, CO: Colorado Associated University Press, 1973), ix.
12. Kaser, *American Academic Library Building*, 119.
13. Metcalf, *Planning*, 15.
14. Ibid., 8.
15. Ralph E. Ellsworth, *Planning the College and University Library Building: A Book for Campus Planners and Architects* (Boulder, CO: Pruett Press, 1960), 6.
16. Keyes D. Metcalf, *Planning Academic and Research Library Buildings*, 2nd ed., edited by Philip D. Leighton and David C. Weber (Chicago: American Library Association, 1986), xi.
17. David Kaser, "Twenty-Five Years of Academic Library Building Planning," *College and Research Libraries* 45 no. 4 (July 1984): 268–81, doi:10.5860/crl_45_04_268.
18. See for example, Renee Feinberg, "B&N: The New College Library?" *Library Journal*, February 1, 1998, 49–51.
19. Barbara Fister, "Repositioning Library Space," in *New Roles for the Road Ahead: Essays Commissioned for ACRL's 75th Anniversary*, edited by Nancy Allen, 43–45 (Chicago: Association of College and Research Libraries, December 5, 2014), 43, http://www.ala.org/acrl/sites/ala.org.acrl/files/content/publications/whitepapers/new_roles_75th.pdf.
20. Christopher Stewart, *The Academic Library Building in the Digital Age: A Study of Construction, Planning, and Design of New Library Space* (Chicago: Association of College and Research Libraries, 2010), 78.
21. Lizanne Payne, "Library Storage Facilities and the Future of Print Collections in North America" (Dublin, OH: OCLC Programs and Research, September 2007), 10, www.oclc.org/programs/publications/reports/2007-01.pdf.
22. Ibid., 6.
23. See the National Center for Education Statistics (NCES) Library Statistics Program, http://nces.ed.gov/surveys/libraries/Academic.asp, for various reports.

24. Paul N. Courant and Matthew "Buzzy" Nielson, "On the Cost of Keeping a Book," in *The Idea of Order: Transforming Research Collections for 21st Century Scholarship*, 81–105 (Washington, DC: Council on Library and Information Resources, June 2010), 96, http://www.clir.org/pubs/reports/pub147/pub147 .pdf.

25. Ibid., 102.

26. Ibid., 96.

27. See, for example, Lorcan Dempsey, Brian Lavoie, Constance Malpas, Lynn Silipigni Connaway, Roger C. Schonfeld, J. D. Shipengrover, and Günter Waibel, *Understanding the Collective Collection: Towards a System-wide Perspective on Library Print Collections* (Dublin, OH: OCLC Research, December 2013), http://www.oclc.org/research/publications/library/2013/2013-09.pdf.

28. The HathiTrust Digital Library is a digital preservation repository and highly functional access platform managed by a consortium of academic libraries. It provides long-term preservation and access. As of October 2015, it contained more than 13.7 million volumes, more than 5.3 million of which are in the public domain. See https://www.hathitrust.org.

29. An architectural review with pictures and floor plans of the Hunt Library can be found in Deane Madsen, "James B. Hunt Jr. Library, Designed by Snøhetta," *Architect: The Journal of the American Institute of Architects*, June 25, 2013, http://www.architectmagazine.com/design/buildings/james-b-hunt-jr -library-designed-by-snhetta_o.

30. "Stanford Prize for Innovation in Research Libraries (SPIRL)—2014 Prizes," *Stanford University Libraries*, http://library.stanford.edu/projects/stanford-prize-innovation-research-libraries-spirl/2014-prizes.

31. Meredith Schwartz, "Tomorrow, Visualized: Library by Design," *Library Journal*, September 18, 2013, 1, http://lj.libraryjournal.com/2013/09/buildings/lbd/tomorrow-visualized-library-by-design.

32. Leadership in Energy and Environmental Design (LEED) is one of the most popular green building certification programs used worldwide. Developed by the nonprofit US Green Building Council (USGBC), it includes a set of rating systems for the design, construction, operation, and maintenance of green buildings. Silver is the third-highest of four ratings.

33. An architectural review with pictures and floor plans of the Pew Library can be found at "GVSU Pew Library/Stantec," *ArchDaily*, August 8, 2014, http://www.archdaily.com/534586/gvsu-pew-library-stan tec.

34. A good exploration of these issues can be found in Michael Wescott Loder, "Academic Libraries with a Future: How Are Academic Library Usage and Green Demands Changing Building Designs?" *College and Research Libraries* 71, no. 4 (July 2010): 348–60, doi:10.5860/crl-37r1.

35. Louise Schaper, "New Landmark Libraries 2012 #3: William Oxley Thompson Memorial Library, Ohio State University," *Library Journal*, June 28, 2012, http://lj.libraryjournal.com/2012/06/buildings/nation al-landmark-academic-library-3-william-oxley-thompson-memorial-library-ohio-state-university/#_.

36. Patricia Steele, David Cronrath, Sandra Parsons Vicchio, and Nancy Fried Foster, *The Living Library: An Intellectual Ecosystem* (Chicago: Association of College and Research Libraries, 2015), 83–115.

37. Steve Kolowich, "5 Things We Know about College Students in 2014," *Chronicle of Higher Education*, December 17, 2004, http://chronicle.com/blogs/wiredcampus/5-things-we-know-about-college-stu dents-in-2014/55313.

38. Brian Mathews, "Why Do People Who Love Libraries Love Libraries?" *The Ubiquitous Librarian: In the Pursuit of User-Sensitive Librarianship, Chronicle of Higher Education*, September 19, 2014, http://chron icle.com/blognetwork/theubiquitouslibrarian/2014/09/19/why-do-people-who-love-libraries-love -libraries.

39. Heather Lea Jackson and Trudi Bellardo Hahn, "Serving Higher Education's Highest Goals: Assessment of the Academic Library as Place," *College and Research Libraries* 72, no. 5 (September 2011): 436, doi:10.5860/crl-123.

40. Freeman, "Library as Place," 6.

41. Ray Oldenburg, *The Great Good Place: Cafés, Coffee Shops, Community Centers, Beauty Parlors, General Stores, Bars, Hangouts, and How They Get You through the Day* (New York: Paragon House, 1989).

42. Ibid., 33.

43. Scott Bennett, "Learning Behaviors and Learning Spaces," *portal: Libraries and the Academy* 11, no. 3 (July 2011): 3, doi:10.1353/pla.2011.0033.

44. The National Survey of Student Engagement (NSSE) is a survey mechanism used to measure the level of student participation at universities and colleges as it relates to learning and engagement. The survey is administered and assessed by Indiana University School of Education Center for Postsecondary Research (http://nsse.indiana.edu).

45. Fister, "Repositioning Library Space," 43.

46. Lynda M. Duke and Andrew D. Asher, eds., *College Libraries and Student Culture: What We Now Know* (Chicago: American Library Association, 2012); Nancy Fried Foster and Susan Gibbons, eds., *Studying Students: The Undergraduate Research Project at the University of Rochester* (Chicago: Association of College and Research Libraries, 2007); Steele et al., *Living Library*.

47. John K. Stemmer and David M. Mahan, "Investigating the Relationship of Library Usage to Student Outcomes," *College and Research Libraries* 77, no. 3 (May 2016), doi:10.5860/crl.77.3.359.

48. *Active Learning Spaces: Insights, Applications + Solutions* (Steelcase Education, 2015), 8–9.

49. *Gensler Research Catalog*, vol. 1 (Washington, DC: Gensler Research, 2014), 136.

50. "How Do Students Envision the Present and Future Academic Library?" *Gensler Research*, 2016, http://www.gensler.com/research-insight/research/students-on-libraries.

51. Brian Mathews and Leigh Ann Soistmann, *Encoding Space: Shaping Learning Environments That Unlock Human Potential* (Chicago: Association of College and Research Libraries, 2016), 12.

12

Serving Campus and Remote Students and Faculty

ONLINE LEARNING, DISTANCE EDUCATION, AND MOOCS

Debbie Faires

Introduction

Today's students and faculty members carry out their academic work from a variety of locations and use devices ranging from desktop or laptop computers to mobile tablets and phones. Add to this mix the increasing adoption of distance learning in the online environment; students and faculty may be located in separate states and beyond. Library resources and services must be available to all users wherever they may be working. Academic librarians must understand the needs of these students and faculty and how best to serve them.

Online Learning and Distance Education

The line between on-campus students and distance students, once a clear demarcation, has become blurred in today's technology-rich environment. Students who attend classes on campus may access library resources online—even while working within the library building itself. Campus students may take classes that are fully or partially online. Other students, located far from campus, may be taking distance education classes. The online environment opens opportunities for students enrolled in classes on campus to access lectures, conduct research, and collaborate without actually traveling to campus. How are these students to be classified? How and where does the library meet their needs?

What do we mean when we refer to "distance education"? In the late 1800s, some educators began using parcel post to deliver course materials and communicate with students.[1] Technology developments introduced content delivery via broadcast media.[2] As the Internet, particularly the World Wide Web, was developed, opportunities and enrollment in online courses grew dramatically, beginning in the 1990s.[3] Hope E. Kentnor offers a straightforward definition: "Distance education is defined as a method of teaching where the student and teacher are physically separated."[4] Note that the definition does not include the mode of instruction. This reflects the history of the various delivery modes that serve to carry out teaching and learning at a distance. Russ Poulin and Terri Taylor Straut define a distance education course as a "course in which the instructional content is delivered exclusively via distance education," adding that "requirements for coming to campus for orientation, testing, or academic support services do not exclude a course from being classified as distance education."[5]

Most of today's distance education takes place via online learning. In 2010, the US Department of Education published a meta-analysis of research on online education and defined it as "learning that takes place partially or entirely over the Internet."[6] Recognizing the broad range of the proportion of online content that might be offered in a class, one guideline defines an online course as one in which at least 80 percent of the content is delivered online.[7]

The terms *distance learning* and *online learning* are sometimes used interchangeably. But distance education is not always conducted online. Similarly, online learning does not always occur at a distance.

The distinction between distance learning and online learning becomes further blurred in reference to libraries because distance students and faculty want access to a full range of library services and resources online, as do those who come to campus. As Sheila Bonnand and Mary Anne Hansen have argued, the rising proportion of students in online and distance education "makes narrowing the gap in services for on- and off-campus students even more important."[8]

Distance education, shaped by forces that include the behavior of information consumers, technology, and economics, has reached a tipping point in today's educational environment.[9] The number of distance education enrollments continues to rise at rates exceeding those of overall higher education.[10] In fall 2014, 28 percent of higher education students were enrolled in at least one course at a distance.[11] During the same period, 14 percent (equivalent to one in seven) of currently enrolled students took *all* of their courses online.[12] As the authors state in the foreword of the 2015 Babson Survey report, "When more than one-quarter of higher education students are taking a course online, distance education is clearly mainstream."[13]

Student Achievement in Online versus Face-to-Face Models

How does the variety of delivery models in use today affect student achievement and learning? Researchers have been studying and comparing the outcomes for more than two decades. The 2010 US Department of Education meta-analysis of research in this area noted, "In recent experimental and quasi-experimental studies contrasting blends of online and face-to-face instruction with conventional face-to-face classes, blended instruction has been more effective."[14] The report also noted, "Students in online learning conditions performed modestly better, on average, than those learning the same material through traditional face-to-face instruction."[15] The report commented on weaknesses in the research studies included in the meta-analysis, and the authors offered several caveats for interpreting the data, such as differences in factors like time spent, curriculum, and pedagogy employed in the various environments. Therefore, it remains difficult to compare the results of learning in these different modalities with any certainty.

Kami J. Silk and colleagues cited numerous studies that compare the effectiveness of library instruction in online, in-person, and blended models. They noted the challenges in research design and the ability to evaluate the comparative effectiveness of each environment definitively and stated, "without strict experimental controls in research designs, determining under which situations either type of instruction is better or worse is virtually impossible."[16] In their own study, they found mostly nonsignificant differences between the modes of instruction and concluded, "Whether or not student learning occurs likely has more to do with the quality of the material and teaching rather than the type of modality."[17] In another study, Karen Anderson and Frances A. May found that the method of instruction does not influence students' retention of information literacy skills and stated, "All methods of instruction can be equally as effective."[18]

While researchers continue to study and compare results in these environments, educators form their opinions based on data and perception. The percentage of academic leaders rating the learning outcomes in online education as the same or better than those in face-to-face instruction was measured at 57.2 percent in 2003 and rose to 77 percent in 2012 and then declined to 71.4 percent in 2015.[19] These academic leaders expressed far more positive opinions concerning the results of blended courses compared with face-to-face courses, with only 13.9 percent citing inferior results.[20] The number of chief academic officers (CAOs) agreeing that "online education is critical to the long-term strategy of my institution" rose from less than 50 percent in 2003 to 63.3 percent in 2015. That number peaked at 70.8 percent in 2014 but dropped in 2015. Simultaneously, the number of CAOs who reported that they disagreed with the statement rose correspondingly in the same time period, an increase interpreted to indicate that institutions that had not been providing distance learning had abandoned plans to do so.[21] The Babson Survey found that, in the past twelve years, no more than a third of the CAOs surveyed reported that their faculty accepted the value and legitimacy of online education.[22] CAOs at institutions with large distance education enrollments reported significantly higher faculty acceptance rates at 60.1 percent.

Regarding the effectiveness of existing online courses and programs, a 2016 report noted that 30 percent of CAOs at all institutions rated their online courses and programs as very effective, with 52 percent ranking them as somewhat effective.[23] Fully 79 percent reported plans for expanding online programs and offerings.[24] This constitutes a significantly higher rate than the 63.3 percent of CAOs in the most recent Babson Survey who agreed that online education will prove crucial to their institutions' long-term strategies. What might account for this difference? More significantly, what do these numbers indicate regarding the future trends in online learning?

Comparing Teaching and Learning in the Online and Face-to-Face Environments

How, from a student's perspective, does the online environment differ from the brick-and-mortar-classroom? Students beginning their first online courses will likely bring a set of expectations developed through their experiences in traditional classes.[25] They may not realize that online instructors often serve as facilitators rather than lecturers and that the learning process will be less structured and require significant input from each student. The first practical issues they face are self-discipline and time management. Students must develop realistic views of how much time they will need to devote to their online work if they hope to succeed. Some may approach an online course with the mistaken preconception that it will prove easier and less demanding than a face-to-face course; they soon learn otherwise. Students must be able to adhere to a consistent practice of regularly logging in to the class site (discussed later under "Learning Management Systems") and paying strict attention to due dates. They must also communicate actively and in an appropriate manner (typically called "netiquette") with the instructor and with others in the class.

Effective pedagogy in the online environment incorporates good teaching practices from traditional settings. Defining learning outcomes and aligning course materials, activities, and assessments to support student success in achieving those outcomes prove crucial regardless of whether a course runs online, face to face, or in a blended format. And as noted earlier, in the online classroom, the instructor often functions as a so-called guide on the side rather than the so-called sage on the stage that students may be used to from previous teaching and learning experiences.[26]

The community of inquiry (CoI) constitutes an important model for online teaching and learning. Randy Garrison, Terry Anderson, and Walter Archer developed a model for computer-mediated communication among members of a group of individuals who work collaboratively to learn together.[27] They describe three important elements of successful educational experiences: social presence,[28] teaching presence,[29] and cognitive presence.[30] Their early work, a series of papers published from 1999 through 2001, has formed a foundation for significant additional research and the development of a survey instrument that can be used to measure and compare the CoI elements of courses. Librarians can incorporate the CoI principles by ensuring that students have opportunities to interact effectively with other students, with the librarian/instructor, and with the lesson content in their online learning experiences.

Instructors have a variety of technology tools available to use in working with groups of students. All such tools should support the achievement of learning outcomes and not simply be used for their own sakes. The latter portion of this chapter introduces several important technologies employed in online learning that can assist librarians and instructors in facilitating successful learning experiences for students.

Library Services for Distance and Online Learners

Wherever students and faculty are located and regardless of whether they use the library on campus or online, they are entitled to full access to library resources and interaction with library personnel. The Association of College and Research Libraries (ACRL) provides standards for library services for distance learning in order to define and encourage quality library support for distant students and online or off-campus programs. These guidelines were developed by the distance learning section of ACRL and were first approved in 2008 and then revised in 2016.[31] The ACRL "Standards for Distance Learning Library Services" begin with an introduction of the access entitlement principle:

> All students, faculty members, administrators, staff members, or any other members of an institution of higher education are entitled to the library services and resources of that institution, including direct communication with the appropriate library personnel, regardless of where they are physically located in relation to the campus; where they attend class in relation to the institution's main campus; or the modality by which they take courses. Academic libraries must, therefore, meet the information and research needs of all these constituents, wherever they may be. This principle of access entitlement, as applied to individuals at a distance, is the undergirding and uncompromising conviction of the Standards for Distance Learning Library Services, hereinafter designated as the Standards.[32]

Academic accrediting organizations also recognize the importance of library services for all students, including those who attend at a distance from campus. For example, the Southern Association of Colleges and Schools' Commission on Colleges' "Distance and Correspondence Education Policy Statement" includes this standard: "Students have access to and can effectively use appropriate library resources."[33] On a broader scale, the council representing all regional accrediting organizations in the United States published guidelines for evaluation of distance education programs. Two of the nine guidelines address adequate support for academic services and specifically include the library as an example.[34]

How well have academic libraries succeeded in carrying out this responsibility? Online students report fairly high satisfaction with library services. A 2015–2016 survey and report of online students enrolled in undergraduate and graduate courses found that 79 percent of students at four-year institutions identified online library services as a strength. Students expressed slightly less satisfaction at community colleges, with 70 percent reporting adequate access to online library services.[35]

After reviewing the ACRL standards for distance learning and related accreditation standards, we can see that all students and faculty associated with a college or university should expect library support. The situation for people outside this official group remains unclear. What should be available to members of the general public who may visit the library on campus or online? For example, should online reference services be available to anyone who uses the library website? Does some type of authentication need to be completed before a question can be answered? Consider, too, the fact that some academic libraries serve both a university community as well as the public. Decisions must be made regarding access to such resources as expensive databases and e-books, as well as the print resources within the library. One possible solution would be to offer access to licensed electronic materials only to the academic community but also make these resources available to anyone who physically comes into the library. These details must be worked out in license agreements with

Debbie Faires

commercial information providers, such as EBSCO or ProQuest. Open courses that an institution may offer pose another challenge for libraries. Librarians must thoughtfully work to negotiate the issue of access to licensed content by those who are not matriculated students or faculty. I explore this subject in greater detail next (see "MOOCs and Libraries").

MOOCs and Libraries

Massive open online courses (MOOCs) exploded onto the educational scene between 2008 and 2013, and enrollments continue to expand at a steady pace. What is a MOOC? The *Oxford English Dictionary* added the term in 2013[36] and defined it as a "course of study made available over the Internet without charge to a very large number of people."[37] It is an online course that (usually) has the following attributes:

- designed for massive enrollment numbers (thousands or even hundreds of thousands);
- open enrollment—participants are not required to be registered students of a particular educational institution; and
- no cost for enrollment.

Proponents claim MOOCs provide affordable education opportunities for huge populations and that they serve as a form of education entirely appropriate for today's interactive digital environment. Detractors have labeled them a "shiny new toy in the toolbox that is [Cornell, Princeton, and Yale Universities'] online education offerings"[38] and wonder how soon the appeal of this new format will fade. Some see MOOCs as the "next great technological disruption in education,"[39] one that could threaten the demise of as many as half the colleges and universities in the United States, with only the most elite institutions like Harvard, currently a leading MOOC provider, surviving to meet the educational needs of millions of students.[40] More significantly, detractors legitimately question learning effectiveness[41] and point to high rates of noncompletion in MOOCs.[42]

Development of MOOCs

MOOCs developed during a time when such forces as technology, rising costs of higher education, and greater commitments to open access were shaping higher education. Paul Kim observed, "As many areas of society have undergone rapid changes enabled by technology, the education sector has been by comparison in a dormant state for some time. Thus, it was inevitable that technology enthusiasts and experimenters would create something like MOOCs and use technology to open up new educational possibilities."[43]

The term *MOOC* is believed to have originated in an online chat between George Siemens and Dave Cormier in 2008.[44] Siemens and Stephen Downs are generally credited with organizing the first MOOC in 2008. More than two thousand external online learners joined the students in a class at the University of Manitoba. In 2011, Sebastian Thrun and Peter Norvig, two professors at Stanford University, offered their course on artificial intelligence for open enrollment and made headlines with enrollments of more than 160,000 online students.[45] At this point MOOCs began to appear frequently in the headlines of educational publications. The number of MOOC-related articles in LIS publications peaked during 2013.[46] Three major MOOC providers emerged during this time: Coursera, edX, and Udacity.[47] In 2015, FutureLearn,[48] a MOOC provider located in the United Kingdom, offered what has been, to date, the largest MOOC, with 440,000 students enrolled in the course titled "Understanding IELTS: Techniques for English Language Tests."[49]

How large is the MOOC movement? Survey data gathered from CAOs in the United States during 2012–2015 indicate that only a small number of higher education institutions either had or were planning a MOOC. In 2012, the number was 12 percent, and in 2015, it was 13.6 percent, down a little after peaking in 2013 at 14.3 percent.[50] The survey concludes adoption levels seem to be plateauing.[51] By contrast, consider the numbers offered by Class-central.com, an aggregator of statistics from MOOC providers, which indicate that more people signed up for MOOCs in 2015 than the combined total in the period from 2011–2013. This source estimates that more than 35 million students have signed up for at least one MOOC over the years the courses have been offered. Far from plateauing, the number of MOOC offerings continues to climb.[52]

What could account for this contradiction in reports regarding the growth of MOOCs? Perhaps it is because the data from CAOs reflects the number of *institutions* involved in MOOCs while the Class-central data reports the number of MOOC *courses*. The number of institutions offering MOOCs might remain level even though each of those institutions could be increasing the number of MOOCs it offers. Also, the Class-central data includes not only MOOCs that originate in higher education institutions but also those from commercial entities that may not be formally linked with universities. We should also consider the fact that Class-central.com data reflects international offerings, while the other report focuses on US institutions.

Experimentation has been a hallmark of the MOOC environment as providers have sought to find a sustainable model. Without student tuition, other sources of revenue must be identified to cover the costs of course preparation and delivery. In one early model, all students who completed a course were awarded a free certificate. Currently, however, such certificates can generally only be obtained for a fee. Some courses require a fee for those who want access to their graded assignments. MOOC providers have developed their own extended certifications through such programs as Udacity's Nanodegrees, Coursera's Specializations, and edX's XSeries.[53] At the same time, edX has been developing partnerships that will allow students to earn credits for their successful work in MOOCs.[54] The question of whether to award credit for participation in a MOOC has been difficult to settle. Determining exactly what the requirements would be for earning credit or degrees and verifying completion constitute just two of the challenges involved. When commenting on MIT's stance that only formally admitted students would receive course credit or be granted MIT degrees (that is, no credit or degree will be awarded for edX participation), Katy Mahraj observed, "Ironically, the openness that makes MOOCs invaluable simultaneously undermines that value."[55]

In spite of the reported growth of MOOCs and the massive open opportunities they offer, they are still relatively unknown to the large majority of the population. In 2014, an OCLC survey of 3,700 online information consumers of all ages reported that only 13 percent of the respondents were familiar with the term *MOOC*, and 3 percent had participated in a course. The survey found higher awareness among college students, with a quarter of the students indicating familiarity with the term and 8 percent participation.[56]

MOOCs and Libraries

The emergence of MOOCs has brought with it a host of questions for libraries associated with the institutions that offer these courses. The issue of the massive enrollment by itself worries many librarians. As Christina Mune wrote, "Concerns over the time demands associated with embedded librarianship in the average online course pale in comparison to the idea of supporting tens or hundreds of thousands of students in a MOOC."[57] Services that libraries with currently strained budgets provide to students and faculty could be further burdened if those resources had to be extended to all MOOC participants.[58] Support to the faculty who are developing a MOOC could require significant time spent in managing copyright and content licensing.[59] Cameron Barnes pointed out that the demands depend not only on the number of participants involved but also on the policies of the library.[60]

In spite of these challenges, there are important reasons that libraries should be involved in campus MOOC initiatives. Active participation in planning will reinforce the library's role in supporting instruction at the university. This support might involve providing expertise in relevant content, managing copyright and licensing issues and solutions, promoting quality open educational resources, or offering instruction in information literacy or input on instructional design. Clearly, the library should be at the table to help to shape the policies that will guide the institution's MOOC development. A report on an expert panel on MOOCs at the 2014 ALA midwinter conference concluded, "If the mission of the university is the creation and dissemination of knowledge, how can the academy not be involved? Libraries must be involved as well."[61] Indeed, Barnes reported that librarians have already been identified as important team members in MOOC development at many Coursera-affiliated institutions, and we can see a similar trend within the edX network.[62]

Librarian Support of MOOCs

How can librarians support campus MOOC initiatives without overwhelming their existing resources? Writers have suggested a wide variety of possible librarian roles; these roles are not new to academic librarians.

Copyright and Licensing

Librarians could provide guidance on which materials can be used in a MOOC. Because only members of an educational institution (faculty, staff, and students) have permission to access most licensed electronic library resources (e.g., e-books, e-journals, databases), MOOC participants from outside the institution are generally excluded. Negotiations with copyright holders may be required in order to legally use some materials.[63]

Open Educational Resources (OER)

Librarians could be valued partners in selecting content for a MOOC[64] and could promote the use of OER. In some situations, it may be problematic for faculty members to use even their own published works in their MOOCs because of restrictions.[65] Such constraints provide situations where librarians could highlight the value of OER and use of Creative Commons licensing.[66] Encouragement of the use of open materials in MOOCs could lead to greater adoption in other classes on campus.[67]

Another matter for librarian consultation might be the question of the status of the materials created by MOOC participants. Hannah Gore wrote, "As learners are actively encouraged to search for learning materials to analyze, discuss, and remix during their MOOC study, then it could be argued that they are collectively advancing the learning process and therefore undertaking the role of co-creators of content."[68] Who owns this content and determines how it will be used? If the MOOC has an open license, then the content creators have copyright over the content but do not have control over its use and dissemination.[69] Librarians could provide valuable assistance in managing these issues.

Information Literacy Instruction

Because librarians already support the development of information literacy (IL) in their academic work, this contribution could be crucial to a MOOC in which many participants may not be well prepared.[70] Many of the IL materials developed could be shared for use by other libraries involved in MOOC support. This collaborative work will improve everyone's access to information and help to reduce duplication of effort.

Librarians involved in MOOCs may have access to system data regarding the learning activities of the students. For example, a librarian could study how many times an information literacy resource in the course site was accessed or how many times the instructions in that resource were followed. The analysis of the very large data sets generated by the actions of thousands of students in the MOOC (i.e., the "big data") could yield insights for librarians and instructors concerning the effectiveness of the instructional strategies in the course.[71]

Support Pages

Librarians could prepare support pages on the library website specifically modified for MOOC participants.[72] These could include FAQs, resource guides, and tutorials. Modifications include indicating clearly which resources are available to MOOC participants, removing any references to local termi-nology that may not apply in the context of the MOOC, and possible removal of individual librarian contact information (perhaps replacing it with an e-mail account that several librarians monitor).[73]

Accessibility

The librarian could promote awareness of techniques and resources that will ensure that MOOC participants using assistive technology have full access to the course resources.[74] In order to be accessible to all, audio content should also be provided in text format. Options for creating text captions include outsourcing to a third-party service provider or using speech-to-text software and then manually correcting errors. Either of these options requires resources that need to be allocated in the planning stages. Text equivalents benefit many users beyond those who may have hearing impairments. For example, English language learners and those who are accessing materials in en-vironments where they cannot play audio aloud will also find the text versions helpful. In addition, images and graphs included in course materials should be accompanied by text descriptions so that those who have visual impairments and are using screen-readers will be able to understand the content.

Embedded Librarian

A librarian could be embedded in the MOOC and actively participate in discussions and provide other types of support.[75] This type of participation can yield rich insights into the activities and needs of the participants. A team approach could help with workload management. The librarians could give direct feedback on such topics as research questions and ethical use of information and encourage students to explore the resources provided by their local libraries.

Should the library devote resources to supporting MOOCs? Each campus will need to evaluate its position carefully and consider not only the costs in terms of hours and resources but also the bene-fits of collaboration and support of the institution's academic mission. Participating with colleagues throughout the college or university will benefit the library and improve its visibility as a highly valued partner in education initiatives. One study of academic library strategic plans found an emphasis on traditional services and little attention devoted to emerging trends.[76] While there may be risk associ-ated with new initiatives, there could also be a "cost to not taking a risk—a danger that libraries will become stuck in a niche that becomes smaller and smaller."[77]

Technology Tools

Today's technology-rich environment offers a multitude of tools for librarians to use in supporting students and faculty. Using these products, it is possible to provide information that can be accessed at the time when learners need guidance rather than only at the time the librarian is speaking to the class. In addition, students and faculty members do not have to travel to the library for assistance. Effective instruction, convenience, and flexibility are facilitated through the use of technology. In this section, I look at a variety of technologies that can be successfully used in the online environment.

Learning Management Systems (LMS)

Most campuses have adopted a learning management system (LMS), also known by such terms as virtual learning environment (VLE) or course management software (CMS), which hosts the course sites for classes that have an online presence.[78] The library should have a prominent presence in the LMS so that it can provide resources and services in a location visible to all users of the system. The library should be as visible and accessible in an LMS as it is on a physical campus. Librarians who work to promote the library in the campus LMS face several challenges.[79] Barriers might be related to both technology and human collaboration[80] and include:

- lack of an integrated library component in most LMSs,[81]
- lack of a librarian-specific role in the LMS,[82]
- frequent lack of librarian involvement in the administration and management of the LMS,[83]
- reliance on faculty for access to seemingly impenetrable walls of each course site,[84] and
- poor awareness among faculty of how incorporating library resources into their course sites could benefit their teaching or the learning of their students.[85]

Several LMS products have been widely adopted and include Blackboard Learn, Moodle, Canvas, D2L Brightspace, eCollege, and Sakai, as well as numerous campus-specific systems.[86] These systems typically include such features as content management, discussion boards, assignment submission, gradebooks, messaging, and quizzes that can be automatically graded. Success in effectively providing library services and resources to students through the LMS does not depend on the system used; rather it is the librarian's response to working online that has been found to make a significant difference in the use of the LMS.[87]

Librarians have developed a number of strategies for incorporating library resources and services into this online course environment. Strategies can be incorporated at a system-wide level or at the course level. Prominently displaying a link to the library website or catalog in the general toolbar of the LMS constitutes one example of a system-wide initiative. This ensures a consistently placed link that automatically appears in every course.

In addition to system-wide LMS customizations, course-level customizations can be set up to more directly address student needs in particular classes. The following list itemizes a variety of these approaches:

- Electronic reserves can be managed at the course level, with readings conveniently accessible directly within course sites.
- Reading lists can be set up within course sites that provide permalinks that students can use to efficiently access digital materials in the library's collection. This strategy has been shown to improve rates of student access to materials.[88]
- RSS feeds from information sources and social media tools can automatically import continuously updated content into a course site. Examples of this type of content include a listing of new acquisitions in a particular subject, the table of contents from each new issue of a particular journal, or bookmarked resources collected by students in the class.
- Course-specific research guides can be added to the course site. These guides could include links to existing tutorials, videos, selected databases, such library services as online reference assistance, and librarian contact information. In addition, a librarian may create new course-specific instructional materials that could be included in course-level guides.
- An embedded librarian can be added as a member in the course site, perhaps with a specific administrative role[89] that would allow the librarian to manage a discussion board, conveniently communicate, and add and update content in the site. The librarian could be involved in the course for a short period of time to support a particular project or throughout the semester and should provide contact information and updates regarding availability; response time; and, where needed, back-up support.

Another strategy combines the efficiency of a system-wide resource with the customization of a course-level resource. Some LMSs offer a system-wide repository for storage of files. Librarians can develop a resource and save it in the repository. The content can then be imported into one or more course sites as needed. This provides a convenient central location for the content, which may be updated and used in future semesters.

How can librarians discover and develop the possibilities for instruction afforded through their campus LMSs? Training, support, and collaboration are crucial. Campus faculty development or IT departments should offer training and support in using the LMS. Because librarians may be looking for additional and creative ways to incorporate resources and services, they should develop collegial relationships with system experts and the campus LMS administrator in order to discuss needs and possible solutions. Whenever a campus explores the possibility of adopting a new LMS, the library should play an active role in discussing its own presence in the system from the beginning of the process. Collaborating with faculty members is crucial if librarians wish to gain course-level access and provide service directly within the course sites.

Content Management Systems (CMS)

Permission to post content on the library's website was once restricted to those who knew HTML and had access to the server. All updates required requests to the authorized person who managed all updates for the organization. Fortunately, there are now many user-friendly tools that allow those who may not know HTML to build and manage web content directly without having to rely on an intermediary. These tools can be used for entire websites or for specific resources that are incorporated as part of the larger library website. Using a content management system (CMS) offers the advantage that the work of maintaining a website can be distributed among a group of people. Each person can be responsible for maintaining a particular group of pages and can edit that portion of the website directly. This distributed model provides the opportunity for quick updates and posting of current content.

LibGuides, a CMS developed by Springshare, offers a user-friendly interface for creating customized library research guides. Using the point-and-click interface, librarians can create subject guides and even entire websites without needing advanced technology skills. The pages can include a variety of types of content, including links, uploaded files, and embedded multimedia. In the open source CMS category, Drupal and Joomla are both popular choices. Large and small libraries use these database-driven software systems to simplify the management of their websites.

Other types of software can also function as content management systems. WordPress is primarily known as a blogging tool. However, it is actually a CMS and is a tool for building web pages. It features a user-friendly editing interface and effectively manages large numbers of pages and a variety of types of content. Editing is easy and instantaneous. It is an open source product, and content can be hosted either on the WordPress.com site or on a local server with code available from WordPress.org. WordPress has proven to be the significant leader in the CMS category and powers at least a quarter of all CMS-driven websites.[90] A librarian at an academic library could build an information resource using this tool. The resource could address the specific needs of a class, or it could document work associated with a particular project. Comments can be enabled or disabled as desired.

Wiki software can also be used for managing online content. Many wiki tools do not require knowledge of coding, and they feature options to permit others to edit or simply view content. Wikis allow for collaborative content building. One or many contributors can create content on a wiki. Matthew M. Bejune identified four models for library-related wikis: between libraries, among library staff, between library staff and patrons, and between patrons.[91] Wikis have been successfully deployed to organize and coordinate information among staff members at various desks within a library[92] and to jointly build and maintain a technical services manual to be used by multiple cooperating campuses.[93] Examples of popular wiki tools include MediaWiki, an open source product used to power sites like Wikipedia and commercial providers like PBworks and Wikispaces.

Recording Tools

Recordings can be effective resources that are always available for just-in-time viewing by students and faculty who need assistance. Short recordings showing screen video accompanied by audio narration have proven to be popular offerings that meet needs at any time of the day or night. These videos do not require an extensive video crew but can be recorded on a computer using commercial software, such as Panopto, TechSmith's Camtasia, Adobe Captivate, or Articulate. Jing (from TechSmith) and Screencast-O-Matic are free tools that are available for both Windows and Mac operating systems.

Web-Based Synchronous Communication Tools

When serving students online, synchronous communication is an efficient means of answering questions, conducting reference interviews, or discussing research strategies. Conversations conducted in real time are sometimes preferable to those conducted via e-mail. Several types of web-based tools are available for these conversations, including instant messaging and web conferences (with or without webcam video). While the telephone may or may not be connected to the Internet, it is, of course, another excellent option for conversations.

When making a decision about which tool to use, a librarian needs to consider the needs of the particular situation. Students or faculty members may want short, quick responses to fairly straightforward questions. For these situations, instant messaging may be the perfect choice. Alternatively, a student who is located in a distant area might need a more extended research consultation. In this case, a web conference tool might be the best choice because it would allow cobrowsing of online resources and simultaneous discussion.

Instant Messaging (IM)

Instant messaging (also referred to as online chat), a convenient and straightforward text-based tool, has proven to be useful for real-time communication. It has been widely adopted for virtual reference. This tool offers not only quick responses to inquiries but also the benefit of a text record of the interactions. A 2013 study of libraries at one hundred top US universities revealed that 91 percent were using IM to provide online reference services.[94] Chat was found to have the highest usability rating in a 2014 study of five different virtual reference tools.[95]

Web Conferencing

Web conferencing features synchronous communication via the web and includes such tools as audio, video, text chat, a collaborative whiteboard, and desktop sharing. This type of product offers the ability for an individual to meet with one or many people, each at his or her own computer. Everyone in the session can see the same content on the screen and discuss it. Enterprise-level web conference tools often used in the academic environment include Adobe Connect, Blackboard Collaborate, WebEx, and Zoom. Other freely available tools that provide most of these functions include such products as Skype and Google Hangouts. When selecting a product, it is important to carefully identify requirements, such as the need for closed captioning, breakout rooms, recordings, and the maximum number of participants a session can support. Collaborating with other units on campus that may be investing in this technology is strategic in effective use of resources.

This technology provides a good online environment for class orientation or information literacy instruction sessions, one-on-one reference appointments, and librarian meetings. Geographic location does not matter as long as each participant has the necessary technology (a computer and adequate Internet connection or a mobile device with the appropriate app installed).

Montana State University's library has used web conferencing to serve students who are located not only on campus but also throughout rural areas of the state. Bonnand and Hansen provide the following list of best practices for online sessions:[96]

- Have the faculty member included in the session.
- Have students login several minutes before the session is to begin.
- Limit sessions to one hour or less.
- Schedule sessions at two separate times to accommodate different time zones.

- Interact through polls and chat.
- Greet students when they enter the session.
- When possible, have two librarians conduct the session so that one of them can focus on the instruction and the other can monitor chat or deal with technical issues.

Regardless of which technology tool is used, it is most important to focus on meeting the learning needs of the students. Anne Barnhart and Andrea Stanfield confirm that technology-mediated interaction should focus on communication and not on the technology itself.[97]

Cloud-Based Tools for Sharing and Storage

Cloud-based services can be effective tools for file storage and sharing. The *2009 Horizon Report* defined cloud-based applications as those that "do not run on a single computer; instead they are spread over a distributed cluster, using storage space and computing resources from many available machines as needed."[98] Google Drive and Dropbox are two examples of such tools. They use a "freemium" model of access: Free service is available, and additional services and storage can be added with paid accounts.

Files can be stored on cloud-based servers and can be synchronized with local copies through use of an application on one or more local computers or mobile devices. This functionality provides great efficiency and version management because a file updated in one location can then be automatically updated in all other locations. The files can be shared with others so that everyone has continuous access to the most recent version.

Academic librarians can use these services to efficiently share files with colleagues or library users. Large files, such as image-rich presentations or videos, which would be too big to share as e-mail attachments, can be uploaded and then either shared with a limited number of people or made widely available. Librarians can collaborate on such projects as writing articles or preparing presentations. Mobile apps are available that provide additional access to materials stored in these cloud-based tools. Cloud-based storage offers improved security of archived data because it can provide additional copies of important files. Every computer will fail at some point, so backing up local data to a cloud-based service has proven to be an important strategy in responsible data management.[99]

This off-site storage and management of files might itself create problems, however. Trust in the security and reliability of the cloud service is crucial. Local copies of data should be kept in addition to the cloud-based versions. Privacy constitutes another concern, and service provider policies should be carefully examined and reviewed for compliance with institutional requirements. Legal issues should also be examined for possible interstate or international access policies.[100]

Conclusion

Whether a university provides courses in the online environment or supports distance education or not, students and faculty members will be using online resources and accessing information through the library's website. The days of providing service exclusively within the physical library are gone. Today's academic librarian needs to develop an understanding of how best to provide the necessary information in the environment where users are working in order to meet their needs, support their educational objectives, and enhance their opportunities to learn and explore.

Discussion Questions

1. What are some common misconceptions about the relative quality of online versus face-to-face education? Provide evidence for your position that these ideas are incorrect.
2. Contrast the differences between face-to-face and online teaching and learning. What do instructors need to do in order to facilitate effective learning in the online environment? What do students need to do in order to be successful online learners?

3. How can the library develop a presence in the campus learning management system? Which other units on campus will librarians need to work with in order to establish a connection to students and faculty through their online course sites? How can this collaboration be initiated and sustained?
4. Consider the case of a university that is offering a MOOC. Does the library have a responsibility to provide resources and services to all of the MOOC participants? If so, how could this be done? If not, how can the information needs of the MOOC participants be met?

Assignment

Assume the role of a librarian who has been assigned to support a class that meets mostly online. Develop a plan for how to integrate library resources and services within the course site in the learning management system. How will you incorporate the following?

- Your contact information
- Options for consulting with you
- Information on how to get answers to questions when you are not available
- Instructions on how to conduct a specific research task (e.g., using the online catalog, finding a peer-reviewed article, selecting course-appropriate databases and other resources)
- Other materials you develop to support specific assignments

Use a variety of tools to support the students' learning.

Notes

1. Hope E. Kentnor, "Distance Education and the Evolution of Online Learning in the United States," *Curriculum and Teaching Dialogue* 17, nos. 1–2 (2015): 23–24.
2. Ibid., 24–28.
3. Ibid., 28.
4. Ibid., 22.
5. Russ Poulin and Terri Taylor Straut, *WCET Distance Education Enrollment Report 2016* (WICHE Cooperative for Educational Technologies, 2016), 7, http://wcet.wiche.edu/sites/default/files/WCETDistance EducationEnrollmentReport2016.pdf.
6. Barbara Means, Yukie Toyama, Robert Murphy, Marianne Bakia, and Karla Jones, *Evaluation of Evidence-Based Practices in Online Learning: A Meta-Analysis and Review of Online Learning Studies* (Washington, DC: US Department of Education, Office of Planning, Evaluation, and Policy Development, 2010), 9, http://www2.ed.gov/rschstat/eval/tech/evidence-based-practices/finalreport.pdf.
7. Elaine Allen, Jeff Seaman, Russell Poulin, and Terri Taylor Straut, *Online Report Card: Tracking Online Education in the United States* (Babson Park, MA: Babson Survey Research Group and Quahog Research Group, 2016).
8. Sheila Bonnand and Mary Anne Hansen, "From Two Dot to Turkey: Reaching Online Library Users via Web Conferencing," *Urban Library Journal* 18, no. 1 (2012): 2.
9. Cathy De Rosa, Joanne Cantrell, Peggy Gallagher, Janet Hawk, Irene Hoffman, and Reneé Page, *At a Tipping Point: Education, Learning and Libraries* (Dublin, OH: OCLC, 2014), 79, http://www.oclc.org/content/ dam/oclc/ reports/tipping-point/215133-tipping-point.pdf.
10. Allen et al., *Online Report Card*, 4.
11. Ibid., 12.
12. Ibid., 10.
13. Ibid., 3.
14. Means et al., *Evaluation of Evidence-Based Practices*, xviii.
15. Ibid., xiv.

16. Kami J. Silk, Evan K. Perrault, Sharon Ladenson, and Samantha A. Nazione, "The Effectiveness of Online versus In-Person Library Instruction on Finding Empirical Communication Research," *Journal of Academic Librarianship* 41, no. 2 (2015): 150, doi:10.1016/j.acalib.2014.12.007.

17. Ibid., 154.

18. Karen Anderson and Frances A. May, "Does the Method of Instruction Matter? An Experimental Examination of Information Literacy Instruction in the Online, Blended, and Face-to-Face Classrooms," *Journal of Academic Librarianship* 36, no. 6 (2010), 498, doi:10.1016/j.acalib.2010.08.005.

19. Allen et al., *Online Report Card*, 29–30.

20. Ibid., 31–32.

21. Ibid., 21–23.

22. Ibid., 6.

23. Scott Jaschik and Doug Lederman, *The 2016 Inside Higher Ed Survey of College and University Chief Academic Officers* (Washington, DC: Gallup and Inside Higher Ed, 2016), 31, https://www.insidehighered.com/booklet/2016-survey-college-and-university-chief-academic-officers.

24. Ibid., 36.

25. Rena M. Palloff and Keith Pratt, "Beyond the Looking Glass: What Faculty and Students Need to Be Successful Online," in *Handbook of Online Learning*, 2nd ed., edited by Kjell Erik Rudestam and Judith Schoenholtz-Read (Thousand Oaks, CA: Sage, 2010), 380.

26. Susan Ko and Steve Rossen, *Teaching Online: A Practical Guide* (New York: Routledge, 2010), 13.

27. D. Randy Garrison, Terry Anderson, and Walter Archer, "Critical Inquiry in a Text-Based Environment: Computer Conferencing in Higher Education," *Internet and Higher Education* 2, nos. 2–3 (2000): 87–105, doi:10.1016/S1096-7516(00)00016-6.

28. Liam Rourke, Terry Anderson, D. Randy Garrison, and Walter Archer, "Assessing Social Presence in Asynchronous Text-Based Computer Conferencing," *Journal of Distance Education* 14, no. 2 (1999): 50–71.

29. Terry Anderson, Liam Rourke, D. Randy Garrison, and Walter Archer, "Assessing Teaching Presence in a Computer Conferencing Context," *Journal of Asynchronous Learning Network* 5, no. 2 (2001): 1–17.

30. D. Randy Garrison, Terry Anderson, and Walter Archer, "Critical Thinking, Cognitive Presence, and Computer Conferencing in Distance Education," *American Journal of Distance Education* 15, no. 1 (2001): 7–23, doi:10.1080/08923640109527071.

31. "Standards for Distance Learning Library Services," *Association of College and Research Libraries*, revised June 2016, http://www.ala.org/acrl/standards.

32. Ibid.

33. "Distance and Correspondence Education: Policy Statement," *Southern Association of Colleges and Schools Commission on Colleges*, July 2014, 3, http://www.sacscoc.org/pdf/DistanceCorrespondenceEducation.pdf.

34. Middle States Commission on Higher Education, *Distance Education Programs: Interregional Guidelines for the Evaluation of Distance Education (Online Learning)* (Philadelphia: Middle States Commission on Higher Education, 2011), 12–13, https://www.msche.org/publications/Guidelines-for-the-Evaluation-of-Distance-Education-Programs.pdf.

35. Ruffalo Noel Levitz, *2015–16 National Online Learners Satisfaction and Priorities Report* (Cedar Rapids, IA: Ruffalo Noel Levitz, 2016), 6, https://www.ruffalonl.com/papers-research-higher-education-fundraising/2016/2015-16-national-online-learners-satisfaction-and-priorities-report.

36. Chris Parr, "'MOOC' Makes Oxford Online Dictionary," *Times Higher Education*, August 28, 2013, https://www.timeshighereducation.com/news/mooc-makes-oxford-online-dictionary/2006838.article.

37. "MOOC," *Oxford Dictionaries*, accessed April 30, 2016, http://www.oxforddictionaries.com/definition/english/mooc.

38. Carl Straumsheim, "Still Questioning the Model," *Inside Higher Ed*, February 21, 2014, para. 2, http://www.insidehighered.com/news/2014/02/21/elite-universities-face-lower-stakes-familiar-concerns-mooc-space.

39. Geoffrey Fowler, "An Early Report Card on Massive Open Online Courses," *Wall Street Journal*, October 8, 2013, http://www.wsj.com/articles/SB10001424052702303759604579093400834738972.

40. Nathan Harden, "The End of the University as We Know It," *American Interest* 8, no. 3 (Winter 2013): 55.

41. "The Hope and Hype of MOOCs," *NextSpace*, June 30, 2014, https://www.oclc.org/publications/nextspace/articles/issue23/thehopeandhypeofmoocs.en.html.
42. Matthew B. Hoy, "MOOCs 101: An Introduction to Massive Open Online Courses," *Medical Reference Services Quarterly* 33, no. 1 (January 2014): 87, doi:10.1080/02763869.2014.866490.
43. Paul Kim, *Massive Online Courses* (New York: Routledge, 2015), vii.
44. Dave Cormier, "The CCK08 MOOC—Connectivism Course, 1/4 Way," *Dave's Educational Blog* (blog), October 2, 2008, http://davecormier.com/edblog/2008/10/02/the-cck08-mooc-connectivism-course-14-way.
45. George L. Mehaffy, "Challenge and Change," *EDUCAUSE Review* 47, no. 5 (September–October 2012): 40, http://er.educause.edu/~/media/files/article-downloads/erm1252.pdf.
46. Anna Kaushik and Ashok Kumar, "Periodical Literature on MOOCs and LIS Domain," *International Journal of Information Dissemination and Technology* 5, no. 1 (2015): 39.
47. Coursera is a for-profit MOOC provider that partners with universities and organizations to offer their courses. It was founded in 2012 by Andrew Ng and Daphne Koller, computer science professors from Stanford University. See https://www.coursera.org. EdX is a nonprofit MOOC provider that runs courses on open-source software. EdX was founded by the Massachusetts Institute of Technology and Harvard in 2012. Numerous other schools and organizations offer courses through edX. See https://www.edx.org. Udacity is a for-profit MOOC provider cofounded by Sebastian Thrun and David Stavens. It began offering classes in 2012. See https://www.udacity.com.
48. FutureLearn is a private company owned by the Open University and founded in 2012. Its partners include numerous universities and other organizations, including the British Museum and the British Library. See https://www.futurelearn.com.
49. Dhawal Shah, "By the Numbers: MOOCS in 2015," *Class Central*, last modified December 21, 2015, https://www.class-central.com/report/moocs-2015-stats.
50. Allen et al., *Online Report Card*, 38.
51. Ibid.
52. Shah, "By the Numbers."
53. Udacity Nanodegrees, https://www.udacity.com/nanodegree; Coursera Specializations, http://coursera.tumblr.com/post/73994272513/coursera-specializations-focused-programs-in; edX XSeries, https://www.edx.org/xseries.
54. Dhawal Shah, "Less Experimentation, More Iteration: A Review of MOOC Stats and Trends in 2015," *Class Central*, last modified December 30, 2015, https://www.class-central.com/report/moocs-stats-and-trends-2015.
55. Katy Mahraj, "Using Information Expertise to Enhance Massive Open Online Courses," *Public Services Quarterly* 8, no. 4 (2012): 363, doi:10.1080/15228959.2012.730415.
56. De Rosa et al., *At a Tipping Point*, 24.
57. Christina Mune, "Massive Open Online Librarianship: Emerging Practices in Response to MOOCs," *Journal of Library and Information Services in Distance Learning* 9, nos. 1–2 (2015): 94, doi:10.1080/1533290X.2014.946350.
58. Hoy, "MOOCs 101," 87.
59. Hannah Gore, "Massive Open Online Courses (MOOCs) and Their Impact on Academic Library Services: Exploring the Issues and Challenges," *New Review of Academic Librarianship* 20, no. 1 (2014): 12, doi:10.1080/13614533.2013.851609; Hoy, "MOOCs 101," 87–88.
60. Cameron Barnes, "MOOCs: The Challenges for Academic Librarians," *Australian Academic and Research Libraries* 44, no. 3 (August 2013): 169, doi:10.1080/00048623.2013.821048.
61. "Hope and Hype of MOOCs."
62. Barnes, "MOOCs," 166.
63. Michael Stephens, "Lessons from #hyperlibMOOC," *Library Journal* 139, no. 7 (April 15, 2014): 45.
64. Ibid.; "Hope and Hype of MOOCs."
65. Ashley E. Faulkner, "MOOCs and Libraries: Many Hats, Many Questions," *Virginia Libraries* 61, no. 1 (2015): 6.
66. Creative Commons licensing provides a standardized method to provide permission for use of content according to the choice of the content creator. For example, licenses can allow others to share and even modify a creator's work. See https://creativecommons.org/about.

67. Gene R. Springs, "Just How Open? Evaluating the 'Openness' of Course Materials in Massive Open Online Courses," *Virginia Libraries* 61, no. 1 (January 2015): 15.
68. Gore, "Massive Open Online Courses," 13.
69. Samantha Bernstein, "MOOCs, Copyright, and the Many Meanings of 'Open,'" in *Massive Online Courses: The MOOC Revolution*, ed. Paul Kim (New York: Routledge, 2015), 109.
70. Gloria Creed-Dikeogu and Carolyn Clark, "Are You MOOC ing Yot? A Review for Academic Libraries," *Kansas Library Association College and University Libraries Section Proceedings* 3, no. 1 (2013): 12, http://dx.doi.org/10.4148/culs.v1i0.1830.
71. Carmen Kazakoff-Lane, *Environmental Scan and Assessment of OERs, MOOCs and Libraries: What Effectiveness and Sustainability Means for Libraries' Impact on Open Education* (Chicago: Association of College and Research Libraries, n.d.), 37, http://www.ala.org/acrl/sites/ala.org.acrl/files/content/publications/whitepapers/Environmental%20Scan%20and%20Assessment.pdf.
72. Bernd W. Becker, "Connecting MOOCs and Library Services," *Behavioral and Social Sciences Librarian* 32, no. 2 (June 2013): 138, doi:10.1080/01639269.2013.787383; Faulkner, "MOOCs and Libraries," 7; Mune, "Massive Open Online Librarianship."
73. Becker, "Connecting MOOCs," 138.
74. Barnes, "MOOCs," 168.
75. Kazakoff-Lane, *Environmental Scan and Assessment*, 34–35.
76. Laura Saunders, "Academic Libraries' Strategic Plans: Top Trends and Under-Recognized Areas," *Journal of Academic Librarianship* 41, no. 3 (May 2015): 285–91, doi:10.1016/j.acalib.2015.03.011.
77. Council on Library and Information Resources, *No Brief Candle: Reconceiving Research Libraries for the 21st Century*, CLIR Report Publication, no. 142 (Washington, DC: Council on Library and Information Resources, 2008), 2, http://www.clir.org/pubs/reports/pub142/pub142.pdf.
78. Eden Dahlstrom, Christopher Brooks, and Jacqueline Bichsel, *The Current Ecosystem of Learning Management Systems in Higher Education: Student, Faculty, and IT Perspectives* (Louisville, CO: EDUCAUSE Center for Analysis and Research, 2014), 4, https://net.educause.edu/ir/library/pdf/ers1414.pdf.
79. Sheila Corrall and Jonathan Keates, "The Subject Librarian and the Virtual Learning Environment," *Program* 45, no. 1 (2011): 33, doi:10.1108/00330331111107385.
80. Ibid., 33–34.
81. Chris Leeder and Steven Lonn, "Faculty Usage of Library Tools in a Learning Management System," *College and Research Libraries* 75, no. 5 (September 2014): 641–42, doi:10.5860/crl.75.5.641.
82. Ibid., 642.
83. Ibid., 641–42.
84. Corrall and Keates, "Subject Librarian," 39.
85. Ibid., 34.
86. Dahlstrom, Brooks, and Bichsel, *Current Ecosystem*, 6.
87. Corrall and Keates, "Subject Librarian," 45.
88. Penny Dale and Kathryn Cheshir, "Collaboration between Librarians and Learning Technologists to Enhance the Learning of Health Sciences Students," *New Review of Academic Librarianship* 15, no. 2 (2009): 207, doi:10.1080/13614530903240593.
89. Leeder and Lonn, "Faculty Usage of Library Tools," 644–45.
90. "Historical Trends in the Usage of Content Management Systems for Websites," *W3 Techs*, 2016, http://w3techs.com/technologies/history_overview/content_management/all.
91. Matthew M. Bejune, "Wikis in Libraries," *Information Technology and Libraries* 26, no. 3 (September 1, 2007): 29–31.
92. Melanie J. Dunn, "Wikis: The Perfect Platform for Library Policies and Procedures," *Southeastern Librarian* 60, no. 3 (Fall 2012): 3–7; Katherine Stiwinter and Patricia R. Jordan, "TMI: Using a Library Staff Wiki to Manage Information and Improve Communication," *Library Hi Tech News* 32, no. 8 (2015): 16–18, doi:10.1108/LHTN-04-2015-0031.
93. Erin Boyd, Olga Casey, Ruth Elder, and Jana Slay, "Collaboration at the Troy University Libraries," *Cataloging and Classification Quarterly* 51, nos. 1–3 (2013): 202–13, doi:10.1080/01639374.2012.733796.
94. Frank Boateng and Yan Quan Liu, "Web 2.0 Applications' Usage and Trends in Top US Academic Libraries," *Library Hi Tech* 32, no. 1 (2014): 126, doi:10.1108/LHT-07-2013-0093.

95. Anthony S. Chow and Rebecca A. Croxton. "A Usability Evaluation of Academic Virtual Reference Services," *College and Research Libraries* 75, no 3 (May 1, 2014): 318.
96. Bonnand and Hansen, "From Two Dot to Turkey," 7–8.
97. Anne Barnhart and Andrea Stanfield, "When Coming to Campus Is Not an Option: Using Web Conferencing to Deliver Library Instruction," *Reference Services Review* 39, no. 1 (2011): 58, doi:10.1108/00907321111108114.
98. Larry Johnson, Alan Levine, and Rachel Smith, *The 2009 Horizon Report* (Austin, TX: New Media Consortium, 2009), 11, http://www.nmc.org/pdf/2009-Horizon-Report.
99. Marshall Breeding, "Digital Archiving in the Age of Cloud Computing," *Computers in Libraries* 33, no. 2 (March 2013): 24.
100. Tom Ipri, "Where the Cloud Meets the Commons," *Journal of Web Librarianship* 5, no. 2 (April 2011): 137, doi:10.1080/19322909.2011.573295.

Bibliography

Allen, I. Elaine, Jeff Seaman, Russell Poulin, and Terri Taylor Straut. *Online Report Card: Tracking Online Education in the United States.* Babson Park, MA: Babson Survey Research Group and Quahog Research Group, 2016.

Anderson, Karen, and Frances A. May. "Does the Method of Instruction Matter? An Experimental Examination of Information Literacy Instruction in the Online, Blended, and Face-to-Face Classrooms." *Journal of Academic Librarianship* 36, no. 6 (2010): 495–500. doi:10.1016/j.acalib.2010.08.005.

Anderson, Terry, Liam Rourke, D. Randy Garrison, and Walter Archer. "Assessing Teaching Presence in a Computer Conferencing Context." *Journal of Asynchronous Learning Network* 5, no. 2 (2001): 1–17.

Barnes, Cameron. "MOOCs: The Challenges for Academic Librarians." *Australian Academic and Research Libraries* 44, no. 3 (August 2013): 163–75. doi:10.1080/00048623.2013.821048.

Barnhart, Anne, and Andrea Stanfield. "When Coming to Campus Is Not an Option: Using Web Conferencing to Deliver Library Instruction." *Reference Services Review* 39, no. 1 (2011): 58–65. doi:10.1108/00907321111108114.

Becker, Bernd W. "Connecting MOOCs and Library Services." *Behavioral and Social Sciences Librarian* 32, no. 2 (June 2013): 135–38. doi:10.1080/01639269.2013.787383.

Bejune, Matthew M. "Wikis in Libraries." *Information Technology and Libraries* 26, no. 3 (September 1, 2007): 26–38.

Bernstein, Samantha. "MOOCs, Copyright, and the Many Meanings of 'Open,'" in *Massive Online Courses: The MOOC Revolution*, ed. Paul Kim, 106–16 (New York: Routledge, 2015).

Boateng, Frank, and Yan Quan Liu. "Web 2.0 Applications' Usage and Trends in Top US Academic Libraries." *Library Hi Tech* 32, no. 1 (2014): 120–38. doi:10.1108/LHT-07-2013-0093.

Bonnand, Sheila, and Mary Anne Hansen. "From Two Dot to Turkey: Reaching Online Library Users via Web Conferencing." *Urban Library Journal* 18, no. 1 (2012): 1–13.

Boyd, Erin E., Olga Casey, Ruth Elder, and Jana Slay. "Collaboration at the Troy University Libraries." *Cataloging and Classification Quarterly* 51, nos. 1–3 (2013): 202–13. doi:10.1080/01639374.2012.733796.

Breeding, Marshall. "Digital Archiving in the Age of Cloud Computing." *Computers in Libraries* 33, no. 2 (March 2013): 22–26.

Chow, Anthony S., and Rebecca A. Croxton. "A Usability Evaluation of Academic Virtual Reference Services." *College and Research Libraries* 75, no. 3 (May 1, 2014): 309–61.

Cormier, Dave. "The CCK08 MOOC—Connectivism Course, 1/4 Way." *Dave's Educational Blog* (blog). October 2, 2008. http://davecormier.com/edblog/2008/10/02/the-cck08-mooc-connectivism-course-14-way.

Corrall, Sheila, and Jonathan Keates. "The Subject Librarian and the Virtual Learning Environment." *Program* 45, no. 1 (2011). 29–49. doi:10.1108/00330331111107385

Council on Library and Information Resources. *No Brief Candle: Reconceiving Research Libraries for the 21st Century*. CLIR Report Publication, no. 142. Washington, DC: Council on Library and Information Resources, 2008. http://www.clir.org/pubs/reports/pub142/pub142.pdf.

Creed-Dikeogu, Gloria, and Carolyn Clark. "Are You MOOC-ing Yet? A Review for Academic Libraries." *Kansas Library Association College and University Libraries Section Proceedings* 3, no. 1 (2013): 9–13. http://dx.doi.org/10.4148/culs.v1i0.1830.

Dahlstrom, Eden D., Christopher Brooks, and Jacqueline Bichsel. *The Current Ecosystem of Learning Management Systems in Higher Education: Student, Faculty, and IT Perspectives*. Louisville, CO: EDUCAUSE Center for Analysis and Research, 2014.

Dale, Penny, and Kathryn Cheshir. "Collaboration between Librarians and Learning Technologists to Enhance the Learning of Health Sciences Students." *New Review of Academic Librarianship* 15, no. 2 (2009): 206–18. doi:10.1080/13614530903240593.

De Rosa, Cathy, Joanne Cantrell, Peggy Gallagher, Janet Hawk, Irene Hoffman, and Reneé Page. *At a Tipping Point: Education, Learning and Libraries*. Dublin, OH: OCLC, 2014. http://www.oclc.org/content/dam/oclc/ reports/tipping-point/215133-tipping-point.pdf.

"Distance and Correspondence Education: Policy Statement." *Southern Association of Colleges and Schools Commission on Colleges*. July 2014. http://www.sacscoc.org/pdf/DistanceCorrespondenceEducation.pdf.

Dunn, Melanie J. "Wikis: The Perfect Platform for Library Policies and Procedures." *Southeastern Librarian* 60. no. 3 (Fall 2012): 3–7.

Faulkner, Ashley E. "MOOCs and Libraries: Many Hats, Many Questions." *Virginia Libraries* 61, no. 1 (2015): 5–8.

Fowler, Geoffrey. "An Early Report Card on Massive Open Online Courses." *Wall Street Journal*. October 8, 2013. http://www.wsj.com/articles/SB10001424052702303759604579093400834738972.

Garrison, D. Randy, Terry Anderson, and Walter Archer. "Critical Inquiry in a Text-Based Environment: Computer Conferencing in Higher Education." *Internet and Higher Education* 2, nos. 2–3 (2000): 87–105. doi:10.1016/S1096-7516(00)00016-6.

———. "Critical Thinking, Cognitive Presence, and Computer Conferencing in Distance Education." *American Journal of Distance Education* 15, no. 1 (2001): 7–23. doi:10.1080/08923640109527071.

Gore, Hannah. "Massive Open Online Courses (MOOCs) and Their Impact on Academic Library Services: Exploring the Issues and Challenges." *New Review of Academic Librarianship* 20, no. 1 (2014): 4–28. doi:10.1080/13614533.2013.851609.

Harden, Nathan. "The End of the University as We Know It." *American Interest* 8, no. 3 (Winter 2013): 54–62.

"Historical Trends in the Usage of Content Management Systems for Websites." *W3 Techs*. 2016. http://w3techs.com/technologies/history_overview/content_management/all.

"The Hope and Hype of MOOCs." *NextSpace*. June 30, 2014. https://www.oclc.org/publications/nextspace/articles/issue23/thehopeandhypeofmoocs.en.html.

Hoy, Matthew B. "MOOCs 101: An Introduction to Massive Open Online Courses." *Medical Reference Services Quarterly* 33, no. 1 (January 2014): 85-91. doi:10.1080/02763869.2014.866490.

Ipri, Tom. "Where the Cloud Meets the Commons." *Journal of Web Librarianship* 5, no. 2 (April 2011): 132–41. doi:10.1080/19322909.2011.573295.

Jaschik, Scott, and Doug Lederman. *The 2016 Inside Higher Ed Survey of College and University Chief Academic Officers*. Washington, DC: Gallup and Inside Higher Ed, 2016. https://www.insidehighered.com/booklet/2016-survey-college-and-university-chief-academic-officers.

Johnson, Larry, Alan Levine, and Rachel Smith. *The 2009 Horizon Report*. Austin, TX: New Media Consortium, 2009. http://www.nmc.org/pdf/2009-Horizon-Report.pdf.

Kaushik, Anna, and Ashok Kumar. "Periodical Literature on MOOCs and LIS Domain." *International Journal of Information Dissemination and Technology* 5, no. 1 (2015): 37–40.

Kazakoff-Lane, Carmen. *Environmental Scan and Assessment of OERs, MOOCs and Libraries: What Effectiveness and Sustainability Means for Libraries' Impact on Open Education*. Chicago: Association of College and Research Libraries, n.d. http://www.ala.org/acrl/sites/ala.org.acrl/files/content/publications/whitepapers/Environmental%20Scan%20and%20Assessment.pdf.

Kentnor, Hope E. "Distance Education and the Evolution of Online Learning in the United States." *Curriculum and Teaching Dialogue* 17, nos. 1–2 (2015): 21–34.

Kim, Paul. *Massive Open Online Courses*. New York: Routledge, 2015.

Ko, Susan, and Steve Rossen. *Teaching Online: A Practical Guide*. New York: Routledge, 2010.

Leeder, Chris, and Steven Lonn. "Faculty Usage of Library Tools in a Learning Management System." *College and Research Libraries* 75, no. 5 (September 2014): 641–63. doi:10.5860/crl.75.5.641.

Levitz, Ruffalo Noel. *2015–16 National Online Learners Satisfaction and Priorities Report*. Cedar Rapids, IA: Ruffalo Noel Levitz, 2016. https://www.ruffalonl.com/papers-research-higher-education-fundraising/2016/2015-16-national-online-learners-satisfaction-and-priorities-report.

Mahraj, Katy. "Using Information Expertise to Enhance Massive Open Online Courses." *Public Services Quarterly* 8, no. 4 (2012): 360–68. doi:10.1080/15228959.2012.730415.

Means, Barbara, Yukie Toyama, Robert Murphy, Marianne Bakia, and Karla Jones. *Evaluation of Evidence-Based Practices in Online Learning: A Meta-Analysis and Review of Online Learning Studies*. Washington, DC: US Department of Education, Office of Planning, Evaluation, and Policy Development, 2010. http://www2.ed.gov/rschstat/eval/tech/evidence-based-practices/finalreport.pdf.

Mehaffy, George L. "Challenge and Change." *EDUCAUSE Review* 47, no. 5 (September–October 2012): 25–42. http://er.educause.edu/articles/2012/9/challenge-and-change.

Middle States Commission on Higher Education. *Distance Education Programs: Interregional Guidelines for the Evaluation of Distance Education (Online Learning)*. Philadelphia: Middle States Commission on Higher Education, 2011. https://www.msche.org/publications/Guidelines-for-the-Evaluation-of-Distance-Education-Programs.pdf.

"MOOC." *Oxford Dictionaries*. Accessed April 30, 2016. http://www.oxforddictionaries.com/definition/english/mooc.

Mune, Christina. "Massive Open Online Librarianship: Emerging Practices in Response to MOOCs." *Journal of Library and Information Services in Distance Learning* 9, nos. 1–2 (2015): 89–100. doi:10.1080/1533290X.2014.946350.

Palloff, Rena M., and Keith Pratt. "Beyond the Looking Glass: What Faculty and Students Need to Be Successful Online." In *Handbook of Online Learning*, 2nd ed., edited by Kjell Erik Rudestam and Judith Schoenholtz-Read, 370–86. Thousand Oaks, CA: Sage, 2010.

Parr, Chris. "'MOOC' Makes Oxford Online Dictionary." *Times Higher Education*. August 28, 2013. https://www.timeshighereducation.com/news/mooc-makes-oxford-online-dictionary/2006838.article.

Poulin, Russ, and Terri Taylor Straut. *WCET Distance Education Enrollment Report 2016*. WICHE Cooperative for Educational Technologies, 2016. http://wcet.wiche.edu/initiatives/research/WCET-Distance-Education-Enrollment-Report-2016.

Rourke, Liam, Terry Anderson, D. Randy Garrison, and Walter Archer. "Assessing Social Presence in Asynchronous Text-Based Computer Conferencing." *Journal of Distance Education* 14, no. 2 (1999): 50–71.

Saunders, Laura. "Academic Libraries' Strategic Plans: Top Trends and Under-Recognized Areas." *Journal of Academic Librarianship* 41, no. 3 (May 2015): 285–91. doi:10.1016/j.acalib.2015.03.011.

Shah, Dhawal. "By the Numbers: MOOCS in 2015." *Class Central*. Last modified December 21, 2015. https://www.class-central.com/report/moocs-2015-stats.

———. "Less Experimentation, More Iteration: A Review of MOOC Stats and Trends in 2015." *Class Central*. Last modified December 30, 2015. https://www.class-central.com/report/moocs-stats-and-trends-2015.

Silk, Kami J., Evan K. Perrault, Sharon Ladenson, and Samantha A. Nazione. "The Effectiveness of Online versus In-Person Library Instruction on Finding Empirical Communication Research." *Journal of Academic Librarianship* 41, no. 2 (2015): 149–54. doi:10.1016/j.acalib.2014.12.007.

Springs, Gene R. "Just How Open? Evaluating the 'Openness' of Course Materials in Massive Open Online Courses." *Virginia Libraries* 61, no. 1 (January 2015): 11–16.

"Standards for Distance Learning Library Services." *Association of College and Research Libraries*. Revised June 2016. http://www.ala.org/acrl/standards.

Stephens, Michael. "Lessons from #hyperlibMOOC." *Library Journal* 139, no. 7 (April 2014): 45.

Stiwinter, Katherine, and Patricia R. Jordan. "TMI: Using a Library Staff Wiki to Manage Information and Improve Communication." *Library Hi Tech News* 32, no. 8 (2015): 16–18. doi:10.1108/LHTN-04-2015-0031.

Straumsheim, Carl. "Still Questioning the Model." *Inside Higher Ed*. February 21, 2014. http://www.insidehighered.com/news/2014/02/21/elite-universities-face-lower-stakes-familiar-concerns-mooc-space.

13

Open Access, Institutional Repositories, E-Science and Data Curation, and Preservation

Brian Owen

Foundations

Academic libraries experienced substantial growth alongside their parent institutions in the aftermath of World War II, as science and knowledge of all kinds began to play an increasing role in the industrialization of society. New universities, community colleges, and other postsecondary institutions appeared in the 1950s and 1960s to accommodate the educational demands of a growing baby boomer cohort. However, this halcyon period did not last. From the 1970s forward, academic libraries were assailed by reductions in institutional budgets as well as cost increases. Fortunately, academic libraries enjoyed a concurrent growth in the adoption of technology, initially to automate internal processes and increasingly to provide enhanced services to students and faculty. Technology provided libraries with a powerful set of tools to counter their economic challenges; it also precipitated a significant shift in mind-set that encouraged creative and positive responses to issues.

The foundations of the transformative technology innovations for academic libraries and their collections and services go back to the 1970s and 1980s. During those decades, many libraries implemented computer-based systems that automated their operational processes and work flows for acquisitions, cataloging, circulation, and serials management. These backroom systems had limited direct or visible consequences for library users other than the computer-enabled checkout systems libraries put into place using cathode ray terminals (CRTs) and barcode scanners.

During this time, libraries realized the classic benefits of workplace automation—operational work flows improved substantially, and many manual procedures became automated. Consequently, libraries were able to manage general budget reductions during this period while also introducing many improvements for collections management and public services. As libraries automated, they began to create, store, and access large databases of bibliographic data, such as MAchine Readable Catalog (MARC) records, but occasionally ventured into other areas—local pamphlet files, bibliographies, and indexes. These functions generated database management and computer storage requirements that pushed the boundaries of the computer systems support available on many academic campuses. A commercial niche market of vendors developing, marketing, and supporting automated library systems appeared by the end of the 1970s and flourished in the 1980s and 1990s.

By the end of the 1980s, most academic libraries stopped maintaining their card catalogs (a practice described at the time as closing the card catalog) and began implementing the first primitive online public access catalogs (OPACs). These early systems replicated the access methods of the recently closed library card catalogs and often followed the identical author, title, subject, and shelf list conventions. Libraries often expended considerable effort in an attempt to emulate the traditional filing practices of card catalogs until thankfully the American Library Association released the *ALA Filing Rules* in 1980, which recognized that computers were increasingly responsible for sorting catalog data and required simple and logical filing rules.[1] Online displays were exclusively text-based, and many libraries went to great lengths to re-create the equivalent format of a 3"×5" printed catalog card. To be fair, this practice often resulted from the limited software in use at the time and the lack of any sophisticated user interface or user experience methodologies for the design and presentation of online environments.

In 1993, online computer systems changed dramatically when Mosaic, the first widely deployed web browser, appeared. By the mid-1990s, every library systems vendor was offering a web-based OPAC interface, and many academic libraries were creating local websites that provided access not just to the OPAC but also to a much wider range of online services and databases. Technology was now transforming the very way in which libraries delivered services and provided access to their collections and other resources. Faculty and students became increasingly accustomed to accessing the library in a growing variety of virtual and remote ways.

By the late 1990s, technology was also creating a major change in the way that commercial providers could make scholarly content available. Unfortunately, traditional publishers of scholarly journals insisted on subscription-pricing models anchored by the traditional print format. They offered access to electronic versions of journals as a value-added option, usually at a surcharge of 15 to 25 percent over the standard print subscription cost. And libraries did not always have the option to purchase only the electronic version; it was sometimes bundled with the parallel print product, a sales technique that translated into a significant increase for collections budgets that still had not recovered from the serials crisis of the early 1990s. Preceding this print-to-digital shift, many university and college libraries undertook massive serials cancellation projects that were brought on in part by journal price increases well beyond inflation and often exacerbated by currency fluctuations. The traditional balance between journal subscriptions and other collections purchases, especially monographs, became destabilized and led to major long-term consequences for the orderly and systematic growth of collections, with concomitant implications for teaching and research.

In the first decade of the twenty-first century, both publishers and library systems vendors were undergoing consolidation. Previously separate journal collections became single large offerings, giving libraries more materials but making budget reductions more difficult to administer. These "big deal" collections bundled a large number of journals at what appeared to be a very compelling price, especially when the license was negotiated by a library consortium on behalf of multiple sites. However, this also made it difficult for an individual library to renegotiate for a reduced subset of titles, let alone consider a complete cancellation. In conjunction with the fact that more than 50 percent of today's published journal output is now concentrated in the hands of the five largest commercial publishers,[2] libraries are now confronted by a new strain of the serials crisis. On the library system vendors' side, the option of choosing from ten to twelve competitive systems was reduced to five to six appropriate options for the academic market. And most of these were increasingly legacy-based systems that had not kept pace with other more rapidly evolving online services and systems, such as Google and Amazon. These commercial systems provided more intuitive interfaces and offered powerful functionality for searching and displaying content. Consolidation in the library systems marketplace seemed driven by the need to maintain and (ideally) increase market share in North America and Europe, where most libraries that needed an automated system had already acquired one. In a limited growth marketplace, the pace of ongoing software enhancement and improvement from vendors slowed, especially in the area of acquiring and managing digital collections that required new software.

It was not all bad news as academic libraries entered the new decade. Building on the previous decades of automation, many academic libraries had assembled extensive technological infrastructure along with groups of employees who had the expertise to operate and support it. Academic librarians became increasingly comfortable creating, maintaining, and navigating the digital landscape in a hands-on way. Of more significance, the growing expertise of librarians coupled with online environments that offered a range of new software tools stimulated a resurgence of local, in-house software development at some libraries. Frustrated with the slow pace of development in the library systems marketplace, some libraries began to create digital collections management platforms, link resolvers, electronic resource management systems, and other applications as a less expensive alternative to commercial equivalents—if such products were even available for purchase.

Libraries also began to realize the power of working in concert to challenge the commercial publishing sector and to insist on more balanced license agreements and pricing models. Library purchasing consortia appeared at the regional (OhioLink, California Digital Library) and national levels (Canadian Research Knowledge Network in Canada, Jisc in Great Britain).[3] In 1996, the International Coalition of Library Consortia (ICOLC) appeared; it currently has two hundred members. In a short period, these consortia were largely responsible for flipping the content subscription model from a print to a digitally based one and substituting library-created model licenses for vendor-provided ones.

The widespread adoption and increasingly sophisticated use of technology in conjunction with the realization that collaboration could be an effective and powerful change agent set the context for what has become apparent during the past five years. We see a radical transformation underway in academic libraries, as they confidently position themselves in the digital realm and develop and offer a wide range of new services and support for the scholarly communities they serve.

Open in All Its Manifestations

In 1977, the *Times Literary Supplement* declared that the battle for open access had been won. The assertion appeared in a book review of *The History of Public Libraries in Great Britain*.[4] It is an ironic historical footnote, but open access had a different connotation for libraries in the nineteenth century and into the twentieth. It referred to the practice of closed stacks, where patrons were not permitted to browse the shelves and find materials; rather, they would request their materials at a service desk, and library staff would retrieve them. Fortunately, libraries abandoned this practice as the twentieth century progressed and declared their stacks to be open.

In 2002, another open access declaration was issued. Known as the Budapest Open Access Initiative, it provided the definition of *open access* that has become the most widely used expression of this principle:

> By "open access" to this literature, we mean its free availability on the public internet, permitting any users to read, download, copy, distribute, print, search, or link to the full texts of these articles, crawl them for indexing, pass them as data to software, or use them for any other lawful purpose, without financial, legal, or technical barriers other than those inseparable from gaining access to the internet itself.[5]

Open access in conjunction with transformational technology changes has become a primary driver for many of the new services and systems now appearing in university and college libraries. But the concept of openness is much broader than just the provision of full public access to scholarly articles and related content. It encompasses open source software, open data, open educational resources, open government, and a still-growing array of "open" concepts. In early 2016, the Scholarly

Publishing and Academic Resources Coalition (SPARC), one of the leading advocates for open access to scholarship since 1998, expanded their focus to what they declared as the open agenda—open access, open data, and open education for the benefits of practitioners, investors, and the public.[6]

Open source software—freely available for anyone to download, use, and improve—and open access have an interesting relationship. Apart from the obvious similarities of being free and publicly available, the two communities that have coalesced around these concepts share many common traits—collaboration and attribution being two of the more significant ones. Both have developed similar ways to codify these concepts in licenses. Creative Commons licenses[7] have been widely adopted for open access publishing: Popular open source licenses include Berkeley Software Definition (BSD), GNU General Public License (GPL), and Massachusetts Institute of Technology License (MIT).

Unfortunately, there are some significant variations in both environs for the most popular licenses, and internally, there are often different versions or options that can be invoked. A significant difference among the more popular open source licenses is whether they are copylefted, which means that derivative works[8] or software that incorporate code must also be distributed under the same license terms. A GPL is copylefted, whereas BSD and MIT are more relaxed and allow their codes to be incorporated with proprietary software without the same license propagation. The advocates for copylefted licenses believe this is the best way to ensure that any software enhancements will continue to be openly available, whereas critics view these licenses as less permissive and likely to inhibit wider adoption, especially in the proprietary realm.

Creative Commons (CC) licenses enable content creators to select from a range of options that reserve or waive their rights or both. It is important to remember that a CC license does not replace or supersede the creator's basic copyright; it merely codifies the permissions negotiation that would otherwise have to be repeated between the creator and every prospective user. In 2014, there were "over 882 million pieces of CC-licensed (or CC0, i.e., public domain) content on the web. Roughly 56% of that content is shared under CC tools whose terms allow both adaptations and commercial use."[9] There are six basic CC license options,[10] ranging from CC BY (only attribution required) and CC-BY-SA (attribution required, share alike; i.e., derivatives permitted but apply the same CC license) to CC BY-NC-ND (attribution required, noncommercial use only, no derivatives permitted). In addition to the international set of CC licenses, there are also more than fifty ported or jurisdictional CC license suites that are still based on the core CC licenses but carefully modified primarily for translation purposes, although these may also reflect local nuances for specifying terms and conditions.[11] Creative Commons has indicated that they do not intend to port version 4.0 of the international suite unless they see compelling reasons to do so. The availability of options has generated considerable debate in the open access (OA) community, especially around the NC (noncommercial use only) stipulation versus the most unrestricted option of CC BY (only attribution required). The latter appears to be gaining ascendancy, as such funding agencies as the Wellcome Trust and Research Councils UK mandate its use along with growing adoption in the commercial sector.

Another important intersection with open source software is its increasing adoption by university and college libraries to provide the technical infrastructure for many of these new open services. The Open Access Directory lists fifteen open source journal management software packages[12] and more than twenty repository systems.[13] Their availability and use reaffirm two previous points: Often commercial alternatives were not readily available at the time many libraries implemented these services, and we see a growing comfort and expertise within libraries to adapt open source software for local institutional use. Yet I must add a cautionary note here: Not all of these software packages may be complete, well-documented, widely used, or even still under active development.

Open educational resources (OER) also enjoy increased attention from academic libraries. OER encompass a diverse range of teaching and learning materials—courses (full, modules, learning objects), textbooks, guides, streaming videos, tests, software, and so on—that are freely and openly available. Libraries already generate a significant amount of content that is often designated as OER and have been participating in OER initiatives for years. One of the more recent developments in this sector has been the appearance of open textbook initiatives, which also overlap significantly with the other publishing areas described previously. Two good examples are Open SUNY Textbooks—an academic library-based publishing enterprise—and the BC Campus Open Textbook Project.

Yochai Benkler wrote extensively[14] in the early 2000s about the phenomenon he observed primarily in the open source software world and described it as "commons based peer production." He defined this as a

> socio-economic system of production that is emerging in the digitally networked environment. Facilitated by the technical infrastructure of the Internet, the hallmark of this socio-technical system is collaboration among large groups of individuals, who cooperate effectively to provide information, knowledge or cultural goods without relying on either market pricing or managerial hierarchies to coordinate their common enterprise.[15]

This concept also stresses the equally significant component of virtuous behavior that prompts individuals to engage in often large-scale production activities without any expectation of financial reward.

The same altruistic motivation has also been manifest in the expansion of the openness concept to academic scholarship and research and expressed as open data, open educational resources, open scholarship, open science, and so on. Open source and open access are relatively mature concepts in comparison, and even they are still grappling with fundamental issues surrounding sustainability and persistence. Additionally, the more recent and emerging scholarly areas must still come to terms with the fundamental tenets of openness, such as repurposing and attribution. As long as promotion and tenure committees hold sway in universities and colleges, the competitive nature of academic appointments may remain fundamentally at odds with the more altruistic elements of openness. Many faculty may be uncomfortable making their research data widely available or publishing their results while still engaged in the tenure process. In more applied disciplines, such as engineering and computing science, there may also be patent and other intellectual property considerations at play, where both faculty and their universities may have a significant financial stake.

The most fundamental challenge for the OA movement is to develop a business model that will sustain OA publishing. Article processing charges (APCs), whereby the author pays a fee to have his or her article published and openly available immediately, are quickly gaining ascendency. The Max Planck Digital Library published a study in 2015 that suggested it would be possible to flip current library collections budgets to an APC model[16] and also launched the OA2020 initiative[17] to pursue the large-scale international implementation of this goal. However, some academic libraries expressed concern that APCs have effectively allowed the commercial publishing sector to monetize OA publishing and that APC charges are not based on a transparent or consistent financial model. Some commercial publishers have also introduced a hybrid payment model, whereby authors pay an APC to provide open access to their articles and the library continues to pay an annual subscription fee. And the proliferation of so-called predatory publishers in the last five years owes much to the APC model.[18]

There is growing interest in a non-APC model for OA publications that will better serve the academics who create the content, the numerous noncommercial scholarly society publishers who manage journals, and academic libraries, which are chiefly responsible for paying for the content. In 2006, Raym Crow, a consultant for SPARC, proposed the creation of publishing cooperatives that would be managed and operated for the collective benefit of the key stakeholders: authors, academic journals and societies, and libraries.[19] This concept would effectively return the control of scholarly publishing to the academy. It finally received consideration in 2015 as a viable alternative to APCs.[20]

Libraries and Publishing

Publishing is most immediately and commonly understood to mean the commercial activity of pre-paring and making available books, journals, and other materials (including their online manifesta-tions) for purchase. The *Oxford English Dictionary* reminds us that the most fundamental meaning of *publish* is "to make public," and one of the variations its editors identify, notwithstanding its religious origins, provides a more appropriate and inclusive meaning when applying the concept of publishing to academic libraries: "To make public or generally known; to declare or report openly or publicly; to announce; (also) to propagate or disseminate (a creed or system)."[21] All of the services and activi-ties—institutional repositories, journal hosting, digital collections—discussed in this section are well-served by this definition, especially when coupled with the concept of "open."

With the appearance of open source software, such as DSpace[22] in 2002, academic libraries began to offer support for institutional repositories (IRs). In the words of Clifford A. Lynch, IRs are a

> set of services that a university offers to the members of its community for the management and dissemination of digital materials created by the institution and its community members. IRs rep-resent an organizational commitment to the stewardship of digital materials, including long-term preservation where appropriate, as well as organization and access or distribution.[23]

Initially, library-based IRs provided overly optimistic offerings, and many libraries were puzzled and disappointed by the limited participation of the teaching faculty. Inertia, discipline-based norms of self-promotion, and reward systems have been identified as key barriers. Many libraries are now developing IR strategies intended to be more effective, such as making it easier for researchers to provide content as they move forward to acquire and preserve research data. With the increasing implementation of OA mandates at the institutional and national levels, IRs have also become one of the most effective green OA[24] options for authors and researchers to comply with these new publi-cation requirements.

Closely related to the development and implementation of institutional repositories in the early 2000s is the local creation of digital collections. These digitization projects are commonly based on the unique holdings that most academic libraries have in their archives, special collections, or rare book areas and should be distinguished from the mass digitization initiatives that the Internet Archive and Google Books have undertaken. Karen Coyle provided a useful definition of and distinction between *mass digitization*[25] and other variants: "Mass digitization is more than just a large-scale project. It is the conversion of materials on an industrial scale. That is, conversion of whole libraries without making a selection of individual materials."[26] These library-based digitization projects are carefully selected and include every conceivable type of content and format—rare books; manuscripts; archival collections; sound recordings; photographs; newspapers; and such cultural ephemera as postcards, posters, and waybills, and so on. They are often presented in conjunction with extensive contextual information and employ a variety of software platforms and tools to make the content searchable and accessible, along with presentation features that allow the content to fully exploit their digital environment.

The appearance of these digital collections is a significant indicator of what the future might hold for collections and services in academic libraries. They are one of the most accessible digital initiatives an academic library can embark on, whether it be a large ARL or a small community college. A modest digitization project can be undertaken using relatively inexpensive consumer equipment in conjunc-tion with a wide variety of free open source content management systems. These digital collections may also prove to be harbingers of the development of library collections that are based increasingly on providing access in digital form to the unique content only available at one location. Libraries will no longer be solely dependent on purchasing their collections; instead, they will be creating and curating them directly. Similarly, catalogers and other metadata specialists will no longer be chiefly occupied with editing MARC records increasingly purchased as bulk commodities; instead, they will be more gainfully employed to create truly original descriptive information for their unique local holdings.

However, libraries must be mindful of copyright considerations and whether they have obtained sufficient permissions to digitize and make items accessible online. Copyright law is complex, with different requirements for different forms of materials, and includes concepts like "fair use" that permit limited use (particularly for educational, research, and preservation purposes) of copyrighted material without obtaining permission from the rights holder. Many collections that are ideal digitization candidates may have been acquired at a time when the focus was the physical artifact and not the ability to create digital facsimiles from them. Consequently, the terms in gift agreements that may have been appropriate for using items in the library do not extend to digitization. Developing a basic understanding of copyright law, carefully reviewing content, and including copyright requirements as part of any digitization project have become crucial.[27]

In a keynote address at the spring 2015 meeting of the Coalition for Networked Information (CNI),[28] Brewster Kahle, the founder of the Internet Archive, described how, every time they expanded the content they wanted to collect without necessarily obtaining the necessary rights or permissions, the inevitable legal advice he received was "bad things would happen." Invariably, the Internet Archive proceeded with their latest plans, and "nothing happened." In the rare instances in which a rights holder challenged them, their immediate response was simply to remove the offending content, thus resolving the issue. The intent of mentioning this strategy is not to encourage libraries to flagrantly ignore copyright law but rather to suggest that risk assessment and management can be an effective way to proceed with digitizing content. Some academic libraries have begun to apply a copyright risk assessment process as one of the ways to determine whether to proceed with a digitization project for materials with a dubious provenance or that present complexities with respect to the application of copyright law.

Library-based digital journal hosting constitutes another logical extension of the support for scholarly publishing and communication that libraries initiated with institutional repositories. Academic librarians initiated journal hosting programs as another way to support scholarly communication by providing equivalent support for electronic journals via either an existing IR platform, commercial services such as Digital Commons by bepress, or open source software like Open Journal Systems (OJS). Library journal hosting coincides with the continuing growth of the open access movement in scholarly publishing and the associated interest in alternative publishing models to support it. In the same way that many scholars were exploring open access publishing, librarians were equally interested in encouraging alternative publishing models that might provide some relief from the control large commercial publishers exercise over the marketplace.

As early as 2008, Karla Hahn determined in an ARL report that "44% of the 80 responding ARL member libraries reported they were delivering publishing services and another 21% were in the process of planning publishing service development."[29] By 2012, a proposal emerged for the creation of the Library Publishing Coalition (LPC), with the mission to promote the "development of innovative, sustainable publishing services in academic and research libraries to support scholars as they create, advance, and disseminate knowledge."[30] The 2016 LPC Directory (third edition) provides information on the publishing activities of their 115 college and university library members in North America and elsewhere. In less than ten years, many libraries have become directly involved in supporting scholarly journal publishing, and numbers will likely continue to increase in the future.

Many library-based journal hosting services primarily provide an online publishing platform and related technical support. Publishing activities, such as article review processes, copyediting, and subscription or membership management, generally remain the responsibility of the journal. However, this is also evolving as some library publishing operations proactively expand their services. The University of Pittsburgh Library offers a full suite of services, including consultation on editorial work flow management, graphic design services, ISSN and DOI registration, and promotional support.[31] The

Center for Digital Research and Scholarship (CDRS) at Columbia University offers multiple support tiers ranging from Hosting with Help, through Native Digital Publication to Companion Site to Print Publication.[32] Smaller institutions also offer comprehensive publishing services. Providence College in Rhode Island, for example, has a digital publishing services unit with more than six FTE staff that offers a range of publishing options, copyright advice, scanning and digitization, text processing and encoding, and other services.[33]

Library hosting services in conjunction with the availability of open source software for journal publishing often support a new kind of scholarly publishing. In a 2009 survey of 998 journals using the OJS software, Brian D. Edgar and John Willinsky identified the "scholar-publishers" responsible for the majority of the journals in their survey as a growing alternative to the traditional commercial publisher.[34] Many of the journals making use of these hosting services are start-up, born digital publications that rely heavily on the volunteer efforts of their editorial boards and free (or low-cost) hosting. Their revenue streams remain limited because many have adopted an open publishing model and so do not have predictable income sources, such as subscriptions.

Scholarly monograph publishing faces multiple challenges: decreasing library monograph collections budgets, increasing publication costs from a diminishing number of publishers, and a technology-driven shift from print to digital platforms and formats. This has also had implications for university presses, one of the primary publishers of scholarly books. In response to pressure from their parent institutions to be more self-sustaining and the decrease in sales to cash-strapped academic libraries, many have shifted their publishing focus to the more general retail market, sometimes at the expense of less marketable scholarly monographs. Many still struggle with the implications of a digital publishing environment and the transition this requires for their traditional production activities. Overlaying all of this is the growing demand for an open access publishing model to be applied to their scholarly publications.

The 2007 report "University Publishing in a Digital Age" by Ithaka S+R[35] encapsulated these trends and also suggested collaborative partnerships, particularly with academic libraries, as a potential way forward. Charles Watkinson, director of the University of Michigan Press and associate university librarian for publishing, stated that in 2014 there were twenty-one members of the Association of American University Presses reporting to libraries, an increase from the 2009 figure of fourteen.[36] In 2016, 30 of the 115 Library Publishing Coalition members identified at least one university press partner.[37] In 2015, the Mellon Foundation announced a new funding program of more than $10 million to support the investigation and development of new digital publishing services that would require the collaborative efforts of university presses, academic libraries, faculty, and other partners.[38] A significant number of ARL libraries—Brown, California Digital Library, Indiana, and Michigan—are participating in these initiatives.

Libraries and Research and Development

The concept of the library as a laboratory, especially for the humanities and social sciences, has a long history. In 1878, Justin Winsor noted in his first report as librarian of Harvard University (and also the first president of the American Library Association) that a "great library should be a workshop as well as a repository. It should teach the methods of thorough research and cultivate in readers the habit of seeking the original sources of learning."[39] This concept has been frequently and fondly cited by academic libraries, but it may finally be achieving fuller expression, as the technology infrastructure and digital content provided by libraries intersect with scholars from the humanities who are adapting digital tools and resources. The digital humanities (DH) field has grown rapidly during the past decade and is attracting a new generation of academics who are adapting and incorporating technology as a direct component of their research. This activity often intersects with library content from archival and special collections that have been recently digitized and readily lends itself to many of the digital research techniques and tools that DH scholars employ.

The DH community is also producing an array of research outputs—websites, online databases, data sets—often coupled with specialized software tools. These scholarly products are often more accessible and functional than traditional print equivalents, but they also have new support and "publication" requirements. Fortunately, they are often an appropriate fit with related activities already well-established in many academic libraries: content digitization; development and implementation of applications software for the description, discoverability, curation, and preservation of scholarly products and related online content; provision and management of online research environments; and familiarity with open source software life cycle management.

A new relationship is also emerging in these collaborative ventures between academic librarians and digital humanists. Librarians have long enjoyed especially close ties with their local humanities scholars, but now they bring an expert knowledge of their potential technology requirements in addition to the extensive collections and bibliographic knowledge that formed the foundation of the library's support and services in this area. Like all researchers, digital humanists rely heavily on grant funding that is also shifting to a focus on larger, collaborative initiatives involving researchers, other research projects, graduate students, librarians, software developers, and other technology specialists. The INKE (Implementing New Knowledge Environments) project[40] led by Ray Siemens of the University of Victoria in Canada is a good example. The project is funded by a $2.5 million, seven-year Major Collaborative Research Initiative (MCRI) grant from Canada's Social Sciences and Humanities Research Council (SSHRC), plus an additional $10.4 million in contributions from institutional and research partners. The international INKE Research Group consists of thirty-five researchers across twenty institutions and twenty-one partner agencies, with work involving some nineteen postdoctoral research fellows and fifty-three graduate research assistants over the life of the project.[41] Two library consortia—the Canadian Association of Research Libraries (CARL) and the Canadian Research Knowledge Network (CRKN)—serve as project partners along with a number of Canadian academic libraries and librarians. The participants from the library sector bring to the mix their technology expertise and infrastructure, along with significant digital collections.

An even larger expression of digitally based research is the growth of E-science in all disciplines, which has "big" (literally) implications for academic libraries. Since its first use in the early years of this century, the definition of this concept has also expanded significantly. Shannon Bohle's is one of the more inclusive and oft-cited:

> E-science is the application of computer technology to the undertaking of modern scientific investigation, including the preparation, experimentation, data collection, results dissemination, and long-term storage and accessibility of all materials generated through the scientific process. These may include data modeling and analysis, electronic/digitized laboratory notebooks, raw and fitted data sets, manuscript production and draft versions, preprints, and print and/or electronic publications.[42]

The popular term *big data* has also become associated with E-science, and although it has often been too loosely and readily applied, it emphasizes the most distinctive features of E-science: the magnitude of raw research data being generated and the associated requirements to manage it. The petabyte (1,000 terabytes) has quickly eclipsed the terabyte (1,000 gigabytes) as the lingua franca to describe the extent of data, and it seems inevitable that the exabyte (1,000 petabytes) will soon replace this current unit of measurement.

Academic libraries are poised to become key E-science participants at many major points in the research life cycle but especially for data management planning, subsequent accessibility and dissemination, and ultimately long-term preservation. Again, their role is based on the expertise libraries have developed as a consequence of maintaining institutional platform repositories, undertaking digitization projects, and using metadata schemas—essentially "data about data" associated with a specific type of information resource or subject area—to describe a wide array of digital content. These activities have also led to an increased emphasis on long-term digital preservation and the platforms, data packaging tools, and specialized metadata schemas intended for this purpose. All of this is collectively brought together in the creation of data management plan templates intended to address all the life cycle requirements for research data. The California Digital Library has developed DMPTool,[43] which assists researchers in meeting the data management requirements that are increasingly mandated by the major funding agencies. Many US academic libraries have adopted this tool in order to support researchers at their local institutions. Libraries in other jurisdictions are developing and implementing similar DMP tools.[44]

The same dynamics that have driven open access and the response of academic libraries to support OA through the provision of institutional repositories and journal publishing platforms have also become considerations for E-science. The initial OA mandates implemented by many research funding agencies are expanding to include research data to make it accessible by others and, what's more important, to ensure that it is preserved for the long term. In early 2016, the SHERPA/JULIET website identified 42 funders (27 percent) who required data archiving and 18 (11 percent) who encouraged it, out of a total of 157 funders.[45] An increasingly familiar "life cycle" has become associated with the development and implementation of these policies. They start as recommended behaviors that also initiate a review and feedback process. Once those recommendations have been sufficiently refined, they proceed to the status of mandated requirements associated with research grants and ultimately become enforced. OA mandates for research data remain at a relatively early point of policy evolution, and it is still not apparent whether any of them will achieve the final stage of full enforcement.

Conclusion

Transformative Changes in the Last Five Years

The digital environment in which academic libraries now find themselves has accelerated numerous transformative changes especially during the past five years. These changes have many positive implications for librarians and their roles at their universities and colleges. Many academic libraries are not just buying systems and online services: They are adapting open source software to implement services that are not yet available or too expensive to purchase and integrating them into a variety of other campus and external systems and services. Academic libraries no longer act as simple consumers of content, both print and digital, provided by vendors; they now create and curate digital collections often based on the unique local materials held in their special collections, rare books, and archives units. Additionally, they are providing systems and related services to enable their faculty and students to publish scholarly journals, textbooks, and monographs.

The strong tradition of collaboration among academic libraries has provided a foundation for new, innovative consortial projects at the regional and national levels. Libraries have worked together to negotiate license agreements for electronic resources that not only leverage collective buying power to obtain the best financial deals but also flip purchasing models and replace vendors' agreements with model licenses that the library community has developed. Now library alliances and consortia are applying concerted strategies to support open access publishing models and to assist authors in understanding and insisting on their rights to retain control over their published content. Academic libraries have coalesced around open source development projects to cultivate community-based alternatives for integrated library systems, institutional repositories, electronic resource management, scholarly publishing, digital content management, research data management repositories, and digital preservation platforms.

All this activity has created a growing confidence in how academic libraries and librarians interact with their scholarly communities; we have witnessed a major shift from an often passive and reactive service culture to a proactive one in which we take the initiative and are even ready to assume risks.

This shift might be best exemplified by the fact that a growing number of librarians now engage directly in research projects and are welcomed as contributors who bring a range of expertise that is in high demand. This expertise includes bibliographic and specialized metadata knowledge, digital content management and curation, project management skills, and a familiarity with and expertise in the infrastructure and software that is increasingly a prerequisite for research in all disciplines. Librarians are not merely viewed as academic support: We are embraced as active partners.

A younger colleague of mine, a 2010 graduate from an MLIS program, further exemplifies this transformation. He is currently embedded with a Compute Canada Research Data Management development team, and the following description of his expertise featured in a recent grant proposal to the Canadian Foundation for Innovation:

> Alex Garnett is a Research Data Management & System Librarian at Simon Fraser University (SFU) Library, and also holds an appointment as a System Developer for the Public Knowledge Project (PKP) that is based at the SFU Library. He brings a diverse range of specialised expertise to these overlapping assignments that ranges from knowledge of research data lifecycles to scholarly publishing workflows. He was the project leader for PKP on a successful project to develop inter-operability between two leading open source platforms that are representative of this intersection—Dataverse, a research data repository framework and Open Journal Systems (OJS) which is PKP's online publishing platform. At the SFU Library, he was instrumental in the development and implementation of Radar, a local data research repository utilizing Islandora and Archivematica, two widely adopted open source platforms. He has been a participant in several national research data initiatives during the past few years: the Globus, Archivematica, Compute Canada, CPDN Pilot within the RDC sponsored Federated Pilot Project; and the Canadian Association of Research Libraries (CARL) Portage Project. He provides support to Compute Canada's Research Data Management activities: by bringing experience and knowledge of existing repository technologies, communities, platforms, standards and metadata schemas; by developing a toolset for indexing and parsing metadata from existing data repositories across Canada, and by providing a stakeholder perspective on data management activities. Alex has a broad base of expertise in Python, SQL, XSLT, shell scripting, and data manipulation of all kinds. He helps to ensure the work being done by Compute Canada is mutually intelligible to libraries, archives, and academic faculty.

Discussion Questions

1. Not all academic libraries have developed sufficient technology expertise and infrastructure capacity to support or sustain new digital services. Instead they have chosen to rely on other campus partners (e.g., the computing center) or external service providers (e.g., ILS vendors). Is this a good or a bad strategy? How might technology developments in the next five years have implications for either approach?
2. Does the large-scale redefinition of library services and librarians' roles made possible by this new digital environment have the potential to weaken the historical foundations of our profession, or does it strengthen them?
3. Open access is a compelling concept for many academic librarians. It holds the promise of providing a more affordable and accessible model for content and resonates strongly with traditional library values. Article processing charges (APCs) have emerged as the primary funding model for OA publishing. Is this the only or most desirable way to sustain it? Is green OA a more desirable and sustainable model than gold OA?
4. Most libraries that currently offer journal publishing services provide the basic infrastructure and hosting support. The editorial and publishing work flows are still the purview of the journal's

editorial staff. Should libraries expand to a full-service offering? Do academic librarians have sufficient expertise in this area?

5. If libraries are increasingly involved in creating and maintaining content (e.g., digitization projects and institutional repositories) and this content is increasingly considered as part of the library's "collections," then is it viable to propose that part of the traditional collections budget should be diverted to funding these endeavors?

6. What is a reasonable expectation for the extent of technological expertise a new academic librarian should possess? For example, should he or she be proficient with coding and scripting languages, or is applications expertise (e.g., metadata schemas) sufficient?

Assignment

Your library has decided to undertake some major digitization projects and has to acquire a digital collections management system. A number of system strategies could be applied—purchase or acquire a propriety vendor system or an open source system and install it locally, subscribe to a "software as a service" cloud-based solution, or outsource the entire activity to a campus or external third party. Undertake an environmental scan of potential systems and service solutions, analyze the pros and cons of each one, and prepare a five-page report with recommendations for your dean of libraries.

This assignment will be scored as follows: environmental scan, 25 percent; analysis of pros and cons, 45 percent; recommendations, 20 percent; and overall clarity and conciseness, 10 percent.

Notes

1. American Library Association, *ALA Filing Rules* (Chicago: American Library Association, 1980).
2. Vincent Larivière, Stefanie Haustein, and Philippe Mongeon, "The Oligopoly of Academic Publishers in the Digital Era," *PLoS ONE* 10 (2015): 6, accessed June 8, 2016, doi:10.1371/journal.pone.0127502.
3. A national licensing consortium has not taken hold in the United States, although the scope and scale of the larger regional consortia rival those at the national level in many other jurisdictions. It is interesting to speculate whether this reflects an optimum size limit for a national undertaking or a tradition of limited state intervention at the national level. State funding and other support has often been a crucial component in the establishment of national consortia elsewhere.
4. Richard Hoggart and D. J. Urquhart, "Books for the People," *Times Literary Supplement*, December 30, 1977, accessed April 30, 2016, Times Literary Supplement Historical Archive.
5. *Budapest Open Access Initiative*, accessed April 30, 2016, http://www.budapestopenaccessinitiative .org/read.
6. "Why Open Matters," *SPARC*, accessed April 30, 2016, http://sparcopen.org/why-open-matters.
7. *Creative Commons*, accessed April 30, 2016, https://creativecommons.org.
8. A derivative work is a subsequent creation that is based on and may even incorporate elements of a previous work by somebody else. The modification or adaptation must be sufficiently substantial to be considered new or original. In an open source context, this practice is commonly referred to as "forking," when developers take a copy of the software code and start a completely separate development path. Although this is permitted under an open source license, it can often create confusion and contention.
9. "State of the Commons," *Creative Commons*, accessed April 30, 2016, https://stateof.creativecommons.org/report.
10. "About the Licenses," *Creative Commons*, accessed April 30, 2016, https://creativecommons.org/licenses.
11. "CC Affiliate Network," *Creative Commons*, accessed April 30, 2016, https://wiki.creativecommons.org/wiki/CC_Affiliate_Network.
12. "Free and Open-Source Journal Management Software," *Open Access Directory*, last modified March 10, 2015, http://oad.simmons.edu/oadwiki/Free_and_open-source_journal_management_software.
13. "Free and Open-Source Repository Software," *Open Access Directory*, last modified December 6, 2015, http://oad.simmons.edu/oadwiki/Free_and_open-source_repository_software.

14. Yochai Benkler, *The Wealth of Networks: How Social Production Transforms Markets and Freedom* (New Haven, CT: Yale University Press, 2006).

15. Yochai Benkler and Helen Nissenbaum, "Commons-Based Peer Production and Virtue," *Journal of Political Philosophy* 14, no. 4 (2006): 394–419.

16. Ralf Schimmer, Kai Karin Geschuhn, and Andreas Vogler, "Disrupting the Subscription Journals' Business Model for the Necessary Large-Scale Transformation to Open Access" (preprint, 2015), accessed January 25, 2016, doi:10.17617/1.3.

17. "OA2020—The Initiative," *OA2020*, accessed April 30, 2016, http://oa2020.org.

18. The concept of predatory publishers remains controversial. Jeffery Beall, a librarian at the University of Colorado, started publishing a list in 2010 of so-called predatory publishers who operated fee-based article publishing journals with dubious, if not nonexistent, editorial processes and other questionable business practices. Beall's list has been a continuous source of controversy. Many think he is providing an important service; others question his focus on open access journals only as opposed to subscription-based journals associated with traditional commercial publishers and the manner in which he applies his criteria. Beall's list of predatory publishers is available at https://scholarlyoa.com/publishers.

19. Raym Crow, "Publishing Cooperatives: An Alternative for Non-profit Publishers," *First Monday* 11, no. 9 (2006), doi:10.5210/fm.v11i9.1396.

20. "The Open Access Publishing Cooperative Study," *Public Knowledge Project*, accessed April 30, 2016, http://oa-cooperative.org.

21. *Oxford English Dictionary*, accessed April 30, 2016.

22. *DSpace*, accessed April 30, 2016, http://www.dspace.org.

23. Clifford A. Lynch, "Institutional Repositories: Essential Infrastructure for Scholarship in the Digital Age," *ARL Bimonthly Report*, no. 226, (February 2003): 1–7, accessed April 30, 2016, http://www.arl.org/storage/documents/publications/arl-br-226.pdf.

24. Green OA refers to the practice of self-archiving in an institutional or subject (discipline) repository, while gold OA is publishing a work in an open access journal. The OA community has expended considerable energy debating the merits and drawbacks of both models, even though the outcome is the same—content has been made freely and openly available.

25. The Google Books Project is perhaps the best known and most controversial example of a mass digitization project. Google has scanned around 30 million volumes, but the project remains in hiatus in 2016 because copyright lawsuits and concerns about the giant company's motivations have stalled it.

26. Karen Coyle, "Mass Digitization of Books," *Journal of Academic Librarianship* 32, no. 6 (November 2006): 641, doi:10.1016/j.acalib.2006.08.002.

27. Bobby Glushko, "Keeping Library Digitization Legal: Overcoming the Legal Hurdles Surrounding Digitization," *American Libraries* (May–June 2011), accessed April 30, 2016, http://americanlibrariesmagazine.org/2011/05/02/keeping-library-digitization-legal.

28. Brewster Kahle, "Providing Universal Access to Modern Materials—and Living to Tell the Tale," presentation, Coalition for Networked Information, spring 2015 meeting, Seattle, WA, April 13–14, 2015, last modified April 28, 2015, https://www.cni.org/news/video-brewster-kahle-on-universal-access-to-modern-materials.

29. Karla Hahn, *Research Library Publishing Services: New Options for University Publishing* (Washington, DC: Association of Research Libraries, 2008), 5, accessed April 30, 2016, http://www.arl.org/storage/documents/publications/research-library-publishing-services-mar08.pdf.

30. "About Us: Mission," *Library Publishing Coalition*, accessed April 30, 2016, http://www.librarypublishing.org/about-us/mission.

31. Allison P. Brown, ed., *Library Publishing Toolkit* (Geneseo, NY: IDS Project Press, 2013), 81, accessed April 30, 2016, http://opensuny.org/omp/index.php/IDSProject/catalog/book/25.

32. Ibid., 111–16.

33. Ibid., 163.

34. Brian D. Edgar and John Willinsky, "A Survey of Scholarly Journals Using Open Journal Systems," *Scholarly and Research Communication* 1, no. 2 (2010), accessed April 30, 2016, http://www.src-online.ca/index.php/src/article/view/24/41.

35. Rebecca J. Griffiths, Matthew Rascoff, Laura Brown, and Kevin M. Guthrie, "University Publishing in a Digital Age," *Ithaka S+R*, last modified July 26, 2007, http://sr.ithaka.org?p=22345.

36. Charles Watkinson, "Three Challenges of Pubrarianship," *Charles Watkinson's Blog* (blog), January 16, 2015, accessed April 30, 2016, http://charleswatkinson.blogspot.ca.

37. Sarah K. Lippincott, ed., *Library Publishing Directory 2016* (Atlanta, GA: Library Publishing Coalition, 2015), vii, accessed April 30, 2016, http://www.librarypublishing.org/sites/librarypublishing.org/files/documents/Library_Publishing_Directory_2016.pdf.

38. Carl Straumsheim, "Piecing Together Publishing," *Inside Higher Ed*, February 25, 2015, accessed April 30, 2016, https://www.insidehighered.com/news/2015/02/25/researchers-university-press-direc tors-emboldened-mellon-foundation-interest.

39. Justin Winsor, "First Report (1878) of Justin Winsor, Librarian of Harvard University," *Google Books*, 1, accessed April 30, 2016, https://books.google.ca/books?id=yXJVAAAAYAAJ&pg=PA52-IA33&lp g=PA52-IA33&dq=justin+winsor+harvard+report&source=bl&ots=N9fwf2V6u9&sig=MAU gYawLM5BNQR58Q5DnILMhF9Q&hl=en&sa=X&ved=0ahUKEwjV7u68iLzKAhVW9WMKHYc 9DrQQ6AEIOjAG#v=onepage&q=workshop&f=false.

40. *Implementing New Knowledge Environments*, accessed April 30, 2016 http://inke.ca.

41. "About," *Implementing New Knowledge Environments*, accessed April 30, 2016. http://inke.ca/projects/about.

42. Shannon Bohle, "What Is E-science and How Should It Be Managed?" *SciLogs* (blog), June 12, 2013, accessed April 30, 2016, http://www.scilogs.com/scientific_and_medical_libraries/what-is-e-science -and-how-should-it-be-managed.

43. "DMPTool," *California Digital Library*, accessed April 30, 2016, https://dmp.cdlib.org.

44. The Canadian Association of Research Libraries has established a national research data management initiative called Portage; one of the first services they have created is DMP Assistant (https://portage-network.ca), which incorporates the requirements of the Canadian research funding agencies.

45. "Some JULIET Statistics," *SHERPA/JULIET*, accessed April 30, 2016, http://www.sherpa.ac.uk/juliet/stats.php?la=en&mode=simple.

14

Assessment and Evaluation, Promotion, and Marketing of Academic Library Services

Nisa Bakkalbasi

Introduction

In the past decade, the interest in library assessment and evaluation has expanded greatly, in particular to provide evidence and context for organizational, operational, and strategic planning; priority-setting; and decision-making. In order to evaluate the quality and effectiveness of library services, collections, and facilities, the number of assessment activities has grown rapidly. Previously, the occasional assessment task was assigned as "other duties" to a library staff member who had an interest in it or a specific area of expertise. However, the demand for assessment and evaluation expertise has led to full-time positions and sometimes evaluation units charged with the sole responsibility of providing leadership, coordination, and support to carry out assessment activities geared toward evidence-based decision-making. Although the field of library assessment and evaluation has advanced considerably during the past three decades, strides still need to be made in administrative commitment, technical training, or reskilling to ensure high quality and rigorous assessment program implementations.

This chapter provides a broad overview of the history and current state of library assessment, offering an examination of key concepts, best practices, and tools. This chapter is not intended as a primer in assessment but instead aims to help students to develop critical thinking skills in identifying the appropriate uses of methods and tools essential to undertaking a rigorous assessment project. Collecting, analyzing, and presenting evidence require a number of essential steps, including establishing clear objectives, collecting data from multiple sources, and then processing it to obtain understandable and actionable results for stakeholders. Furthermore, the assessment cycle cannot be considered complete until results have been disseminated and used to inform operational and strategic planning. All these essential steps in the assessment cycle are tightly interwoven and affect each other in complex ways. In order to lend structure to a complex and expanding array of library assessment activities, for the remainder of this chapter, I have divided the main topic into five subheadings: (1) "History and Current State of Library Assessment," which covers the progression from data collection to assessment, the impetus for assessment activities, and the needs of a user-centered and data-driven organization; (2) "Assessment Process," which offers an in-depth examination of each component in a five-step assessment process as the engine that drives an iterative cycle of improvement; (3) "Research Methods and Design," which introduces a wide variety of standardized or locally developed methods and instruments; (4) "User Privacy and Confidentiality," which provides an overview of protecting user privacy and welfare as research subjects within the context of organizational research; and (5) "Promotion and Marketing," which discusses the relationship between assessment and marketing.

History and Current State of Library Assessment

Academic libraries have a long history of compiling detailed data at a local level and comparative data across libraries in an attempt to help library administration and management solve practical problems. More than a century ago, in 1906, James Thayer Gerould, a librarian at the University of Minnesota, proposed a scheme to collect and publish data on facilities, size of collections, expenditures, and various internal processes. Furthermore, he emphasized the importance of comparative data across libraries:

> No questions arise more frequently in the mind of the progressive librarian than these: Is this method the best? Is our practice, in this particular, adopted to secure the most effective administration? Are we up to the standard set by similar institutions of our class? These questions are of the most fundamental type, and upon the success with which we answer them depends much of the success of our administration.[1]

Gerould's efforts led to the first compilation of annual statistics, known as Gerould Statistics (1907/08–1961/62), for college and university libraries, which eventually became the Association of Research Libraries (ARL) Statistics. While these early statistics help us to document the historical development of American academic libraries, we possess little evidence of how they were actually used in improving operations and aiding decision-making.

Since Gerould, libraries have seen a century of progress in the development of more robust quantitative methods to capture library inputs and outputs and the increased use of qualitative methods to better understand the needs and expectations of the user communities they serve. Put simply, inputs (e.g., operating expenditures, personnel salaries, or investments in collections) are the resources that are put into a process to obtain desired outputs (library visits, instruction sessions, circulation, etc.). In "From Measurement to Management: Using Data Wisely for Planning and Decision-Making," Steve Hiller and James Self[2] provide a historical summary of measurement, evaluation, and assessment in libraries, tracing the development of each step toward the present: traditional uses of data in libraries, organizational development and data use, user-centered libraries, organizational barriers, and pioneer libraries that have successfully integrated assessment results into their operational and strategic planning. In the same article, the authors argue that the introduction of strategic planning in the 1980s proved to be a key catalyst in the evolution of measurement and assessment for improving library performance. Overall, the major components of a strategic planning process include identifying goals and objectives, planning actions to achieve a set of goals, implementation, monitoring, and evaluation. In the course of this process, data is collected and used to assess existing operations and measure progress toward achievement of goals and objectives. As strategic planning has become an accepted practice in many academic libraries, the need for developing performance measures closely linked to strategic goals, objectives, and initiatives has grown.

Initially fostered by internal strategic planning processes and progressively transformed by high user expectations, the concept of the user-centered library emerged. In ARL's "SPEC Kit 303: Library

Assessment,"[3] reporting findings of a survey that examined the state of library assessment, Stephanie Wright and Lynda S. White observe that the survey of libraries revealed that:

> while a modest number of libraries in the 1980s and earlier engaged in assessment activities beyond annual ARL statistics gathering, the biggest jump in activity occurred between 1990 and 2004. The overwhelming majority of responses indicate the impetus was service driven and user centered, and came from within the library itself rather than from an outside source. Respondents' top impetus for beginning assessment activities (63 respondents or 91%) was the desire to know more about their customers.

Across all types of academic institutions, operating in an environment of high user expectations for convenience and immediacy in getting information, library management strategies emphasized the need to focus on gathering information about users' preferences, perceptions, needs, expectations, and information-seeking and -using behaviors rather than organizational inputs and outputs. As a result, the user-centered libraries began to utilize new data collection methods, such as usability testing, user satisfaction and service quality surveys, observation studies, interviews, and focus groups. More recently, the impetus for assessment activities came from external sources: a rapidly changing information environment, increasing demand for accountability across higher education, mandated accreditation of an institution or program, and competition for public and private funds.

In order to proactively navigate an increasingly customer-oriented, digital, competitive, global, and budget-conscious higher education environment, libraries have been forced to expand their range of decision-making considerations and to demonstrate their value in ways that their users and stakeholders will find meaningful. In an environment that stresses the importance of assessing user needs related to the library process of educating, selecting resources, and providing access, libraries not only need to utilize new assessment and evaluation methods and tools but also must transform themselves into learning and innovation organizations through organizational research and analysis. Many libraries have recognized that it will take more than strategy and making accommodations for new assessment methods and tools to respond effectively to users' needs and efficiently meet their expectations—it will require a cultural change within the organization. In the past decade or so, Amos Lakos[4] has promoted the concept of establishing a positive organizational climate for data-driven decision-making through the development of a culture of assessment in libraries. A widely accepted definition of *culture of assessment* that conceptualizes an environment sought for many libraries is an

> organizational environment in which decisions are based on facts, research and analysis, and where services are planned and delivered in ways that maximize positive outcomes and impacts for customers and stakeholders. A Culture of Assessment exists in organizations where staff care to know what results they produce and how those results relate to customers' expectations. Organizational mission, values, structures, and systems support behavior that is performance and learning focused.[5]

While it may be a daunting task to introduce new concepts and a set of new activities to implement a continuous cycle of assessment in an established library environment, it is reassuring to know that many libraries have successfully provided multiple pathways to organization-wide assessment. Whenever possible, more and more libraries aim to base decisions on facts, carefully designed studies, and analysis, while recognizing the value of domain knowledge to help convert data into knowledge and give context for actions. Domain knowledge can be defined as library function-specific knowledge, such as e-resource management, collection development, preservation, and so on, and it is a key ingredient to success in giving meaning to data. As of the writing of this chapter, the most up-to-date publication, "Driving with Data: A Roadmap for Evidence-Based Decision Making in Academic Libraries,"[6] on the current state of evidence-based decision-making within the academic library, was published by Ithaka S+R, a strategic consulting and research service organization. In this article, Deanna Marcum and Roger C. Schonfeld state that "while there is more to be done, library leaders have extensive experience with data for several vital decision-making and advocacy purposes," contending that libraries' use of data is increasingly improving but still a work in progress.

Fueled by a number of internal and external forces, assessment seems to be everywhere and seems likely to stay with us for the foreseeable future. Discussing the future of assessment, James G. Neal predicts that "accountability and evaluation will continue to expand and intensify as part of the culture and politics of North American higher education. The governments and boards that administer them will expand their expectations and mandate for rigorous assessment."[7] It appears probable that much of the trend we have seen in the last three decades will continue as academic libraries collect data more rigorously and systematically to further the interest and needs of users and advance education and scholarship. The current trend seems to point toward further dynamic development of assessment, evaluation, analytics, and data visualization. The next section covers broadly the major components of an assessment process that renders constructive results instead of gathering data endlessly without use or purpose.

Assessment Process

Though it may be only one simple word, *assessment* comprises many definitions. Within the context of higher education, *assessment* means different things to different people, depending on whom you ask—faculty, information technology professionals, instructional designers, librarians, administrators, and others. Some assessment activities focus on student learning outcomes, and others intend to evaluate effective implementation of instructional technology, while still others concentrate on meeting administrative needs. We have no commonly accepted definition for the term *assessment*—neither in higher education nor in the community of library assessment practitioners. Pam Ryan offers this helpful, although broad, definition for the library assessment community: "any activities that seek to measure the library's impact on teaching, learning, and research, as well as initiatives that seek to identify user needs or gauge user perceptions or satisfaction. The overall goal is data based and user centered continuous improvement of library collections and services."[8] Regardless of how we define it, good assessment follows a reflective and thoughtful process of design, implementation, evaluation, and integration. To support, advance, and sustain assessment efforts, we must put in place an effective process that will ensure that libraries gather appropriate, valid, and accurate evidence to promote and support a culture of assessment. We should consider assessment an iterative and continuous cycle of experimentation and evaluation that begins with developing objectives, as figure 14.1 illustrates.

Before beginning the assessment process, it is beneficial to consider the context within which the library operates. Depending on the type of institution and its environment (e.g., research university, four-year teaching university, or community college), the mission, core values, and priorities vary greatly across higher education institutions. A well-designed assessment is feasible, produces actionable results, and is linked to the mission of the institution.

1. Developing the Assessment Question or Objective

The first part of the assessment cycle involves identifying what we want to know. The development of an assessment design requires that we have a clear and shared idea of precisely what we seek to achieve. In a toolkit to provide a standardized, step-by-step mechanism to create assessment plans, I and colleagues Donna L. Sundre and Keston Fulcher[9] have found the establishment of objectives to be "one of the most important and rewarding stages of the assessment process." At this step, we must engage multiple stakeholders to delineate the purpose of assessment—to improve the quality of services, to aid in decision-making, or to meet external agencies' requirements (accountability)—to

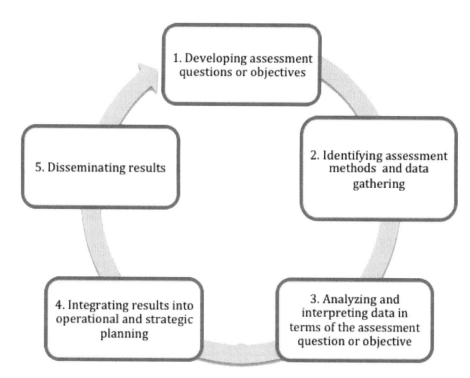

Figure 14.1. Assessment as a continuous cycle of experimentation

ensure that the information we gather remains aligned with the needs of the audience (e.g., an accrediting agency, funding authorities, or library users). It is crucial that assessment objectives are linked to the operational and strategic goals of the library to ensure that we gather relevant and actionable data that can be used to support organizational development and change.

2. Identifying Assessment Methods and Data Gathering

Once we have developed our assessment objectives, the second step in the assessment process will be to identify and select the most appropriate assessment methods and instruments. Well-written objectives provide the basis and guidance for the design and selection of best methods for assessment use. Many academic libraries boast a strong tradition of producing "homegrown" instruments for surveys, focus groups, and observations. Some libraries prefer other methods and instruments already available in the marketplace; for example, the International Organization for Standardization (ISO)[10] performance indicators designed for activities commonly undertaken in libraries or LibQUAL+, a survey designed to measure service quality. However, marketplace availability, while convenient, should not influence the specification of assessment objectives nor the selection of the best method for assessment use. We must pay close attention to identifying the target population, discussing the appropriate sampling technique, encouraging participant motivation, and specifying the data collection period. Ensuring the reliability and validity of the data will be equally important during data collection and the next stage—analysis and interpretation.

3. Analyzing and Interpreting Data in Terms of the Assessment Question or Objective

After data collection has been completed, the data is analyzed and prepared for reporting. This step of the assessment process concerns how data will be analyzed and interpreted into meaningful and significant conclusions that stakeholders can understand and use. In most academic libraries, assessment officers or units with relevant expertise assume primary responsibility for ensuring comprehensive, appropriate, and accurate data analysis and reporting. The assessment practitioners and domain experts (i.e., librarians with function-specific expertise or other perspectives) should share responsibility for the interpretation of the results produced in order to ensure that meaningful conclusions are drawn from the findings. In addition, engaging domain experts not only improves the conclusions but also enhances the potential usefulness of the findings to influence improvements. At this step, all parties involved should be aware of data limitations and report these honestly. For instance, certain limitations might mean that the views or perspectives gathered through interviews with a group of biology faculty cannot be generalized to the larger population of all faculty across all disciplines.

4. Integrating Results into Operational and Strategic Planning

The fourth step of the assessment process involves integrating the results into operational improvements and strategic directions of the library, as well as marketing and communication to promote library services. It is not enough simply to lay satisfying groundwork for methods and data collection and then employ rigorous statistical analysis and interpretation; we then need to use the findings to make recommendations and close the gaps identified. I see little point in having an assessment program if we do not follow through and make meaningful use of the results. If assessment generates results that are not immediately actionable due to lack of resources or results that are not actionable due to a flaw in assessment design, then the library should determine an appropriate way to communicate it to those who participated in the study.

5. Disseminating Results

We should develop and implement a transparent communication plan to share the assessment results with all stakeholders, particularly those in charge of library programs and services. I and my colleagues Sundre and Fulcher have argued that the most important contribution one could possibly make to the development of a culture of assessment would be to seek input from the community by asking the following question: "Are our methods and results of sufficient quality to warrant the inferences we wish to make?" In order to develop, sustain, and advance a culture of assessment, we must share results with stakeholders and report on the decisions we made based on the collected data.

Assessment should be considered an iterative process that seeks to expand our knowledge and understanding through research and analysis. We should also be looking to continuously improve the assessment process itself. In "Assessing Assessment: A Framework to Evaluate Assessment Practices and Progress for Library Collections and Services,"[11] I and my colleagues provide an assessment progress template and a rubric to evaluate the quality and rigor of the assessment plans implemented and attain excellence in assessment design over time.

Research Methods and Design

In order to respond to a wide spectrum of data needs and requirements, libraries employ a diverse variety of methods in their assessment work, ranging from surveys to anthropological fieldwork. Furthermore, the areas being assessed can be as varied as the methods employed. Broadly speaking, we can divide the evaluation methods into two main groups, namely *quantitative* and *qualitative methods*. As the name implies, the purpose of *quantitative methods* is to quantify data in order to allow generalizations of the results from a sample to an entire population of interest; for instance, the students' views and perceptions of library space in a given sample. Quantitative methods involve the process of collecting, analyzing, and interpreting numerical data collected through satisfaction surveys, organizational climate surveys, and systems-generated transactional data from web logs, library management systems, interlibrary loan systems, and facilities access data, to name a few examples. Researchers consider *qualitative methods* to be particularly suitable for gaining an in-depth understanding of underlying reasons and motivations in user studies. Within the context of libraries, qualitative data is collected through interviews, focus groups, open-ended survey questions, observation studies, usability testing, and wayfinding studies (i.e., user experience of orientation and navigation within the library building). However, what might possibly constitute qualitative data seems limitless, given that we are seeing more and more creative use of sources, such as recorded observations (both audio and video recordings), photo diaries, drawings solicited through participatory design processes, mapping surveys, and social media data. The main differences between quantitative and qualitative research can be found in all key components of a research method: data sample; data collection; data analysis; and, last but not least, findings and outcomes.

Regardless of the methodology employed—quantitative or qualitative—no single method can tell us all we might wish to know about library use and library users. Different research questions will require different methods (and possibly more than one) to capture all aspects of a topic under examination. For example, while we may rely on a quantitative approach, such as a survey, to identify user needs to produce generalizable results, combining it with a qualitative approach, such as a series of in-depth interviews, provides insights and perspectives into library users' rationales behind a particular need. Insufficient or inaccurate data or inappropriate evaluation methods may generate inconclusive or even misleading results. Robust assessment plans feature multiple and mixed methods (i.e., a combination of quantitative and qualitative) research. In academic libraries today, researchers ever more frequently pair quantitative and qualitative methods in order to benefit from the strengths of each approach. In recent library and information science literature, we frequently see quantitative research followed by qualitative research with an aim to explore select findings further. Alternatively, qualitative research may be used to gain insights and generate hypotheses for later quantitative research.

A lot of work has been done to get to where we find ourselves now. Libraries have struggled for years with how to make the best use of statistics and other data to enhance library effectiveness. Since the late 1980s, as the interest in assessment and evaluation, driven by strategic planning, has grown, so, too, have the questions about the validity and relevance of commonly employed methods. At that time, Geoffrey G. Allen posed the following questions to the library community at a conference:

> The failure of library statistics to solve all the problems that library management would have them solve may not . . . be entirely the fault of the statistics. A number of questions may reasonably be asked. Do librarians collect the appropriate statistics? Are the statistics collected either accurate or compatible among similar libraries? Do we ask valid questions of the data? And above all, do we know how to manipulate and interpret statistical information? All too often the answers to these questions is "no."[12]

Such concerns voiced at professional gatherings encouraged a change from input standards and measures (e.g., size of collections, expenditures, staff size, facilities, transactional data from internal processes) to output standards and measures (e.g., gate counts, circulation and download statistics, reference or instruction statistics). The demand for methods to measure outcome and demonstrate impact and value led to the development of highly sophisticated standardized data collection procedures, international performance measurements, and instruments that allow peer benchmarking.

Although libraries have traditionally designed their own local instruments, which can be tailored to meet their specific needs, many of them have recognized the need to move beyond the boundaries of locally developed data definitions, instruments, and tools so that they might benefit from new initiatives at the national or international levels. One of the early international initiatives, launched in March 2002, was Project COUNTER (Counting Online Usage of Networked Electronic Resources),[13] developed to serve librarians, publishers, and intermediaries by setting standards that facilitate the recording and reporting of online usage statistics in a consistent, credible, and compatible way. The widespread availability of reliable usage data for electronic resources has made it possible to calculate cost per use and perform cost and usage analysis. In order to assist the library community by indicating and defining useful, quantifiable information to measure the resources and performance of libraries and to provide a body of valid and comparable data concerning American libraries, the American National Standards Committee (ANSC) developed the ANSI/NISO Z39.7-2013 Data Dictionary.[14] At the international level, the ISO prepared and has continuously revised documentation, ISO 11620:2014 Library Performance Indicators,[15] to be used by all types of libraries to offer accepted, tested, and publicly accessible methodologies and approaches to measuring the performance of a range of library services. These strides in collecting appropriate statistics were not limited to quantifying outputs and outcomes but included qualitative methods to demonstrate impact and value.

In order to enable libraries to articulate their value, the ARL Statistics and Assessment Program[16] has engaged at the national and international levels to develop qualitative and quantitative methods and benchmarking tools. Some of the most widely used surveys include LibQUAL+, ClimateQUAL (a survey designed to understand organizational climate and diversity perceptions of library staff), and MINES for Libraries (a transaction-based survey that collects data on the purpose of use of electronic resources). Ithaka S+R developed the Local Faculty and Student Surveys for Libraries[17] program in response to the increasing interest of library managers in gaining better insight into the perceptions of their faculty members and students. In order to accommodate the unique needs of special collections, the Archival Metrics[18] project sought to promote a culture of assessment among archivists by creating standardized user-based evaluation tools and other performance measures. The benefits of using these ready-made tools and services are so diverse and numerous that it would be practically impossible to list them exhaustively in a short chapter. Suffice it to say that they include validated, tested questionnaires; administration and coding instructions; and comparisons between libraries, thereby identifying best practices and helping all institutions to improve their user services.

Whatever the choice, standardized or homegrown, maturing assessment programs have been increasingly using mixed-method approaches to look at the research question from various angles. In the social sciences, the practice of using two (or more) data sources or methods, known as data triangulation, will often be advocated in a given study in order to validate that study's claims. In order to make library assessment strategic, diverse, and effective in demonstrating library impact and value, as well as alignment with the university's mission and initiatives, we must emphasize the value of mixed-method studies and reiterate the importance of engaging domain experts in interpretations to draw meaningful conclusions.

User Privacy and Confidentiality

Assessment and evaluation work almost always involves obtaining data about or from people. Dramatic increases in the availability of quantitative data in academic libraries enable nonintrusive, continuous, and low-cost means of capturing rich demographic information, making community-specific user research more feasible. Data sources (e.g., circulation, interlibrary lending, and facilities access) provided by the numerous systems operating in academic libraries represent the behavioral patterns of various user communities. However, there remain challenges related to capturing and archiving library user data from systems, which often contain personally identifiable information. Qualitative methods, capturing rich, detailed accounts of library experience or the research process through unstructured interviews, also present unique challenges in maintaining participant confidentiality. As a result, legitimate concerns about the security and privacy of both quantitative and qualitative data sometimes hamper their collection and use. In "Questions of Data Ownership on Campus,"[19] Kyle M. L. Jones, John Thomson, and Kimberly Arnold explore questions of data ownership on campus and provide talking points toward a shared ownership model that would "support the institution's data needs, protect students' privacy, and inform individual students about personally identifiable data use on campus and what rights they have to it."

As in any other field of research involving human participants, organizational research raises a host of ethical issues and challenges concerning participant privacy and confidentiality. Privacy risks in library assessment include the identifiability of participants and the potential harm they may experience from the collection, use, and disclosure of personal information. Privacy risks arise at all stages of the research life cycle, including initial collection of information, use and analysis to address research questions, dissemination of findings, storage and retention of information, and disposal of records or devices containing sensitive information. When researchers collect, use, share, and access different types of information or data about participants, they must determine whether the information or data proposed in their research may reasonably be expected to identify an individual, either directly or indirectly.

All staff involved in assessment and evaluation activities are expected to maintain the ethical standards set out by their institutions to protect the privacy and confidentiality of research participants. Academic institutions provide extensive guidance to researchers about ethical issues and requirements. In the United States, local committees, institutional review boards (IRB), are responsible for oversight functions for research conducted with human subjects. In most American academic institutions, faculty, students, and staff who plan to use human subjects in their research need to find out whether their research activities require institutional board review. The issues examined by IRBs include the rationale for data collection, recruitment of participants and informed consent, voluntary participation, strategy for data collection, processing and storing raw data, confidentiality, risk to participants, and dissemination of findings. Sharing research data that relates to people can often be achieved using a combination of obtaining informed consent, anonymizing data, reporting aggregate results, and regulating data access.

Promotion and Marketing

Earlier in the chapter, I introduce the concept of a culture of assessment as a key ingredient in keeping academic libraries relevant to their communities in a new information environment. A culture of assessment strives to move the organization forward by focusing on positive outcomes for its community of users. A culture of assessment encourages reflection, promotes open communication, and values information transparency among library staff, users, and other stakeholders. In order to establish and maintain a culture of assessment, assessment, evaluation, promotion, and marketing activities must join forces. Assessment and marketing bear a strong relationship: Library services cannot be promoted effectively and efficiently without understanding users' needs and expectations, and library impact cannot be evaluated effectively and efficiently unless users know what libraries have to offer. John Sumsion[20] describes this relationship in a nutshell by stating, "'Marketing' and 'user studies' may employ different terminology but, in reality, they are two sides of the same coin."

With the growth of digital bulletins, social media, blogs, and press releases, marketing and communication has gained recognition as a niche area within libraries. Libraries allocate valuable resources to help spread the word, both on campus and off, about their resources and services and the expertise of their staff. Understanding users' needs and expectations allows libraries to deploy marketing resources efficiently and campaign effectively by targeting appropriate user groups. In "Marketing and Assessment in Academic Libraries: A Marriage of Convenience or True Love?"[21] Lynne Porat documents the benefits of a successful collaboration between assessment and marketing teams, not only to promote libraries, but also to enlist the goodwill of users to motivate them to participate in future assessment studies.

Conclusion

In the one-hundred-plus years since Gerould's compilation of annual statistics, libraries have seen tremendous changes and made great strides in data collection and purpose. In the past three decades, library assessment has been transformed by internal factors, such as strategic planning processes, and external sources, such as user expectations influenced by Amazon, Google, Netflix, and other web services; technology; accreditation requirements; and competition for public and private funds. In particular, the last decade has witnessed a remarkable shift from collecting inputs and outputs to reporting outcomes and demonstrating impact and value.

In the foreseeable future, digital technologies will continue to change assessment. We have witnessed a growing movement around exploiting activity data in higher education. An influential report published by the United Kingdom's Jisc[22] defines *activity data* as the "record of human actions in the online or physical world that can be captured by computer."[23] The analysis of such data and placing it in a visual context to expose patterns, trends, and correlations can lead to new insights about library use. Furthermore, combining activity from systems with detailed information from interviews, focus groups, and social media can help libraries to tell a complex story through engaging infographics (i.e., a visual image, such as a chart or diagram, used to represent data.).

While change may be inevitable and is often unpredictable, the mission of assessment remains the same. The underlying philosophy and principle of assessment is to increase our level of knowledge and understanding of a subject and inform action. In a dynamic environment, one needs an enduring map to successfully undertake the long journey toward building an organizational assessment program. Working for well over a decade as an assessment practitioner, Sundre[24] draws from her experience to provide a pathway to an institution-wide assessment program. Sundre's exemplary model includes six successive components, each one leading logically to the next: vision, high standards, commitment, resources, structure, and integration. Undoubtedly, a certain level of administrative commitment, broad engagement in assessment activities, and the various positive personal attributes that researchers who succeed at collaborative work typically possess, combined with individual enthusiasm and organizational rewards for continuous reskilling, must all be considered important parts of practicing successful library assessment. However, in an ever-changing world of decision-making considerations, abundance and variation of data sources, and proliferation of new data analysis and visualization tools, the ultimate success of a far-reaching assessment program consistently depends on our ability to make sensible use of data.

Discussion Questions/Assignment

Assessment and Evaluation Proposal Assignment

Write a research proposal of at least 1,000 words to describe an assessment project you intend to pursue for an academic library. Building on the five-step assessment process discussed in this chapter, this should be set out in five subheadings:

1. Goals and Objectives: Provide background information with references that are related to the need to conduct this study. State assessment objectives or questions clearly and precisely.
2. Study Design or Methodology: Describe the methodology that will be used in this study.
3. Analysis and Reporting: Provide sufficient details about procedures that will be used in analysis and a brief report outline.
4. Findings: Discuss how potential findings or hypothetical results might affect decision-making or contribute to the improvement of the library.
5. Dissemination: Provide a communication plan to disseminate results.

Timeline: Include a timeline for your project.

Notes

1. James Thayer Gerould, "A Plan for the Compilation of Comparative University and College Library Statistics," *Library Journal* 31 (1906): 761–63.
2. Steve Hiller and James Self, "From Measurement to Management: Using Data Wisely for Planning and Decision-Making," *Library Trends* 53, no. 1 (2004): 129–55.

3. Stephanie Wright and Lynda S. White, "SPEC Kit 303: Library Assessment" (Washington, DC: Association of Research Libraries, 2007), 11, http://publications.arl.org/Library-Assessment-SPEC-Kit-303/11?ajax.

4. Amos Lakos, "Culture of Assessment as a Catalyst for Organizational Culture Change in Libraries," in *Proceedings of the Fourth Northumbria International Conference on Performance Measurement in Libraries and Information Services: "Meaningful Measures for Emerging Realities,"* edited by Joan Stein, Martha Kyrillidou, and Denise Davis, 311–19 (Washington, DC: Association of Research Libraries, 2002), http://www.libqual.org/documents/admin/4np_secure.pdf.

5. Ibid., 313.

6. Deanna Marcum and Roger C. Schonfeld, "Driving with Data: A Roadmap for Evidence-Based Decision Making in Academic Libraries," *Ithaka S+R,* 2014, http://www.sr.ithaka.org/wp-content/uploads/2014/05/SR_BriefingPaper_DrivingData.pdf.

7. James G. Neal, "On the Horizon: Future Thinking about Assessment in the Academic Library," in *Reviewing the Academic Library: A Guide to Self-Study and External Review*, ed. Eleanor Mitchell and Peggy Seiden (Chicago: ACRL, 2015), 315.

8. Pam Ryan, "About," *Library Assessment*, 2006, http://libraryassessment.info/?page_id=7.

9. Nisa Bakkalbasi, Donna L. Sundre, and Keston Fulcher, "Assessing Assessment: A Framework to Evaluate Assessment Practices and Progress for Library Collections and Services," in *Proceedings of the 2012 Library Assessment Conference: Building Effective, Sustainable, Practical Assessment*, ed. Steve Hiller, Martha Kyrillidou, Angela Pappalardo, Jim Self, and Amy Yeager (Washington, DC: Association of Research Libraries, 2012), http://libraryassessment.org/bm~doc/proceedings-lac-2012.pdf.

10. International Organization for Standardization (ISO) is an independent, nongovernmental, standard-setting body that provides common standards between nations to support innovation and provide solutions to global challenges. For more information about this body, see http://www.iso.org/iso/home/about.htm.

11. Bakkalbasi, Sundre, and Fulcher, "Assessing Assessment."

12. Geoffrey G. Allen, "The Management Use of Library Statistics," *IFLA Journal* 11, no. 3 (October 1, 1985): 211–22, doi:10.1177/034003528501100305.

13. *COUNTER*, 2016, http://www.projectcounter.org.

14. "ANSI/NISO Z39.7-2013, Information Services and Use: Metrics and Statistics for Libraries and Information Providers—Data Dictionary," *NISO*, March 2013, http://z39-7.niso.org. ANSI/NISO stands for American National Standards Institute/National Information Standards Organization.

15. "ISO 11620:2014: Information and Documentation—Library Performance Indicators," *ISO*, n.d., http://www.iso.org/iso/home/store/catalogue_ics/catalogue_detail_ics.htm?csnumber=56755.

16. "Statistics and Assessment," *Association of Research Libraries*," n.d., http://www.arl.org/focus-areas/statistics-assessment#.Vso-QxjXK80.

17. For more information, see "Local Faculty and Student Surveys for Libraries," *Ithaka S+R*, 2016, http://www.sr.ithaka.org/work-with-us/surveys.

18. "About Archival Metrics," *Archival Metrics*, n.d., http://www.archivalmetrics.org.

19. Kyle M. L. Jones, John Thomson, and Kimberly Arnold, "Questions of Data Ownership on Campus," *EDUCAUSE Review* (August 25, 2014), http://www.educause.edu/ero/article/questions-data-ownership-campus#.U_zxhqlmcyA.twitter.

20. John Sumsion, "Library Statistics for Marketing," *IFLA Journal* 27, no. 4 (January 1, 2001): 221–31, doi:10.1177/034003520102700404.

21. Lynne Porat, "Marketing and Assessment in Academic Libraries: A Marriage of Convenience or True Love?" in *Proceedings of the 2010 Library Assessment Conference: Building Effective, Sustainable, Practical Assessment*, 743–48 (Washington, DC: Association of Research Libraries, 2011).

22. Jisc (formerly Joint Information Systems Committee) is a UK nondepartmental public body whose role is to support higher education and research by providing advice, digital resources, and technology services. For more information about Jisc, see https://jisc.ac.uk.

23. David Kay and Mark van Harmelen, "Activity Data—Delivering Benefits from the Data Deluge," *Jisc*, January 15, 2015, http://www.jisc.ac.uk/guides/activity-data-delivering-benefits-from-the-data-deluge.

24. Donna L. Sundre, "A Pathway for an Institution-Wide Assessment Program: Are We There?" in *Volume IV: What Works, What Matters, What Lasts* (2005), http://works.bepress.com/donna_l_sundre/17.

15

A Vision for the Future

NEW ROLES FOR ACADEMIC LIBRARIANS

Ronald C. Jantz

Introduction: Vision and Transformation

Academic library leaders have long acknowledged the need for the library to transform itself in order to meet the needs of the twenty-first-century university. The transformation implies a major change in form and function, suggesting that library organizational structures and functions will change along with how professional librarians conduct the work of the library. To guide the transformation, a vision will be needed, one that creates a compelling mental image of what the library should become. Vision bridges the present with the future, establishes a standard of excellence, and informs the strategic planning process.[1] Creating a vision is a challenge; it is difficult to imagine, verbalize, and communicate a future preferred state.

Today, academic librarianship is overburdened and preoccupied with attending to the details of providing traditional services to students and faculty. For library leaders and librarians, it is a time for independent thinking, innovation, and the courage to undertake risk and embrace major change. Library professionals will not only look forward but, according to John M. Budd, will also need to step back and examine the profession—"purpose, ethos and the world we live in."[2] In the end, courageous leadership and management will be required, as Jordan M. Scepanski affirms, "to abandon what has worked and often worked well, to strike off on a new and perhaps perilous course."[3]

A well-articulated vision can lead naturally to the development of new competencies, the associated knowledge, and the requisite skills. In contributing to a vision of the future, this chapter takes an approach in which new roles for academic librarians are extrapolated from emerging functions in the academic library and my observance of incongruities that suggest we in the profession should be doing something differently. Totally new services will emerge with these roles and, in all likelihood, will require changes in the traditional organizational structure of the library and related management processes and practices. Some in today's world will consider the new roles unusual, unorthodox, and perhaps even detrimental to the profession, for they fear these changes might conflict with the norms and traditions of librarianship. Jesse H. Shera aptly characterizes the dilemma and the opportunity for the academic library: "On the one hand there are the traditionalists, who cling close to the solid earth of library convention and shun the heights of innovation. . . . Against them are arrayed the innovators, the intrepid explorers, who reject convention as the traditionalists fear the unknown. . . . In the conflict between these two groups librarianship suffers."[4]

This chapter proposes that academic libraries will undergo change, even radical change, in order to address the information needs of the university. This premise suggests a reorientation to a service model, one that significantly extends the range and depth of creative work undertaken by faculty and students and in the process creates dynamic new roles for professional librarians.[5]

Organizational Dynamics and the Profession

Understanding the dynamics of organizational change will be important for leaders to successfully introduce and support new roles in the library. The library, an institution with well-established professional norms and traditions, will need to become more creative, continuing to support traditional services while simultaneously launching new ones. The associated new roles will develop and flourish within a more inventive culture. Although culture can constrain our actions, it can also become a vehicle for change in which library employees are empowered to search for innovation opportunities. Strategy, organizational structure, and a more turbulent external environment can stimulate ingenuity and change in the library, disrupting the status quo but also creating the space for new roles to emerge.[6] The future academic library will look quite different, yet change will be difficult in an environment where the university is embedded in an institutional bureaucracy, further restricted by faculty norms, union contracts, and the traditions of the library profession.

We all believe that librarianship is a profession. The casual observer understands that academic librarians provide access to information and are able to describe and organize scholarly works. The librarian acts as the guardian, caretaker, and curator of the world's knowledge. Librarians provide instruction to educate students in navigating the complexities of the library and to help them to understand how to interpret and evaluate information. In the ongoing dialogue and evolution of the academic library profession, Shera captures the challenge we all face: "The first responsibility of a profession is to know itself, which means, first, knowing what a profession is; second, knowing what kind of a profession it is; and third, knowing what differentiates it from all other professions."[7] Keeping Shera's admonition uppermost in our thinking, this chapter outlines emergent roles in academic libraries that will not only advance the mission of the library and the university but also help us to develop a deeper understanding of the profession.

Technology, Research, and Marketing: Building New Knowledge and Skills

The implications of a rapidly changing technology environment, stakeholders' demands that demonstrate value, and the need for more active engagement throughout the university will lead to new academic library roles. The impact of technological discontinuities on our society has been widely publicized. Universities and their libraries are not immune to these events. To paraphrase Henry Lucas's rhetorical question,[8] libraries and universities almost certainly will be disrupted in ways similar to for-profit firms, such as Kodak and Borders. Of course, mortality and bankruptcy are not in store for the library. However, change can be more subtle and slow moving in academia, allowing for complacency and lack of action within the leadership team and a much-diminished library presence in the university.

Research

James G. Neal has argued that academic librarianship is an "information poor" profession where "decisions are routinely not supported by evidence" and "research in the field is poorly understood, communicated, and applied."[9] If we hope to facilitate a library transformation, we can scarcely overstate the benefits of research and exploration. We will require an increased investment in research in order to properly assimilate and deploy new knowledge and in turn create forward-looking service roles. An emerging role in the research domain would focus on advancing the profession, bringing in novel ideas, exploiting external technologies, and championing innovation.

So, what does the *research librarian* do, and how is this person positioned in the library organization? In terms of traditional R&D, the research librarian focuses more on the *D* (development) rather than the basic research implied by the *R*. For this reason, the person in this new role spends a considerable amount of time spanning and exploring the external world, looking for new ideas, cutting-edge technologies, and process initiatives that will benefit the library. The research librarian facilitates and expedites the transfer of new technologies, processes, and related software into the library to be customized for library applications. In pursuing these initiatives, we heed Budd's caution regarding the application of technology in the library: "We are concerned with how the technology is used, how it may be transformative, how it may privilege some people over others, the economics of technology, the politics of technology, and other factors."[10]

If the research librarian expects to be successful, he or she will need to facilitate the flow of an idea across the organization, championing this idea throughout the decision-making and implementation processes. An associated function supporting the flow of ideas includes the development of an idea database. Robert C. Litchfield and Lucy L. Gilson[11] have proposed an approach for the management of ideas that uses a museum metaphor for curating idea collections. The idea curators do not take responsibility for the ideas, nor do they necessarily generate or develop work plans to support a particular one. These curators typically seek a strategic balance in idea collections and will organize these resources to support both traditional services and emerging services. Litchfield and Gilson have combined the curator function with idea management to create a unique new role for academic libraries, one that fits nicely with the traditions and culture of the library. The research librarian might serve as the idea curator, constantly scavenging for old ideas within the organization that can be reapplied in new contexts. The curator thus keeps old ideas alive by communicating across the organization, emphasizing how these ideas might once again prove viable in different ways. In effect, the idea database becomes an information exchange and knowledge management tool, facilitating the growth of individual and organizational intelligence in the library.

As an example, research and technology-focused initiatives include the examination of applications of artificial intelligence, expert systems, and natural language processing. Artificial intelligence (AI) applications will have an impact on the library commensurate with that of the Internet and mobile computing. Some twenty-five years ago Charles W. Bailey Jr., digital artist and publisher of the journal *Digital Scholarship*, articulated the challenge of artificial intelligence for library applications, noting that our conceptual horizons are limited by a lack of understanding of this important area.[12] AI offers the promise to create systems that rival human intelligence and, in doing so, affect or even disrupt traditional reference and bibliographic instruction services. The research librarian will not develop AI applications; rather, he or she will assist in organizational learning about AI and act as a technology transfer agent to bring systems in from the external world that could be used to offer new library services.

Organizationally, the research librarian is best positioned to support all units in the library. Embedding this role in the traditional public or technical services units would likely result in traditional innovations specific to those units. To maximize benefit to the organization, then, the research librarian should report to either the library director or a unit that bears overall responsibility for research and organizational planning. He or she will also require different academic credentials. Given that many developments will be technology-based, the research librarian might need an engineering or computer science degree in addition to the MLS.

Marketing

The value of the library to the institution's mission and the continued support of library resources cannot be assumed. Over a forty-year period starting in the mid-1970s, the library budget as a percentage of the institution's expenditures has dropped from 5 percent to less than 2 percent. An ARL study of forty research libraries demonstrated a decline from 3.7 percent to 1.8 percent of the institution's expenditures in the period 1982–2011.[13] Library directors can hardly ignore the not-so-subtle message that administrators now value library contributions less and increasingly reallocate portions of the library budget to other units. Public relations activities and marketing can have a huge impact on sustaining and increasing library resources, yet academic libraries have been slow to recognize the importance of this form of self-promotion.[14]

Looking to the future, Charles Martell[15] suggests that we need to create new services in the twenty-first century that were unthinkable in the twentieth. Introducing a new service will require significant marketing efforts, not only to understand client needs, but also to facilitate the introduction of this service. Kathryn J. Deiss describes the marketing challenge for academic librarians as a "failure to match the introduction of a new service with the customers' readiness to adopt new behaviors."[16] Faculty and students form their impressions of the library based on longstanding services and seem unlikely to propose new services beyond the traditional library portfolio. Thus, marketing library value, introducing creative new services, and communicating the concept of a broader role for the academic librarian becomes increasingly important.

The *marketing librarian* matches client needs with the services and resources of the library. In doing so, this role provides an important bridge between ongoing library research that generates new knowledge and ideas and the evolving needs of students and faculty. The convergence of new ideas, technology, and client needs can result in the specification for a totally new library service. As an example, the marketing librarian might work with a student group that is advocating for open e-textbooks in order to reduce the expense of commercial textbooks. Undergraduates are expected to spend some $1,200 annually on textbooks, an unaffordable sum that causes many of these students not to purchase required texts or to take fewer courses in order to reduce expenses. After understanding the students' requirements and communicating with faculty who are interested in developing an open e-textbook, the marketing librarian works with the research librarian and other institutional partners, such as the university press, to develop specifications for an open e-textbook service. In this publishing endeavor, a range of solutions might be possible, from the use of existing open e-textbook libraries[17] to actually providing a service for faculty members to publish their own open e-textbooks.

In a case study at the University of New Mexico (UNM) Library, the value of a marketing strategy was clearly demonstrated. Camila A. Alire describes the initiative at UNM to conduct word-of-mouth marketing. The initial strategy focused on the Faculty Senate Library Committee, with an objective of having faculty talk to other faculty about the value of library services. The resulting successful marketing campaign added $700,000 to the library budget to maintain the journal collection.[18]

Organizationally, the marketing librarian constitutes a new role, one whose duties differ from the marketing and outreach conducted by the library liaison. The marketing librarian spans all the scholarly disciplines and spends much of his or her time outside the library, communicating with faculty, students, and administrators. Perhaps one of the more important functions in the marketing role might be understanding how stakeholders think—legislators, provosts, and administrators.[19] Gaining this knowledge will enable the marketing librarian to assess the effectiveness of a new service and communicate value and impact to all stakeholders. In effect, the marketing librarian becomes a leader in advancing the entrepreneurial mission of the library, creating new programs and new revenue streams, and enabling the library to become a successful competitor in the information marketplace.[20]

Digital Library Architect

Broadly speaking, an architect is one who designs a plan or undertaking and advises in the ongoing construction of the resulting project. Architecting a system largely entails taking system concepts as embodied in principles, requirements, and prototypes and mapping them to physical components. The work of the architect can be undertaken at many different levels.

Ronald C. Jantz

At the software level, the *digital library architect* maps requirements to a variety of components, including data structures, databases, objects, protocols, subroutines, modules, scripts, and other similar artifacts. The architect will break down complex software applications into more manageable and smaller components. In these tasks, the architectural activity relates primarily to new library software applications, the institutional repository, and the underlying digital library architecture. However, as in most complex systems, there is architectural entropy, so the digital library architect must also serve as an advocate for renewal to take advantage of new technologies and software methodologies.

At another level, the digital library architect addresses the information requirements of the digital object, including metadata, byte streams, and special scripts that govern dynamic behavior. There are many different digital object types reflecting the formats of physical objects—books, maps, photographs, and media. In each case, the architect must decide how to present the object to the end user and what should be preserved. In this activity, the architect works with the digital archivist to ensure authenticity and trust for these resources.[21] The resulting digital object must be managed as a whole. If the repository is organized in such a way that bits and pieces of the object are scattered throughout storage, it becomes difficult, perhaps impossible, to keep track of all these pieces, risking the possibility of not preserving all the relevant material as one unit.

Archiving, Publishing, and Research Data: Leveraging Existing Roles

In this section, I build on the traditional skills of the academic librarian to propose new functions for existing roles that represent opportunities for librarians to extend into interesting and challenging new areas. In the digital world, we are interested in more than just the published article or book. The scholarly communication process generates models, research data, working papers, blogs, e-mails, and lab notes. According to Lorcan Dempsey, "All of these become materials to manage and disclose effectively to interested parties elsewhere."[22] By developing new knowledge in how these resources are created and used, the librarian can leverage existing skills to preserve and provide access to these emerging new formats, thereby enriching the scholarly communications process.

Digital Preservation and Archiving

Our society produces electronic information at increasing rates, while we see a pressing need to digitize cultural artifacts housed in special collections and other institutional archives. Much of the gray literature and ephemera along with many cultural artifacts from disadvantaged nations suffer from neglect. Scholars, archivists, and the general public have quite disparate views of the value of artifacts, ephemera, and the detritus produced by our global society; however, the risks of not preserving these resources are almost impossible to evaluate. Digital preservation, archiving, and curation are natural extensions of traditional roles in academic libraries. These new roles are so compelling and so intimately related to the academic library's mission in the university that it seems only natural that digital preservation should become an integral part of this mission.

Many important functions of the *digital archivist*[23] are well established in academic libraries. Much has been accomplished in existing open source digital library platforms to provide capabilities for preserving digital objects, including the now ubiquitous-features, such as persistent identifiers, integrity checks, audit trails, and resource versioning.[24] A major task and part of life cycle management involves the migration forward of archival master files to new formats and standards. Although many libraries have a digital archivist or curator in their ranks, what is new about this position is the opportunity to extend it into previously untapped areas. These new areas include providing archival and preservation services and assuming the role of a trusted archival agent for the university.

Some examples will illustrate these new functions and services. New types of research can be conducted by using the digital surrogate as in the study of ancient artifacts. The metal coins of antiquity were the principal mass media that conveyed a government's chosen image, displaying important information on a small surface through symbols and allusive images. Because of library security issues and the logistics of organizing access to a physical coin collection, digital portals become even more important in providing access to these special collections for study and teaching. The Badian Collection of Roman Republican Coins[25] is just one example of how the digital surrogate extends access to students and scholars who previously had only limited use of this unique collection. A classics scholar may be studying the control marks on these coins, while a doctoral student uses the digital images to test pattern recognition software, projects that would be virtually impossible to conduct with the physical collection.

A second example involves the archiving and preservation of e-mail related to research and university policies and constitutes an important new service, one that could be offered by means of collaboration between the library and the university archivist and librarians. The institution's e-mail will likely prove to be of major administrative, historical, and legal value—each area possessing its own unique set of technical and policy issues. In addition to administrative e-mail, faculty may also want to preserve their research-related e-mail as part of their legacy upon retirement. The typical e-mail package consists of headers, message bodies, and attachments. Andrea Goethals and Wendy Gogel note that the storage format for e-mail has not been standardized.[26] The message format might be plain text or HTML, and attachments can include almost any file type. Security is a major concern because e-mail messages might contain viruses or spam content. E-mail can contain sensitive personal data, and archiving would need to satisfy security and privacy requirements, complying with laws at multiple levels of governance, as well as local security policies and practices.

For these new services, the university community has an expectation of trustworthiness, albeit one that is not well defined. Trust is a complex, multifaceted concept and can exist between individuals or an individual and an institution. There are three dimensions of trust based on benefits, information, and identity.[27] Information-based trust relies on researchers, scholars, and students understanding the processes and mechanisms of the institution. Trust develops over time with repeated interactions between the user and the library. Libraries over the years have built up considerable trust within the communities they serve, originating primarily from traditional services, such as the reference interview and reliable processes for finding a book or journal article. The library and the digital archivist must offer assurance that the institution can be trusted as a digital archival agent. How do we transform libraries to become trusted repositories of digital information?

A scholar or researcher will always want to know that a digital object can be trusted—that it is authentic and reliable. Relatively few of the digital resources in use today receive proper archival and preservation attention. Indeed, one might claim that twenty-first-century scholarship depends on trusted methods for archiving and preserving digital information. Digital objects can be surrogates resulting from a digitization process or objects whose only form is electronic (often referred to as "born digital"). These digital containers work to hold content fixed so that it can be preserved and repeated. *Fixity*, however, is a relative term that takes on different meanings in the world of digital documents. The fixity of microfilm and paper is generally considered to be much greater than that of any of the digital media. How do we guarantee the authenticity of the original content as represented in the digital surrogate, and what does *original* mean in the digital context? In Charles T. Cullen's words,[28] a third party, ideally a trusted librarian, would put a marker on a digital object—a marker that could not be predicted or guessed—that would mark the document's time and date. Ross Atkinson[29] proposes that the academic librarian is better suited than any other information intermediary to assume the role of a trusted third party. The actions of creating an authentic digital object place the digital preservationist and archivist in a key role as a cognitive authority in a trusted scholarly communication process and offer the opportunity to leverage and transform the traditional skills of academic librarianship.

Research Data Librarian

In some respects, research data has been long neglected by academic librarians. Early digital initiatives focused on text documents, providing for full-text indexing and digitization of many special collections.

The role of the social science data librarian appeared relatively recently in academic library history. Today, the Inter-university Consortium for Political and Social Research (ICPSR)[30] provides more than 65,000 data sets for social science research and instruction, covering a wide range of areas, such as population, economics, education, health, political behavior, and political attitudes. ICPSR comprises the world's largest archive of social science data and provides web access to documentation and data files for use with statistical software, such as R, SAS, and SPSS. As part of the vast and growing data realm, the *research data librarian* will also encounter the complexities of science data and data from the emerging digital humanities (DH) disciplines.

The emerging field of E-science and the establishment of data-sharing mandates by the National Science Foundation[31] and the National Endowment for the Humanities[32] have motivated academic libraries to pursue ways in which they might assist faculty and researchers in preserving research data and providing access to scholars for reuse of data.[33] Although academic library directors appear to support data management as an important service for the institution, recent research suggests that libraries are having difficulty defining and getting started with data management services.[34] Many academic librarians feel that they lack the knowledge and skills to undertake this new service. In a recent survey of science librarians, Karen Antell and colleagues[35] report that only 23 percent of 155 respondents felt that they had sufficient skills to take on a data management role, citing unfamiliarity with the data life cycle as a major impediment.

The role of research data librarian in some respects represents the change needed in the traditions and cultural limitations of the academic library profession. Clearly there will be a steep learning curve that will require the data librarian to embed himself or herself in the research process, not only understanding the data life cycle, but also dealing with copyright, data security, and university policies regarding the ownership of research data.[36] Ownership of research data presents its own unique problems, frequently influenced and complicated by institutional, state, and country jurisdictions.[37] In the organizational learning process, the nature of the liaison role changes—the data librarian becomes a collaborator and partner with the scholar. Recent research demonstrates the opportunities and challenges for academic librarians who participate in grant-funded projects as part of the research team.[38] In this role, we can see obvious synergies with other traditional and emerging services in the academic library. Deposited data will require extensive metadata that is specific to the research domain. It will also need to be archived and curated for reuse by researchers, and in this reuse, domain academic libraries become publishers of data.[39]

Scholarly Publishing

The academic library has both mission-oriented and economic reasons to engage in scholarly publishing. One strategic objective of the library is to support scholarly communication, including the creation and dissemination of scholarly information. In contrast to other emerging services, scholarly publishing might be considered relatively mature. The recent Library Publishing Directory[40] indicates that 115 academic libraries have published 404 faculty-driven journal titles. Many academic libraries have the technology and the wherewithal to publish in a variety of formats, including e-journals, blogs, electronic theses and dissertations (ETDs), and monographs. Paul N. Courant and Elisabeth A. Jones offer an economic perspective, suggesting "research libraries are natural and efficient loci for scholarly publication."[41] These authors argue that publishing should lead to new business models for the library. Within the broad area of scholarly publishing, we can identify many opportunities for the research library and the smaller academic library. In the past few years, the designations for these new roles illustrate the involvement of libraries in a variety of publishing initiatives—scholarly communication librarian, digital scholarship librarian, digital initiative librarian, and director of digital publishing.

Of the many titles now in vogue, perhaps the one most relevant for this emerging new service is *publishing director*. One of the most important tasks of the publishing director is to envision and create the business concept and associated business model for a publishing service. This concept will be quite different in each library, depending on the size of the institution, the strategy of the library, and the fit with the requirements of students and faculty. Gary Hamel describes the importance of strategic business innovation that requires individuals "who can think more holistically and concretely about new concepts."[42] For the library, the business concept characterizes the focus, purpose, and impact of publishing, addressing partnerships with the university press, possible revenue streams, the types of publishing that would be undertaken, and how the university's clients would benefit. Publishing initiatives can be directed at different stakeholders in the university. For example, the publishing initiative might focus on collaboration with the university press to publish humanities monographs. This initiative might take the form of a library–university press collaboration.[43] Courant and Jones suggest that in this partnership the library "can teach the press how to give information away free," and the press "can teach the library how to reach beyond the university for authors . . . and how to extract mission-enhancing revenues."[44] This publishing collaboration will likely demonstrate that these two organizations need not be separate entities. In a smaller academic library, publishing might focus on student e-journals. Given the wide availability of mature open source software, such as the Open Journal System,[45] it is quite easy for a technology-oriented librarian to establish the necessary infrastructure for a journal publishing service.

The Small Academic Library

We can examine these new roles from the perspective of a smaller academic library, including four-year teaching colleges, liberal arts colleges, and community colleges. In scouring data from the National Center for Education Statistics, Cy Dillon[46] reports that a small academic library serves a degree-granting institution that enrolls fewer than 2,500 students. A common misconception holds that these smaller academic libraries lack the resources to innovate. Although the mission of smaller libraries will typically focus more on teaching and less on research, these libraries remain subject to the forces of change from the external environment, technological evolution, and budget pressures. However, in many respects, the small library lacks the bureaucratic encumbrances of larger institutions and can therefore be more flexible, innovative, and responsive to student needs. The roles of the research librarian, publishing librarian, and marketing librarian are all relevant for the small library, albeit in a somewhat different form than they are for the larger library. For example, the research librarian might spend part of his or her time scanning the external environment, not so much to conduct research as to look for attractive technologies that might be readily applied in an instructional environment. The publishing librarian might work with faculty to publish an undergraduate journal of the best student papers or provide assistance in teaching students how to create a newsletter based on readily available open-source blogging software. In all of these initiatives, the marketing librarian works with administrators to make sure these emerging roles and services align with the university mission and to articulate the impact of these new service roles. Depending on the size of the library, the marketing and research roles might be easily undertaken by a single individual. Similarly, the publishing role could be merged with the digital initiatives or scholarly communication librarian.

Public Services

Every profession must withstand challenges to its status,[47] and for the public services librarian, the challenge is in the pervasive impact of technology. Public services are crucial but still remain somewhat difficult to define, appearing in both technical and public services units. Public services professionals will need to provide the leadership to introduce and sustain the emerging new roles that have been highlighted in this text. In discussing the qualifications for public services librarians, Barbara I. Dewey[48] indicates that these librarians are motivated to contribute innovative ideas and eager to experiment with new programs.

The reader may ask about how public services roles appear in the transformed academic library of the twenty-first century. In fact, many of the roles already discussed herein have a significant public service component. Dewey[49] notes that public services are shifting to a more proactive and collaborative model that is linked to university research and the teaching mission. This shift is evident in the aforementioned role of the *research data librarian*—a role in which the liaison acts to collaborate with researchers to acquire and preserve science data. The marketing role leverages the traditional skills of the liaison—collegiality, leadership, and management, albeit with a different focus, interacting more with vice presidents, provosts, and administrators rather than students and faculty. Some twenty years ago, Dewey articulated the importance of library research that can lead to new and practical public service models, citing areas for further study, such as information-seeking behaviors, learning technologies, and information literacy.[50] In pursuing these areas, the public service librarian does become a *research librarian*.

There are, however, continuing innovative extensions of the traditional liaison role. Steven Bell has suggested that liaisons reach out to the broader external environment, resulting in a role of the *neighborhood liaison and public education specialist*.[51] The neighborhood liaison works through an existing college department or community relations or an entirely new outreach initiative in order to identify, locate, and communicate with the people who are able to leverage experts and resources to create sustainable services. In a similar new role, Bell proposes the *outreach/community engagement specialist*, who is tasked with connecting to high school students and their parents at the schools, at community meetings, and at public libraries. The specialist is there to create more recognition for his or her institution and to demonstrate that the library is an active participant in contributing to student success.

These extended roles of the public services librarian do not represent new skills but suggest a significant change in emphasis. The public services professional will need to reposition his or her work to engage in all facets of the information experience. This change in emphasis is crucial for creating and sustaining all new roles, helping the parent institution to understand how the library and librarian can become a full partner in the academic experience.[52]

Conclusion

In discussing the future of librarianship, Budd argues that it would be irresponsible for us not to envision a preferred future state, one that is "not accidental; it is a conscious and intentional and attainable state."[53] The accompanying vision is one in which new knowledge undergoes continuous development, where ideas and innovation frequently originate in the external (nonlibrary) environment. For example, it is not too early for library researchers and technologists to explore the possibilities for artificial intelligence applications. IBM Watson[54] is a technology platform that uses natural language processing and machine learning to reveal insights embedded in large amounts of unstructured data and documents. Watson Analytics[55] provides a smart data discovery service available on the cloud that guides data exploration for all types of businesses, including nonprofits. Intelligent software applications will soon be commonplace, and the automated library reference assistant might be a good place to start.

The new roles cited here become part of the vision for the future academic library and, taken as a whole, represent a library that will be quite different from today's institution.[56] The list is not exhaustive, and there are, of course, still other emerging roles that represent promise and change for the library.[57] The skills and competencies embodied in these roles emphasize the impact of the external world—technology, politics, and economics—highlighting the importance for each librarian to take a leadership role in the transformation of the academic library.

This transformation requires a reorientation, moving from the print, automated, and electronic libraries of previous eras[58] to a model that embraces new digital services and new digital formats. The transformation suggests that library leaders and librarians should engage in an in-depth reflection, resulting in a theory of librarianship that links the broad and classical functions of librarianship with new roles into a comprehensive whole. In this process, organizational change becomes a fact of life, undertaken with a sense of urgency but always honoring the traditions and ethical norms of librarianship.

Discussion Questions

1. All the new roles discussed in this chapter require leadership, not only from library management, but also from those who are undertaking these new roles. Leadership requires vision—a preferred future state. Will the current vision and strategy of the academic library accommodate and support these new roles, or will there need to be a significant change in vision and strategy?
2. Should academic libraries provide revenue-generating services? Which services would be candidates, and what would be the business model?
3. Academic libraries are notorious for not being able to defund and cancel services that are no longer valuable for the university community. Assume the queries at your library reference desk have been dramatically reduced in recent years, and you have decided that students can handle most questions. How would you manage this transition? Comment on how the change should be communicated to the members of the library, the opportunities, and the issues of reassigning and retraining professional librarians.
4. Given that many of the new services in an academic library will be technology-based, how would the ratio of technical staff to professional librarians change?
5. Under which conditions should an academic library become a "bookless" library?
6. Provosts and administrators are demanding more evidence of the library's impact on the university. What would be the quantitative indicators that might demonstrate this impact?

Assignments

1. Your library has started to publish e-journals as a service for faculty who want to launch a new journal. The journals are peer-reviewed and are freely available to the world. The wide availability of open source platforms (such as OJS) makes it relatively easy for your library to take on this new role. You, as scholarly publications librarian, are asked to develop criteria for acceptance of new journals to be published by the library.
2. Discuss the implications of a revenue-generating service. How does such a service fit into the norms and traditions of the library profession, and how might revenue be generated for a specific service (e.g., a data service that seeks to defray the costs of storing and preserving large data sets)?
3. As a marketing librarian, can you think of a totally new service that meets the needs of one of the library's clients—faculty, students, and administrators? Describe the concept and the business model—strategy, client interface, resources, partners, and potential revenue.
4. As the digital library architect, you want to have your library certified as a trusted archival agent. Which steps would you take to achieve this certification? (Hint: See the Center of Research Libraries work for certification at https://www.crl.edu/archiving-preservation.)

Notes

1. Donald E. Riggs, "Visionary Leadership," in *Leadership and Academic Libraries*, edited by Terrence F. Mech and Gerard B. McCabe, 55–65 (Westport, CT: Greenwood Press, 1998).
2. John M. Budd, *Self-Examination: The Present and Future of Librarianship* (Westport, CT: Libraries Unlimited, 2008), 2.
3. Jordan M. Scepanski, "Forecasting, Forestalling, Fashioning: The Future of Academic Libraries and Librarians," in *Academic Libraries: Their Rationale and Role in Higher Education*, edited by Gerard B. McCabe and Ruth J. Person, 167–76 (Westport, CT: Greenwood Press, 1995), 173–74.
4. Jesse H. Shera, *"The Compleat Librarian" and Other Essays* (Cleveland: Press of Case Western University, 1971), 64.

Ronald C. Jantz

5. "Changing Roles of Academic and Research Libraries," *Association of College and Research Libraries*, 2007, http://www.ala.org/acrl/issues/value/changingroles.

6. Ronald C. Jantz, "The Determinants of Organizational Innovation: An Interpretation and Implications for Research Libraries," *College and Research Libraries* 76, no. 4 (2015): 512–36, doi:10.5860/crl.76.4.512.

7. Jesse H. Shera, *Foundations of Education for Librarianship* (New York: John H. Wiley and Sons, 1972), 350.

8. Henry Lucas, "Disrupting and Transforming the University," *Communications of the ACM* 57, no. 10 (2015): 32–35.

9. James G. Neal, "The Research and Development Imperative in the Academic Library: Path to the Future," *portal: Libraries and the Academy* 6, no. 1 (2006): 1–3.

10. John M. Budd, *Knowledge and Knowing in Library and Information Science* (Lanham, MD: Scarecrow Press, 2001), 328.

11. Robert C. Litchfield and Lucy L. Gilson, "Curating Collections of Ideas: Museum as Metaphor in the Management of Creativity," *Industrial Marketing Management* 42, no. 1 (2013): 106–12, doi:10.1016/j.indmarman.2012.11.010.

12. Charles W. Bailey Jr., "Intelligent Library Systems: Artificial Intelligence Technology and Library Automation Systems," *Advances in Library Automation and Networking* 4 (1991): 1–23.

13. "Library Expenditure as % of Total University Expenditure," *Association of Research Libraries*, 2013, http://www.libqual.org/documents/admin/EG_2.pdf.

14. Nancy J. Marshall, "Public Relations in Academic Libraries: A Descriptive Analysis," *Journal of Academic Librarianship* 27, no. 2 (2001): 116–21.

15. Charles Martell, "The Disembodied Librarian in the Digital Age," *College and Research Libraries* 61, no. 1 (2000): 10–28, doi:10.5860/crl.61.1.10.

16. Kathryn J. Deiss, "Innovation and Strategy: Risk and Choice in Shaping User-Centered Libraries," *Library Trends* 53, no. 1 (2004): 17–32.

17. *Open Textbook Library*, n.d., http://open.umn.edu/opentextbooks.

18. Camila A. Alire, "Word-of-Mouth Marketing: Abandoning the Academic Library Ivory Tower," *New Library World* 108, nos. 11–12 (2007): 545–51.

19. Helen H. Spalding and Jian Wang, "The Challenges and Opportunities of Marketing Academic Libraries in the USA," *Library Management* 27, nos. 6–7 (2006): 494–504.

20. James G. Neal, "The Entrepreneurial Imperative: Advancing from Incremental to Radical Change in the Academic Library," *portal: Libraries and the Academy* 1, no. 1 (2001): 1–13. The marketing role might complement or be combined with the outreach or community engagement specialist, as reported in the recent ACRL study. Steven Bell, "Building Community through Collaboration," in *New Roles for the Road Ahead: Essays Commissioned for ACRL's 75th Anniversary*, by Steven Bell, Lorcan Demsey, and Barbara Fister, edited by Nancy Allen (Chicago: Association of College and Research Libraries, 2015), 47, http://www.ala.org/acrl/sites/ala.org.acrl/files/content/publications/whitepapers/new_roles_75th.pdf.

21. Henry M. Gladney, *Preserving Digital Information* (Berlin: Springer-Verlag, 2007), 93–107.

22. Lorcan Dempsey, "Introduction: Rules and Roles," in *New Roles for the Road Ahead*, 12.

23. For rhetorical simplicity, the role is referred to here as "digital archivist," which embodies the functions of archiving, preservation, and curation. It is acknowledged that many variations on this title can be found in academic libraries.

24. Ronald C. Jantz, "An Institutional Framework for Creating Authentic Digital Objects," *International Journal of Digital Curation* 1, no. 9 (2009): 71–83, http://www.ijdc.net/index.php/ijdc/article/viewFile/103/86.

25. "The Badian Collection: Coins of the Roman Republic," *Rutgers University Libraries*, 2013, http://coins.libraries.rutgers.edu/romancoins.

26. Andrea Goethals and Wendy Gogel, "Reshaping the Repository: The Challenge of Email Archiving," *Austrian Computer Society*, 2010, http://www.ifs.tuwien.ac.at/dp/ipres2010/papers/goethals-08.pdf.

27. Niki Panteli and Siva Sockalingam, "Trust and Conflict within Virtual Interorganizational Alliances: A Framework for Facilitating Knowledge Sharing," *Decision Support Systems* 39, no. 4 (2005): 599–617.

28. Charles T. Cullen, "Authentication of Digital Objects: Lessons from a Historian's Research," in *Authenticity in a Digital Environment*, 1–7 (Washington, DC: Council of Library and Information Services, 2000), http://www.clir.org/PUBS/reports/pub92/pub92.pdf.

29. Ross Atkinson, "Transversality and the Role of the Library as Fair Witness," *Library Quarterly* 75, no. 2 (2005): 169–89.

30. "ICPSR—A Partner in Social Science Research," *Inter-university Consortium for Political and Social Research*, 2016, https://www.icpsr.umich.edu.

31. "NSF ENG Data Management Plan Requirements," *National Science Foundation, Directorate of Engineering*, n.d., https://www.nsf.gov/eng/general/dmp.jsp.

32. Jason Rhody, "Data Management Plans From Successful Grant Applications (2011–2014) Now Available," *National Endowment for the Humanities*, November 4, 2015, http://www.neh.gov/divisions/odh/grant-news/data-management-plans-successful-grant-applications-2011-2014-now-available.

33. As an example, the NSF Engineering Directorate requests that proposals include a document of no more than two pages labeled "Data Management Plan." This supplementary document describes how the proposal will conform to NSF policy on the dissemination and sharing of research results.

34. Carol Tenopir, Robert J. Sandusky, Suzie Allard, and Ben Birch, "Research Data Management Services in Academic Research Libraries," *Library and Information Science Research* 36, no. 2 (2014): 84–90.

35. Karen Antell, Jody Bates Foote, Jaymie Turner, and Brian Shults, "Dealing with Data: Science Librarians' Participation in Data Management at Association of Research Libraries Institutions," *College and Research Libraries* 75, no. 4 (2014): 557–74, doi:10.5860/crl.75.4.557.

36. Laura B. Palumbo, Ron Jantz, Yu-Hung Lin, Aletia Morgan, Minglu Wang, Krista White, Ryan Womack, Yingting Zhang, and Yini Zhu, "Preparing to Accept Research Data: Creating Guidelines for Librarians," *Journal of eScience Librarianship* 4, no. 2 (2015), http://dx.doi.org/10.7191/jeslib.2015.1080.

37. Kristen Briney, Abigail Goben, and Lisa Zilinski, "Do You Have an Institutional Data Policy? A Review of the Current Landscape of Library Data Services and Institutional Data Policies," *Journal of Librarianship and Scholarly Communication* 3, no. 2 (2015): eP1232, doi:10.7710/2162-3309.1232.

38. Shailoo Bedi and Christine Walde, "Transforming Roles: Canadian Academic Librarians Embedded in Faculty Research," *College and Research Libraries* (forthcoming, 2017), http://crl.acrl.org/content/early/2016/03/22/crl16-871.abstract?papetoc.

39. Patricia Hswe, "Peering Outward: Data Curation Services in Academic Libraries and Scientific Data Publishing," in *Getting the Word Out: Academic Libraries as Scholarly Publishers*, edited by Maria Bonn and Mike Furlough, 221–48 (Chicago: Association of College and Research Libraries, 2015).

40. Sarah K. Lippincott, *Library Publishing Directory 2016* (Atlanta: Library Publishing Coalition, 2015), vi.

41. Paul N. Courant and Elisabeth A. Jones, "Scholarly Publishing as an Economic Public Good," in *Getting the Word Out: Academic Libraries as Scholarly Publishers*, edited by Maria Bonn and Mike Furlough (Chicago: Association of College and Research Libraries, 2015), 17.

42. Gary Hamel, *Leading the Revolution* (Boston: Harvard Business School Press, 2000), 61.

43. Janneke Adema and Birgit Schmidt, "From Service Providers to Content Producers: New Opportunities for Libraries in Collaborative Open Access Book Publishing," *New Review of Academic Librarianship* 16, no. 1 (2010): 28–43.

44. Courant and Jones, "Scholarly Publishing," 35.

45. "Open Journal System," *Public Knowledge Project*, 2014, https://pkp.sfu.ca/ojs.

46. Cy Dillon, "College Libraries," in *Running a Small Library: A How-to-Do-It Manual for Librarians*, 2nd ed., edited by John A. Moorman, 3–14 (Chicago: Neil-Schuman, 2015).

47. Stephen E. Atkins, *The Academic Library in the American University* (Chicago: American Library Association, 1991), 161.

48. *Libraries*, 85–97.

49. Barbara I. Dewey, "In Search of Practical Applications: A Public Services Research Agenda for University Libraries," *Journal of Academic Librarianship* 23, no. 5 (1997): 371–79.

50. Ibid.

51. Bell, Dempsey, and Fisher, "Building Community through Collaboration."

52. Susan Sharpless Smith and Lynn Sutton, "The Embedded Academic Librarian," in *Reference Reborn: Breathing New Life into Public Services Librarianship*, edited by Diane Zabel, 93–104 (Santa Barbara: Libraries Unlimited, 2010).

53. Budd, *Self-Examination*, 249–50.

54. "What Watson Can Do for You," *IBM Watson*, n.d., http://www.ibm.com/smarterplanet/us/en/ibm watson/what-is-watson.html.
55. "What Is Watson Analytics?" *IBM Watson*, n.d., www.ibm.com/WatsonAnalytics.
56. Ronald C. Jantz, *Managing Creativity: The Innovative Research Library* (Chicago: Association of College and Research Libraries, 2016), 137–39.
57. Steven Bell, Lorcan Demsey, and Barbara Fister, *New Roles*.
58. David W. Lewis, "From Stacks to the Web: The Transformation of Academic Library Collecting," *College and Research Libraries* 74, no. 2 (2013): 159–76.

Index

Bohle, Shannon, 205
Bolin, Mary K., 32, 35
BookBots, 162, 166, 167, 168, 169
Boolean logic, 117
BorrowDirect (BD), 107, 112n21
Brown University, 112n21, 204
Budapest Open Access Initiative, 199
budgets, 62; academic library, 2, 7, 8, 10, 29, 33, 47–48, 52–58; acquisitions, 74, 76, 102, 106–07, 115, 116, 136, 198, 201, 204, 208; models, 53–54; operating, 48–50, 60, 62; reductions in, 1, 6, 13, 61, 147, 182, 197, 225–26
Butler Library, Columbia University, 163

California Digital Library, 199, 204, 206
California State University in Fresno, 31
Canadian Association of Research Libraries (CARL), 205, 207, 210n44
Canadian Foundation for Innovation, 207
Canadian Research Knowledge Network (CRKN), 199, 205
Canvas (learning management system), 20, 89, 133, 185
Capella University, 103
card catalogs, library, 9, 198
Carnegie Classification of Institutions of Higher Education, 102, 111n3
Carnegie Corporation, 16
Carnegie Mellon University, 12
Carnegie, Andrew, 7
Casalini (vendor), 103, 104
catalog records, library, 10, 15, 29, 83, 104, 115, 117, 119, 127n3
cataloging librarian. See librarians, academic
Center for Digital Research and Scholarship (CDRS), Columbia University, 204
Center for Research Libraries (CRL), 56
Clery Act, 25
Cleveland State University, 102
ClimateQUAL, 218
cloud-based tools for sharing and storage, 125–26, 188, 208
Coalition for Networked Information (CNI), 203
collection development, in academic libraries, 2, 24, 47, 48–49, 54–56, 58, 60, 61, 63, 69, 70, 83, 84, 101–110, 116, 131, 134, 135–36; collection-building as a service, 108
Columbia University Libraries/Information Services, 32
community college librarian. See librarians, academic
Community College Library Consortium (CCLC), 56
community colleges. See higher education, institutions of

conservation. See preservation of library materials
Consortium of Liberal Arts Colleges (CLAC), 19
content management systems (CMS), 133, 185–86, 202
copyleft, 200
copyright, 11, 12, 14, 19, 25, 58, 76, 80n35, 105, 115, 135, 140, 182, 183, 200, 203, 229; fair use, 203; importance of understanding the law, 203; risk assessment, 203. See also authors' rights
Cornell University, 14, 72, 107, 181; Libraries, 14, 107, 112n21
Council on Library and Information Resources (CLIR) Postdoctoral Fellowship Program, 65n34, 149
Council on Library Resources (CLR), 10
Courant, Paul N., 81n51, 167, 175n24, 229–30
course managements systems (CMS), 20
Coursera, 181, 182, 183, 191n47
Creative Commons licensing, 183, 191n66, 200
critical information literacy. See instruction
Crow, Raym, 201
Cullen, Charles T., 228
culture of assessment, 141, 213–14, 216, 218, 219

D2L (learning management system), 89, 185
Darnton, Robert, 12
data management librarian. See librarians, academic
data: analysis, 106, 215; "big," xi, 145; curation, xi, 3, 58, 77, 105, 149, 197; gathering, 97, 105, 106, 215; interpretation, 105, 216; life cycle of, 229; linked, 83, 117, 120, 121–22, 125, 127, 145; management, 23, 57, 89, 143, 146, 148; mining, 106; sets, 74, 75, 76, 77, 106, 107, 109, 134; storage, 108, 112n28; university policies regarding the ownership of research, 229; visualization, 75, 89, 90, 105
databases, electronic. See electronic library resources
data-driven acquisitions (DDA). See patron-driven acquisitions (PDA)
DDA. See patron-driven acquisitions (PDA)
Dempsey, Lorcan, 109, 144, 150, 227
DePaul University, 102
development, in institutions of higher education. See fund-raising
digital archivist. See librarians, academic
Digital Commons (bepress), 203
digital content curation, 75, 108, 140, 205, 207. See also data curation
digital humanities (DH), 75, 140, 145, 204–05, 229; labs, 59
digital humanities librarian. See librarians, academic
digital initiative librarian. See librarians, academic

digital library architect. *See* librarians, academic
digital preservation. *See* preservation
digital projects, guidelines for the evaluation of, 74
Digital Public Library of America (DPLA), 5, 12
digital scholarship librarian. *See* librarians, academic
digital scholarship, new forms of, 75, 77; acceptance of, 74
director of digital publishing. *See* librarians, academic
discrimination, 23, 25, 139, 147, 150. *See also* diversity
distance education librarian. *See* librarians, academic
distance education, xi, 130, 133, 140, 149, 177–78, 180, 188; distinguished from online learning, 178
diversity, 3, 5, 17, 20, 22, 23–24, 87, 94, 111n3, 135, 136, 139, 143, 147, 149, 150, 151, 152, 218
DMPTool, 206
domain knowledge, 213
Drexel University, 102
Dropbox (software), 188
Drupal (content management system), 133, 186
DSpace, 202
Dublin Core (metadata), 121, 125

Earlham College, 9; library, 9
Eastern Michigan University, 95, 102
e-books. *See* electronic library resources
EBSCO (vendor), 11, 13, 56, 104, 181
education: graduate, 22, 28, 69; high school, 8, 131; for librarianship, 3, 16, 30, 131, 139, 148–49, 225; undergraduate, 8–9, 10, 16, 21, 28, 69, 91–92, 95. *See also* postgraduate residency programs
edX, 181–83, 191n47
effort study, 52
e-journals. *See* electronic library resources
electronic library resources, 1, 2, 5, 13, 35, 55, 56, 57, 59, 60, 74, 75, 80n39, 87, 102, 104, 106, 107, 110, 116, 118, 120, 122, 125, 126, 127, 130, 136, 140, 145, 147, 180, 183, 185, 198, 203, 205, 206, 218, 229, 230, 232
electronic resource management systems (ERMS), 57, 199
electronic resources librarian. *See* librarians, academic
Ellsworth, Ralph E., 165, 168
Elmborg, James K., 94
Elsevier (publisher), 71, 104
embedded librarian. *See* librarians, academic
employees. *See* staff, academic library
Encoded Archival Description (EAD), 121, 125
endowments, college and university, 13, 47, 48, 49, 50–51, 130; effects of the 2008 financial crisis on, 13

ENIAC (Electronic Numerical Integrator and Computer), 9
ERIAL Project, 170
E-science, 3, 140, 197, 205, 206, 229
ethics and compliance, in institutions of higher education, 17, 18, 24
Ex Libris (vendor), 117, 119

faculty senate, 17, 18, 21, 31, 32
faculty status, academic librarians and, 21, 31–32, 92, 146; debate surrounding, 40n3, 40n10, 129, 131–32, 136, 144, 148, 151
faculty, in institutions of higher education: relationships with academic librarians, 2, 9, 73, 74, 88–89, 92, 96, 133, 148, 206–07; research, 74–78, 79n20, 88, 101, 103, 105–06, 108, 110, 116, 117, 124, 130–31, 145–46, 151; research, applied, 73; research productivity, expectations of, 6, 37, 70, 72–77; teaching, 2, 6, 31, 36, 37, 38, 40, 49, 52, 53, 57, 58, 61, 69, 70, 71, 72, 73, 89, 92, 131, 133, 148, 202
Farber, Evan, 9
Federation of European Publishers, 107
FERPA (Family, Educational Rights and Privacy Act), 25
Financial Accounting Standards Board (FASB), 48, 63n3
Fister, Barbara, 144–45, 150, 166, 170
Florida Atlantic University, 102
Florida State University, 75
Ford Foundation, 10
Frankfurt Book Fair, 11
Functional Requirements for Authority Data (FRAD), 120–21
Functional Requirements for Bibliographic Records (FRBR), 120–22, 124, 128, 145
Functional Requirements for Bibliographic Records, Library Reference Model (FRBR-LRM), 120–21, 124, 128
Functional Requirements for Subject Authority Data (FRSAD), 121
fund-raising, in institutions of higher education, 20, 24, 25–26, 31, 33, 47, 51, 61

Gale Cengage (vendor), 104
Geisel Library, University of California, San Diego, 165
general counsel, office of, in institutions of higher education, 5, 17, 20, 25
Georgia Southern University, 102
Gerould, James Thayer, 212, 219
Gettysburg College library, 36
Gingrich, Newt, 11
Ginsparg, Paul, 14, 72
GNU General Public License (GPL), 200

Google, 11–12, 15, 119, 126, 198, 219; Books, 5, 11–12, 167, 202; Drive, 188; Hangouts, 134, 187; Print Program, 11; Print Library Project, 11; Scholar, 112n28, 145

Gorman, Michael, 31

governance, college and university, 2, 5, 17–28, 131, 148

governing boards, college and university, 18, 219

government documents librarian. *See* librarians, academic

grants, 47, 50; demonstration, 13; funding through, 8, 10, 16n1, 40, 51, 72, 90, 146, 205, 229; proposal writing, 37, 62, 146; research, 8, 10, 14, 15, 22, 40, 52, 206, 229

GreenGlass, 56

Hahn, Karla, 203

Hanley, Edna Ruth, 163–64

Harnad, Stevan, 72

Harrassowitz (vendor), 103, 104

Harvard Institute for Academic Librarians, 149

Harvard University, 8, 13, 14, 181, 191n47, 204; Libraries, 9, 12, 106, 107, 112n21, 112n23, 166–67; Widener Library, 163–64

Hayes, Robert M., 8

higher education, institutions of: community colleges, 1, 8, 10, 13, 15, 17, 18, 19, 28, 31, 32, 38, 49, 50, 52, 53, 70, 73, 129, 131, 132, 134–36, 144, 197, 202, 214; four-year colleges, 1, 15, 17, 31, 32, 38, 70, 73, 129, 131, 134, 137, 144, 214, 230; liberal arts colleges, 9, 10, 22, 36, 70, 72, 73, 74, 129, 230; research universities, 1, 8, 10, 15, 17, 19, 28, 31, 32, 38, 49, 69, 70, 72, 73, 74, 129, 134, 135, 136, 202, 214. *See also* Carnegie Classification of Institutions of Higher Education

HIPAA (Health Insurance Portability and Accountability Act), 25

Hirsch, J. E., 73

human genome project, 74

IBM Watson, 231

Implementing New Knowledge Environments (INKE) project, 205

Indiana University, 204

Indianapolis Public Central Library, 165

information commons. *See* learning commons

Information Delivery Services Project (IDS), 56

information literacy instruction (ILI). *See* instruction

Information Technology (IT) units, 5, 6, 20–21, 29, 31, 34, 57, 186; mergers with academic libraries, 6, 29, 35–36, 38, 87

Ingram, Robert T., 18

Innovative Interfaces (vendor), 116–17, 119

Institute for Scientific Information (ISI), 73

Institute of Museum and Library Services (IMLS), 12

institutional repositories (IRs), xi, 3, 6, 23, 51, 76, 80n35, 108, 134, 140, 145, 197, 202, 203, 206, 208, 227

instruction librarian. *See* librarians, academic

instruction, 2, 14, 83, 85, 86, 88, 133, 177, 178, 182, 184, 186, 188; active learning, 83, 93–94, 96; bibliographic, 9, 91, 225; classroom assessment techniques (CATS), 96; critical information literacy (CIL), 83, 94; information literacy instruction (ILI), 2, 9, 37–38, 58, 70, 83, 85, 91–97, 129–33, 136, 140, 178, 182, 183, 187, 231; learning styles, 9, 83, 94, 96

intellectual property. *See* copyright

International Coalition of Library Consortia (ICOLC), 199

International Organization for Standardization (ISO), 215

Internet Archive, 12, 16n9, 202, 203

Inter-university Consortium for Political and Social Research (ICPSR), 75

invisible college, 70

Iowa State University, 9

ISO 11620:2014 Library Performance Indicators, 218

Ivy League universities, 102

Jaggars, Damon E., 150–51

James B. Hunt Jr. Library, North Carolina State University, 139, 167–68

Jisc, 199

journal impact factors, 73, 77

journals, academic: article processing charges (APCs), 14, 140, 207; big deal packages, 103–04, 107, 198; rising costs of, 6, 10, 55, 60, 69, 74, 76, 106, 116; serials crisis of the early 1990s, 35, 198

JSTOR, 11, 15, 60, 116

Kahle, Brewster, 12, 203

Kanopy (video streaming service), 104

Kaser, David, 165

Kerr Library, Oregon State University, 166

Kilgour, Frederick, 10

knowledge management (KM), 53

Knowledge Unlatched, 77

Kuhn, Warren, 9

labor unions, in libraries, 17, 22, 30, 139, 149, 224

Lakos, Amos, 213

Lancaster, Frederick Wilfrid, 8

Leading Change Institute, 149

learning commons, 3, 95, 139, 166–67

learning management systems (LMS), 57, 89, 133, 135 179, 184, 189

LEED (Leadership in Energy and Environmental Design), 167, 168, 175n32

lesbian, gay, bisexual, and transgender persons, 23

LexisNexis (vendor), 11, 104

liaison librarian. *See* librarians, academic

LibAnswers (software), 88

LibGuides (software), 88, 133, 186

LibQUAL+, 215, 218

librarians, academic: mentorship of, 3, 139, 146–49, 152–53; need to demonstrate their value, 13–14, 85, 96, 213, 218; new roles for, 3, 77, 87, 146, 148, 206–07, 223–32; professional development for, 3, 33, 35, 51, 95, 131, 139, 143–51; professional positions, 1–2, 15, 29–32, 35, 36, 57, 58, 77, 86–87, 130, 136, 139, 145–46, 148–49, 211, 225, 231; recruitment of, 150, 152. *See also* diversity. *See also* staff, academic library

libraries as sacred spaces, 161, 169, 171

libraries, academic: college, 3, 15, 32–34, 36, 49, 52–53, 55, 84, 87, 101, 103, 109, 129–30, 132–37; community college, 3, 9, 13, 32–34, 36, 51–53, 56, 58, 61, 84, 87, 90, 94, 101, 103, 109, 129–30, 132–37; liberal arts college, 9, 103, 129; organizational structure, 33–36; research, 3, 7, 10, 11, 15, 25, 51, 56, 74, 87, 101–02, 104, 106–09, 130, 134–35, 145, 148, 203, 226, 229.

libraries, public, 19, 124, 132, 134, 135

library building design, academic: creative renovation, 165; utilitarian versus iconic, 162

Library of Congress, 9, 11, 83, 117–18, 122

Library Publishing Coalition (LPC), 203, 204

library spaces, academic: carrels, 162, 171; furniture, 162, 171; group study, 61, 162, 165, 168, 171–72; individual study, 162, 164, 165; modular design, 162, 165; noise in, 61, 171; virtual, 3; weight-bearing stack core, 162–65. *See also* library building design. *See also* storage facilities, book

license agreements, vendor, 13, 25, 180, 199, 206

Licklider, J. C. R., 10

Lynch, Clifford A., 202

Machine Readable Cataloging (MARC) records, 9–10, 83, 116–28, 145, 197, 203

Marcum, Deanna, 5, 161, 214

marketing librarian. *See* librarians, academic

marketing of academic library services, 3, 140–41, 211–12, 216, 219, 224–26, 230–32

Marquette University, 102

Mary Idema Pew Library Learning and Information Commons, Grand Valley State University, 167–68, 172

Massive Open Online Courses. *See* MOOCs

Master's degree in Library and Information Science (MLS or MLIS), 39, 58, 146, 150, 225; perceived value of, 30, 39, 58, 146–50. *See also* ALA-accredited programs in library and information studies

Max Planck Digital Library, 201

Medical Library Association (MLA), 144

MEDLINE, 8

metadata librarian. *See* librarians, academic

metadata, 2, 12, 58, 75, 77, 83, 116, 118, 121–22, 145, 147, 207, 227, 229; costs, 60; schemas, 118, 125, 205–08; standards, 1

Metcalf, Keyes D., 165, 168

Michigan State University Libraries, 124

Middle States Commission on Higher Education (MSCHE), 92

Million Book Project, 12

MINES for Libraries, 218

Modern Language Association (MLA), 74

Montana State University library, 187

MOOCs, xi, 140, 171, 177, 181–84, 189

NASIG, 144

National Center for Education Statistics, 50, 52, 57, 133, 230

National Collegiate Athletics Association (NCAA), 24

National Education Association (NEA), 30

National Endowment for the Humanities (NEH), 12, 72

National Historical Publication and Records Commission (NHPRC), 72

National Information Standards Organization (NISO), 144

National Library of Canada, 102

National Library of Medicine, 8

National Science Foundation (NSF), 229

National Survey of Student Engagement (NSSE), 170

Neal, James G., 214, 224

New York Public Library, 12

New York State Foundation for Education Association (NYSFEA), 51

Nielson, Matthew "Buzzy," 167, 175n24

Northwestern University, Main Library, 165

Notation3, 123

OA2020, 201

Obama, Barack, 13

OCLC, 10-11, 15, 56, 75, 182; Connexion, 122; Sustainable Collection Services (SCS), 64n23

offices of research, in institutions of higher education, 22

Ohio College Association, 10

OhioLink, 199

Oldenburg, Ray, 169
online college courses, xi, 3, 13, 14, 22, 86, 89, 131, 133, 136, 140, 177-80, 188-89. *See also* MOOCs
Open Access Directory, 200
open access, xi, 140, 145-46, 181, 197-207; for federally funded research, mandated, 75, 80n43; gold OA, 207, 209n24; green OA, 202, 207, 209n24
Open Content Alliance (OCA), 12
open educational resources (OER), 14, 135, 183, 200-01
Open Journal Systems (OJS), 203-04, 207, 232
Open Library of Humanities, 77
open textbook initiatives: Open SUNY Textbooks, 201; BC Campus Open Textbook Project, 201
outreach librarian. *See* librarians, academic
outsourcing (business strategy), 59
OverDrive (vendor), 104
Oviatt Library, California State University Northridge, 167

paraprofessionals (or nonprofessionals). *See* staff, academic library
patron-driven acquisitions (PDA), 13, 56, 63, 104, 107, 116
PDA. *See* patron-driven acquisitions (PDA)
peer review, 2, 6, 14, 70-72, 94; blind, 77; crowdsourced, 72, 77
personal librarian. *See* librarians, academic
persons with disabilities, 23
plagiarism, 24
postgraduate residency programs, for academic librarians, 148
preservation: digital, xi, 3, 130, 140, 146, 175n28, 202, 205, 206, 227-28; of federally funded data and research, 19, 23, 75; of library materials, xi, 1, 13, 51, 110, 167, 171, 197
Primo, 124
privacy, patron, 125, 129, 132-33, 161, 171, 188, 212, 218-19
professional librarians. *See* staff, academic library
Project COUNTER (Counting Online Usage of Networked Electronic Resources), 217
promotion and tenure process, faculty, 21-22, 70, 72-74, 77, 116, 131, 134, 201
promotion. *See* marketing of academic library services
ProQuest (vendor), 11, 13, 56, 104, 181
Providence College, 204
Public Library of Science, 14
public services librarian. *See* librarians, academic
publishers: academic libraries as, 15, 77-78, 134, 140, 202-04, 206-08, 229-30, 232; commercial, 14-15, 57, 71, 76, 103, 116, 118,

198-99, 201, 203; librarians in the role of, 70, 77; nonprofit, 71, 76, 201, 203-04, 226
publishing, scholarly. *See* scholarly communication

Radford University, 88
reference librarian. *See* librarians, academic
reference service models, academic library, 85-91
research activity, levels of, in institutions of higher education, 102-03
Research Councils UK, 200
research data librarian. *See* librarians, academic
research librarian. *See* librarians, academic
Research Libraries Group (RLG), 10, 102, 112n21
Resource Description and Access (RDA), 119-24, 128, 145
Resource Description Framework (RDF), 117, 121-25, 128
roving librarian. *See* librarians, academic

scholarly communication librarian. *See* librarians, academic
scholarly communication, xi, 1, 2, 3, 6, 13, 14, 15, 25, 49, 58, 69-71, 74-75, 77-78, 101, 107, 134, 145, 203-07, 227-30, 232
Scholarly Publishing and Academic Resources Coalition (SPARC), 19, 78, 80n43, 200-01
Schonfeld, Roger C., 214
semantic web, 83, 116-18, 121-22, 124-26, 145
serendipity, 124
serials. *See* journals, academic
service quality surveys, 213, 215, 218
sexual harassment, 23, 25
SHERPA/JULIET website, 206
Siemens, Ray, 205
Simon Fraser University, 207
SirsiDynex (vendor), 117
Skype, 134
Sloan Sky Survey, 74
smart classrooms, 3, 139
SMART goals, 36-39
Smith, Adam (philosopher, political economist), 61
social media, 71, 87, 149, 185, 217, 219-20
social science data librarian. *See* librarians, academic
Society of American Archivists (SAA), 144
SPARC. *See* Scholarly Publishing and Academic Resources Coalition (SPARC)
SPARQL (query language), 117
Springer (publisher), 71, 104
Springshare (vendor), 88, 133, 186
SQL (query language), 117, 207
staff, academic library: paraprofessional (or nonprofessional), 3, 6, 29-30, 33, 38, 57, 58, 88, 130, 139, 144, 145, 147-49, 151, 152;

About the Editor and Contributors

Todd Gilman taught literature and writing at the University of Toronto, Boston University, and MIT before embarking on a career in academic librarianship. Since 2001, he has served as librarian for literature in English at Yale University, where he builds humanities collections for Sterling Memorial Library and, as library liaison to various humanities departments, assists undergraduate and graduate students with their library research.

Since 2004, Gilman has served as a part-time member of the faculty of the School of Information at San Jose State University, where he teaches graduate courses on academic libraries, reference, and book and library history. He holds a bachelor's degree in English from the University of Michigan–Ann Arbor, a master's and PhD in English from the University of Toronto, and a master's in library and information science from Simmons College. He has contributed numerous articles on the subject of academic librarianship to the *Chronicle of Higher Education* and authored the "Academic Libraries" chapter featured in Sandra Hirsh's recently published LIS textbook *Information Services Today: An Introduction* (Lanham, MD: Rowman & Littlefield, 2015). With Thea Lindquist, he coauthored two articles published in the journal *portal: Libraries and the Academy*, both based on their international survey of nearly seven hundred academic and research librarians holding subject doctorates.

Gilman also remains an active scholar in his subject area. He has published many articles on seventeenth- and eighteenth-century English theater and music. Most recently he published a major scholarly biography, *The Theatre Career of Thomas Arne*, about eighteenth-century London's preeminent native-born composer for the stage, the culmination of nearly two decades of academic library and archival research.

Nisa Bakkalbasi serves as assessment coordinator at Columbia University Libraries (CUL). She is responsible for fostering a culture of assessment within CUL, enabling data-driven decision-making, and promoting information transparency in the work environment. Prior to joining Columbia University, Nisa was the director of planning and assessment at James Madison University and held previous positions at Yale University Libraries. As an adjunct professor, she taught courses for the Information and Library Science Department at Southern Connecticut State University.

Nisa is a member of the peer review board of *Performance Measurement and Metric* journal, a past member of the ARL Library Assessment Conference Planning Committee, a past chair of the Special Library Association's Physics-Astronomy-Mathematics (PAM) Division, and a past member of the Project COUNTER Executive Committee. She holds an MS in library and information science from Long Island University and a BA in mathematics, as well as an MS in applied statistics from the University of Alabama.

Marta Brunner is college librarian of Lucy Scribner Library at Skidmore College. She came to Skidmore from UCLA, where she served as interim director of teaching and learning services and head of Powell Library and, before that, as subject librarian and head of the Collections, Research, and Instructional Services Department at the Charles E. Young Research Library. Marta joined UCLA Library in 2006 as a Council on Library and Information Resources postdoctoral fellow, after working as an access services library assistant at the University of Chicago. She obtained her doctoral degree from the History of Consciousness Program at UC–Santa Cruz. She also holds a master's in English (rhetoric and composition) from the University of Arizona and a bachelor's in English from Goshen College.

Barbara I. Dewey is dean of university libraries and scholarly communications at Penn State University. Previously she was dean of libraries, University of Tennessee, Knoxville. She has also held several administrative positions at the University of Iowa Libraries, including interim university librarian. Prior to her work at Iowa, she held positions at Indiana University's School of Library and Information Science, Northwestern University Libraries, and Minnesota Valley Regional Library in Mankato, Minnesota. She is the author or editor of seven books and has published articles and presented papers on research library topics, including digital libraries, technology, user education, publishing, fund-raising, diversity, organizational change, and human resources. She holds an MA in library science, a BA in sociology and anthropology from the University of Minnesota, and a public management certificate from Indiana University.

Debbie Faires serves as director of online learning at San Jose State University's School of Information. She earned her master of library and information science degree at SJSU and has taught classes about web technologies. In addition to her current administrative responsibilities, she has worked in the areas of faculty development, website management, and effective facilitation of synchronous online sessions.

Autumn Faulkner serves as assistant head of cataloging and metadata services at Michigan State University; supervises copy cataloging staff; manages work flows and procedures for all formats; and contributes to cataloging of problem materials, non-Roman language resources, and music formats.

Zoe Fisher is an assistant professor and pedagogy and assessment librarian at Auraria Library in Denver, Colorado. Before joining Auraria, she was an associate professor and reference and instruction librarian at Pierce College in Puyallup, Washington, where she worked with community college students for four years. She serves on the editorial board for *CHOICE* magazine as well as on the Information Literacy Standards Committee of the Association of College and Research Libraries. Zoe holds degrees from Oberlin College and Emporia State University.

Carrie Forbes, associate professor and associate dean for student and scholar services, heads the public service units of the University of Denver Libraries, including reference and instructional services, circulation, interlibrary loan, and reserves. She coedited *Rethinking Reference for Academic Libraries: Innovative Developments and Future Trends*, published by Rowman and Littlefield in 2014. She received her MLS from Indiana University, Bloomington, and her MA in higher education from the University of Denver.

Starr Hoffman (PhD, MLS, MA) is head of planning and assessment at the UNLV Libraries. In that role, she plays a key part in the strategic planning process and leads the assessment of library progress toward strategic goals. She holds a doctorate in higher education, with a focus on the administration and planning of academic organizations, and her dissertation examines how academic library administrators prepared for their administrative roles. She previously served as head of the Journalism Library at Columbia University and head of government documents at the University of North Texas Libraries.

Ronald C. Jantz holds a BA and an MA in mathematics from the University of Kansas and the University of Michigan, respectively. He worked for many years as a software developer and manager in one of the world's best-known research and development (R&D) organizations: Bell Laboratories. In 1996, he returned to academia and earned a master's degree in library science and a PhD from the School of Communication and Information at Rutgers University. At Rutgers University Libraries, he serves as the digital library architect and continues his research into the innovativeness and organizational performance of nonprofit institutions.

Peggy Keeran is a professor and the arts and humanities reference librarian at the University of Denver Libraries. She coedits the Rowman & Littlefield Literary Research: Strategies Sources series, is coauthor of three of the volumes, and coedited *Research within the Disciplines: Foundations for Reference and Library Instruction*. She received her MLIS and her MA in art history from the University of California–Berkeley.

David W. Lewis holds a BA from Carleton College and an MLS from Columbia University. He began his library career as a reference librarian and became a library administrator. Since 2000, he has been the dean of the university library at Indiana University–Purdue University, Indianapolis. Mr. Lewis has published more than forty articles and chapters. His 1988 article "Inventing the Electronic University" was selected as one of seven "landmark" articles to be republished in the seventy-fifth anniversary issue of *College and Research Libraries*. His book *Reimagining the Academic Library* was published by Rowman & Littlefield in 2016.

Joan K. Lippincott serves as associate executive director of the Coalition for Networked Information (CNI), a joint program of the Association of Research Libraries (ARL) and EDUCAUSE. Joan is a widely published author and frequent conference speaker. She is past chair of the Association of College and Research Libraries (ACRL) new publications board; serves on the boards of the New Media Consortium, *portal*, *The Reference Librarian*, and the Networked Digital Library of Theses and Dissertations (NDLTD); and is on the advisory board of the *Horizon Report* and the *Journal of Learning Spaces*. Prior to joining CNI, Joan was a librarian at Cornell, Georgetown, and George Washington Universities and SUNY–Brockport. Joan received her PhD in higher education from the University of Maryland, an MLS from SUNY–Geneseo, and a BA from Vassar College.

Sarah K. Lippincott is a librarian with a background in scholarly communications and the humanities. She currently serves as program director of the Library Publishing Coalition (LPC), an independent, community-led membership association that supports an evolving, distributed range of library publishing practices. She earned her MSLS from the University of North Carolina–Chapel Hill and her BA in the College of Letters and French Studies from Wesleyan University. Before joining the LPC, she worked as an independent communications consultant for the Association of Research Libraries (ARL), SPARC, and the open access journal *eLife*. Her professional interests include the intersection of scholarly communications and undergraduate teaching and learning, digital scholarship, and how librarians can facilitate new forms of scholarly inquiry.

Deanna B. Marcum, in her capacity as Ithaka S+R managing director, leads the research and consulting services that assist universities and colleges, libraries, publishers, and cultural institutions as they make the transition to the digital environment. She heads a growing staff of program directors and analysts with wide-ranging expertise.

From 2003 to 2011, Deanna served as associate librarian for library services at the Library of Congress. She managed 53 divisions and offices, whose 1,600 employees are responsible for acquisitions, cataloging, public service, and preservation activities; services to the blind and physically handicapped; and network and bibliographic standards for America's national library. She was also responsible for integrating the emerging digital resources into the traditional artifactual library, the first step toward building a national digital library for the twenty-first century. In 1995, Deanna was appointed president of the Council on Library Resources and president of the Commission on Preservation and Access. She oversaw the merger of these two organizations into the Council on Library and Information Resources (CLIR) in 1997 and served as president until August 2003. Deanna served as director of public service and collection management at the Library of Congress from 1993 to 1995. Before that she was the dean of the School of Library and Information Science at the Catholic

University of America. From 1980 to 1989, she was first a program officer and then vice president of the Council on Library Resources.

Deanna holds a PhD in American studies, a master's degree in library science, and a bachelor's degree in English. She was awarded a doctorate in humane letters by North Carolina State University in 2010 and received the Melvil Dewey Medal, the highest award conferred by the American Library Association, in June 2011. Deanna was appointed to the Japan–US Friendship Commission, which seeks "to strengthen the US-Japan relationship through educational, cultural, and intellectual exchange," in 2013.

Jennifer Osorio serves as interim head of the Collections, Research and Instructional Services (CRIS) Department at UCLA's Charles E. Young Research Library, where she has worked since 2007. She also serves as the subject librarian for Latin American studies, Iberian studies, and ethnic studies. In addition to an MLIS from UCLA, she holds an MA in Latin American studies. Her research interests include academic library leadership and succession planning; open access in Latin America; and teaching, particularly with rare and unique materials.

Brian Owen serves as associate university librarian for technology services and special collections at the Simon Fraser University Library in Burnaby, British Columbia. He has more than twenty-five years of senior management experience in large academic libraries—SFU and the University of British Columbia—with the development, implementation, and maintenance of library software and systems, both proprietary and open source, and the application of information technology to creating, maintaining, accessing, and preserving information resources. He is also the managing director for the Public Knowledge Project (PKP), which is responsible for the development and support of Open Journal Systems (OJS), an open source software publishing platform actively used by almost 10,000 scholarly journals in 2015. He is an associate with SFU's Canadian Institute for Studies in Publishing and SFU's Master of Publishing Program. He received the award for distinguished service to research librarianship from the Canadian Association of Research Libraries (CARL) in 2007.

Tahir Rauf is finance and planning manager for River Campus Libraries, University of Rochester. He has more than thirty years' experience working in different organizations, such as banking, corporate finance, industrial loans, student loans, and health care finance, and has been associated with academic library finance for the last sixteen years.

Kim Read is an assistant professor and distance education librarian at Concordia University in Portland, Oregon. She received her master of education in learning design and leadership from the University of Illinois Urbana–Champaign, her master of library science from Emporia State University, and her bachelor of anthropology from Colorado College. Prior to working at Concordia University, Kim served as an instructor and librarian at community college libraries and both small and large college and university libraries.

Lidia Uziel serves as the head of the Western Languages Division at Harvard University Library. She is the unit's leader and catalyst in building and then implementing its vision and strategy for collection development of materials in humanities and social science originating in Western European and English-speaking countries to support the FAS and university goals related to research, teaching, and learning. Uziel has a PhD in comparative literature from both the University of Montreal in Canada and Jean Moulin Lyon 3 University in France, a master's in French literature from Jean Moulin Lyon 3 University, a master's in library and information science from the University of Montreal, and a bachelor of arts in Romance languages from the Jagiellonian University of Krakow, Poland. Prior to Harvard, Uziel worked as the librarian for Western European humanities and coordinator for humanities collections at the Yale University Library.